PLACE–NAME CHANGES
1900—1991

Compiled by
ADRIAN ROOM

The Scarecrow Press, Inc.
Metuchen, N.J., & London
1993

British Library Cataloguing-in-Publication data available

Library of Congress Cataloging-in-Publication Data

Room, Adrian.
    Place–name changes 1900–1991 / compiled by Adrian
Room.
        p.   cm.
    Includes bibliographical references.
    ISBN 0-8108-2600-3 (alk. paper)
    1. Gazetteers.   I. Title.
G103.5.R657   1993
910'.3—dc20   93-5159

CONTENTS

FOREWORD

The world has moved on since the first edition of this book appeared in 1979. Several new African countries have emerged, East and West Germany have united to form a single state, and perhaps most spectacularly of all, the Soviet Union has broken up (or down) into the non-Communist Commonwealth of Independent States. Yugoslavia and Czechoslovakia, too, have essentially followed in her footsteps.

In short, there has been enough change and progress to justify a new edition of this book, and several new place-name changes have emerged as suitable candidates for inclusion. At the same time the opportunity has been taken to revise and correct the whole of the original text as thoroughly as possible. The result should be not simply a more up-to-date book, but a bigger and better one.

Initial acknowledgments for the first edition still stand, of course. In addition, I should now like to thank all those who have commented on that edition, with suggestions for new entries and amendments, and those who have contributed further material. They include Paul Woodman, of the Permanent Committee on Geographical Names for British Official Use, London; Steve Duke, of Victoria, Australia; and P.W. Hagelthorn, Senior Information Attaché at the Zimbabwe High Commission, London.

As before, however, I shall always appreciate indications of any suspected errors or omissions noted, and would ask that they be sent me either care of the publisher in the United States or to my home address in England: 12, High Street, St. Martin's, Stamford, Lincolnshire PE9 2LF.

Adrian Room
May, 1993

INTRODUCTION

For many countries of the world, the first nine decades of the 20th century have brought an era of change unparalleled in history. Hardly a single state has escaped the consequences of either a global war or a more local conflict. In Russia and China two age-old imperial dynasties have been overthrown, and in Africa, more recently, colonial ties have been broken and new democratic or dictatorial regimes established.

A frequent result of an old order yielding to a new, whether painfully or painlessly, is a change of another kind. It is this change—the renaming of places in a particular country—that is the concern of the present book, which aims to record many of the renamings that have taken place in the world since the beginning of the present century. Since the broad principle holds, that the more turbulent the history of a country, the more numerous are its renamings, it is self-evident that the name changes of some countries will be more fully represented than others. There have simply been more of them.

The highest proportion of renamings will thus be found to be those in China and the former Soviet Union.

Since the last of the Chinese emperors abdicated in 1912, the history of the country has been both troubled and complex. First torn by civil wars, then split between Nationalists and Communists, China was eventually proclaimed a People's Republic in 1949. Political unrest during those nearly forty years was further aggravated by an open war with Japan. Even since 1949 the road has been anything but smooth, and the 1980s have seen the adoption of a new state constitution and violent student demonstrations for a genuine kind of democracy in a radical swing from communism to conservatism.

Of the thousands of place-name changes during this period, only a representative selection can be included here, and these chiefly belong to the pre-1949 era. Chinese place-name changes are moreover complex affairs, so that county seats, for example, take their name with them when they are transferred from one region to another. Many places, too, change their names seasonally. To complicate matters further, hundreds of places share the same name, and several are known by different names at any given time.

In the former Soviet Union, where the political pendulum swung dramatically from right to left, only to rebound with almost indecent momentum in the early 1990s, place-name changes since the 1917 Revolution have been legion. It has been estimated that of the total number of around 700,000 populated places in the old USSR, probably as many as half had their names changed in some way in the first sixty years following the Revolution. Today, three-quarters of a century on, several of them have already changed back to their pre-Revolutionary original, often as a result of keen public demand for such a reversion. Some of the changes have been remarkable. Until quite recently it was near impossible to envisage a day when St. Petersburg would once again appear on world maps as Russia's "Athens of the North," and when even the name of the Soviet Union itself would disappear from our atlases and our daily newspapers. But now these momentous events have actually occurred, and the once familiar Leningrad and Union of Soviet Socialist Republics are no more.

Despite this, many places in the former USSR have so far retained their old names. When and even if they will resume their old name is as yet unknown or at best uncertain. This means that the present new edition of *Place-Name Changes* still contains a sizeable proportion of names paying tribute to Lenin, May Day, and the October Revolution. Logically all of these names would be expected to revert, or at any rate to convert to something non-Communist, and doubtless many of them are now in the process of doing so. But until notification is officially received, they must stay recorded as they are (or were until recently), so that a third edition of the book will be needed to complete the Russian renaming process. This is not exactly satisfactory, but at least all major ex-Soviet renamings have been entered here, as far as they are known, and they may well give a taste of the "more of the same" that will presumably follow.

Similar reversions to those in Russia, although on nothing like such a grandiose scale, have also been implemented elsewhere in eastern Europe, so that places named for former Communist leaders, such as Germany's Karl-Marx-Stadt and Czechoslovakia's Gottwaldov, are once more familiar under their old names of Chemnitz and Zlín. (For recent political developments in Yugoslavia and Czechoslavakia, and their effect on the location of place-names, see p. xxi.)

Other regions of the world have also had radical renaming programs. This has been particularly noticeable in Africa, where countries such as Algeria, Angola, Mozambique and Zimbabwe have replaced colonial European names (respectively French, Portuguese, and English) with indigenous ones. Many countries have themselves been renamed, such as Bechuanaland, Belgian Congo, Dahomey, Gold Coast, Nyasaland, Rhodesia, Sudanese Republic, Upper Volta. These eight names illustrate the pattern well enough, and show that not all renamings have been from European colonial to African indigenous. Dahomey is an African name, for example, as is Benin, its successor. An exception to the rule is Côte d'Ivoire, which has officially adopted a French name, ultimately of colonial origin, in place of its traditional English one, Ivory Coast.

The colonization of America by English speakers has also involved a remarkably high incidence of renamings. In this case, however, it has mostly not been a matter of one race speaking one language superseding another race speaking another, but of settlers frequently unable to fix on a name for a new settlement. Furthermore, a place with a modest name may need a more imposing one as it expands and becomes increasingly important. Without going into the motives behind the particular choices made for this name or that, a study that would make a book in itself, suffice it to say that many places in the United States have undergone not one or two but several renamings. Many of them predate 1900, so (unfortunately) fall outside the historical parameters for the present book. But mention should be made of one or two specific examples, simply to show that such instances exist. Glen Ellyn, a residential district of western Chicago, takes its present name from the wife of Thomas E. Hill, the village president at the time when this name was adopted. But in 1833 it was originally Babcock's Grove, for the first settlers, Ralph and Morgan Babcock, then successively DuPage Center (1834), Stacy's Corners (1835), Newton's Station (1849), Danby (1851), and Prospect Park (1882), finally acquiring its present name in 1889. Seven changes of name in well under an average human being's lifetime is a fair bid for the record books. Nor is this an isolated case. Portland, Maine, was first settled by the English in 1632, and during its early years underwent at least six name changes: Machigonne, Indigreat, Elbow, The Neck, Casco, and Falmouth, before finally settling for Portland in 1786.

Elsewhere, local or even national authorities have clearly paid considered attention to the aesthetic aspect of names. France, perhaps expectedly, is notable in this respect, and renamed five of her departments in the period 1941–70 on such grounds. Three of the names contained the component "Inférieure," while two had "Basses." And although these simply denoted a geographical or topographical reality, that the region was lower or further south than another that was higher or further north, the names were seen by some as suggesting that the places were "inferior" or "low" in a social sense. Accordingly the offending elements were replaced respectively with "Maritime" and "Atlantique," a purely coastal description that can upset nobody.

In among the old Soviet Union's political renamings, too, one finds several changes of this type, with an unattractive or misleading name replaced by a more salubrious or unambiguous one. In Belorussia, for instance, the community previous known as Zagryazye ("dirty place") was renamed Bereznyanka ("birch trees"), while Yazvy ("ulcers") was sanitized to Vostochnaya ("eastern"). In several other countries of the world, however, the residents of places with names like these, or names that could (sometimes mistakenly) be interpreted unfavorably, have been quite happy to have them remain unchanged. In England, for example, villagers are almost proud to live in places called Ugley, Nasty, Foul Hole, and Swineshead. It's something to do with a nation's corporate historical consciousness and an awareness of a country's linguistic and toponymical heritage.

Of course, there are other reasons why a place should be renamed, apart from such political, practical, and aesthetic considerations. During a world war, for example, "enemy" names are clearly out of favor. In 1918, in one such consequence, the South Australian government outlawed all German place-names except that of Adelaide, so that, for example, Hahndorf became Ambleside and Lobethal turned into Tweedvale. It restored them in 1935, however. Similar bans were enforced elsewhere.

Some individual name-changes conceal a story that, alas, is not the concern of the present book, which has the more sober responsibility of simply recording the changes themselves. But perhaps one such tale may be briefly recounted here, simply to show the sort of things that can occur.

The small New Zealand town of Otorohanga adopted the name Harrodsville in 1986. The reason? It was all because the prestigious London store, Harrods, had sent lawyers' letters to several businesses in New Zealand complaining about their using the name Harrods. Otorohanga (pop. 2,500) decided to cash in on the controversy and change the name of the entire town to Harrodsville. The visitor is now greeted with a road-sign "Welcome to Harrodsville" and one local store (Harrods, of course) has a prominent window poster recommending customers "Please visit our London branch when on your next U.K. holiday."

Not all name-changes are therefore implemented as the result of po-faced political or administrative decrees.

There have been very few place-name changes in Britain since 1900, although many county names were abolished on the reorganization of local government boundaries in the mid-1970s. One apparent name-change gained a certain notoriety, however. It is still popularly supposed by some that Windscale, Cumbria, was renamed Sellafield when in 1981 the controversial British Nuclear Fuels reprocessing plant there adopted the latter name for its operations in place of the familiar former one. But in fact both places still exist, and the "change" was due simply to a managerial reorganization of the site.

There are some countries in the world where there appear to have been no name changes at all, at least in the period covered by this book. None has been recorded for Iceland, for example, so that geographical names in that land have been appropriately "frozen" to match the natural environment.

DEFINITION OF A NAME CHANGE

The renamings recorded in the present book are, for the most part, those that have been officially decided or decreed. "For the most part" since certain renamings, although widely recognized and generally adopted, have not actually had governmental or legal sanction. In Ireland, for example, the five towns Navan, Queenstown, Kells, Naas, and Kingstown were all officially renamed, by local government act, prior to 1946. On the other hand, King's County and Queen's County were respectively renamed Offaly and Laoighis in 1920 without legal authorization. Yet clearly the renaming is valid enough and has certainly been generally accepted.

In many cases a renaming is a one-sided affair carried out by an occupying or invading power in time of war or conflict. Some names of this type may well become official, even if for a limited historical period, such as the German names imposed on Polish places in World War II. (A number of these were actual reversions to names that had previously existed, for reasons that the history books will best reveal.) In other instances the name lives only a brief, unofficial life, and is generally unrecognized by the world at large. The 1980s saw such examples. When Britain challenged the Argentines for control of the Falkland Islands in 1982, for example, the Spanish-speaking occupiers twice renamed Port Stanley, the islands' capital, calling it first Puerto Argentino, then Puerto Rivero (for an Argentine hero), all within a few weeks. But these names were as short-lived as they were unacceptable, and Port Stanley remains firmly on the map today, just as it officially prevailed during the period of occupation.

More recently, when Iraq occupied Kuwait in 1990, it renamed Kuwait City, that country's capital, as Khadima. Yet this name, too, was not generally recognized, any more than was the occupation itself.

Such renamings are very much in a minority in this book, but since they did actually occur, albeit unilaterally and illegally, they deserve inclusion if only "for the record." There may well be some future historian or high school student, after all, who needs to know what the Argentines called Port Stanley in their attempt to annex the Falkands, or what name Saddam Hussein imposed on Kuwait City when he staked his ill-advised claim on a neighboring state.

Some renamings are purely a "correction" to a native form that has been corrupted by occupying powers or colonists. A recent example occurred in 1989 when Burma's military rulers passed a law changing the country's name to Myanmar and that of its capital, Rangoon, to Yangon. These are in each case one and the same name, of course, but the new forms more closely reflect the native original. The *B* of "Burma" and *R* of "Rangoon" are merely western approximations of the Burmese sounds that actually begin the names, respectively more like *M* and *Y*. More interesting, perhaps, from an English speaker's point of view, are the names of the Pacific state of Kiribati and its island of Kiritimati, which evolved as respective "corrected" indigenous forms of the earlier English (colonial) names of Gilbert Islands and Christmas Island. (Gilbertese has a simplified phonetic alphabet that does not cater for English refinements.)

Many changes of country name are more a change of official title, brought about by the introduction of a new politicial or other structure. An example is that of the alteration of the name of the Democratic Republic of Afghanistan to the Republic of Afghanistan in 1987. Since, as mentioned, these are mostly changes of title rather than basic name, they will largely be absent from this book. However, all the retitlings of the former Soviet republics have been recorded, not only because they mark a political change of world importance, but because several of them had a genuine name change at some stage in the past anyway. Also recorded is the renaming of the old Soviet Union, on its disintegration, as the Commonwealth of Independent States, a name that was the third to evolve in almost as many months. This umbrella title may well itself give way to some other name (or be annulled) in the years ahead.

Some spelling adjustments to a name are so fine that they hardly merit the description "change." In India, for instance, Adirampatnam was "changed" to Adirampattinam, and Kanauj to Kannauj. On the whole adjustments of this type are not entered in the book, since they would have been included at the expense of the many major, more radical renamings. But even so a few will be found, especially where important places are concerned, such as the change in spelling for the Bangladeshi capital Dacca to Dhaka in 1982.

This is perhaps the point to clarify what apparent name changes are *not* included in the book. They amount to the following:

1. Alternate spellings, such as Berkhamstead/Berkhamsted, Portchester/Porchester, both in England.

2. Alternate names in different languages, such as Åbo (Swedish)/Turku (Finnish) in Finland, or Liège (French)/Luik (Flemish) in Belgium. Even if one name of the two is subsequently officially adopted, there will still have been a dubious category of name change.

3. New names arising as the result of local administrative reorganizations where the new territory does not correspond to the old, such as many of the new English and Welsh counties already referred to. In fact, there were no genuine renamings at all in the full sense of the word, since new counties with new names (such as Avon and Cumbria in England, and Clwyd, Dyfed, Gwent, Gwynedd, and Powys in Wales) were either larger in area than the combined regions they superseded or simply did not correspond geographically. The same holds true of the Scottish regions.

4. New names resulting simply from a merging or amalgamation of adjoining regions, even where the merged territories retain their former boundaries. An example is the new English county of Hereford and Worcester, formed when the old separate counties of Herefordshire and Worcestershire were merged as a single administrative unit in 1974. Even if the new county had been given a quite different name, it would still not be a "full" name change in the proper sense of the word. (If Herefordshire alone had been renamed, it would, of course.)

5. Specialized or restricted renamings, such as code names used for a town in a military operation. These, after all, do not replace the true name, which continues in general use.

Finally, it has to be said that habit dies hard, and that if a place is renamed many people will continue to refer to it by its old name, either because they object to the new name for some reason, or simply because the old name is the familiar one. There were thus Russians who, long after the renaming of St. Petersburg as Leningrad, continued to refer to the city by its old familiar nickname of *Piter*. In Britain, too, there are a number of people, by no means all of them crusty colonels or died-in-the-wool conservatives, who for two decades now have refused to use the new county names, even when sending mail. (Some, more circumspectly, use the old county name *and* the new one, if only because they do not wish to see their mail delayed through improper addressing.)

So a name change noted in this book is simply a historic record, nothing more, and there is no legal obligation on anyone to observe it!

ARRANGEMENT OF THE ENTRIES

The main entries and the cross-references run continously in alphabetical order.

For any given place, each entry will normally give five pieces of information, viz., ①present name, ②identification, ③location, ④former name(s), ⑤year or years of renaming. Thus in the entry

  ①   ②   ③   ④   ⑤
Daniels.   Village, Maryland, USA : Alberton (–1940)

the information given is that a village called Daniels in the state of Maryland, in the United States, was until 1940 called Alberton. To take each point separately.

①. PRESENT NAME

The normal or conventional name of the place in English or appropriate foreign language is given, with diacritics (accents) as necessary. The spelling of the name is the regular one given in its source, as crossed-checked wherever possible with *Webster's New Geographical Dictionary,* the *Columbia-Lippincott World Gazetteer,* and *The Times Atlas of the World* (see Bibliography). Only a minority of names occur outside these works.

Most Chinese names have alternate spellings in square brackets. These are the ones given in *Columbia-Lippincott,* and represent the Wade-Giles rendering of the name, as distinct from the English conventional version. Thus traditional English *Tungliao* has a Wade-Giles equivalent spelling *T'ung-liao.* Today Pinyin is widely used in many maps of China, but on the whole it is not regularly represented in this book, unless it happens to coincide with the conventional English, as it does for *Harbin,* for instance. This is not to be reactionary or awkward, but simply because Pinyin is still unfamiliar to many, and has not been adopted universally even now for many atlases (although it has for *The Times Atlas*).

Russian names also present problems, since transliteration from Cyrillic can be worked in different ways. The city that is now again Nizhny Novgorod but that was formerly *Gorky,* for example, can have its old name rendered as *Gor'kiy, Gorkiy, Gor'kij* or *Gorkij.* The most appropriate transliteration here seems to be one that is straightforward, widely recognized, and reasonably accurate. A simplified system is thus systematically used. (It is very similar to that adopted by the *Encyclopaedia Britannica*.)

Places with identical spellings are numbered (1), (2), etc., in alphabetical order of their former name, or earliest former name, if there are more than one.

A place having part of its name in round brackets, such as *Krosno (Odrzańskie),* means that the parenthesized element is a defining or mainly optional word, often added where more than one place of the name exist. The alphabetical order for such names takes account of the bracketed element, however, even when it comes first, so that *(Ilirska) Bistrica* will be found under *I,* not *B.* There are in fact very few such names.

②. IDENTIFICATION

Each place is followed by a describer which states its nature, whether "man-made" (the majority), such as town, village, settlement, and the like, or natural, such as mountain, river, island, and so on. For inhabited places, the describer aims to give an accurate idea of the nature of the place and its size, without necessarily indicating its precise political status. But status describers are none the less given wherever possible. Readers are reminded that "city" need not necessarily denote a large town. In many countries, the status of "city" can be held by quite small settlements, which would elsewhere be little more than "village." This particularly applies in North and South America, notably the United States and Brazil, where a "city" may have literally only a few hundred inhabitants. By contrast, at least in the United States, a "village" may have a population running into several thousands.

In populated places in the Commonwealth of Independent States (the former Soviet Union), a frequent status is that of "urban settlement" (more precisely, though not used in this book, "settlement of urban type"). Places so designated are in status midway between a village and a town, with a population of at least 2,000. Many Russian towns, on the other hand, are so large and important that elsewhere they would certainly be designated "city." But this is a category that does not exist in the CIS, and which is therefore mostly missing from the book.

Towns or cities that are capitals of a country or state are usually simply identified as capital, with no further status describer or even locational information.

Where the nature of a place is clear from its name, such as *Acadia National Park,* there is no need for an additional describer, although in a few cases one will be given, mostly where there could otherwise be ambiguity. Some towns, for example, are named after the river on which they stand, with *River* as an integral element of their name. The city of *Coos Bay* is similarly named for its bay, and the village of *Moi's Bridge* for the bridge where it arose.

③. LOCATION

The location of a place is fixed in one of two ways. It will either have a directional "compass-point" indication, such as "northern", "southeastern", "west-central" or the like, or it will be entered with the name of its administrative region, such as county, state, province, and so on. The second system is mostly followed for English-speaking countries, since on the whole these will be meaningful to English speakers, even to those not resident in the country concerned.

One notable exception, however, has been made for the Commonwealth of Independent States, and especially Russia, which because of its sheer size demands a more precise locating system. Here, the basic administrative region is given within the particular state. In many cases this is an *oblast*. In some republics, however, there are no *oblasts,* while in others there are both *oblasts* and other types of administrative district.

It should be noted that where the name of the administrative district only is given, the "directional" location of the place concerned within it will not additionally be supplied. The narrowing down of the location site to the particular district should suffice for the particular place to be identified accurately.

For English-speaking countries the administrative units entered for locating purposes are as follows: by state in the United States, by province or territory in Canada, by county (or region) in the United Kingdom and Ireland, by state or territory in Australia, and by province in South Africa. Places in New Zealand are located as being in North Island, South Island, or on one of the smaller islands.

Where a country has a large number of islands within its territory, such as Greece or Japan, the particular island will be entered for the given place. Further, if the island is sizeable or important, such as Honshu, Hokkaido, Shikoku or Kyushu in Japan, "directional" location will also be given. In the Philippines, however, location is given by province rather than by individual island, if only because there may be 66 provinces, but there are over 7,000 islands!

Places in India and China are fixed by "directional" location rather than state or province, despite the size of these countries, as such locations will normally be more meaningful. It is felt to be more helpful to say that a place is in "northwestern India" rather than in Rajasthan, and in "south-central China" rather than in Szechwan. Geographers may object, but one has to consider the practical aspect: many readers would need to establish the location of the territory itself in order to gain an idea of the actual site of the place within the country as a whole.

Conversely, a "directional" or compass-point location is given for all countries in Africa (apart from the self-explanatory South Africa), since although "darkest Africa" is now largely a historic concept, there can be some uncertainty regarding the geographical position of certain African states. (Some African countries, moreover, have confusingly similar names to a western ear, such as Zambia, Zaïre and Zimbabwe, Mali and Malawi, Guinea, Guinea-Bissau and Equatorial Guinea, Niger and Nigeria, even Liberia and Libya.)

In a very few instances a place may extend over the territory of two adjacent countries or regions, or be shared by them. Where this occurs, the names of both will be given with a dividing virgule (/), such as "Arkansas/Oklahoma", "Uganda/Zaïre."

Political developments and even civil war in eastern Europe from the early 1990s have resulted in the disintegration not only of the Soviet Union but of other Communist bloc countries, notably Yugoslavia and Czechoslovakia. In consequence, places in Yugoslavia are located in one of the six former constituent republics: Bosnia-Herzegovina, Croatia, Macedonia, Montenegro, Serbia, and Slovenia. Of these, four declared their independence in 1991, while the remaining two, Serbia and Montenegro, proclaimed the foundation of a new and much reduced Yugoslavia in April 1992. (As reported in the *New York Times* on May 7, 1992, Greece was not happy about Macedonia's retention of its historic name, and claimed it as her own. The name should be changed to Skopje, said Greece, for the state capital. But, to date, the name remains.)

In June 1992 the Czechs and Slovaks, having originally united in 1918 to form the new state of Czechoslovakia, announced that they were again going their separate ways. The Czech and larger portion of the country, west of the White Carpathian Mountains, and politically established as the Czech Socialist Republic in 1968, became known as the Czech Lands, and is referred to as such in this book. (The name is provisional, however, and unlikely to endure: historically the region is familiar in its larger, western part as Bohemia, and in its smaller, eastern section as Moravia. The former name may be the one to prevail.) The Slovak and smaller part, east of the White Carpathians, and politically established as the Slovak Socialist Republic in 1968, reverted to its historic name of Slovakia. This name will thus also be found for locational purposes. Prior to 1918 it was familiar as that of a region which for centuries was part of Hungary.

④. FORMER NAME(S)

The former name of a place is given, as is the current one, in the accepted standard English or foreign-language spelling. In a few instances, a non-English version of a name may be given, especially if it is as familiar as the English one. An example is *Moyen Congo* as well as *Middle Congo* for the former (French) name of what is now just Congo.

If there has been more than one renaming since 1900, the former names are given in chronological order. Where a place formerly belonged, with a different name, to another country, as happened in certain central European states, the former country name is given at the end of the entry, after the year of renaming. An example is the following:

Chernyakhovsk. Town, Kaliningrad Oblast, Russia : Insterburg (–1946), Germany (–1945).

This means that the Russian town of Chernyakhovsk, now in the Kaliningrad Oblast, was in German hands until 1945 when it passed to the Soviet Union, who renamed it a year later. (Strictly speaking such "German" places were in Prussia, but the latter was a northern German state until the end of World War II, so the national descriptive is valid.)

Indications of former nationality are not normally given when the occupying or annexing power was acting in a colonial capacity, as France was in Algeria, for example, or Italy in Ethiopia.

Alternate former names appear in square brackets as they do for current names.

⑤. YEAR(S) OF RENAMING

Where the year of renaming is known, it is given following the former name. Since the book deals only with name changes that have occurred since 1900 (inclusive), no indication will normally be given of any name change before that date. Thus a form such as "(–1938)" means that a place had its former name from at least 1900 to 1938, and possibly for some time before 1900. In a few cases, however, a year before 1900 is given. This happens when a "new" name adopted after 1900 is the same as one held before that year. An example is:

Bethpage. Village, New York, USA : Central Park (1841–1936).

This means that Bethpage has not only been the name of the village since 1936, but was its name before 1841, in which year it was renamed Central Park. Reversions to names held earlier than 1800 are on the whole not included, since this would involve complex historic nomenclature, as well as being outside the strict parameters of the book.

From the late 1980s onward many places in the former Soviet Union have reverted to their old names, so that certain names antedating 1900 will be found.

In some cases it has not been possible to fix the precise year of renaming. In such instances either an approximation is given, such as "(1912–c. 1940)" or "(–early 1930s)", or else a question mark replaces the expected year, such as "(1920–?)."

Where a single year is not preceded by a hyphen, such as "(1982)", this means that the name was in use for less than a year, or at most for just that one year.

An apparent gap in a run of dates implies that the present name was borne earlier by the place in the years of the gap period. Thus in the entry

Lugansk.　Capital of Lugansk Oblast, Ukraine : Voroshilovgrad (1935–58, 1970–90)

the gap between 1958 and 1970 indicates that the town of Lugansk was earlier known by this name between those years. In other words, it now bears the name for the third time, having been called *Voroshilovgrad* twice.

SYMBOLS

The two symbols, asterisk (*) and dagger (†), need an explanation.

An asterisk before a year indicates that the name then came into use for the first time, perhaps because the place concerned was originally settled then, or administratively organized that year. An asterisk thus implies that there was no earlier name, since there was no earlier place!

The dagger indicates that the named place no longer exists. This will mostly apply to an administrative district that has been either abolished or incorporated into a larger unit of some kind, so losing its identity.

In a few instances a territory was abolished only to be reinstated some years later. Dates will thus be found with both dagger, denoting the demise, and asterisk, indicating the restoration.

In other instances the territory was abolished for good. An example is:

Izmail Oblast (1954†). Ukrainian SSR : Akkerman Oblast (*1940)

This shows that a region named *Akkerman Oblast* was created in 1940 in what was then the Ukrainian SSR, was renamed the same year as *Izmail Oblast,* and was abolished in 1954. Although Ukraine is no longer a Soviet Socialist Republic (SSR), its old title is given as that was the one which was current for the duration of the name entered.

CROSS-REFERENCES

Every former name is cross-referenced to its present or last existing name with the notation "*see.*" An example is:

Haas *see* Camp Morton

Former variant spellings are similarly cross-referenced. Present variant spellings cross-refer to a more common or conventional spelling of a name by means of an equals sign (=), as notably from Wade-Giles versions of Chinese names to conventional English ones. (Where a Wade-Giles spelling is exactly the same as the conventional one, however, and differs only in its punctuation, there will be no cross-reference. Thus Ch'ang-shun will not be cross-referred to Changshun, even though the former Wade-Giles version of the name will appear in square brackets next to the latter conventional form.)

Where the former name is identical for more than one current name, the cross-reference enumerates the names in alphabetical order. An example is:

Hochow *see* (1) Hochwan [Ho-ch'uan]; (2) Hohsien; (3) Linsia [Lin-hsia]

A former name cross-referencing to a current name followed by a number means that the current name is identical for more than one place. An example is:

Kruglyakov *see* Oktyabrsky (5)

meaning that it is the fifth Oktyabrsky listed that was formerly called Kruglyakov.

Since numbers thus appear (for different purposes) both before and after a name, care may be needed when dealing with cross-references of this type:

Kirova, imeni *see* (1) Bank; (2) Kirovo (1), (2); (3) Kirovsk (2)

meaning that the name imeni Kirova was formerly borne by one place now called Bank, by two (respectively numbered) now called Kirovo, and by one (the second of those listed) now known as Kirovsk. A semicolon closes each of the numbered former names, whether or not itself followed by a sequence number. (Russian *imeni* in names like this means "named for", and in name headings follows the alphabetized name.)

PLACE-NAME CHANGES 1900–1991

Abaeté *see* Abaetutuba

Abaetutuba. City, northern Brazil, South America : Abaeté (–1944)

Abakan. Capital of Khakass Autonomous Oblast, Krasnoyarsk Kray, Russia : Ust-Abakanskoye (–1925), Khakassk (1925–31)

Abakanskoye *see* Krasnoturansk

Abakumova *see* Dzhansugurov

Abariringa. Island, Kiribati, western Pacific : Canton Island (–1981)

Abay (1). Village, Chimkent Oblast, Kazakhstan : Abay-Bazar (–c. 1960)

Abay (2). Town, Karaganda Oblast, Kazakhstan : Churubay-Nura (–1961)

Abay *see* Karaul

Abay-Bazar *see* Abay (1)

Abbazia *see* Opatija

Abdalyar *see* Lachin

Åbenrå. City, southeastern Denmark : Apenrade (–1920), Germany

Abercorn *see* Mbala

Ablan. Barrio, Ilocos Norte, Philippines : Barat (–1969)

Ableman *see* Rock Springs

Abovyan. Town, Armenia : Elar (–1963)

Abrene *see* Pytalovo

Abunã. Town, northwestern Brazil, South America : Presidente Marques (–1944)

Acacia Park. Residential area, Cape Province, South Africa : Sassar (1947–1959)

Acadia National Park. Maine, USA : Sieur de Monts National Monument (*1916–19), Lafayette National Park (1919–29)

Acate. Village, southeastern Sicily, Italy : Biscari (–c. 1937)

Achalpur. Town, central India : Dadra (–1966)

Acheng [A-ch'eng]. Town, northeastern China : Ashihho (–1909)

Achkoy-Martan. Village, Chechen-Ingush Autonomous Republic, Russia : Novoselskoye (1944–c. 1965)

Acul *see* Vidin

Adelphi *see* Westwold

Ademi *see* Adimi

Adernò *see* Adrano

1

Adimi. Urban settlement, Primorsky Kray, Russia : Ademi (–c. 1940)

Adrano. Town, eastern Sicily, Italy : Adernò (–1929)

Adrar. District, west-central Mauritania, western Africa : Septième (–c.1979)

Adygey Autonomous Oblast. Krasnodar Kray, Russia : Cherkess (Adygey) Autonomous Oblast (*1922), Adygey (Cherkess) Autonomous Oblast (1922–36)

Adygey (Cherkess) Autonomous Oblast *see* Adygey Autonomous Ablast

Adygeysk *see* Teuchezhsk

Adyk. Settlement, Kalmyk Autonomous Republic, Russia : Yuzhny (–c. 1960)

Adzhibakul *see* Kazi-Magomed

Afars and Issas *see* Djibouti

Affreville *see* Khemis Miliana

Afonso Pena *see* Conceição do Almeida

Agbulakhi *see* Tetri-Tskaro

Aggelóna. Village, southern Greece : Agkylóna (–1960s)

Agkylóna *see* Aggelóna

Agnessa *see* Shokalsky

Agnew. Railway point, Manitoba, Canada : Monda (–1905)

Agram *see* Zagreb

Agrigento. Province and its capital, southern Sicily, Italy : Girgenti (–1927)

Aguaí. City, southeastern Brazil, South America : Cascavel (–1944)

Aguathuna. Village, Newfoundland, Canada : Limeville (–1911)

Ahfir. Village, northeastern Morocco, northwestern Africa : Martimprey-du-Kiss (–c. 1959)

Aichow [Yaichow] *see* Aihsien

Aiga. Town, southern Honshu, Japan : Oka (–1934)

Aigrefeuille *see* Aigrefeuille-sur-Maine

Aigrefeuille-sur-Maine. Village, western France : Aigrefeuille (–1934)

Aihsien. Town, southeastern China : Aichow [Yaichow] (–1912)

Ainaži. Town, Latvia : Gainash (–1917)

Aïn Benian. Town, northern Algeria, northern Africa : Guyotville (–c.1962)

Aïn Berda. Village, northeastern Algeria, northern Africa : Penthièvre (–c. 1962)

Aïn Defla. Village, northern Algeria, northern Africa : Duperré (–c. 1962)

Aïn el Hammam. Village, northern Algeria, northern Africa : Michelet (–c. 1962)

Aïn el Kebira. Village, northeastern Algeria, northern Africa : Périgotville (–c. 1962)

Aïn Mokra *see* Berrahal

Aïn Oulmene. Village, northeastern Algeria,

northern Africa : Colbert
(–c. 1962)

Aïntab *see* Gaziantep

Aïn Touta. Town, northeastern Algeria, northern Africa : MacMahon (–c. 1962)

Aiud. Town, west-central Romania : Strassburg (–c. 1939), Germany

Aizpute. Town, Latvia : Gazenpot (–1917)

Akchi-Karasu *see* Toktogul

Akhali-Afoni *see* Novy Afon

Akhalkhevi. Village, Georgia : Itum-Kale (–1944)

Akhangaran. River, Tashkent Oblast, Uzbekistan : Angren (–c. 1960)

Akhigria *see* Icaria

Akhoúria Vavouríou *see* Platános

Akhta *see* Razdan (1)

Akhtala. Urban settlement, Armenia : Nizhnyaya Akhtala (–1939)

Akhunbabayev. Town, Andizhan Oblast, Uzbekistan : Sufikishlak (–1975)

Akhuryan. Village, Armenia : Duzkend (–1945)

Akkerman *see* Belgorod-Dnestrovsky

Akkerman Oblast *see* Izmail Oblast

Akmal-Abad *see* Gizhduvan

Akmangit *see* Belolesye

Ak-Mechet *see* (1) Chernomorskoye; (2) Kzyl-Orda

Akmolinsk *see* Tselinograd

Akmolinsk Oblast *see* Tselinograd Oblast

Akow *see* Pingtung [P'ingtung]

Akrolímne. Village, northern Greece : Gymná (–1960s)

Aksay. Town, Uralsk Oblast, Kazakhstan : Kazakhstan (–1968)

Ak-Sheikh *see* Razdolnoye

Ak-Suu. Town, Issyk-Kul Oblast, Kirgizia : Pervomaysky (–1985)

Aktam. Village, Osh Oblast, Kirgizia : Chanach (–c. 1960)

Aktau. Town, Guryev Oblast, Kazakhstan : Shevchenko (1963–91)

Alagoa de Baixo *see* Sertânia

Alagoa Nova. City, northeastern Brazil, South America : Laranjeiras (1939–43)

Alagoas *see* Marechal Deodoro

Alagyoz *see* Aragats

Alaid *see* Atlasova

Alais *see* Alès

Al-Anbar. Province, western Iraq : Al-Dilame (–1971)

Alanskoye. Village, North Ossetian Autonomous Republic, Russia : Psedakh (–1944)

Alawiya *see* Latakia

Alba Iulia. City, west-central Romania : Weissenburg (-?), Germany, Karlsburg (?–c. 1918), Germany

Albalat de Segart *see* Albalat de Taronchers

Albalat de Taronchers. Village, eastern Spain : Albalat de Segart (–1949)

Albany. City, California,
    USA : Ocean View
    (1908–09)
Albat *see* Kuybyshevo (1)
Albert, Lake *see* Mobutu Sese
    Seko, Lake
Albert-Edward, Lake *see* Ed-
    ward, Lake
Albertinia. Town, Cape
    Province, South Africa :
    Riversdale (–1904)
Albert National Park *see*
    Virunga National Park
Alberton. Town, Transvaal,
    South Africa : Elandsfon-
    tein (–1904)
Alberton *see* Daniels
Albertville *see* Kalemi
Albor *see* Libyo
Alcazarquivir *see* Ksar el Ke-
    bir
Alchevsk *see* Kommunarsk
Alcobaça *see* Tucuruí
Aldan. Town, Yakut Auton-
    omous Republic, Russia :
    Nezametny (–1939)
Aldea del Rey *see* Aldea Real
Aldea Real. Village, north-
    central Spain : Aldea del
    Rey (–1920)
Al-Dilame *see* Al-Anbar
Alejandro Selkirk. Island,
    Juan Fernandez group,
    Chile, South America :
    Más Afuera (–1962), Pi-
    loto Juan Fernandez
    (1962–66)
Aleksandropol *see* Kumayri
Aleksandrov Dar *see* Rakhma-
    novka
Aleksandrovka *see* (1) Lozno-
    Aleksandrovka; (2) Ord-
    zhonikidze (1)
Aleksandrovsk. Town,

Perm Oblast, Russia :
    Aleksandrovsky (–1951)
Aleksandrovsk *see* (1) Belo-
    gorsk (1); (2) Polyarny;
    (3) Zaporozhye
Aleksandrovsk-Grushevsky
    see Shakhty
Aleksandrovsk Guberniya =
    Zaporozhye Guberniya
Aleksandrovskoye *see*
    Kirovskoye (1)
Aleksandrovsk-Sakhalinsky.
    Town, Sakhalin Oblast,
    Russia : Aleksandrovsky
    Post (–1926)
Aleksandrovsky *see* Aleksan-
    drovsk
Aleksandrovsky Post *see* Alek-
    sandrovsk-Sakhalinsky
Alekseyevsk *see* Svobodny
Alekseyevskoye *see* Len-
    inskoye (1)
Alès. Town, southeastern
    France : Alais (–1926)
Alexandria *see* Arlington
Alexandroúpolis. City, north-
    eastern Greece : Dede-
    ağaç (–1919), Turkey
Alfredo Chaves *see* Veranópo-
    lis
Al-Hawtah *see* Lahij
Al-Hoceima. Town and
    province, northern Mo-
    rocco, northwestern Af-
    rica : Villa Sanjurjo
    (*1926–c. 1958)
Aliabad *see* Shahi
Ali Butus *see* Slavjanka
Alice Springs. Town, North-
    ern Territory, Australia :
    Stuart (–1933)
Alija del Infantado. Village,
    northwestern Spain : Alija
    de los Melones (–c. 1960)

Alija de los Melones *see* Alija
del Infantado
Al Ikhwan. Island group,
Gulf of Aden : The
Brothers (–1975)
Al-Ittihad *see* Madinat ash-
Shab
Alitus. Town, Lithuania :
Olita (–1917)
Alkatvaam. Village, Ma-
gadan Oblast, Russia :
Valkatlen (–c. 1960)
Al-Khalil *see* Hebron
Allenburg *see* Druzhba (1)
Allenstein *see* Olsztyn
Alleroi *see* Shuragat
Alma. City. Quebec, Can-
ada : Saint-Joseph-
d'Alma (–1954)
Alma-Ata. Capital of Ka-
zakhstan : Verny (–1921)
Almalii *see* Yabalkovo
Al-Marj. Town, northern
Libya, northern Africa :
Barce (–?)
Almazar. Urban settlement,
Tashkent Oblast, Uzbeki-
stan : Vrevsky (–1963)
Almenara. City, southeast-
ern Brazil, South Amer-
ica : Vigia (–1944)
Almeria *see* Kawayan
Al-Muntafak *see* Dhi Qar
Alouette Lake. Lake, Brit-
ish Columbia, Canada :
Lillooet Lake (–1914)
Alpargatal *see* Vicente Noble
Alpes-de-Haute-Provence.
Department, southeast-
ern France : Basses-Alpes
(–1970)
Alpicat. Village, northeast-
ern Spain : Villanueva de
Alpicat (–c. 1950)

Al-Qadisiya. Province,
south-central Iraq : Di-
waniya (–1971)
Alsóközpont *see* Mórahalom
Alsószentgyörgy *see* Jászal-
sószentgyörgy
Altamirano. City, southwest-
ern Mexico, North Amer-
ica : Pungarabato (–1936)
Altanbulak. Town, northern
Mongolia : Maymachen
(–1921)
Altdamm *see* Dabie
Altentreptow. Town, north-
western Germany : Trep-
tow (an der Tollense)
(–1940s)
Alt Gaarz *see* Rerik
Altofonte. Village, northern
Sicily, Italy : Parco
(–1931)
Alto Parnaíba. City, north-
eastern Brazil, South
America : Vitória do Alto
Parnaíba (–1944)
Altsohl *see* Zvolen
Alūksne. Town, Latvia :
Marienburg (–1917)
Alyoshki *see* Tsyurupinsk
Amamlu *see* Spitak
Amandelboom *see* Williston
Amangeldy. Village, Kus-
tanay Oblast, Kazakhstan
: Batbakkara (–1936)
Amapari *see* Ferreira Gomes
Amara *see* Maysan
Amarração *see* Luís Correia
Amasiya. Village, Armenia
: Gukasyan (–c. 1960)
Amatitlán. Town, southeast-
ern Mexico, North Amer-
ica : Amatlán (–1938)
Amatlán *see* Amatitlán
Ambarica *see* Levski

Ambleside *see* Hahndorf
Ambridge. Town, Pennsylvania, USA : Economy (–1906)
Ambrizete *see* Nzeto
Ambrolauri. Town, Georgia : Yenukidze (–mid-1930s)
Americana. City, southeastern Brazil, South America : Villa Americana (–1938)
Amerika *see* (1) Nakhodka; (2) Sovetskaya (1)
Amherst *see* Kyaikkami
Ami *see* Kaiyüan [Kai-yüan]
Amlan. Municipality, Negros Oriental, Philippines : New Ayuquitan (–1950)
Amu-Darya. Urban settlement, Chardzhou Oblast, Turkmenistan : Samsonovo (–1962)
Amursk. Town, Khabarovsk Kray, Russia : Padali (–1958)
Amvrosiyevka. Town, Donetsk Oblast, Ukraine : Donetsko-Amvrosiyevka (–c. 1955)
Anadyr. Capital of Chukot Autonomous Okrug, Magadan Oblast, Russia : Novo-Mariinsk (–1920)
Analândia. City, southeastern Brazil, South America : Anápolis (–1944)
Analostan Island *see* Theodore Roosevelt Island
Ananyevo. Village, Issyk-Kul Oblast, Kirgizia : Sazanovka (–1942)
Anao-aon *see* San Francisco (1)
Anápolis *see* (1) Analândia; (2) Simão Dias

Anatsogno. Village, southwestern Madagascar, southeastern Africa : St. Augustin (–1981)
Anchieta *see* Piatā
An-ching = Anking
Ancienne-Lorette. Town and airport, Quebec, Canada : Notre-Dame-de-Lorette (–1967)
Andalaly *see* Nozhay-Yurt
Andalusia *see* Jan Kempdorp
Andersen Air Force Base. Guam, Mariana Islands, western Pacific : North Field (*1945–49)
Anderson Siding *see* St. Quentin
Andirá. City, southern Brazil, South America : Ingá (–1944)
Andoany. Town, northwestern Madagascar, southeastern Africa : Hell-Ville (–1981)
Andreyev *see* Jędrzejów
Andreyevsk *see* Tezebazar
Andreyevskoye *see* Dneprovskoye
Andropov *see* Rybinsk
Anfu *see* Linli
Angaco Norte. Town, western Argentina, South America : Kilómetro 924 (–?)
Angel Albino Corzo *see* Jaltenango
Angerapp *see* Ozyorsk
Angerburg *see* Węgorzewo
Angoche. City, eastern Mozambique, southeastern Africa : Vila António Enes (–1970), António Enes (1970–76)

Angola. Republic, south-
western Africa : Portu-
guese West Africa
(–1951)
Angora *see* Ankara
Angren *see* Akhangaran
Angshui *see* Sansui
Angus (1975†). County,
eastern Scotland, UK :
Forfarshire (–1928)
Anhwa *see* (1) Ipeh [Ipei], (2)
Tehkiang [Te-chiang]
Anikšiai. Town, Lithuania :
Onikšty (–1917)
Aniva. Town, Sakhalin Ob-
last, Russia : Rudaka
(1905–46), Japan (–1945)
Anjen *see* Yükiang [Yü-
chiang]
Ankaboa, Tanjona. Cape,
southwestern Madagas-
car, southeastern Africa :
St. Vincent, Cap (–1981)
Ankang [An-kang]. Town,
central China : Hingan
(–1913)
Ankara. Capital of Turkey :
Angora (–1930)
An Khe. Town, southern
Vietnam : An Tuc (–c.
1980)
Ankhialo *see* Pomoriye
Anking [An-ching]. City,
eastern China : Hwaining
[Huai-ning] (1911–49)
An-kuo = Ankwo
Ankwo [An-kuo]. Town,
northeastern China : Chi-
chow (–1914)
An Loc *see* Hon Quan
Anlu. Town, northeastern
China : Teian (–1912)
Anlu *see* Chungsiang [Chung-
hsiang]

Anlung. Town, southern
China : Hingi (–1913),
Nanlung (1913–31)
Annaba. Town, northeast-
ern Algeria, northern Af-
rica : Bône (–c. 1962)
Annenfeld *see* Shamkhor
Annino *see* Shamkhor
Annobón *see* Pagalu
Áno Exántheia *see* Exántheia
Áno Leukímme. Village,
Corfu, Greece : Rig-
gládes (–1960s)
Anpeh [Anpei]. Town,
northern China : Tashetai
(–1925)
Anpei = Anpeh
Anping *see* Makwan [Ma-
kuan]
An-shan. City, northeastern
China : Shaho(chen)
(–1934)
Ansu *see* Süshui [Hsü-shui]
Antananarivo. Capital of
Madagascar, southeast-
ern Africa : Tananarive
(1895–1975)
Antarctic Peninsula. Region
of Antarctica : Graham
Land (claimed by UK),
Palmer Peninsula
(claimed by USA),
O'Higgins Land (claimed
by Chile), San Martín
Land (claimed by Argen-
tina) (–1961)
Antatet *see* Luna (1)
Anting *see* (1) Changtze
[Chang-tzu]; (2) Tingsi
[Ting-hsi]
Antipolo. Barrio, Marin-
duque, Philippines : Hi-
nubuan (–1957)
António Enes *see* Angoche

Antono-Kodintsevo *see* Kominternovskoye

Antratsit. Town, Lugansk Oblast, Ukraine : Bokovo-Antratsit (–1962)

Antrea *see* Kamennogorsk

An-tse = Antseh

Antseh [An-tse]. Town, central China : Yoyang (–1914)

Antseranana. Town, northern Madagascar, southeastern Africa : Diégo-Suarez (–1979)

An Tuc *see* An Khe

Antung *see* (1) Lienshui; (2) Tantung

Antze [An-tzu]. Town, northeastern China : Tungan (–1914)

An-tzu = Antze

An Uaimh *see* Navan

Anyang. City, north-central China : Chang-te (–1913)

Anzaldo. Town, central Bolivia, South America : Paredón (–1900s)

Anzeba *see* Chekanovsky

Aparecida *see* Bertolínia

Ape. Town, Latvia : Oppekaln (–1917)

Apeírathos. Village, Naxos, Cyclades Islands, Greece : Apýranthos (–1960s)

Apenrade *see* Åbenrå

Appila. Town, South Australia, Australia : Yarowie (–1941)

Aprelsk. Urban settlement, Irkutsk Oblast, Russia : Nadezhdinsky Priisk (–1925)

Apsheronsk. Town, Krasnodar Kray, Russia : Apsheronskaya (–1947)

Apsheronskaya *see* Apsheronsk

Apuania *see* Massa-Carrara

Apýranthos *see* Apeírathos

Aq Qaleh. Town, northern Iran : Pahlavi Dezh (–1980)

Arabistan *see* Khuzestan

Arab Republic of Egypt [Egypt]. Republic, northeastern Africa : Egypt (–1958), United Arab Republic [jointly with Syria, 1958–61] (1958–71)

Araçá *see* Mari

Araceli. Municipality, Palawan, Philippines : Dumaran (–1954)

Araçoiaba da Serra. City, southeastern Brazil, South America : Campo Largo (–1944)

Aracruz. City, southeastern Brazil, South America : Santa Cruz (–1944)

Aragats. Urban settlement, Armenia : Alagyoz (–c. 1955)

Araguacema. City, north-central Brazil, South America : Santa Maria do Araguaia (–1944)

Araguaçu *see* Paraguaçu Paulista

Araguatins. City, north-central Brazil, South America : São Vicente (–1944)

Arak. City, west-central Iran : Sultanabad (–mid-1930s)

Aral *see* Kuybyshevsky (1)
Aranyosmarót *see* Zlaté Moravce
Araquari. City, southern
   Brazil, South America :
   Parati (–1944)
Araripina. City, northeastern Brazil, South America : São Gonçalo (–1944)
Arborea. Village, western
   Sardinia, Italy : Villaggio
   Mussolini (–c.1935), Mussolinia di Sardegna
   (c.1935–c. 1944)
Arcangel. Barrio, Ilocos
   Norte, Philippines : Santo
   Tomas (–1971)
Arcoverde. City, northeastern Brazil, South America : Rio Branco (–1944)
Ardino. Village, southern
   Bulgaria : Yegri-Dere
   (–1934)
Area *see* Mundelein
Arėgala. Town, Lithuania :
   Eiragola (–1917)
Areia *see* Ubaíra
Arensburg *see* Kuressaare
Argenta *see* North Little Rock
Arkansas National Forest *see*
   Ouachita National Forest
Arkhaíai Kleonaí.Village,
   southern Greece : Kontóstablos (–1960s)
Arkhangelo-Pashisky Zavod
   see Pashiya
Arkhangelskoye. Village,
   Bashkir Autonomous Republic, Russia : Arkhangelsky Zavod (–c. 1930)
Arkhangelsky Zavod *see* Arkhangelskoye
Arktichesky. Cape, Komsomolets Island, Severnaya

Zemlya, Krasnoyarsk
   Kray, Russia : Molotov
   (?–c. 1957)
Arlington. County, Virginia, USA : Alexandria
   (–1920)
Armenia. Republic, southeastern Europe : Armenian SSR (*1920–91)
Armenian SSR *see* Armenia
Arnswalde *see* Choszczno
Ar Rachidiya. Town, eastcentral Morocco, northwestern Africa : Ksar es
   Souk (–1979)
Arroyo de la Luz. Village,
   western Spain : Arroyo
   del Puerco (–c. 1940)
Arroyo del Puerco *see* Arroyo
   de la Luz
Arsenyev. Town, Primorsky
   Kray, Russia : Semyonovka (–1952)
Artashat. Town, Armenia :
   Kamarlu (–c. 1955)
Artesia. City, New Mexico,
   USA : Stegman (–1905)
Arti. Urban settlement,
   Sverdlovsk Oblast, Russia : Artinsky Zavod
   (–1929)
Artigas. City, northwestern
   Uruguay, South America
   : San Eugenio (–1930s)
Artigas *see* Río Branco
Artinsky Zavod *see* Arti
Artsiz. Town, Odessa Oblast, Ukraine : Artsyz
   (1940–44)
Artsyz *see* Artsiz
Artur de Paiva *see* Kuvango
Artyoma, imeni. Suburb of
   Krivoy Rog, Dnepropetrovsk Oblast, Ukraine :

Galkovsky Rudnik (–c. 1926), Artyomovsky Rudnik (c. 1926–?)

Artyomovo. Town, Donetsk Oblast, Ukraine : Nelepovsky (–1921)

Artyomovsk (1). Town, Donetsk Oblast, Ukraine : Bakhmut (–1924)

Artyomovsk (2). Town, Krasnoyarsk Kray, Russia : Olkhovsky (*1911–30)

Artyomovsk (3). Town, Lugansk Oblast, Ukraine : Yekaterinovka (–1921)

Artyomovsky. Town, Sverdlovsk Oblast, Russia : Yegorshino (–1938)

Artyomovsky Rudnik see Artyoma, imeni

Aruanã. Town, central Brazil, South America : Leopoldina (–1944)

Arumeru. District, northern Tanzania, eastern Africa : Arusha (–1974)

Arunachal. Town, northeastern India : Masimpur (–1950s)

Arunachal Pradesh. Union territory, northeastern India : North East Frontier Agency (–1972)

Arusha see Arumeru

Arviat. Settlement, Northwest Territories, Canada : Eskimo Point (–1989)

Arys see Orzysz

Arzila see Asilah

Asaka. City, central Honshu, Japan : Hizaori (–1932)

Asba Littoria see Asba Tafari

Asba Tafari. Town, east-central Ethiopia, northeastern Africa : Asba Littoria (1936–41)

Asbest. Town, Sverdlovsk Oblast, Russia : Asbestovyye Rudniki (–1928), Kudelka (1928–33)

Asbestovyye Rudniki see Asbest

Asé Goniá. Village, western Crete, Greece : Asigonía (–1960s)

Asenovgrad. Town, southern Bulgaria : Stanimaka (–1934)

Asha. Town, Chelyabinsk Oblast, Russia : Asha-Balashevsky Zavod (–c. 1928)

Asha-Balashevsky Zavod see Asha

Ashihho see Acheng [A-ch'-eng]

Ashkhabad. Capital of Turkmenistan : Askhabad (–1919), Poltoratsk (1919–27)

Ashraf see Behshahr

Asht. Village, Leninabad Oblast, Tajikistan : Shaydan (–c. 1960)

Asigonía see Asé Goniá

Asilah. Town, northern Morocco, northwestern Africa : Arzila (–c. 1959)

Askhabad see Ashkhabad

Askraía. Village, central Greece : Panagía (–1960s)

Asnières see Asnières-sur-Seine

Asnières-sur-Seine. Town,

northern France :
Asnières (–1968)
Assab. Town, northern Ethi-
opia, northeastern Africa
: Dancalia Meridionale
(–1941)
Assaba. District, southern
Mauritania, western Af-
rica : Troisième (–c.
1979)
Assake *see* Leninsk (2)
Assiniboia. Town, Sas-
katchewan, Canada :
Leeville (–1913)
Assuruá *see* Santo Inácio
Astapovo *see* Lev Tolstoy
Astarabad *see* Gorgan
Astrabad *see* Gorgan
Astrakhan-Bazar *see* Dzhalila-
bad
Astrida *see* Butare
Atella di Caserta. Town,
southern Italy : Atella di
Napoli (1927–45)
Atella di Napoli *see* Atella di
Caserta
Atentze *see* Tehtsin [Te-chin]
Atig. Urban settlement,
Sverdlovsk Oblast, Rus-
sia : Atigsky Zavod
(–1929)
Atigsky Zavod *see* Atig
Atkinson Field *see* Timerhi
Atlasova. Island, Sakhalin
Oblast, Russia : Alaid
(–c. 1955)
Attock. District, northwest-
ern Pakistan : Camp-
bellpur (–?)
Attock City. Town, north-
western Pakistan : Camp-
bellpur (–?)
Auerbakhovsky Rudnik *see*
Rudnichny

Auezov. Urban settlement,
Semipalatinsk Oblast, Ka-
zakhstan : Bakyrchik
(–1967)
Augusto Cardosa *see* Metan-
gula
Aulenbach *see* Kalinovka (1)
Auliye-Ata *see* Dzhambul
Aulowönen *see* Kalinovka (1)
Aulus *see* Aulus-les-Bains
Aulus-les-Bains. Village,
southern France : Aulus
(–1938)
Aumale *see* Sour el-Ghozlane
Aumont *see* Aumont-Aubrac
Aumont-Aubrac. Village,
southern France :
Aumont (–1937)
Aurisina. Village, northeast-
ern Italy : Nabresina (–c.
1920)
Aurora. City, Colorado,
USA : Fletcher (–1907)
Aurora *see* San Francisco (2)
Auschwitz *see* Oświęcim
Auspitz *see* Hustopeče
Aussig *see* Ústí nad Labem
Aust-Agder. County, south-
ern Norway : Nedenes
(–1918)
Austerlitz *see* Slavkov
Australian Capital Terri-
tory. Territory, south-
eastern Australia : Yass-
Canberra (–1911), Fed-
eral Capital Territory
(1911–38)
Auyuittuq National
Park. Northwest Terri-
tories, Canada : Baffin Is-
land National Park
(*1972–75)
Avelavo Bay *see* Vaila Voe
Bay

Avellaneda. City, eastern Argentina, South America : Barracas al Sur (–1904)
Avesta see Erickson
Aviateur-Lécrivain see Mellah Sidi Brahim
Avli-Koi see Zhivkovo
Avlona see Vlorë
Avondale. Village, Newfoundland, Canada : Salmon Cove (–1906)
Avraamovskaya see (1) Khvoynaya Polyana; (2) Partizanskaya
Avşar see Türkeh
Ayaguz. Town, Semipalatinsk Oblast, Kazakhstan : Sergiopol (*1931–39)
Ayat. Urban settlement, Sverdlovsk Oblast, Russia : Ayatskoye (–1944)
Ayatskoye see Ayat
Ayer's Cliff. Village, Quebec, Canada : Ayer's Flat (–1904)
Ayer's Flat see Ayer's Cliff
Ayni. Village, Leninabad Oblast, Tajikistan : Zakhmatabad (–c. 1960)
Ayni see Zafarabad (1)
Ayuquitan. Barrio, Negros Occidental, Philippines : Old Ayuquitan (–1950)
Ayutinsky. Urban settlement, Rostov Oblast, Russia : Vlasova-Ayuta (–c.1960)
Azad Shahr. Town, northeastern Iran : Shah Pasand (–1980)
Azaña see Numancia de la Sagra

Azaran. Town, northwestern Iran : Sar Eskand Khan (–1980)
Azar Shahr. Town, northwestern Iran : Dehkhvareqan (–1980)
Azerbaijan. Republic,southeastern Europe : Azerbaijan SSR (*1920–91)
Azerbaijan SSR see Azerbaijan
Azetfoun. Village, northcentral Algeria, northern Africa : Port-Gueydon (–c. 1962)
Azizbekov. Urban settlement, Armenia : Pashalu (–c. 1935), Soylan (c. 1935–1956)
Azizbekov see Zaritap
Azovskoye. Urban settlement, Crimean Oblast, Ukraine : Kolai (–1944)
Azuma see Ninomiya
Azurduy. Town, south-central Bolivia, South America : Pomabamba (–1900s)

Babelsberg†. Suburb of Potsdam, southwestern Germany : Nowawes (–1938)
Babil. Province, central Iraq : Hilla (–1971)
Babimost. Town, western Poland : Bomst (–1945), Germany
Babol [Babul]. Town, northern Iraq : Barfurush (–1930)

Babolser. Town, northern
Iraq : Meshkhede-Ser
(–1930)
Baborów. Town, southern
Poland : Bauerwitz
(–1945), Germany
Bab Sebta. Village, north-
ern Morocco, northwest-
ern Africa : Farahal
(–c. 1959)
Babul = Babol
Babushkin (1). Suburb of
Moscow, Moscow Oblast,
Russia : Losino-Os-
trovskaya (–1939)
Babushkin (2). Town,
Buryat Autonomous Re-
public, Russia : Mysovsk
(–1941)
Babushkina, imeni. Village,
Vologda Oblast, Russia :
Ledengskoye (–c. 1940)
Bachaty see Starobachaty
Bachinsky see Solzavod
Bacuit see El Nido
Bad Altheide see Polanica
Zdrój
Baddeck Lakes see Bell Lakes
Bad Düben. Town, east-
central Germany : Düben
(–1948)
Bad Flinsberg see Swieradów
Zdrój
Bad Hofgastein. Town,
west-central Austria :
Hofgastein (–1936)
Bad Kudowa see Kudowa
Zdrój
Bad Landeck see Lądek Zdrój
Bad Polzin see Połczyn Zdrój
Bad Radein see Slatina Rad-
enci
Bad Reinerz see Duszniki
Zdrój

Bad Salzbrunn see Szczawno
Zdrój
Bad Sankt Leonhard im Lav-
anttale.Village, southern
Austria : Sankt Leonhard
(–1935)
Bad Schönfliess in Neumark
see Trzcińsko Zdrój
Bad Segeberg. Town, north-
western Germany : Sege-
berg (–1924)
Bad Warmbrunn see Cieplice
Śląskie Zdrój
Badyaly see Krinichnaya
Baffin Island National Park
see Auyuittuq National
Park
Bagara see Kirovskoye (2)
Bagdadi. Town, Georgia :
Mayakovsky (1940–91)
Bagenalstown see Muine
Bheag
Bagni della Porretta see Por-
ette Terme
Bagni San Giuliano see San
Giuliano Terme
Bagnorea see Bagnoregio
Bagnoregio. Town, central
Italy : Bagnorea
(–1922)
Bagrationovsk. Town,Kalin-
ingrad Oblast, Russia :
Preussisch Eylau (–1946),
Germany (–1945)
Bailen see General Emilio
Aguinaldo
Bailundo. Town, western
Angola, southwestern Af-
rica : Teixeira da Silva
(–c. 1979)
Bairak see Kalininsk (1)
Baixo Mearim see Vitória do
Mearim
Bajabonico see Imbert

Bakal. Town, Chelyabinsk
Oblast, Russia : Bakalsky
Zavod (–1928)
Baker. City, Montana, USA
: Lorraine (–1908)
Bakhmut see Artyomovsk (1)
Bakht. Town, Syrdarya Ob-
last, Uzbekistan : Veliko-
alekseyevsky (–1963)
Bakhtaran. Town, western
Iran : Qahremanshar
(–1980), Kermanshah
(1980–c. 1985)
Baki see Krasnyye Baki
Baktalórántháza.Town,
northeastern Hungary :
Nyírbakta (*1932–33)
Bakwanga see Mbuji-Mayi
Bakyrchik see Auezov
Balabaia see Egito
Balagtas. Municipality, Bu-
lacan, Philippines : Bigaa
(–1966)
Balanda see Kalininsk (2)
Balatonkiliti. Town, west-
central Hungary : Kiliti
(–1922)
Balatonmária see Balaton-
máriafürdő
Balatonmáriafürdő.Town,
west-central Hungary :
Balatonmária (–1927)
Balbunar see Kurbat
Baldenburg see Bialy Bór
Baldzhuan see Boldzhuan
Baley. Town, Chita Oblast,
Russia : Novo-Troitskoye
(–1938)
Balfour. Town, Transvaal,
South Africa : McHat-
tiesburg (–1905)
Balindong. Municipality,
Lanao, Philippines : Wa-
ter (–1956)

Balkansky Priisk see Balkany
Balkany. Settlement, Ch-
elyabinsk Oblast, Russia :
Balkansky Priisk (–1929)
Balkhash. Town, Dzhez-
kazgan Oblast, Ka-
zakhstan : Bertys (*1929–
?), Pribalkhash (?–1937)
Balla Balla see Mbalambala
Ballescas. Barrio, Antique,
Philippines : Barasanan
(–1957)
Ballydesmond. Town,
County Cork, Ireland :
Kingwilliamstown
(–c. 1950)
Balombo. Town, western
Angola, southwestern Af-
rica : Vila Norton de
Matos(–c. 1979)
Balsas. City, northeastern
Brazil, South America :
Santo Antônio de
Balsas(–1944)
Baltiysk. Town, Kaliningrad
Oblast, Russia : Pillau
(–1946), Germany (–
1945)
Baltiysky (Port) see Paldiski
Baltser see Krasnoarmeysk (1)
Banaba. Island, Kiribati,
western Pacific : Ocean
(Island) (1804–1979)
Bancroft see Chililabombwe
Banda Atjeh. Town, Suma-
tra, Indonesia :
Kutaradja (–c. 1966)
Bandar see Masulipat(n)am
Bandar-e Anzali [En-
zeli]. Town, northwest-
ern Iran : Bandar-e
Pahlavi [Pehlevi] (–1980)
Bandar-e Khomeyni [Bandar
Khomeyni].Town, south-

western Iran : Bandar-e
Shahpur [Bandar
Shahpur] (–1980)
Bandar-e Pahlavi [Pehlevi] *see*
Bandar-e Anzali [Enzeli]
Bandar-e Shah [Bandar Shah]
see Bandar-e Torkeman
[Bandar Torkeman]
Bandar-e Shahpur [Bandar
Shahpur] *see* Bandar-e
Khomeyni [Bandar
Khomeyni]
Bandar-e Torkeman [Bandar
Torkeman]. Town,
northern Iran : Bandar-e
Shah [Bandar Shah] (–
1980)
Bandar Khomeyni = Banda-e
Khomeyni
Bandar Penggaram *see* Batu
Pahat
Bandar Seri Bega-
wan. Capital of Brunei,
Borneo, southeastern
Asia : Brunei Town
(–1970)
Bandar Shah *see* Bandar-e
Torkeman
Bandar Shahpur *see* Bandar-e
Khomeyni
Bandundu. Town, western
Zaïre, central Africa :
Banningville (–1966)
Bangladesh. Republic,
southern Asia : East Paki-
stan (*1947–71)
Banjul. Capital of Gambia,
western Africa : Bathurst
(–1973)
Bank. Urban settlement,
Azerbaijan : Narima-
nova, imeni (–1939),
Kirova, imeni (1939–c.
1940)

Banki *see* Krasnogorsk (1)
Banningville *see* Bandundu
Bannovsky *see* Slavyanogorsk
Bannu. City, northwestern
Pakistan : Edwardesabad
(–1903)
Banská Bystrica. Town,
eastern Slovakia : Ne-
usohl (–1918, 1939–45),
Germany
Banská Štiavnica. Town,
central Slovakia : Schem-
nitz (–1918, 1939–45),
Germany
Banto-Anin *see* Bukal
Banzyville *see* Mobayem-
bongo
Baquba *see* Diyala
Baran. Town, Vitebsk Ob-
last, Belorussia : Krasny
Oktyabr (c. 1918–1920s)
Baranchinsky. Urban settle-
ment, Sverdlovsk Oblast,
Russia : Baranchinsky
Zavod (–1928)
Baranchinsky Zavod *see* Ba-
ranchinsky
Barangay *see* Hilario Valdez
(1)
Baranovichi. Town, Brest
Oblast, Belorussia : Bara-
nowicze (1921–39), Po-
land
Baranowicze *see* Baranovichi
Barão de Cocais. City,
southeastern Brazil,
South America : Morro
Grande (–1944)
Barasanan *see* Ballescas
Barat *see* Ablan
Barba de Puerco *see* Puerto-
Seguro
Barbará *see* Santa María de
Barbará

Barce *see* Al-Marj
Barczewo. Town, northeastern Poland : Wartenburg (–1945), Germany
Bardejov. Town, northeastern Slovakia : Bartfeld (–1918, 1939–45), Germany
Bardily *see* Zaleshany
Bardo. Town, southwestern Poland : Wartha (–1945), Germany
Barfurush *see* Babol
Bar Harbor. Town, Maine, USA : Eden (–1918)
Baria *see* Dewgard Baria
Barlinek. Town, northwestern Poland : Berlinchen (–1945), Germany
Barmaksizi *see* Tsalka
Bärn *see* Moravský Beroun
Barnegat City *see* Barnegat Light
Barnegat Light. Borough, New Jersey, USA : Barnegat City (–1948)
Barnsdall. City, Oklahoma, USA : Bigheart (–1921)
Baronsk *see* Marks
Barotse *see* Western
Barra Bonita *see* Ibaiti
Barracas al Sur *see* Avellaneda
Barrit-Luluno *see* Luba
Barshatas. Village, Semipalatinsk Oblast, Kazakhstan : Chubartau (–c. 1960)
Bartang. Village, Gorno-Badakhshan Autonomous Oblast, Tajikistan : Sipon(d)zh (–c. 1935)
Bartenstein *see* Bartoszyce
Bartfeld *see* Bardejov

Bartolo *see* Betanzos
Bartoszyce. Town, northeastern Poland : Bartenstein (–1945), Germany
Barville. Town, Quebec, Canada : Val-Laflamme (*1950–54)
Bärwalde (in Neumark) *see* Barwice (1)
Bärwalde (in Pommern) *see* Barwice (2)
Barwice (1). Town, northwestern Poland : Bärwalde (in Neumark) (–1945), Germany
Barwice (2). Town, northwestern Poland : Bärwalde (in Pommern) (–1945), Germany
Baryshnikovo *see* Krasnogorskoye (1)
Basargechar *see* Vardenis
Bashanta *see* Gorodovikovsk
Bashkicheti *see* Dmanisi
Bashkir Autonomous Republic. West-central Russia : Bashkir Autonomous SSR (*1919–91)
Bashkir Autonomous SSR *see* Bashkir Autonomous Republic
Bashtanka. Town, Nikolayev Oblast, Ukraine : Poltavka (–c. 1930)
Basses-Alpes *see* Alpes-de-Haute-Provence
Basses-Pyrénées *see* Pyrénées-Atlantiques
Bassopiano Orientale *see* Massawa [Mitsiwa]
Basutoland *see* Lesotho
Bata. Town, Río Muni, Equatorial Guinea, western Africa : Macías

Nguema Bijogo (1973–79)

Batalha. City, northeastern Brazil, South America : Belo Monte (–1949)

Batalhão see Taperoá

Batalpashinsk see Cherkessk

Batalpashinskaya see Cherkessk

Batamshinsky. Urban settlement, Aktyubinsk Oblast, Kazakhstan : Kimpersaysky (–1945)

Batang see Paan

Bata-Siala. Town, western Zaïre, central Africa : Kai-Mbaku (–1972)

Batavia see Jakarta

Batbakkara see Amangeldy

Bathurst see Banjul

Batingan see Narra (1)

Batken. Village, Osh Oblast, Kirgizia : Batken-Buzhum (–1945)

Batken-Buzhum see Batken

Batovany see Partizánske

Batu Pahat. City, southern Malaya, southeastern Asia: Bandar Penggaram (–?)

Batuli see San Isidro

Bat Yam. City, west-central Israel : Ir Gannim (*1925–36)

Batz see Batz-sur-Mer

Batz-sur-Mer. Village, western France : Batz (–1931)

Baudens see Belarbi

Baudouinville see Virungu

Bauerwitz see Baborów

Bauguen see Salcedo

Bauman see Shafirkan

Baumanabad see Pyandzh

Bay see Bay Village

Bayag see Calanasan

Bayan-Tumen see Choybalsan

Bayetovo. Village, Issyk-Kul Oblast, Kirgizia : Dyurbeldzhin (–1981)

Baymak. Town, Bashkir Autonomous Republic, Russia : Baymak-Tanalykovo (– 1944)

Baymak-Tanalykovo see Baymak

Bay Village. Suburb of Cleveland, Ohio, USA : Bay (*1903–50)

Bayville see Kirkwood

Bazargic see Tolbukhin

Bazarjik see Tolbukhin

Bazar-Yaypan see Yaypan

Beauaraba see Pittsworth

Beaver River see Beaverton

Beaverton. Town, Ontario, Canada : Beaver River (–1928)

Bečej. Village, northern Serbia : Stari Bečej (–c. 1947)

Béchar. Town, western Algeria, northern Africa : Colomb-Béchar (–c. 1962)

Bechuanaland see Botswana

Becsehely. Town, western Hungary : Beksénypólya (*1941–42)

Beda see Noviki (1)

Bedeau see Ras el Ma

Bedeyeva Polyana. Village, Bashkir Autonomous Republic, Russia : Bedeyevo (–c. 1940)

Bedeyevo see Bedeyeva Polyana

Bedford see North Bedfordshire

Bedfordview. Township, Transvaal, South Africa : Geldenhuis Estate Small Holdings (–1926)

Bedloes Island see Liberty Island

Bednodemyanovsk. Town, Penza Oblast, Russia : Spassk (–1925)

Będzin. City, southern Poland : Bendin (–1919), Russia; Bendsburg (1939–45), Germany

Begovat see Bekabad

Behshahr. Town, northern Iran : Ashraf (–mid-1930s)

Beijing = Peking

Beilau see Pilawa

Beira see Sofala

Beitsch see Biecz

Béjaïa. Town, northern Algeria, northern Africa : Bougie (–c. 1962)

Bekabad. Town, Tashkent Oblast, Uzbekistan : Begovat (–1964)

Bek-Budi see Karshi

Beksénypólya see Becsehely

Bektemir see Narimanov (1)

Bela Aliança see Rio do Sul

Bělá pod Bezdězem. Town, northern Czech Lands : Weisswasser (–1918, 1939–45), Germany

Belarbi. Village, northwestern Algeria, northern Africa : Baudens (–c. 1962)

Bela Slatina see Byala Slatina

Bela Vista see (1) Echaporã; (2) Katchiungo

Belaya Kalitva. Town, Rostov Oblast, Russia : Ust-Belokalitvenskaya (–c. 1935), Belokalitvenskaya (late 1930s)

Belém see Palmeirais

Belgard see Bialogard

Belgian Congo see Zaïre

Belgorod-Dnestrovsky. Town, Odessa Oblast, Ukraine : Akkerman (–1918), Cetatea Albă (1918–40, 1941–44), Romania

Belingwe see Mberengwa

Belinsky. Town, Penza Oblast, Russia : Chembar (–1948)

Belize. UK crown colony, Central America : British Honduras (1840–1973)

Bella Unión. Town, northwestern Uruguay, South America : Santa Rosa (–1930s)

Bella Vista. Town, southern Mexico, North America : San Pedro Remate (–1934)

Belle Glade. City, Florida, USA : Hillsborough Canal Settlement (–1921)

Bellin. Town, Quebec, Canada : Payne Bay (–1965)

Bellingham. City, Washington, USA : Whatcom (–1903)

Bell Lakes. Lakes, Nova Scotia, Canada : Baddeck Lakes (–1974)

Bellville. Railway station of town of Bellville, Cape Province, South Africa : Durban Road (–1906)

Belmeken see Kolarov

Belmont see Belmont-de-la-Loire

Belmont-de-la-Loire.
Village, southeastern
France : Belmont (–1936)
Belmonte *see* Manissobal
Belogorsk (1).   Town, Amur
Oblast, Russia : Bo-
chkarevo (–1926),
Aleksandrovsk (1926–
35), Kuybyshevka-Vosto-
chnaya (1935–57)
Belogorsk (2).   Town, Cri-
mean Oblast, Ukraine :
Karasubazar (–1945)
Belogorsk (3).   Urban settle-
ment, Kemerovo Oblast,
Russia : Kiya-Shaltyr
(–c. 1960)
Belogorye.   Urban settle-
ment, Khmelnitsky Ob-
last, Ukraine :
Lyakhovtsy (–1946)
Belo Horizonte.   City, south-
eastern Brazil, South
America : Cidade de Mi-
nas (–1901)
Belokalitvenskaya *see* Belaya
Kalitva
Belolesye.   Village, Odessa
Oblast, Ukraine : Ak-
mangit (–c. 1960)
Belolutsk.   Urban settle-
ment, Lugansk Oblast,
Ukraine : Belolutskaya
(–1937)
Belolutskaya *see* Belolutsk
Belo Monte *see* Batalha
Belomorsk.   Town, Karelian
Autonomous Republic,
Russia : Soroka (–1938)
Belorechensk.   Town, Kras-
nodar Kray, Russia : Be-
lorechenskaya (–1958)
Belorechenskaya *see* Belore-
chensk

Beloretsk.   Town, Bashkir
Autonomous Republic,
Russia : Beloretsky
Zavod (–1923)
Beloretsky Zavod *see* Be-
loretsk
Belorussia.   Republic, cen-
tral Europe : Belorussian
SSR (*1922–91)
Belorussian SSR *see* Belorussia
Beloshchelye *see* Naryan-Mar
Belotsarsk *see* Kyzyl
Belovo *see* Zemen
Belovodsk.   Urban settle-
ment, Lugansk Oblast,
Ukraine : Belovodskoye
(–1937)
Belovodskoye.   Village, Kir-
gizia : Stalinskoye (1937–
61)
Belovodskoye *see* Belovodsk
Bely Bychek *see* Chagoda
Bely Klyuch *see* Krasny
Klyuch
Belyye Kresty *see* Sazonovo
Bendel.   State, southwest Ni-
geria, western Africa :
Mid-West Region
(*1963–67), Mid-Western
(State) (1967–76)
Bendery.   Town, Moldova :
Tighina (1918–40, 1941–
44), Romania
Bendin *see* Będzin
Bendix *see* Teterboro
Bendsburg *see* Będzin
Beneditinos.   City, northeast-
ern Brazil, South Amer-
ica : São Benedito
(–1944)
Benefactor *see* San Juan
Bengal.   State, northeastern
India : West Bengal
(*1947–72)

Benin. Republic, western
Africa : Dahomey
(–1975)
Ben Slimane. Town, north-
western Morocco, north-
western Africa : Boulhaut
(–c. 1959)
Bentiaba. Village, south-
western Angola, south-
western Africa : São Ni-
colau (–c. 1979)
Ben Tre. Town, southern
Vietnam : Truc Giang
(–c. 1980)
Berane see Ivangrad
Berdyansk. Town, Zapo-
rozhye Oblast, Ukraine :
Osipenko (1939–58)
Beregovoy. Urban settle-
ment, Omsk Oblast, Rus-
sia : Kharino (–c. 1960)
Berestovitsa see Pogranichny
(1)
Berezanka. Urban settle-
ment, Nikolayev Oblast,
Ukraine : Tiligulo-Be-
rezanka (–c. 1960)
Bereznik. Urban settle-
ment, Arkhangelsk Ob-
last, Russia : Se-
myonovskoye (–c. 1960)
Berezniki. Town, Perm Ob-
last, Russia : Usolye-
Solikamskoye (–1933)
Bereznitsa (1). Village,
Vitebsk Oblast, Belorus-
sia : Lezhni (–1964)
Bereznitsa (2). Village,
Grodno Oblast, Belorus-
sia : Treputikha (–1964)
Bereznyaki. Village,
Vitebsk Oblast, Belorus-
sia : Sinebryukhi (–1964)
Bereznyanka. Village,

Vitebsk Oblast, Belorus-
sia : Zagryazye (–1964)
Berezovichi. Village, Brest
Oblast, Belorussia:
Parshevichi (–1964)
Bergreichenstein see Kašper-
ské Hory
Bergstadt see Leśnica
Beringovsky. Urban settle-
ment, Chukot Autono-
mous Okrug, Magadan
Oblast, Russia : Ugolny
(–1957)
Berkovets see Kotsyubinskoye
Berlengas see Valença do
Piaulí
Berlin see Kitchener
Berlinchen see Barlinek
Bernstadt (in Schlesien) see
Bierutów
Bernstein see Pełczyce
Berrahal. Town, northeast-
ern Algeria, northern Af-
rica : Aïn Mokra (–c.
1962)
Bertolínia. City, northeast-
ern Brazil, South Amer-
ica : Aparecida (–1944)
Bertys see Balkhash
Berwyn see Gene Autry
Beryoza. Town, Brest Ob-
last, Belorussia : Beryoza-
Kartuzskaya
(–1939)
Beryoza-Kartuzskaya see
Beryoza
Beryozov see Beryozovo
Beryozovo. Urban settle-
ment, Khanty-Mansi Au-
tonomous Okrug,
Tyumen Oblast, Russia :
Beryozov (–1926)
Beryozovshchina. Village,
Grodno Oblast, Belo-

russia : Bozhedary
(–1964)
Beryozy. Village, Grodno
Oblast, Belorussia : Mar-
tyshki (–1964)
Berzence. Town, southwest-
ern Hungary : Berzencze
(–1918)
Berzencze see Berzence
Besharyk. Town, Fergana
Oblast, Uzbekistan :
Kirova, imeni (1937–c.
1940), Kirovo (1940–83)
Beskhlebichi see Sosnovichi
Bessarabka. Urban settle-
ment, Moldavia : Roma-
novka (–c. 1960)
Betanzos. Town, southeast-
ern Bolivia, South Amer-
ica : Bartolo (–1900s)
Bethel see Bethel Park
Bethel Park. Suburb of Pitts-
burgh, Pennsylvania,
USA : Bethel (–1960)
Bethpage. Village, New
York, USA : Central
Park (1841–1936)
Bettioua. Village, north-
western Algeria, north-
ern Africa : Saint-Leu (–
c. 1962)
Beuthen see Bytom
Beuthen an der Oder see
Bytom Odrzański
Beverly see Beverly Hills
Beverly Hills. Suburb of Los
Angeles, California,
USA : Beverly (*1907–
11)
Beylagan. Town, Azer-
baijan : Zhdanovsk
(–1989)
Beyuk-Vedi see Vedi
Bezdelichi see Razdolnaya

Bezdružice. Town, western
Czech Lands : Weseritz
(–1918, 1939–45), Ger-
many
Bezhitsa (1956†, when amal-
gamated with Bry-
ansk).Town, Bryansk
Oblast, Russia : Ordzhon-
ikidzegrad (1941–44)
Bezwada see Vijayawada
Biafra, Bight of see Bonny,
Bight of
Biała. Town, southwestern
Poland : Zülz (–1945),
Germany
Biała (Piska). Town, north-
eastern Poland : Geh-
lenburg (–1938), Ger-
many; Bialla (1938–45),
Germany
Bialla see Biała (Piska)
Białogard. Town, northwest-
ern Poland : Belgard
(–1945), Germany
Biały Bór. Town, northwest-
ern Poland : Baldenburg
(–1945), Germany
Biały Kamień. Town, south-
western Poland : Weiss-
stein (–1945), Germany
Bibala. Town, southwestern
Angola, southwestern Af-
rica : Vila Arriaga
(–c. 1979)
Bié. Town, central Angola,
southwestern Africa :
Silva Porto (c. 1900–c.
1976)
Biecz. Town, southeastern
Poland : Beitsch (–1935),
Germany
Bielawa. Town, southwest-
ern Poland : Langenbie-
lau (–1945), Germany

Bielitz *see* Bielsko
Bielsko. City, southern Poland : Bielitz (–1919), Germany
Bierutów. Town, southwestern Poland : Bernstadt (in Schlesien) (–1945), Germany
Biga *see* El Rio
Bigaa *see* Balagtas
Bigheart *see* Barnsdall
Bilimbay. Urban settlement, Sverdlovsk Oblast, Russia : Bilimbayevsky Zavod (–1929)
Bilimbayevsky Zavod *see* Bilimbay
Bílovec. Town, southeastern Czech Lands : Wagstadt (–1919, 1939–45), Germany
Binangoan de Lampon *see* Infanta
Bingerau *see* Węgrów
Binokor *see* Pakhtakor
Bioko. Island territory, Equatorial Guinea, western Africa : Fernando Po (–1973), Macías Nguema Bijogo (1973–79)
Bircao *see* Bur Gao
Birdville *see* Halton City
Bir Jdid. Village, northwestern Morocco, northwestern Africa : Bir Jdid Chavent (–c. 1959)
Bir Jdid Chavent *see* Bir Jdid
Bir Mogreïn. Town, northwestern Mauritania, western Africa : Fort Trinquet (–c. 1958)
Birobidzhan. Capital of Jewish Autonomous Oblast, Khabarovsk Kray,

Russia : Tikhonkaya (–1928)
Biruni. Town, Karakalpak Autonomous Republic, Uzbekistan : Shabbaz (–1958)
Biryuch *see* Krasnogvardeyskoye (1)
Biryusinsk. Town, Irkutsk Oblast, Russia : Suyetikha (–1967)
Birzhi *see* Madona
Birzula *see* Kotovsk (1)
Biscari *see* Acate
Bischoflack *see* Škofja Loka
Bischofsburg *see* Biskupiec (1)
Bischofstal *see* Ujazd
Bischofstein *see* Bisztynek
Bischofswerder *see* Biskupiec (2)
Bisert. Urban settlement, Sverdlovsk Oblast, Russia : Bisertsky Zavod (–1942)
Bisertsky Zavod *see* Bisert
Bishkek. Capital of Kirgizia : Pishpek (–1926), Frunze (1926–91)
Bishopburg *see* Oyen
Biskupiec (1). Town, northeastern Poland : Bischofsburg (–1945), Germany
Biskupiec (2). Town, northeastern Poland : Bischofswerder (–1945), Germany
Bismarckburg *see* Kasanga
Bistrica *see* (1) (Ilirska) Bistrica; (2) (Slovenska) Bistrica
Bisztynek. Town, northeastern Poland : Bischofstein (–1945), Germany

Bitola [Bitolj]. City, southern Macedonia : Monastir (–1913), Turkey
Bitolj = Bitola
Bitschwiller *see* Bitschwiller-lès-Thann
Bitschwiller-lès-Thann. Village, eastern France : Bitschwiller (–1938)
Bitulok *see* Gabaldon
Biyuk-Onlar *see* Oktyabrskoye (1)
Björkö *see* (1) Krasnoostrovsky; (2) Primorsk (2)
Blachownia (Śląska). Town, southern Poland : Blechhammer (–1945), Germany
Black Diamond *see* Pittsburg
Blackfalds. Village, Alberta, Canada : Waghorn (–1903)
Blackwell's Island *see* Franklin D. Roosevelt Island
Blagoevgrad. Town, southwestern Bulgaria : Gorna Djumaya (–1950)
Blagoveshchensk. Town, Bashkir Autonomous Republic, Russia : Blagoveshchensky Zavod (–1942)
Blagoveshchensky Zavod *see* Blagoveshchensk
Blanco *see* Luperón
Blechhammer *see* Blachownia (Śląska)
Bliznetsy *see* Bliznyuki
Bliznyuki. Urban settlement, Kharkov Oblast, Ukraine : Bliznetsy (–c. 1960)
Bloom *see* Chicago Heights

Bloshniki *see* Kalinovaya (1)
Bloshno *see* Podgornaya (1)
Bluden *see* Pervomayskoye (1)
Bluefield. City, Virginia, USA : Graham (–1921)
Bluefields *see* Zelaya
Bluff. Town, South Island, New Zealand : Campbelltown (–1917)
Blumenau *see* Stettler
Blyukherovo *see* Leninskoye (6)
Blyukherovsk *see* Srednyaya Nyukzha
Boa Esperança. City, southeastern Brazil, South America : Dores da Boa Esperança (–1940)
Boa Esperança *see* (1) Boa Esperança do Sul; (2) Esperantina
Boa Esperança do Sul. City, southeastern Brazil, South America : Boa Esperança (–1944)
Boa Vista *see* Tocantinópolis
Boa Vista (do Erechim) *see* Erechim
Bobovozovshchina *see* Urozhaynaya (1)
Bobriki *see* Novomoskovsk
Bocâina. City, southeastern Brazil, South America : São João da Bocâina (–1938)
Bocaiúva *see* (1) Bocaiúva do Sul; (2) Macatuba
Bocaiúva do Sul. City, southern Brazil, South America : Bocaiúva (–1944), Imbuial (1944–48)
Bochkarevo *see* Belogorsk (1)

Bocoio. Town, western An-
gola, southwestern Africa
: Sousa de Lara (–c. 1979)
Bocsarlapujtő see Kar-
ancslapujtő
Bodenbach see Podmokly
Bogatoye. Village, Samara
Oblast, Russia : Pavlovka
(–c. 1960)
Bogatynia. Town, south-
western Poland : Reich-
enau (–1945), Germany
Bogatyye Saby. Village, Ta-
tar Autonomous Oblast,
Russia : Saby (late 1930s)
Boghari see Ksar el Boukhari
Bogodukhovka see Chkalovo
(1)
Bogomdarovanny see Kommu-
nar
Bogor. City, western Java,
Indonesia : Buitenzorg
(–1945)
Bogorodsk see Noginsk
Bogorodskoye see (1)
Kamskoye Ustye; (2)
Leninskoye (2)
Bogoyavlensk see Zhovtn-
evoye (1)
Bogoyavlenskoye see Per-
vomaysky (1)
Boguszów. City, southwest-
ern Poland : Gottesberg
(–1945), Germany
Böhmisch-Brod see Český
Brod
Böhmisch-Kamnitz see Česká
Kamenice
Böhmisch-Leipa see Česká
Lípa
Böhmisch-Skalitz see Česká
Skalice
Böhmisch-Trübau see Česká
Třebová

Bokovo-Antratsit see Antrat-
sit
Boldyuki see Zarechnaya (1)
Boldzhuan. Village, Khat-
lon Oblast, Tajikistan :
Baldzhuan (–c. 1940)
Bolesławice. Village, south-
western Poland : Bun-
zelwitz (–1945), Germany
Bolesławiec. Town, south-
western Poland : Bunzlau
(–1945), Germany
Boleszkowice. Town, north-
western Poland : Fürsten-
felde (–1945), Germany
Bolívar. Town, northwest-
ern Peru, South America
: Cajamarquilla (–1925)
Bolívar see (Cerro) Bolívar
Bolnisi. Town, Georgia :
Yekaterinofeld (–1921),
Lyuksemburg (1921–36),
Lyuksemburgi (1926–43)
Bologhine. Suburb of Algi-
ers, Algeria, northern Af-
rica : Saint-Eugène
(–c. 1962)
Bolshakovo. Village, Kalin-
ingrad Oblast, Russia :
Gross Skaisgirren
(–1938), Germany;
Kreuzingen (1938–45),
Germany
Bolshaya Garmanda see
Evensk
Bolshaya Martyn-
ovka. Village, Rostov
Oblast, Russia : Martyn-
ovka [Martynovskoye]
(–c. 1944)
Bolshaya Novosyolka see
Velikaya Novosyolka
Bolshaya Promyshlenka see
Promyshlennovsky

Bolshaya Tsaryovshchina *see*
Volzhsky
Bolshaya Ussurka. River,
Primorsky Kray, Russia :
Iman (–1974)
Bolshevo. Village, Moscow
Oblast, Russia : Stalinsky
(1928–61)
Bolshiye Arabuzy *see* Per-
vomayskoye (2)
Bolshiye Soli *see* Nekra-
sovskoye
Bolshoy Beryozovy. Island,
Gulf of Finland, Lenin-
grad Oblast, Russia :
Koivisto (–1949), Finland
Bolshoye Ignatovo. Village,
Mordovian Autonomous
Republic, Russia : Igna-
tovo (–c. 1940)
Bolshoy Kosheley *see* Komso-
molskoye (1)
Bolshoy Tokmak *see* Tokmak
(1), (2)
Bolshoy Yanisol *see* Velikaya
Novosyolka
Bolton *see* Stonefort
Bolvan *see* Zagornaya
Bolvanovka *see* Noviki (2)
Bolvany *see* Borovaya (1)
Bóly. Town, southern Hun-
gary : Németbóly (–1950)
Bom Jardim. City, south-
eastern Brazil, South
America : Vergel (1944–
48)
Bom Jardim *see* Bom Jardim
de Minas
Bom Jardim de Minas. City,
southeastern Brazil,
South America : Bom
Jardim (–1944)
Bomst *see* Babimost
Bondyuzhsky *see* Mende-

leyevsk
Bondyuzhsky Zavod *see* Men-
deleyevsk
Bône *see* Annaba
Bonfim *see* (1) Senhor do
Bonfim; (2) Silvânia
Bonito *see* Bonito de Santa Fé
Bonito de Santa Fé. City,
northeastern Brazil,
South America : Bonito
(–1944)
Bonny, Bight of [name used by
Nigeria]. Bay, Gulf of
Guinea, western Africa :
Biafra, Bight of (–1975)
Borchalo *see* Marneuli
Borden. Town, Prince Ed-
ward Island, Canada :
Carleton Point (–1916)
Bordj Bounaama. Village,
northern Algeria, north-
ern Africa : Molière
(–c. 1962)
Bordj el Bahri. Village,
northern Algeria, north-
ern Africa : Cap-Matifou
(–c. 1962)
Bordj el Kiffan. Town,
northern Algeria, north-
ern Africa : Fort-de-l'Eau
(–c. 1962)
Bordj Omar Driss. Town,
east-central Algeria,
northern Africa : Fort
Flatters (–c. 1962),
Zaouet el-Kahla (c.
1962–c. 1979)
Borgo San Donnino *see* Fidenza
Borgotaro *see* Borgo Val di
Taro
Borgo Val di Taro. Town,
north-central Italy : Borgotaro (–c. 1930)

Borisoglebskiye Slobody *see* Borisoglebsky

Borisoglebsky. Urban settlement, Yaroslavl Oblast, Russia : Borisoglebskiye Slobody (–c. 1960)

Borisovgrad *see* Pârvomaj

Borja *see* Sagbayan

Borki Wielkie *see* Velikiye Borki

Borok *see* Polenovo

Borovaya (1). Village, Vitebsk Oblast, Belorussia : Bolvany (–1964)

Borovaya (2). Village, Brest Oblast, Belorussia : Korostovka (–1964)

Borovets. Mountain resort, western Bulgaria : Chamkoriya (–1942)

Borovichi. Village, Gomel Oblast, Belorussia : Gryazliv (–1964)

Borovshchina (1). Village, Vitebsk Oblast, Belorussia : Peredelki (–1964)

Borovshchina (2). Village, Minsk Oblast, Belorussia : Puziki (–1964)

Borovsk [†, now merged with Solikamsk]. Town, Perm Oblast, Russia : Ust-Borovaya (–1949)

Bor u České Lípy *see* Nový Bor

Borzhom *see* Borzhomi

Borzhomi. Town, Georgia : Borzhom (–1936)

Boshnyakovo. Urban settlement, Sakhalin Oblast, Russia : Nishi-shakutan (1905–45), Japan

Bosquet *see* Hadjadj

Botev. Mountain, central Bulgaria : Ferdinandov (?–?), Yumrukchal (?–1950)

Botevgrad. City, western Bulgaria : Orkhaniye (–1934)

Botswana. Republic, southern Africa : Bechuanaland (–1966)

Boucheron *see* El Guara

Boufatis. Village, northwestern Algeria, northern Africa : Saint-Louis (–c. 1962)

Bougaâ. Village, northeastern Algeria, northern Africa : Lafayette (–c. 1962)

Bougainville *see* North Solomon Islands

Bougie *see* Béjaïa

Bou Hanifia el Hamamat. Village, northwestern Algeria, northern Africa : Bou Hanifia les Thermes (–c. 1962)

Bou Hanifia les Thermes *see* Bou Hanifia el Hamamat

Bou Ismaïl. Village, northern Algeria, northern Africa : Castiglione (–c. 1962)

Bou Kadir. Village, northern Algeria, northern Africa : Charon (–c. 1962)

Boulder Dam *see* Hoover Dam

Boulhaut *see* Ben Slimane

Boulogne-Billancourt. Suburb of Paris, France : Boulogne-sur-Seine (–1924)

Boulogne-sur-Seine *see* Boulogne-Billancourt

Bourbourg. Town, northern

France : Bourbourg-Ville
(–1945)
Bourbourg-Ville *see* Bour-
bourg
Bous.   Town, western Ger-
many : Buss (1936–45)
Bovdilovtsy *see* Slobozhany
Boykovo.   Village, Kuril Is-
lands, Sakhalin Oblast,
Russia : Kataoka (1905–
45), Japan
Boynton *see* Boynton Beach
Boynton Beach.   City, Flor-
ida, USA : Boynton
(–1926)
Boynton Beach *see* Ocean
Ridge
Boyoma Falls.   Cataracts,
Congo River, Zaïre, cen-
tral Africa : Stanley Falls
(–1972)
Bozhedarovka *see* Shchorsk
Bozhedary *see* Beryozovshch-
ina
Boží Dar.   Town, northwest-
ern Czech Lands : Got-
tesgab (–1918, 1939–45),
Germany
Bragança *see* Bragança Pau-
lista
Bragança Paulista.   City,
southeastern Brazil,
South America : Bra-
gança (–1944)
Bragg's Spur *see* West Mem-
phis
Brahestad *see* Raahe
Brakna.   District, western
Mauritania : Cinquième
(–c. 1979)
Brandenburg *see* Old Glory
Braniewo.   Town, northeast-
ern Poland : Braunsberg
(–1945), Germany

Brantovka *see* Oktyabrsky (1)
Braşov.   Town, central Ro-
mania : Kronstadt
(–1918), Germany;
Oraşul Stalin (1950–60)
Bratislava.   Capital of Slova-
kia : Pressburg (1939–
45), Germany
Bratsberg *see* Telemark
Bratsk *see* Porozhsky
Brätz *see* Brójce
Braunsberg *see* Braniewo
Brazil.   Federal republic,
east-central South Amer-
ica : United States of Bra-
zil (1891–1967)
Brea.   City, California, USA
: Randolph (1908–11)
Breage *see* Vermilion
Břeclav.   Town, southeast-
ern Czech Lands : Lun-
denburg (–1918, 1939–
45), Germany
Breitenstein *see* Ulyanovo (1)
Brejo da Madre de
Deus.   City, northeast-
ern Brazil, South Amer-
ica : Madre de Deus
(1939–48)
Bremerhaven.   City, north-
ern Germany : Weser-
münde (1938–47)
Bremersdorp *see* Manzini
Breslau *see* Wrockaw
Brest.   Capital of Brest Ob-
last, Belorussia : Brest-
Litovsk (–1921), Brzešč
nad Bugiem (1921–39),
Poland
Brest-Litovsk *see* Brest
Brezhnev *see* Naberezhnyye
Chelny
Brickaville *see* Vohibinany
Brieg *see* Brzeg

Briesen *see* Wąbrzeźno
Brights Grove. Village, Ontario, Canada : Maxwell (–1935)
British Central Africa (Protectorate) *see* Malawi
British East Africa *see* Kenya
British Guiana *see* Guyana
British Solomon Islands (Protectorate) *see* Solomon Islands
Brno. City, southeastern Czech Lands : Brünn (–1918, 1939–45), Germany
Brochów. Town, southwestern Poland : Brockau (–1945), Germany
Brockau *see* Brochów
Brod (Makedonskie). Town, west-central Macedonia : Južni Brod (–c. 1945)
Broderick Falls *see* Webuye
Brodnica. Town, north-central Poland : Buddenbrock (–1945), Germany
Brójce. Town, western Poland : Brätz (–1945), Germany
Broken Bank *see* Victor
Broken Hill *see* Kabwe
Bromberg *see* Bydgoszcz
Bromont. Village, Quebec, Canada : West Shefford (–1966)
Bronkhorstspruit. Town, Transvaal, South Africa : Erasmus (*1904–35)
Brookfield. Village, Illinois, USA : Grossdale (–1905)
Brooklyn *see* Keystone Heights
Brossard. Suburb of Mon-

treal, Quebec, Canada : Brosseau Station (–1958)
Brosseau Station *see* Brossard
Brotas *see* Brotas de Macaúbas
Brotas de Macaúbas. City, eastern Brazil, South America : Brotas (–1944)
Brothers, The *see* Al Ikhwan
Bruckmühl. Village, southwestern Germany : Kirchdorf am Haunpold (–1948)
Brunei Town *see* Bandar Seri Begawan
Brünn *see* Brno
Brunshaupten *see* Kühlungsborn
Bruntál. Town, eastern Czech Lands : Freudenthal (–1919, 1939–45), Germany
Brzeg. City, southwestern Poland : Brieg (–1945), Germany
Brzeg Dolny. Town, southwestern Poland : Dyhernfurth (–1945), Germany
Brzešč nad Bugiem *see* Brest
Brzeziny. Town, central Poland : Löwenstadt (1939–45), Germany
Buayan *see* General Santos
Bucana *see* Suhaile Arabi
Budarinskaya *see* Cherkesovsky
Budatétény. Suburb of Budapest, Hungary : Kistétény (–1915)
Buddenbrock *see* Brodnica
Bűdszentmihály *see* Tiszavasvári
Budweis *see* České Budějovice

Budyonnovka *see* Novoazovsk
Budyonnovsk. Town,
Stavropol Kray, Russia :
Svyatoy Krest (–1920),
Prikumsk (1920–35,
1957–73)
Budyonnoye *see* Krasnog-
vardeyskoye (1)
Budyonny *see* Chat-Bazar
Buenavista. Barrio, Sorso-
gon, Philippines : Gi-
bigaan (–1914)
Bugaz *see* Zatoka
Bugho *see* Javier
Buitenzorg *see* Bogor
Bujumbura. Capital of Bu-
rundi, central Africa :
Usumbura (–1962)
Bukal. Barrio, Marinduque,
Philippines : Banto-Anin
(–1957)
Bukavu. Town, eastern
Zaïre, central Africa :
Costermansville (–1966)
Bukhara. Capital of Bukhara
Oblast, Uzbekistan :
Staraya Bukhara (–1935)
Bukharino *see* Dolgintsevo
Bukittinggi. Town, western
Sumatra, Indonesia : Fort
de Kock (–c. 1966)
Bulbugan *see* Santa Maria
Bulembu. Town, northwest-
ern Swaziland, southern
Africa : Havelock (–1976)
Bunclody. Town, County
Wexford, Ireland : New-
townbarry (–1950)
Bunge Rudnik *see* Yunokom-
munarovsk
Bunker Hill Air Force Base
see Grissom Air Force
Base
Bunzelwitz *see* Boleslawice

Bunzlau *see* Boleslawiec
Bureya-Pristan *see* Novobu-
reysky
Bur Gao [Bircao]. Town,
southern Somalia, east-
ern Africa : Port
Durnford (–c. 1926)
Burgos (1). Municipality,
Ilocos Norte, Philippines
: Nagpartian (–1914)
Burgos (2). Municipality,
Pangasinan, Philippines :
San Isidro de Potot
(–1914)
Burhave *see* Butjadingen
Buribay. Urban settlement,
Bashkir Autonomous Re-
public, Russia : Buryubay
(–1938)
Burkatów. Village, south-
western Poland : Burkers-
dorf (–1945), Germany
Burkersdorf *see* Burkatów
Burkina (Faso). Republic,
western Africa : Upper
Volta (–1984)
Burma *see* Myanmar
Burnas *see* Lebedevka
Bursa. Province, northwest-
ern Turkey : Khodav-
endikyar (–1920s)
Buru. Volcano, western Pan-
ama, Central America :
Chiriquí (–1979)
Burundi. Republic, east-
central Africa : Urundi
(1918–66)
Burunny *see* Tsagan-Aman
Buryat Autonomous Repub-
lic. Southeastern Russia
: Buryat-Mongol Autono-
mous SSR (*1923–58),
Buryat Autonomous SSR
(1958–91)

Buryat Autonomous SSR *see*
Buryat Autonomous Re-
public
Buryat-Mongol Autonomous
SSR *see* Buryat Autono-
mous Republic
Buryubay *see* Buribay
Buss *see* Bous
Buston. Urban settlement,
Leninabad Oblast, Tajiki-
stan : Yantak (–c. 1960)
Butare. Town, southern
Rwanda, east-central Af-
rica : Astrida (–1962)
Butaritari. Island, Kiribati,
western Pacific : Makin
Island (–1981)
Butjadingen. Village, north-
western Germany : Bur-
have (–1936)
Butler. Village, Wisconsin,
USA : New Butler (–1930)
Bütow *see* Bytów
Butterworth *see* Gcuwa
Butuka-Luba. Town, Bioko,
Equatorial Guinea, west-
ern Africa : San Carlos
(–1973)
Butysh *see* Kama
Buynaksk. Town, Dagestan
Autonomous Republic,
Russia : Temir-Khan-
Shura (–1922)
Büyükada. Island, Sea of
Marmara, western Tur-
key : Prinkipo (–?)
Buyun-Uzun *see* Moskovsk
Buzuldza *see* Hadzi Dimitar
Byala Slatina. City, north-
ern Bulgaria : Bela
Slatina (–c. 1945)
Byczyna. Town, southern
Poland : Pitschen
(–1945), Germany

Bydgoszcz. City, north-cen-
tral Poland : Bromberg
(–1919, 1939–45), Ger-
many
Byorksky *see* Krasnoostrovsky
Byorkyo *see* Krasnoostrovsky
Byrd Land. Region, Antarc-
tica : Marie Byrd Land
(*1929–67)
Bystrzyca. River, south-
western Poland : Weis-
tritz (–1945), Ger-
many
Bystrzyca Kłodzka. Town,
southwestern Poland :
Habelschwerdt (–1945),
Germany
Bytom. City, southwestern
Poland : Beuthen (1939–
45), Germany
Bytom Odrzański. Town,
western Poland : Beuthen
an der Oder (–1945),
Germany
Bytów. Town, northwestern
Poland : Bütow (–1945),
Germany

Caála. Town, western Ango-
la, southwestern Africa :
Robert Williams
(–c. 1979)
Cabagan. Municipality, Isa-
bela, Philippines : Ca-
bagan Nuevo (–1914)
Cabagan Nuevo *see* Cabagan
Cabaret *see* Duvalier-Ville
Cabo Agua *see* Ras Kebdana
Cabo Yubi *see* Tarfaya
Cabrália *see* Cabrália Paulista
Cabrália Paulista. Town,
southeastern Brazil,
South America : Cabrália

(–1944), Pirajaí (1944–48)

Cabrera de Mar. Village, northeastern Spain : Cabrera de Mataró (–c. 1970)

Cabrera de Mataró *see* Cabrera de Mar

Cacadu. Town, western Transkei, southern Africa : Glen Grey (–1979)

Cacaguatique *see* Ciudad Barrios

Caçapava *see* Caçapava do Sul

Caçapava do Sul. City, southern Brazil, South America : Caçapava (–1944)

Cáceres. City, western Brazil, South America : São Luiz de Cáceres (–1939)

Cachoeira *see* (1) Cachoeira Paulista; (2) Solonópole

Cachoeira do Sul. City, southern Brazil, South America : Cachoeira (–1944)

Cachoeira Paulista. City, southeastern Brazil, South America : Cachoeira (–1944), Valparaíba (1944–48)

Cachoeiras *see* Cachoeiras de Macacu

Cachoeiras de Macacu. City, southeastern Brazil, South America : Cachoeiras (–1943)

Cachuela Esperanza. Town, northern Bolivia, South America : Esperanza (–1900s)

Cacongo. Town, northwestern Angola, southwestern Africa : Guilherme Capelo (–c. 1975), Landana (c. 1975–c. 1979)

Caddoa Reservoir *see* John Martin Reservoir

Caia. Town, central Mozambique, southeastern Africa : Vila Fontes (–1980)

Caiapônia. City, central Brazil, South America : Rio Bonito (–1944)

Caiuás *see* Rio Brilhante

Caja *see* Čepelarska

Cajamarquilla *see* Bolívar

Calabar. Town, southeastern Nigeria, western Africa : Old Calabar (–1904)

Calamba. Town, Luzon Philippines : Plaridel (–1940s)

Calamunding *see* Lucio Laurel

Calanasan. Municipality, Mountain Province, Philippines : Bayag (–1967)

Calandagan. Barrio, Palawan, Philippines : Tudela (–1957)

Calandula. Town, northern Angola : Duque de Bragança (–c. 1975), Kalandula (c. 1975–c. 1979)

Calanutan *see* Don Felix Coloma

Caldas. City, southeastern Brazil, South America : Parreiras (1940–48)

Callang *see* San Manuel

Caluango *see* Kavungo

Calumet. Village, Michigan, USA : Red Jacket (–1929)

Calumet City. City, Illinois, USA : West Hammond (–1924)

Camacupa. Town, central Angola, southwestern Africa : General Machado (–c. 1979)

Camaquã. City, southern Brazil, South America : São João de Camaquã (–1938)

Camarazal see Mulungu

Camataquí see Villa Abecia

Ca Mau. Town, southern Vietnam : Quan Long (–c. 1980)

Cambé. City, southern Brazil, South America : Nova Dantzig (–1944)

Cambirela see Santa Amaro da Imperatriz

Cambodia. State, southeastern Asia : Khmer Republic (1970–76), Kampuchea (1976–89)

Camembe. Town, western Angola, southwestern Africa : Santa Eulalia (–c. 1976)

Cameron Bay see Port Radium

Camissombo. Town, northeastern Angola, southwestern Africa : Veríssimo Sarmento (–c. 1979)

Cammin see Kamień (Pomorski)

Camp-Bataille see Souk el Arba de l'Oued Beth

Campbell. City, Ohio, USA : East Youngstown (–1926)

Campbellford. Town, Ontario, Canada : Campbell's Ford (–1906)

Campbellpur see (1) Attock; (2) Attock City

Campbell's Ford see Campbellford

Campbelltown see Bluff

Camp Bertaux see Melqa el Ouidane

Camp Cooke see Vandenberg Air Force Base

Camp Coulter see Powell

Camp David. Country estate, Maryland, USA : Shangri-La (*1942–c. 1952)

Campestre see São José do Campestre

Camp Hughes. Locality, Manitoba, Canada : Sewell (–c. 1914)

Camp Morton. Settlement, Manitoba, Canada : Faxa (–?), Haas (?–1925)

Campo Belo see Itatiaia

Campo Florido. City, southeastern Brazil, South America : Campo Formoso (–1944)

Campo Formoso see (1) Campo Florido; (2) Orizona

Campo Largo see Araçoiaba da Serra

Campo Lugar. Village, western Spain : El Campo (–c. 1960)

Campo Quijano. Town, northwestern Argentina, South America : Kilómetro 1172 (–1930s)

Campos see Tobias Barreto

Camrose. City, Alberta, Canada : Sparling (*1905–07)

Canal Dover see Dover

Canarias see (1) Las Palmas; (2) Santa Cruz de Tenerife

Canaveral, Cape : Florida,
USA : Kennedy, Cape
(1963–73)
Canchungo *see* Teixeira Pinto
Cangas de Narcea. Village,
northwestern Spain : Can-
gas de Tineo (–c. 1930)
Cangas de Tineo *see* Cangas
de Narcea
Caniçado *see* Guijá
Cañizar de Argano. Village,
northern Spain : Cañizar
de los Ajos (–c. 1970)
Cañizar de los Ajos *see*
Cañizar de Argano
Canterbury *see* Invermere
Cantin, Cap *see* Meddouza,
Cap
Canton. City, southern
China : Punyü (1913–35)
Canton Island *see* Abariringa
Caoyan *see* Hilario Valdez (2)
Cap Blanc *see* El Jorf Lasfar
Cape Bald *see* Cap-Pelé
Cape Colony *see* Cape of
Good Hope (Province)
Capela. City, northeastern
Brazil, South America :
Conçeicão do Paraíba
(1944–48)
Capelongo. Town, south-
central Angola, south-
western Africa : Folgares
(–c. 1979)
Cape of Good Hope (Prov-
ince) [Cape Prov-
ince]. Southern South
Africa : Cape Colony (–
1910)
Cape Province = Cape of
Good Hope (Province)
Capivari *see* Silva Jardim
Capiz *see* Roxas
Cap-Matifou *see* Bordj el Bahri

Caporetto *see* Kobarid
Cap-Pelé. Village, New
Brunswick, Canada :
Cape Bald (–1950)
Carabao Island *see* San Jose
(1)
Caraguatay *see* La Cordillera
Caraza *see* Santiváñez
Carcross. Village, Yukon,
Canada : Caribou Cross-
ing (–1905)
Caribou Crossing *see* Carcross
Caribrod *see* Dimitrovgrad (1)
Carignan. Town, Quebec,
Canada : Saint-Joseph-
de-Chambly (–1965)
Caririaçu. City, northeast-
ern Brazil, South Amer-
ica : São Pedro (do
Cariry) (–1944)
Carleton Point *see* Borden
Carlingville *see* Crandall
Carlos Reyles. Town, cen-
tral Uruguay, South
America : Molles
(–c. 1945)
Carmanville. Town, New-
foundland, Canada :
Rocky Bay (–1906)
Carmo *see* Carmópolis
Carmona *see* Uige
Carmópolis. City, northeast-
ern Brazil, South Amer-
ica : Carmo (–1944)
Caronno Milanese *see* Car-
onno Pertusella
Caronno Pertusella. Village,
northern Italy : Caronno
Milanese (–c. 1940)
Carstensz Top *see* Jaya, Pun-
cak
Carteret. Borough, New Jer-
sey, USA : Roosevelt
(–1906)

Casas del Puerto *see* Casas de Miravete

Casas del Puerto de Tornavacas *see* Puerto de Castilla

Casas de Miravete. Village, western Spain : Casas del Puerto (–c. 1920)

Cascavel *see* Aguaí

Casim *see* General Toshevo

Čáslav. Town, central Czech Lands : Czaslau (–1918, 1939–45), Germany

Cassaigne *see* Sidi Ali

Castelo *see* (1) Castelo do Piauí; (2) Manuel Urbano

Castelo do Piauí. City, northeastern Brazil, South America : Castelo (–1944), Marvão (1944–48)

Castelrosso *see* Kastellorizon

Castiglione *see* Bou Ismaïl

Castillejos *see* El Fendek

Castillo de San Marcos National Monument. St. Augustine, Florida, USA : Fort Marion National Monument (*1924–42)

Castle Mountain. Mountain, Banff National Park, Alberta, Canada : Mount Eisenhower (1946–79)

Castrogiovanni *see* Enna

Catabola. Town, central Angola, southwestern Africa : Nova Sintra (–c. 1979)

Catambia *see* Catandica

Catandica. Town, west-central Mozambique, southeastern Africa : Vila Gouveia (1915–76), Catambia (1976–80)

Catigbian. Municipality, Bohol, Philippines : San Jacinto (–1954)

Cattaro *see* Kotor

Caucaia. City, northeastern Brazil, South America : Soure (–1944)

Caurel *see* Folgoso de Caurel

Cavazuccherina *see* Iesolo

Caviúna *see* Rolândia

Cawayanon *see* Vintar

Cawnpore *see* Kanpur

Caxias *see* Caxias do Sul

Caxias do Sul. City, southern Brazil, South America : Caxias (–1944)

Ceannanus Mór. Town, County Meath, Ireland : Kells (–c. 1930)

Cebolla de Trabancas *see* San Cristobal de Trabancos

Cedar Grove. Township, New Jersey, USA : Verona (1907–08)

Cedar Hall *see* Val-Brillant

Ceduna. Town, South Australia, Australia : Murat Bay (–1915)

Cedynia. Town, northwestern Poland : Zehden (–1945), Germany

Celebes *see* Sulawesi

Centane. Town, southern Transkei, southern Africa : Kentani (–1976)

Central African Empire *see* Central African Republic

Central African Republic. Republic, central Africa : Ubanghi Shari (–1958), Central African Empire (1976–79)

Central Arctic *see* Kitikmeot

Central Industrial Oblast *see* Moscow Oblast

Central Park *see* Bethpage

Central Provinces *see* Madhya
Pradesh
Čepelarska. River, southern
Bulgaria : Caja (–1967)
Čepinska. River, south-central Bulgaria : Elidere
(–1967)
Cerknica. Village, western
Slovenia : Zirknitz
(–1918), Germany
Cernăuţi *see* Chernovtsy
(Cerro) Bolívar. Mountain,
eastern Venezuela, South
America : La Parida
(–1948)
Cēsis. Town, Latvia : Wenden (–1917)
Česká Kamenice. Town,
northern Czech Lands :
Böhmisch-Kamnitz
(–1918, 1939–45), Germany
Česká Lípa. Town, northern
Czech Lands : Böhmisch-Leipa (–1918, 1939–45),
Germany
Česká Skalice. Town, northern Czech Lands :
Böhmisch-Skalitz (–1918,
1939–45), Germany
Česká Třebová. Town, east-central Czech Lands :
Böhmisch-Trübau
(–1918, 1939–45), Germany
České Budějovice. City,
southwestern Czech
Lands : Budweis (–1918,
1939–45), Germany
Český Brod. Town, central
Czech Lands : Böhmisch-Brod (–1918, 1939–45),
Germany
Český Krumlov. Town,
southwestern Czech
Lands : Krummau (–1918,
1939–45), Germany
Český Těšín. Town, eastern
Czech Lands : Teschen
(–1919, 1939–45), Germany
Cetatea Albă *see* Belgorod
Dnestrovsky
Ceva-i-Ra. Reef, southwestern Fiji, southwestern Pacific : Conway Reef
(–1979)
Ceylanpinar. Village, southeastern Turkey : Resulayn (–c. 1945)
Ceylon *see* Sri Lanka
Chaco. Province, northern
Argentina, South America : Presidente Juán
Perón (1950–55)
Chad *see* Oktyabrsky (2)
Chagoda. Urban settlement,
Vologda Oblast, Russia :
Bely Bychek (–1939)
Chaikang *see* Linnam
Chalakazaki *see* Kyzylasker
Chalantun *see* Yalu
Chalchicomula *see* (Ciudad)
Serdán
Chamkoriya *see* Borovets
Chanach *see* Aktam
Chancay *see* Chancaybaños
Chancaybaños. Village,
northwestern Peru, South
America : Chancay
(–1942)
Chan-chiang. City, southeastern China : Fort
Bayard (1898–1945)
Changan [Ch'ang-an]. Town, central
China : Wangkü (–1942)
Changan *see* Sian [Hsi-an] (1)

Changchai *see* Changshun
[Ch'ang-shun]
Chang-chia-k'ou. City,
northeastern China :
Wan-ch'üan (1911–29)
Changchih [Ch'ang-
chih]. Town, northeast-
ern China : Luan (–1912)
Chang-chiu = Changkiu
Ch'ang-chou = Changchow
Changchow [Ch'ang-chou].
City, eastern China :
Wutsin (1912–49)
Changchow *see* Lungki [Lung-
ch'i]
Changhwa *see* Cheongkong
Changkiu [Chang-chiu].
Town, eastern China :
Mingshui (–1949)
Changku *see* Luho
Changlo *see* Wufeng
Changning [Ch'ang-ning].
Town, southwestern
China : Yutien (–1935)
Changpeh. Town, northeast-
ern China : Sinho (–1918)
Changshan *see* Yaonan
Changshow *see* Yenshow
Changshun [Ch'ang-shun].
Town, southern China :
Changchai (–1942)
Ch'ang-te *see* Anyang
Changting [Ch'ang-t'ing].
Town, southeastern
China : Tingchow
(–1913)
Changtze [Ch'ang-tzu].
Town, central China :
Wayaopu (–c. 1940), Ant-
ing (1940–49)
Ch'ang-tzu = Changtze
Changwucheng *see* Chaotung
Changyeh. Town, north-

central China : Kanchow
(–1913)
Chan-hua = Chanhwa
Chanhwa [Chan-
hua]. Town, southern
China : Chantui (–1912),
Hwaiju (1912–16)
Chanta *see* Lienshan
Chantui *see* Chanhwa [Chan-
hua]
Chanyü. Town, southwest-
ern China : Kaihwachen
(–1915)
Chaoan [Ch'ao-an]. Town,
southeastern China :
Chaochow (–1914)
Chaochow *see* (1) Chaoan
[Ch'ao-an]; (2)
Chaohsien; (3) Fengyi
[Feng-i]
Chaohsien. Town, northeast-
ern China : Chaochow
(–1913)
Chaotung. Town, northeast-
ern China : Changwuch-
eng (–1913)
Chaoyangchwan *see* Shulan
Chapayev. Town, Uralsk
Oblast, Kazakhstan :
Lbishchensk (–1939)
Chapayevka. Left tributary
of Volga River, Samara
Oblast, Russia : Mocha
(–c. 1930)
Chapayevsk. Town, Samara
Oblast, Russia : Ivashch-
enkovo (–1919), Trotsk
(1919–27)
Chapin *see* Edinburg
Chaplygin. Town, Lipetsk
Oblast, Russia : Ra-
nenburg (–1948)
Chapopotla. Town, south-

eastern Mexico, North
America : Ixhuatlán
(–1938)
Chara. Village, Irkutsk Ob-
last, Russia : Ust-Zhuya
(–c. 1960)
Charazani see Villa (General)
Pérez
Chardzhou. Capital of
Chardzhou Oblast, Turk-
menistan : Chardzhuy
(–1924, 1927–40), Len-
insk(-Turkmensky)
(1924–27)
Chardzhuy see Chardzhou
Charente-Inférieure see Char-
ente-Maritime
Charente-Maritime.
Department, western
France : Charente-In-
férieure (–1941)
Charentsavan. Town, Arme-
nia : Lusavan (–1967)
Charlesville see Djokupunda
Charleville see Ráth Luirc
Charlotte Amalie. Capital
of United States Virgin
Islands, West Indies : St.
Thomas (1921–36)
Charon see Bou Kadir
Charsk. Town, Semipala-
tinsk Oblast, Kazakhstan :
Charsky (–1963)
Chat-Bazar. Village, Kir-
gizia : Budyonny (c.
1937–c. 1965)
Châteaudun-du-Rhumel see
Chelghoum-el-Aïd
Château-Salins. Village,
northeastern France :
Salzburgen (1940–44),
Germany
Chatham see East Hampton

Chau Doc. City, southern
Vietnam : Chau Phu
(–c. 1980)
Chau Phu see Chau Doc
Chaykovsky. Town, Perm
Oblast, Russia : Kamskoy
GES, stroiteley (–1962)
Cheb. Town, western Czech
Lands : Eger (–1918,
1939–45), Germany
Chechen-Ingush Autonomous
Oblast see Chechen-In-
gush Autonomous Repub-
lic
Chechen-Ingush Autonomous
Republic. Western Rus-
sia : Chechen-Ingush Au-
tonomous Oblast (*1934–
36), Chechen-Ingush
Autonomous SSR (1936–
44†, *1957–91)
Chechen-Ingush Autonomous
SSR see Chechen-Ingush
Autonomous Republic
Chegutu. Town, north-cen-
tral Zimbabwe, southeast-
ern Africa : Hartley
(–1980)
Chehalis see Grays Harbor
Chejung. Town, southeast-
ern China : Cheyang
(–1945)
Chekalin. Town, Tula Ob-
last, Russia : Likhvin
(–1944)
Chekanovsky. Urban settle-
ment, Irkutsk Oblast,
Russia : Anzeba (–1963)
Chekhov (1). Town,
Moscow Oblast, Russia :
Lopasnya (–1954)
Chekhov (2). Town, Sak-
halin Oblast, Russia :

Noda (1905–47), Japan
(–1945)
Chekmagush. Village,
Bashkir Autonomous Re-
public, Russia : Chekma-
gushi (–1945)
Chekmagushi *see* Chekma-
gush
Chelghoum-el-Aïd. Town,
northeastern Algeria,
northern Africa : Châ-
teaudun-du-Rhumel
(–c. 1962)
Chelmsko Śląskie. Town,
southwestern Poland :
Schömberg(–1945), Ger-
many
Chelny *see* Naberezhnyye
Chelny
Chelyabkopi *see* Kopeysk
Chembar *see* Belinsky
Chemnitz. City, eastern
Germany : Karl-Marx-
Stadt (1953–90)
Chenan *see* (1) Heishan; (2)
Tienpao [T'ien-pao]
Chen-chiang. City, eastern
China : Tan-t'u (1912–18)
Chenchow *see* (1) Chenhsien
[Ch'en-hsien]; (2)
Hwaiyang [Huai-yang]
Chenfan *see* Mintsin [Min-
ch'in]
Cheng-chou = Chengchow
Chengchow [Cheng-chou].
City, east-central China :
Chenghsien (1913–
49)
Chenghsien *see* Chengchow
[Cheng-chou]
Chenhsien [Ch'en-hsien].
Town, south-central
China : Chenchow
(–1913)

Chen-hua = Chenhwa
Chenhwa [Chen-hua].
Town, eastern China :
Ningtsing (–1949)
Chenlai. Town, northeast-
ern China : Chentung
(–1949)
Chenpa. Town, central
China : Tingyüan (–1913)
Chenpien *see* Lantsang [Lan-
ts'ang]
Chenping *see* Chiuling
Chentung *see* Chenlai
Chenyüeh. Town, south-
western China : Yiwu
(–1929)
Cheongkong. Town, south-
eastern China : Chang-
hwa (–1914)
Cheo Reo. Town, central
Vietnam : Hau Bon
(–c. 1980)
Cheremshany. Settlement,
Primorsky Kray, Russia :
Sinancha (–1972)
Cherente *see* Miracema do
Norte
Cherepni *see* Vishnyovaya
(1)
Cherkasskoye *see* Zimogorye
Cherkesovsky. Village, Vol-
gograd Oblast, Russia :
Budarinskaya (–c. 1940)
Cherkess (Adygey) Autono-
mous Oblast *see* Adygey
Autonomous Oblast
Cherkessk. Capital of Kara-
chayev-Cherkess Autono-
mous Oblast, Stavropol
Kray, Russia : Batalpash-
inskaya (–1931), Batalpa-
shinsk (1931–36), Suli-
mov (1936–37), Yezhovo-
Cherkessk (1938–39)

Chernenko *see* (1) Sharypovo; (2) Sholdaneshty

Chernomorka. Health resort, Odessa Oblast, Ukraine : Lyustdorf (–?)

Chernomorskoye. Urban settlement, Crimean Oblast, Ukraine : Ak-Mechet (–1944)

Chernorechye. Suburb of Grozny, Chechen-Ingush Autonomous Republic, Russia : Novyye Aldy (–1940)

Chernorechye *see* Dzerzhinsk (1)

Chernovitsy *see* Chernovtsy

Chernovtsy. Capital of Chernovtsy Oblast, Ukraine : Czernowitz (–1918), Germany, Cernăuţi (1918–40), Romania, Chernovitsy (1940–44)

Chernyakhovsk. Town, Kaliningrad Oblast, Russia : Insterburg (–1946), Germany (–1945)

Chernyayevo *see* Yangiyer

Chernyshevskaya *see* Sovetskaya (2)

Chernyshevskoye. Village, Kaliningrad Oblast, Russia : Eydtkuhnen (–1938), Germany, Eydtkau (1938–45), Germany

Cherry Hill. Township, New Jersey, USA : Delaware (–?)

Chersky. Urban settlement, Yakut Autonomous Republic, Russia : Nizhniye Kresty (–c. 1960)

Chertkov *see* Chortkov

Chertovshchina *see* Rassvet

Cherven. Town, Minsk Oblast, Belorussia : Igumen (–1924)

Chervonoarmeysk (1). Urban settlement, Zhitomir Oblast, Ukraine : Pulin (–c. 1935)

Chervonoarmeysk (2). Town, Rovno Oblast, Ukraine : Radzivilov (–1939)

Chervonoarmeyskoye *see* Volnyansk

Chervonograd. Town, Lvov Oblast, Ukraine : Kristinopol (–1951)

Chervonogrigorovka. Urban settlement, Dnepropetrovsk Oblast, Ukraine : Krasnogrigoryevka (–1939)

Chervonoye (1). Urban settlement, Zhitomir Oblast, Ukraine : Krasnoye (–c. 1935)

Chervonoye (2). Village, Sumy Oblast, Ukraine : Luzhki (–c. 1960)

Cheryomukha. Village, Minsk Oblast, Belorussia : Zatychino (–1964)

Cheryomushki (1). Village, Grodno Oblast, Belorussia : Mondino (–1964)

Cheryomushki (2). Village, Vitebsk Oblast, Belorussia : Poddannyye (–1964)

Chesnokovka *see* Novoaltaysk

Chesterville *see* Kearns

Chetumal. City, southeastern Mexico, North America : Payo Obispo (–1935)

Cheyang *see* Chejung
Chia-hsien = Kiahsien
Chi-an = Kian
Chiang-ch'eng = Kiangcheng
Chiang-k'ou = Kiangkow
Chiang-ling = Kiangling
Chiang-ning (1) = Kiangning;
    (2) *see* Nanking
Chiang Saen. Village, north-
    ern Thailand : King Chi-
    ang Saen (1930s)
Chiao-hsien = Kiaohsien
Chia-shan = Kiashan
Chibia. Town, southwestern
    Angola, southwestern Af-
    rica : João de Almeida
    (–c. 1979)
Chibizovka *see* Zherdevka
Chibyu *see* Ukhta
Chicacole *see* Srikakulam
Chicago Drainage Canal *see*
    Sanitary and Ship Canal
Chicago Heights. Suburb of
    Chicago, Illinois, USA :
    Bloom (–1901)
Chichka *see* Oktyabrsk (1)
Chichow *see* Ankwo
Ch'i-ch'un = Kichun
Chicualacuala. Town, south-
    western Mozambique,
    southeastern Africa :
    Malvérnia (*1956–80)
Chiehchow *see* Chiehsien
    [Chieh-hsien]
Chieh-hsien = Chiehsien
Chiehsien [Chieh-hsien].
    Town, northeastern
    China : Chiehchow
    (–1912)
Ch'ien-ch'ang = Kienchang
Ch'ien-ch'eng = Kiencheng
Chien-ho = Kienho
Ch'ien-hsien = Kienhsien
Chien-ko = Kienko

Ch'ien-ning = Kienning
Chien-ou = Kienow
Chien-te = Kienteh
Chien-yang = Kienyang
Chiesa *see* Chiesa in Val-
    malenco
Chiesa in Val-
    malenco. Village,north-
    ern Italy : Chiesa
    (–c. 1940)
Chih-chiang = Chihkiang
Chih-chin = Chihkin
Chihchow *see* Kweichih [Kuei-
    ch'ih]
Chihkiang [Chih-chi-
    ang]. Town, south-cen-
    tral China : Yüanchow
    (–1913)
Chihkin [Chih-chin]. Town,
    southern China :
    Pingyüan (–1914)
Chihli *see* Hopeh
Chi-hsien = Kihsien
Chihtan. Town, central
    China : Paoan (–1949)
Chih-te = Chihteh
Chihteh [Chih-te]. Town,
    eastern China : Kiupu
    (–1932)
Chike *see* Sünko [Hsün-k'o]
Chikhachyov Bay. Bay, Ta-
    tar Strait, Khabarovsk
    Kray, Russia : De-Kastri
    Bay (–1952)
Chilalin *see* Shihwei
Ch'i-lien = Kilien
Chililabombwe. Town,
    north-central Zambia,
    south-central Africa :
    Bancroft (–late 1960s)
Chililaya *see* Puerto Pérez
Chilumba. Town, northern
    Malawi, southeastern Af-
    rica : Deep Bay (–?)

Chimanimani. Town, south-
eastern Zimbabwe, south-
eastern Africa : Melsetter
(–1980), Mandidzuzure
(1980–82)
Chimkent Ob-
last. Kazakhstan :
South Kazakhstan Oblast
(*1932–62)
Chin-chai = Kinchai
Chin-ch'eng = Tsincheng
Chin-chiang = Tsinkiang
Ch'in-chou *see* T'ien-shui
Ch'ing-chiang(-pu) = Tsing-
kiang(pu)
Ching-ch'uan = Kingchwan
Ching-hsi = Tsingsi
Ching-hsien = Tsinghsien
Ching-ku = Kingku
Ch'ing-lung = Tsinglung
Ch'ing-p'ing = Tsingping
Ching-t'ai = Kingtai
Ching-te-chien =
Kingtehchen
Ching-yü = Tsingyü
Ching-yüan = Kingyüan
Ch'ing-yüan (1) *see* Pao-ting;
(2) = Tsingyüan
Chinhoyi. Town, north-cen-
tral Zimbabwe, southeast-
ern Africa : Sinoya
(–1980)
Chinhsien. Town, northeast-
ern China : Kinchow
(–1945)
Chin-hsien = Tsinhsien (1)
Ch'in-hsien = Tsinhsien (2)
Chini *see* Kalpa
Chi-ning = Tsining
Chinnai *see* Krasnogorsk (2)
Chinnamp'o *see* Namp'o
Chinomiji *see* Tyatino
Chin-p'ing = Kinping
Chin-sha = Kinsha

Chin-t'ang = Kintang
Ch'in = yang = Tsinyang
Chinyüan. Town, northeast-
ern China : Taiyüan
(–1947)
Chios. Island, Aegean Sea,
Greece : Sakiz-Adasi
(–c. 1913), Turkey
Chipata. Town, eastern
Zambia, south-central Af-
rica : Fort Jameson
(–c. 1965)
Chipinga *see* Chipinge
Chipinge. Town, southeast-
ern Zimbabwe, southeast-
ern Africa : Chipinga
(–1980)
Chipuriro *see* Guruwe
Chirchik. Town, Tashkent
Oblast, Uzbekistan : Kir-
giz-Kulak (–1932), Kom-
somolsky (1932–34)
Chirie *see* Kotikovo
Chiriquí *see* Buru
Chişinău *see* Kishinyov
Chistyakovo *see* Torez
Chitaldrug *see* Chitradurga
Chitipa. Town, northern
Malawi, southeastern Af-
rica : Fort Hill (–?)
Chitradurga. Town, south-
ern India : Chitaldrug
(–1966)
Chittaranjan. Village, north-
eastern India : Mihidjan
(–1966)
Chitung [Ch'i-tung]. Town,
eastern China :
Hweilungchen (–1929)
Chiu-chüan = Kiuchüan
Chiuling. Town, southeast-
ern China : Chenping
(–1914)
Ch'iung-lai = Kiunglai

Ch'iung-shan = Kiungshan
Ch'iung-tung = Kiungtung
Chiu-t'ai = Kiutai
Chivhu. Village, central
Zimbabwe, southeastern
Africa : Enkeldoorn
(–1982)
Chkalov. Island, Okhotsk
Sea, Khabarovsk Kray,
Russia : Udd (–c. 1939)
Chkalov see Orenburg
Chkalovo (1). Village, Kok-
chetav Oblast, Ka-
zakhstan : Bogo-
dukhovka (–1939)
Chkalovo (2). Village,
Sakhalin Oblast, Russia :
Kitose (1905–45), Japan
Chkalovo (3). Village,
Dnepropetrovsk Oblast,
Ukraine : Novo-Ni-
kolayevka (–1939)
Chkalovo see Kurchaloy
Chkalov Oblast see Orenburg
Oblast
Chkalovsk. Town, Nizhe-
gorodskaya Oblast, Rus-
sia : Vasilyova Sloboda
(–1927), Vasilyovo
(1927–37)
Chkalovskoye (1). Village,
Chuvash Autonomous
Republic, Russia : Shik-
hirdany (–1939)
Chkalovskoye (2). Village,
Primorsky Kray, Russia :
Zenkovka (–1939)
Chkalovsky see Kayrakkum
Chobienia. Town, south-
western Poland : Köben
(an der Oder) (–1945),
Germany
Choca see Praia da Condúcia
Chochow see Chohsien

Chocianów. Town, south-
western Poland :
Kotzenau (–1945), Ger-
many
Chociwel. Town, northwestern Poland : Freienwalde
(–1945), Germany
Choerhcheng see Talai
Chohsien. Town, northeastern China : Chochow
(–1913)
Chojna. Town, northwest-
ern Poland : Königsberg
(–1945), Germany
Chojnów. City, southwest-
ern Poland : Haynau
[Hainau] (–1945), Ger-
many
Chókué. Town, southern
Mozambique, southeast-
ern Africa : Guijá
(–1960), Vila Alferes
Chamusca (1960–64),
Vila Trigo de Morais
(1964–71), Trigo de Mo-
rais (1971–80)
Choloma. Town, northwest-
ern Honduras, Central
America : El Paraiso
(–early 1930s)
Chomutov. City, northwest-
ern Czech Lands : Komo-
tau (–1918, 1939–45),
Germany
Chon-Ak-Dzhol see Dzhangy-
Dzhol
Chongning see Sunfung
Chortkov. Town, Ternopol
Oblast, Ukraine :
Czortków (1919–39), Po-
land, Chertkov (1939–44)
Chorzów. Suburb of Ka-
towice, southern Poland :
Königshütte (–1921),

Germany, Królewska
Huta (1921–1930s)
Choszczno. Town, north-
western Poland :
Arnswalde (–1945), Ger-
many
Chotzeshan see Lungshen
Chou-ning = Chowning
Chowning [Chou-
ning]. Town, southeast-
ern China : Chowtun
(–1945)
Chowtun see Chowning
[Chou-ning]
Choybalsan. Town, eastern
Mongolia : San-Beyse
(–1921), Bayan-Tumen
(1921–41)
Chozas de la Sierra see Soto
del Real
Christburg see Dzierżgoń
Christian see Ez Zhiliga
Christiania see Oslo
Christmas Island see Kiriti-
mati
Chrzanów. Town, southern
Poland : Krenau (1939–
45), Germany
Chtimba. Town, northeast-
ern Malawi, southeastern
Africa : Florence Bay
(–c. 1964)
Chüanchow see Tsinkiang
Chubarovka see Pologi
Chubartau see Barshatas
Chubek see Moskovsky
Chuchow see (1) Chuhsien
[Ch'u-hsien]; (2) Lishui
Chüchow see Chühsien [Ch'ü-
hsien]
Chuho see Shangchih
Chuhsien [Ch'u-
hsien]. Town, eastern
China : Chuchow (–1912)

Chühsien [Ch'ü-
hsien]. City, eastern
China : Chüchow
(–1913)
Chukotskaya Kultbaza see
Lavrentiya
Chulaktau see Karatau
Chungchow see Chunghsien
Chung-hsiang = Chungsiang
Chunghsien. Town, central
China : Chungchow
(–1913)
Ch'ungmu. City, southeast-
ern South Korea : Ton-
gyŏng (–1955)
Chungpu see Hwangling [Hu-
ang-ling]
Chungshan see Tangkiakwan
[T'ang-chia-kuan]
Ch'ung-shan = Tsungshan
Chungsiang [Chung-
hsiang]. Town, east-
central China : Anlu
(–1912)
Ch'ung-te = Tsungteh
Chungyang. Town, north-
eastern China : Ni-
angsiang (–1914)
Chün-hsien = Künhsien
Churchill. Statistical region,
North Island, New Zeal-
and : South Auckland
(–1963)
Churchill Falls. Waterfall,
Churchill River, New-
foundland, Canada :
Grand Falls (–1965)
Churchill River. River, New-
foundland, Canada : Ha-
milton River (–1965)
Churubay-Nura see Abay (2)
Chusovoy. Town, Perm Ob-
last, Russia : Chusovskoy
Zavod (–1933)

Chusovskoy Zavod *see*
    Chusovoy
Chust *see* Khust
Chutzeshan *see* Weichang
    [Wei-ch'ang]
Chuvash Autonomous Oblast
    see Chuvash Autonomous
    Republic
Chuvash Autonomous Re-
    public.   West-central
    Russia : Chuvash Auton-
    omous Oblast (*1920–
    25), Chuvash Autono-
    mous SSR (1925–91)
Chuvash Autonomous SSR
    see Chuvash Autonomous
    Republic
Chwankow *see* Minho
Chwanping *see* Lankao
Chyormoz.   Town, Perm Ob-
    last, Russia : Chyor-
    mozsky Zavod (–1943)
Chyormozsky Zavod *see*
    Chyormoz
Chyorny Rynok *see* Kochubey
Cidade de Minas *see* Belo
    Horizonte
Ciechocinek.   Town, north-
    central Poland : Her-
    mannsbad (1939–45),
    Germany
Cieplice Śląskie
    Zdrój.   Town, south-
    western Poland : Bad
    Warmbrunn (–1945),
    Germany
Cinquième *see* Brakna
City of The Dalles.   City, Or-
    egon, USA : The Dalles
    [Dalles City] (–1966)
Ciudad Arce.   Town, west-
    central Salvador, Central
    America : El Chilamatal
    (*1921–c. 1948)

Ciudad Barrios.   City, east-
    ern Salvador, Central
    America : Cacaguatique
    (–1913)
Ciudad Gonzáles *see* Doctor
    Hernández Alvarez
Ciudad Madero.   City, east-
    ern Mexico, North Amer-
    ica : Villa Cecilia (*1924–
    30)
Ciudad Porfirio Díaz *see*
    Piedras Negras
(Ciudad) Serdán.   Puebla,
    central Mexico, North
    America : Chalchicomula
    (–1934)
Ciudad Trujillo *see* Santo Do-
    mingo
Clairfontaine *see* El Aouinet
Claviere.   Village, northwest-
    ern Italy : Clavières
    (–c. 1936), France
Clavières *see* Claviere
Clinch-Powell Reservoir *see*
    Norris Lake
Clinton *see* Galena Park
Cloyes *see* Cloyes-sur-le-Loir
Cloyes-sur-le-Loir.   Village,
    northwestern France :
    Cloyes (–1938)
Cluj.   Town, northwestern
    Romania : Klausenburg
    (–1920), Germany
Coal Creek *see* Lake City
Coast *see* Pwani
Coatzacoalcos.   Town,
    south-central Mexico,
    North America : Puerto
    México (–?)
Cóbh.   Town, County Cork,
    Ireland : Queenstown
    (1849–1922)
Coelho Neto.   City, north-
    eastern Brazil, South

America : Curralinho (–1939)

Cofimvaba. Town, southwestern Transkei, southern Africa : St. Marks (–1976)

Cogon-Bingkay *see* Salvacion (1)

Colbert *see* Aïn Oulmene

Coligny. Town, Transvaal, South Africa : Treurfontein (–1923)

Colinas. City, northeastern Brazil, South America : Picos (–1944)

College Park *see* East Lansing

Colleville-Montgomery. Village, northwestern France : Colleville-sur-Orne (–1946)

Colleville-sur-Orne *see* Colleville-Montgomery

Colomb-Béchar *see* Béchar

Colonia *see* Libertad (1)

Colônia Leopoldina. City, northeastern Brazil, South America : Leopoldina (–1944)

Colonia Mineira *see* Sisqueira Campos

Colony Province *see* Ikeja Province

Comandante Arbues *see* Mirandópolis

Comendador *see* Elías Piña

Commonwealth of Independent States. Europe/Asia : Union of Soviet Socialist Republics [Soviet Union, USSR; popularly, Russia] (*1922–91), Union of Free Sovereign Republics (1991), Union of Sovereign States (1991)

Communism Peak [Kommunizma, Pik]. Mountain, Pamirs Range, Tajikistan : Garmo Peak (–1933), Stalin Peak (1933–62)

Comunanza. Village, central Italy : Comunanza del Littorio (c. 1937–45)

Comunanza del Littorio *see* Comunanza

Conceição do Almeida. City, eastern Brazil, South America : Afonso Pena (–1944)

Conceição do Paraíba *see* Capela

Concepcion. Barrio, Masbate, Philippines : Sawmill (–1957)

Concepcion *see* Gregorio del Pilar

Condé-Smendou *see* Zighout Youcef

Congo. Republic, west-central Africa : Middle Congo [Moyen-Congo] (*1902–58), Congo Autonomous Republic (1958–60), Congo (Brazzaville) (1960–70)

Congo *see* Zaïre

Congo Autonomous Republic *see* Congo

Congo Belge *see* Zaïre

Congo (Brazzaville) *see* Congo

Congo Free State *see* Zaïre

Congo (Kinshasa) *see* Zaïre

Congo (Léopoldville) *see* Zaïre

Congonhas. City, southeastern Brazil, South America : Congonhas do Campo (–1948)

Congonhas do Campo *see*
Congonhas
Conquista *see* Vitória da Con-
quista
Constantinople *see* Istanbul
Contrebandiers, Plage des *see*
Sidi el Abed
Conway Reef *see* Ceva-i-Ra
Coos Bay. City, Oregon,
USA : Marshfield (–1944)
Copperbelt. Province, west-
ern Zambia, south-cen-
tral Africa : Western
(–1971)
Copper City *see* Invermere
Coquilhatville *see* (1) É-
quateur; (2) Mbandaka
Cordeiro *see* Cordeirópolis
Cordeirópolis. City, south-
eastern Brazil, South
America : Cordeiro
(–1944)
Cordillera Capetónica *see* Sis-
tema Central
Cordillera Mariánica *see* Si-
erra Morena
Cordillera Oretana *see* Mon-
tes de Toledo
Coreaú. City, northeastern
Brazil, South America :
Palma (–1944)
Corneille *see* Merouana
Corneto (Tarquinia) *see* Tar-
quinia
Corregidora. Town, central
Mexico, North America :
El Pueblito (–1946)
Corumbá *see* Corumbá de
Goiás
Corumbá de Goiás. City,
central Brazil, South
America : Corumbá
(–1944)
Corupá. Town, southern

Brazil, South America :
Hansa (–1944)
Cosel *see* Koźle
Cossette *see* Inwood
Costa Mesa. City, Califor-
nia, USA : Harper
(*1906–21)
Costermansville *see* (1)
Bukavu; (2) Kivu
Côte d'Ivoire. Republic,
western Africa : Ivory
Coast (–1986)
Cotillas *see* Las Torres de Co-
tillas
Cotopaxi. Province, north-
central Ecuador, South
America : León (–1939)
Cotrone *see* Crotone
Cottage City *see* Oak Bluffs
Country Club Estates *see* Mi-
ami Springs
Coxim. City, western Brazil,
South America : Hercu-
lânia (1939–48)
Crandall. Village, Mani-
toba, Canada : Car-
lingville (–1901)
Cristina *see* Cristinápolis
Cristinápolis. City, north-
eastern Brazil, South
America : Cristina
(–1944)
Crosby. Town, Mississippi,
USA : Stephenson
(–1934)
Crossen *see* Krosno (Odr-
zańskie)
Crotone. Town, southern It-
aly : Cotrone (–1928)
Cruzeiro *see* Joaçaba
Cruzeiro do Sul *see* Joaçaba
Csév *see* Piliscsév
Cuamba *see* Nova-Freixo
Cuatro de Junio. Town,

west-central Argentina,
South America : La Toma
(–c. 1945)
Cuevas de Almanzora.
Village, southern Spain :
Cuevas de Vera (–c.
1930)
Cuevas de Vera see Cuevas de
Almanzora
Cuiabá see Mestre Caetano
Culebra see Dewey
Culebra Cut see Gaillard Cut
Cumbe see Euclides da Cunha
Cummings' Island see Vanier
(1)
Cunhinga. Town, central
Angola, southwestern Af-
rica : Vouga (–c. 1979)
Curador see Presidente Dutra
Curba see San Roque
Curralinho see Coelho Neto
Curt-Bunar see Tervel
Cybinka. Town, western Po-
land : Ziebingen (–1945),
Germany
Cypress. City, California,
USA : Waterville
(–1956), Dairy City
(1956)
Czaplinek. Town,northwest-
ern Poland : Tempelburg
(–1945), Germany
Czarne. Town, northwest-
ern Poland : Hammer-
stein (–1945), Germany
Czaslau see Čáslav
Czernina. Town, western
Poland : Tschirnau
(–1937), Germany;
Lesten (1937–45), Ger-
many
Czernowitz see Chernovtsy
Człopa. Town, northwest-
ern Poland : Schloppe

(–1945), Germany
Człuchów. Town,northwest-
ern Poland : Schlochau
(–1945), Germany
Czortków see Chortkov

Daber see Dobra
Dąbie. Town, northwestern
Poland : Altdamm
(–1945), Germany
Dąbromierz. Town, south-
western Poland : Hohen-
friedeberg (–1945), Ger-
many
Dąbrowa Górnicza. Town,
southwestern Poland :
Dombrau (–1945), Ger-
many
Dąbrówno. Town, north-
eastern Poland : Gil-
genburg (–1945), Ger-
many
Dacca see Dhaka
Dachnoye. Village,
Sakhalin Oblast, Russia :
Shimba (1905–45), Japan
Dacudao see General Roxas
Dadra see Achalpur
Dagestan Autonomous Re-
public. Western Russia
: Dagestan Autonomous
SSR (*1921–91)
Dagestan Autonomous SSR
see Dagestan Autono-
mous Republic
Dahomey see Benin
Daingean. Village, County
Offaly, Ireland : Philip-
stown (–1920)
Dairen. City, northeastern
China : Dalny (–1905),
Russia
Dairy City see Cypress

Dajabón. Province, northwestern Dominican Republic, West Indies : Libertador (*1938–61)

Dakhla. Town, western Western Sahara, northwestern Africa : Villa Cisneros (–1976)

Dakhlet Nouâdhibou. District, western Mauritania, western Africa : Huitième (–c. 1979)

Dalagan see San Antonio

Dalatando. Town, northwestern Angola, southwestern Africa : Vila Salazar (1930s–c. 1976)

Dalence see Teniente Bullaín

Dalle see Yirga-Alam

Dalles City see City of The Dalles

Dalnegorsk. Urban settlement, Primorsky Kray, Russia : Tetyukhe (–1972)

Dalnerechensk. Town, Primorsky Kray, Russia : Iman (–1973)

Dalny see Dairen

Dambrowica see Dubrovitsa

Da Nang. City, northeastern Vietnam : Tourane (–?)

Dancalia Meridionale see Assab

Dange. Village, north-central Angola, southwestern Africa : Quitexe (–c. 1979)

Daniels. Village, Maryland, USA : Alberton (–1940)

Danish West Indies see Virgin Islands (of the United States)

Dansalan see Marawi

Danzig see Gdańsk

Dáphne. Village, southern Greece : Koutroumpoúkhion (–1960s)

Daphnokhórion see Glypháda

Darachichag see Tsakhkadzor

Dara Dere see Zlatograd

Daraga. Municipality, Albay, Philippines : Locsin (–1967)

Darasun see Vershino-Darasunsky

Dar el Beïda. Village, northern Algeria, northern Africa : Maison-Blanche (–c. 1962)

Dar es Salaam. District, eastern Tanzania, eastern Africa : Mzizima (–1974)

Darkehmen see Ozyorsk

Darwin. Capital of Northern Territory, Australia : Palmerston (–1911)

Dashev. Urban settlement, Vinnitsa Oblast, Ukraine : Stary Dashev (–c. 1930)

Dashkesan. Town, Azerbaijan : Verkhny Dashkesan (*c. 1945–48)

Dasokhórion. Village, eastern Greece : Zarkhanádes (–1960s)

Datu Piang. Municipality, Cotobato, Philippines : Dulawan (–1954)

Daugavgriva. Fortified port, Riga, Latvia : Ust-Dvinsk (–1917), Russia

Daugavpils. Town, Latvia : Dvinsk (1893–1920), Russia; Dünaburg (1941–44), Germany

Davydkovo see Tolbukhino

Dawley see Telford

Deberai. Peninsula, north-western Irian Jaya, Indonesia : Vogelkop (–1963)

Dębica. Town, southeastern Poland : Dembica (1939–45), Germany

Dęblin. Village, eastern Poland : Ivangorod (–1915), Russia

Debrzno. Town, northwestern Poland : Preussisch Friedland (–1945), Germany

Decemvrie 30, 1947. Suburb of Bucharest, Romania : Principele-Nicolae (–1948)

Děčín. City, northern Czech Lands : Tetschen (–1918, 1939–45), Germany

Dedeağaç see Alexandroúpolis

Dedovsk. Town, Moscow Oblast, Russia : Guchkovo (–1925), Dedovsky (1925–40)

Dedovsky see Dedovsk

Deep Bay see Chilumba

Deep River. Town, Connecticut, USA : Saybrook (–1947)

Deerfield see Deerfield Beach

Deerfield Beach. City, Florida, USA : Hillsboro (–1907), Deerfield (1907–39)

Dégelis. Town, Quebec, Canada : Sainte-Rose-du-Dégelé (*1915–69)

Degtyarka see Degtyarsk

Degtyarsk. Town, Sverdlovsk Oblast, Russia : Degtyarka (–1954)

Dehkhvareqan see Azar Shahr

Deichow see Dychów

De-Kastri Bay see Chikhachyov Bay

Dekhkanabad. Village, Kashkadarya Oblast, Uzbekistan : Tengi-Kharam (–c. 1935)

De Las Mercedes see Sandino

Delaware see Cherry Hill

Del Carmen. Municipality, Surigao del Norte, Philippines : Numancin (–1966)

Delray see Delray Beach

Delray Beach. City, Florida, USA : Linton (–c. 1901), Delray (c. 1901–27)

Demárion. Village, western Greece : Dimarión (–1960s)

Dembica see Dębica

Demidov. Town, Smolensk Oblast, Russia : Porechye (–1918)

Demyanovka see Leninskoye (3)

Denali National Park. Alaska, USA : Mount McKinley National Park (*1917–80)

Denezhkin Kamen. Nature reserve, Sverdlovsk Oblast, Russia : Ivdel (–c. 1960)

Denisovka see Ordzhonikidze (2)

Denwood see Wainwright

Deodoro see Piraquara

Deorha see Jubbal

Derbeshka see Derbeshkinsky

Derbeshkinsky. Urban settlement, Tatar Autonomous Republic, Russia : Derbeshka (–1940)

Derbinskoye see Tymovskoye

Derby. City, Kansas, USA : El Paso (–1957)

Deryaki *see* Gornaya (1)

Derzhavinsk. Town, Tselinograd Oblast, Kazakhstan : Derzhavinsky (–1966)

Derzhavinsky *see* Derzhavinsk

Deschnaer Kuppe *see* Velká Deštná

Desenzano del Garda. Town, northern Italy : Desenzano sul Lago (–1926)

Desenzano sul Lago *see* Desenzano del Garda

Dete. Village, western Zimbabwe, southeastern Africa : Dett (–1980)

Detskoye Selo *see* Pushkin

Dett *see* Dete

Deutsch Brod *see* Havlíčkův Brod

Deutsch Eylau *see* Iława

Deutsch Gabel *see* Jablonné v Podještědí

Deutsch Krone *see* Wałcz

Deutsch Przemysl *see* Przemyśl

Deuxième *see* Hodh el Gharbi

Devin. City, southwestern Bulgaria : Dovlen (–1934)

Dewey. Town, Culebra, Puerto Rico, West Indies : Culebra (–c. 1940)

Dewgard Baria. Town, western India : Baria (–1950s)

Dezh-i-Shahpur *see* Marivan

Dhaka. Capital of Bangladesh : Dacca (–1982)

Dhi Qar. Province, southeastern Iraq : Al Muntafak (–1971)

Diciosânmartin *see* Târnăveni

Diedenhofen *see* Thionville

Diégo-Suarez *see* Antseranana

Dien Bien. Town, northwestern Vietnam : Dien Bien Phu (–c. 1980)

Dien Bien Phu *see* Dien Bien

Dieppe. Town, New Brunswick, Canada : Leger Corner (–1946)

Dievenow *see* Dziwnów

Diez y Ocho de Julio. Village, southeastern Uruguay, South America : San Miguel (–1909)

Dilman *see* Shahpur

Dimarión *see* Demárion

Dimitrov. Town, Donetsk Oblast, Ukraine : Novy Donbass (1937–57), Novoekonomicheskoye (1957–72)

Dimitrovgrad (1). Town, southeastern Serbia : Caribrod [Tsaribrod] (–1950)

Dimitrovgrad (2). Town, Ulyanovsk Oblast, Russia : Melekess (–1972)

Dimitrovo. Village, west-central Bulgaria : Kostenets (–1950)

Dimitrovo *see* Pernik

Dinokot *see* Macias

Díon. Village, northern Greece : Malathriá (–1960s)

Díon *see* Karítsa

Dirizhablstroy *see* Dolgoprudny

Dirrákhion *see* Dyrrákhion

Dirschau *see* Tczew

Divnogorsk. Town,

Krasnoyarsk Kray, Russia : Skit (–1963)
Diwaniya *see* Al-Qadisiya
Dixième *see* Guidimaka
Diyala. Province, eastern Iraq : Baquba (–1971)
Djajapura = Jayapura
Djakarta = Jakarta
Djakova *see* Djakovica
Djakovica. Town, southwestern Serbia : Djakova (–1913), Turkey
Djalma Dutra *see* (1) Miguel Calmon; (2) Poções
Djaya, Puntjak = Jaya, Puncak
Djibouti. Republic, northeastern Africa : French Somaliland (–1967), Afars and Issas (1967–77)
Djokupunda. Town, south-central Zaïre, central Africa : Charlesville (–1972)
Dmanisi. Urban settlement, Georgia : Bashkicheti (–1947)
Dmitriyevsk *see* Makeyevka
Dmitriyevskoye *see* Talas
Dmitriyevsky *see* Makeyevka
Dmitrovsk *see* Dmitrovsk-Orlovsky
Dmitrovsk-Orlovsky : Town, Oryol Oblast, Russia : Dmitrovsk (–1929)
Dneprodzerzhinsk. Town, Dnepropetrovsk Oblast, Ukraine : Kamenskoye (–1936)
Dnepropetrovsk. Capital of Dnepropetrovsk Oblast, Ukraine : Yekaterinoslav (–1796, 1802–1926)
Dneprovskoye. Village, Smolensk Oblast, Russia :

Andreyevskoye (–c. 1960)
Doberei. Peninsula, northwestern Papua-New Guinea, southeastern Asia : Vogelkop (–1963)
Doberlug. Town, eastern Germany : Dobrilugk (–1937)
Dobiegniew. Town, western Poland : Woldenberg (–1945), Germany
Dobra. Town, northwestern Poland : Daber (–1945), Germany
Dobřany. Town, western Czech Lands : Wiesengrund (–1918, 1939–45), Germany
Dobre Miasto. Town, northeastern Poland : Guttstadt (–1945), Germany
Dobrič *see* Tolbukhin
Dobrilugk *see* Doberlug
Dobrinka. Village, Volgograd Oblast, Russia : Nizhnyaya Dobrinka (–c. 1940)
Dobrna. Village, western Slovenia : Neuhaus (–1918), Germany
Dobrodzień. Town, southern Poland : Guttentag (–1945), Germany
Dobropolye. Town, Donetsk Oblast, Ukraine : Svyatogorovsky Rudnik (–c. 1918), Valdgeym [Waldheim] (c. 1918–c. 1935), Rot-Front (c. 1935–41), Krasnoarmeysky Rudnik (1941–46)

Dobrovolsk. Village, Kaliningrad Oblast, Russia : Pillkallen (–1938), Germany, Schlossberg (1938–46), Germany (–1945)

Dobroye. Village, Sakhalin Oblast, Russia : Naibo (1905–45), Japan

Dobrzany. Town, northwestern Poland : Jacobshagen (–1945), Germany

Doctor Hernández Alvarez. City, central Mexico, North America : Ciudad González (–1938)

Dodecanese. Island group, Aegean Sea, Greece : Possedimenti Italiani dell' Egeo (1912–45)

Dogo see Dogoyuno-machi

Dogoyuno-machi. Town, northwestern Shikoku, Japan : Dogo (–1923)

Dokshukino see Nartkala

Dokuchayevsk. Town, Donetsk Oblast, Ukraine : Yelenovskiye Karyery (–1954)

Dolban see Liman

Dolbeau see Sacré-Coeur-de-Jésus

Dolgintsevo. Suburb of Krivoy Rog, Dnepropetrovsk Oblast, Ukraine : Bukharino (1920s–c. 1935)

Dolgoprudny. Town, Moscow Oblast, Russia : Dirizhablstroy (*?–1938)

Dolinovskoye. Urban settlement, Lugansk Oblast, Ukraine : Petro-Golenishchevo (–c. 1960)

Dolinsk. Town, Sakhalin Oblast, Russia : Otiai (1905–46), Japan (–1945)

Dolinskaya. Town, Kirovograd Oblast, Ukraine : Shevchenkovo (mid-1920s, c. 1940–44)

Dolinskoye. Village, Odessa Oblast, Ukraine : Valegotsulovo (–1945)

Dolisie see Loubomo

Doma see Gombe

Domažlice. Town, southwestern Czech Lands : Taus (–1918, 1939–45), Germany

Dombarovka see Dombarovsky

Dombarovsky. Urban settlement, Orenburg Oblast, Russia : Dombarovka (–1939)

Dombasle see El Hachem

Dombrau see Dąbrowa Górnicza

Dombrovitsa see Dubrovitsa

Dominion. Town, Nova Scotia, Canada : Dominion No. 1 (–1906)

Dominion No. 1 see Dominion

Domman-Asfaltovy Zavod see Leninsky (1)

Domnau see Domnovo

Domnovo. Village, Kaliningrad Oblast, Russia : Domnau (–1945), Germany

Doña Alicia see Mabini

Doña Rosario, Barrio, Agusan, Philippines : Victory (–1952)

Donetsk (1). Town, Rostov Oblast, Russia : Gundorovka (–1955)

Donetsk (2). Capital of Don-
etsk Oblast, Ukraine :
Yuzovka (–1924), Stalin
(1924–c. 1935), Stalino
(c. 1935–61)
Donetsko-Amvrosiyevka *see*
Amvrosiyevka
Donetsk Oblast. Ukraine :
Stalino Oblast (*1938–61)
Don Felix Coloma. Barrio,
Pangasinan, Philippines :
Calanutan (–1972)
Don Mariano. Barrio, Ilocos
Norte, Philippines : Sitio
Rawrawang (–1972)
Donskoye (1). Village, Ka-
liningrad Oblast, Russia :
Gross Dirschkeim
(–1945), Germany
Donskoye (2). Village, Li-
petsk Oblast, Russia : Pa-
triarsheye (–1930s),
Vodopyanovo (1930s–c.
1965)
Doonside. Holiday resort,
Natal, South Africa :
Middleton (–1910)
Dor. Settlement, northwest-
ern Israel : Tantura
(–1949)
Dores da Boa Esperança *see*
Boa Esperança
Doristhal *see* Razino
Dorokawa *see* Ulyanovskoye
(1)
Dorchester. Township, On-
tario, Canada : Dorch-
ester Station (–1961)
Dorchester Station *see* Dorch-
ester
Döryzomba *see* Zomba
Dosmahlen *see* Pushkino (1)
Dostluk. Urban settlement,
Chardzhou Oblast, Turk-

menistan: Yuzhny
(–c. 1960)
Dothan. City, Alabama,
USA : Poplar Head
(–1911)
Douchy *see* Douchy-les-Mines
Douchy-les-Mines. Town,
northern France :
Douchy (–1938)
Doué *see* Doué-la-Fontaine
Doué-la-Fontaine. Town,
western France : Doué
(–1933)
Douglas Point. Headland,
Ontario, Canada :
MacPherson's Point
(–1902)
Douzième *see* Inchiri
Dovbysh. Urban settlement,
Zhitomir Oblast, Ukraine
: Markhlevsk (–1944)
Dover. City, Ohio, USA :
Canal Dover (–1920)
Dover *see* Westlake
Dovlen *see* Devin
Dozdab *see* Zakhedan
Draâ Ben Khedda. Village,
northern Algeria, north-
ern Africa : Mirabeau
(–c. 1962)
Draâ Esmar. Village, north-
ern Algeria, northern Af-
rica : Lodi (–c. 1962)
Drable *see* (José Enrique) Ro-
dó
Dragomirovo *see* Proletarsk
(1)
Dramburg *see* Drawsko
Dravograd. Village, north-
ern Slovenia : Unterdrau-
burg (–1918), Germany
Drawno. Town, northwest-
ern Poland : Neuwedell
(–1945), Germany

Drawsko. Town, northwestern Poland : Dramburg (–1945), Germany
Drayton Valley. Town, Alberta, Canada : Power House (*c. 1907–20)
Drekhcha Panenskaya see Kutuzovka
Dresser. Village, Wisconsin, USA : Dresser Junction (–1940)
Dresser Junction see Dresser
Drezdenko. Town, western Poland : Driesen (–1945), Germany
Driesen see Drezdenko
Drissa see Verkhnedvinsk
Drochilovo see Gagarino
Droichead Nua. Town, County Kildare, Ireland : Newbridge (–?)
Drosiá. Village, central Greece : Khalía (–1960s)
Drosokhórion. Village, eastern Greece : Typhloséllion (–1960s)
Drosopegé. Village, southern Greece : Mpásion (–1960s)
Drossen see Ośno
Drozhzhanoye see (Staroye) Drozhzhanoye
Druskeniki see Druskininkai
Druskininkai. Town, Lithuania : Druskeniki (1921–39)
Druzhba (1). Village, Kaliningrad Oblast, Russia : Allenburg (–1946), Germany (–1945)
Druzhba (2). Town, Sumy Oblast, Ukraine : Khutor-Mikhaylovsky (–1962)

Druzhba (3). Town, Khorezm Oblast, Uzbekistan : Sharlauk (–1976)
Druzhkovka. Town, Donetsk Oblast, Ukraine : Gavrilovsky Zavod (–1930s)
Dryazgi see Oktyabrskoye (2)
Drymón. Village, Levkás, Ionian Islands, Greece : Káto Exántheia (–1960s)
Duarte, Pico. Mountain, central Dominican Republic, West Indies : Monte Trujillo (1936–61)
Düben see Bad Düben
Dubovsky. Urban settlement, Lugansk Oblast, Ukraine : Gromovsky (–c. 1960)
Dubrovitsa. Town, Rovno Oblast, Ukraine : Dambrowica (–1939), Poland, Dombrovitsa (1939–45)
Dubrovnik. Town, southern Croatia : Ragusa (–1919), Germany
Dudergof see Mozhaysky
Duders Beach see Umupuia
Dufault see Genthon
Duisburg. City, western Germany : Duisburg-Hamborn (1929–34)
Duisburg-Hamborn see Duisburg
Dulawan see Datu Piang
Dumaran see Araceli
Dumbraveny. Village, Moldavia : Kainary (–1985)
Dünaburg see Daugavpils
Dunaújváros. Town, west-central Hungary : Sztálinváros (*1950–62)

Dundas. Settlement, northwestern Greenland : Thule (–1910)

Dungriga. Town, east-central Belize, Central America : Stann Creek (–1981)

Dun Laoghaire. Town, County Dublin, Ireland : Kingstown (1821–1920)

Duperré *see* Aïn Defla

Dupnitsa *see* Stanke Dimitrov

Duque de Bragança *see* Calandula

Durasovka *see* Ozyornoye

Durazzo *see* Durrës

Durban Road *see* Bellville

Durichi *see* Znamenka (1)

Durnevichi *see* Lugovaya (1)

Durrës. City, western Albania : Durazzo (1939–43), Italy

Dushanbe. Capital of Tajikistan : Dyushambe (–1929), Stalinabad (1929–61)

Dushet *see* Dusheti

Dusheti. Town, Georgia : Dushet (–1936)

Dusti. Urban settlement, Khatlon Oblast, Tajikistan : Pyandzh (–c. 1960)

Duszniki Zdrój. Town, southwestern Poland : Bad Reinerz (–1945), Germany

Dutch Borneo *see* Kalimantan

Dutch East Indies *see* Indonesia

Dutch Guiana *see* Surinam

Duvalier-Ville. Town, Haïti, West Indies : Cabaret (–1963)

Duvanny *see* Gobustan

Duvno. Town, western Bosnia-Herzegovina : Tomislavgrad (1930s–c. 1945)

Duxbury *see* Forestburg

Duzkend *see* Akhuryan

20 let VLKSM, Pik *see* Pobedy, Pik

26 Bakinskikh Komissarov, imeni. Urban settlement, Azerbaijan : Neftechala (–c. 1960)

Dvigatelstroy *see* Kaspiysk

Dvinsk *see* Daugavpils

Dvoryanskaya Tereshka *see* Radishchevo (1)

Dvurechensk. Urban settlement, Sverdlovsk Oblast, Russia : Khrompik (–c. 1960)

Dvůr Králové (nad Labem). Town, northern Czech Lands : Königinhof (an der Elbe) (–1918, 1939–45), Germany

Dychów. Village, western Poland : Deichow (–1945), Germany

Dyhernfurth *see* Brzeg Dolny

Dyrrákhion. Village, southern Greece : Dirrákhion (–1960s)

Dyurbeldzhin *see* Bayetovo

Dyushambe *see* Dushanbe

Dzagidzor *see* Tumanyan

Dzaudzhikau *see* Vladikavkaz

Dzerzhinsk (1). Town, Nizhegorodskaya Oblast, Russia : Chernorechye (–?), Rastyapino (?–1929)

Dzerzhinsk (2). Town, Minsk Oblast, Belorussia : Kaydanovo (–1922)

Dzerzhinsk (3). Village, Gomel Oblast, Belorussia : Radzivilovichi (–1925)

Dzerzhinsk (4). Urban settlement, Zhitomir Oblast, Ukraine : Romanov (–1931)

Dzerzhinsk (5). Town, Donetsk Oblast, Ukraine : Shcherbinovka (–1938)

Dzerzhinskogo, imeni see Naryan-Mar

Dzerzhinskoye (1). Village, Taldy-Kurgan Oblast, Kazakhstan : Kolpakovskoye (–?)

Dzerzhinskoye (2). Village, Krasnoyarsk Kray, Russia : Rozhdestvenskoye (–?)

Dzerzhinsky. Town, Moscow Oblast, Russia : Trudovaya Kommuna imeni Dzerzhinskogo (*1921–38)

Dzerzhinsky see Sorsk

Dzhalal-Ogly see Stepanavan

Dzhalilabad. Town, Azerbaijan : Astrakhan-Bazar (–1967)

Dzhambay. Town, Samarkand Oblast, Uzbekistan : Khoshdala (–1977)

Dzhambul. Capital of Dzhambul Oblast, Kazakhstan : Auliye-Ata (–1936), Mirzoyan (1936–38)

Dzhandar see Sverdlovsk (1)

Dzhangala. Settlement, Uralsk Oblast, Kazakhstan : Kisykkamys (–1975)

Dzhangy-Dzhol. Village, Osh Oblast, Kirgizia : Chon-Ak-Dzhol (–1942)

Dzhansugurov. Urban settlement, Taldy-Kurgan Oblast, Kazakhstan : Abakumova (–c. 1960)

Dzharkent see Panfilov

Dzhetysuy Guberniya (1928†). USSR : Semirechensk Guberniya (–1922)

Dzhezdy. Urban settlement, Dzhezkazgan Oblast, Kazakhstan: Kotabaru (–?), Marganets (?–1962)

Dzhugeli see Zestafoni

Dzhuma. Town, Samarkand Oblast, Uzbekistan : Ikramovo (1930s)

Dzierżgoń. Town, northern Poland : Christburg (–1945), Germany

Dzierżoniów. Town, southwestern Poland : Reichenbach (–1945), Germany

Dziwnów. Town, northwestern Poland : Dievenow (–1945), Germany

Dzoraget. Urban settlement, Armenia : Kolageran (–1978)

Dzurchi see Pervomayskoye (3)

Eagle Nest. Village, New Mexico, USA : Therma (–1935)

Earl Gray see Harding

East Buganda. District, southeastern Uganda,

eastern Africa : East Mongo (–?)

East Detroit. Suburb of Detroit, Michigan, USA : Halfway Village (1924–29)

Eastern Province. Province, northeastern Zaïre, central Africa : Stanleyville (1935–47)

East Hamburg see Orchard Park

East Hampton. Town, Connecticut, USA : Chatham (–1915)

East Lansing. City, Michigan, USA : College Park (–1907)

East Livermore see Livermore Falls

Eastmain see East-Main

East-Main. Town, Quebec, Canada : Eastmain (–1975)

East Milwaukee see Shorewood

East Mongo see East Buganda

East Pakistan see Bangladesh

Eastview see Vanier (1)

East Windsor. Suburb of Windsor, Ontario, Canada : Ford (*1913–29)

East Youngstown see Campbell

Ebenrode see Nesterov (1)

Ebn Ziad. Village, northeastern Algeria, northern Africa : Rouffach (–c. 1962)

Ebor. Settlement, Manitoba, Canada : Sproule (–1907), Ebor Station (1907–09)

Ebor Station see Ebor

Echaporã. City, southeastern Brazil, South America : Bela Vista (–1944)

Ech Chiahna. Village, northern Morocco, northwestern Africa : Rose-Marie (–c. 1959)

Echmiadzin. Town, Armenia : Vagarshapat (–1945)

Echuca. City, Victoria, Australia : Hopwoods Ferry (–?)

Economy see Ambridge

Eden. Town, North Carolina, USA : Leaksville (–c. 1970)

Eden see Bar Harbor

Edenburg see Knox

Edgewood see Homewood

Edinburg. City, Texas, USA : Edinburgh (–1908), Chapin (1908–11)

Edinburgh see Edinburg

Edison. Township, New Jersey, USA : Raritan (–1954)

Edison see Westlock

Edith Cavell, Mount. Mountain, Jasper National Park, Alberta, Canada : Montagne de la Grande Traverse (–1916)

Edith Ronne Land see Ronne Ice Shelf

Edson. Town, Alberta, Canada : Heatherwood (–1911)

Edward, Lake. Uganda/Zaïre, central Africa : Albert Edward, Lake (–1908), Idi Amin Dada, Lake (1973–79)

Edwardesabad see Bannu

Eger *see* Cheb
Egito. Village, western Angola, southwestern Africa : Balabaia (–c. 1979)
Ehrenforst *see* Slawiecice
Eibenschitz *see* Ivančice
Eighty Mile Beach. Coastal strip, Western Australia, Australia : Ninety Mile Beach (–1946)
Eiragola *see* Arėgala
Eire *see* Ireland
Eirunepé. City, northwestern Brazil, South America : São Felippe (–1939), João Pessoa (1939–43)
Eisenbrod *see* Železný Brod
Eisenhower, Mount *see* Castle Mountain
Eisenstein *see* Železná Ruda
Ekaterinburg = Yekaterinburg
Ekaterinenstadt *see* Marks
Ekaterinodar *see* Krasnodar
Ekaterinoslav *see* Dnepropetrovsk
Ekaterinovka *see* Artyomovsk (3)
Ekeli *see* Zahirabad
Ekklesoúla *see* Néa Ekklesoúla
Ekuku. Cape, Río Muni, Equatorial Guinea, western Africa : Nguema Biyogo (1973–79)
Elaión *see* Kamisianá
Elandsfontein *see* Alberton
Elandsfontein Junction *see* Germiston
El Aouinet. Village, northeastern Algeria, northern Africa : Clairfontaine (–c. 1962)
Elar *see* Abovyan

El-Asnam. Town, northern Algeria, northern Africa : Orléansville (–1964)
El Basatine. Village, northern Morocco, northwestern Africa : Meknès l'Oasis (–c. 1959)
El Bayadh. Town, northwestern Algeria, northern Africa : Géryville (–c. 1962)
Elbing *see* Elbląg
Elbląg. Town, northern Poland : Elbling (1939–45), Germany
El Braya. Village, northwestern Algeria, northern Africa : Mangin (–c. 1962)
Elbrus. Town, Kabardin-Balkar Autonomous Republic, Russia : Ialbuzi (–c. 1960)
El Campo *see* Campo Lugar
El Cerrito. City, California, USA : Rust (–1917)
El Chilamatal *see* Ciudad Arce
Eldorado. City, southeastern Brazil, South America : Xiririca (–1948)
Elektrogorsk. Town, Moscow Oblast, Russia : Elektroperedacha (–1946)
Elektroperedacha *see* Elektrogorsk
Elektrostal. Town, Moscow Oblast, Russia : Zatishye (–1938)
Elektrougli. Town, Moscow Oblast, Russia : Kudinovo (–1935)
Elektrovoz *see* Stupino

El Eulma. Town, northeastern Algeria, northern Africa : Saint-Arnaud (–c. 1962)

El Fendek. Town, northern Morocco, northwestern Africa : Castillejos

El Ferrol *see* El Ferrol del Caudillo

El Ferrol del Caudillo. City, northwestern Spain : El Ferrol (–1939)

El Guara. Village, northwestern Morocco, northwestern Africa : Boucheron

El Hachem. Village, northwestern Algeria, northern Africa : Dombasle (–c. 1962)

El Harhouba. Village, northern Morocco, northwestern Africa : Miramar (–c. 1959)

El-Harrach. Suburb of Algiers, Algeria, northern Africa : Maison-Carrée (–c. 1962)

Elías Piña. Town, western Dominican Republic, West Indies : Comendador (–1930)

Elidere *see* Čepinska

Élisabethville *see* (1) Lubumbashi; (2) Shaba

Elista. Capital of Kalmyk Autonomous Republic, Russia : Stepnoy (1944–57)

Elizabeth Hall *see* Melanie Damishana

Elizavetgrad = Yelizavetgrad

Elizavetpol *see* Gyandza

El-Jadida. City, western Morocco, northwestern Africa : Mazagan (–c. 1960)

El Jorf Lasfar. Village and cape, northwestern Morocco, northwestern Africa : Cap Blanc (–c. 1959)

El Jovero *see* Miches

Ełk. City, northeastern Poland : Lyck (–1945), Germany

El-Kala. Town, northeastern Algeria, northern Africa : La Calle (–c. 1962)

Ellesmere *see* Scottsdale

Ellice Islands *see* Tuvalu

Elliotdale *see* Xhora

Ellore *see* Eluru

Ellouizia. Village, northern Morocco, northwestern Africa : St-Jean-de-Fédala (–c. 1959)

Ellsworth Highland *see* Ellsworth Land

Ellsworth Land. Region, Antarctica : Ellsworth Highland (*1935–?)

El Meddah. Village, northern Morocco, northwestern Africa : La Varenne (–c. 1959)

El Menzel. Village, northern Morocco, northwestern Africa : Meknès-Plaisance (–c. 1959)

El Nido. Municipality, Palawan, Philippines : Bacuit (–1954)

El Paraíso *see* Choloma

El Paso *see* Derby

El Poyo *see* Poyo del Cid

El Progreso. City, east-central Guatemala, Central

America : Guastatoya
(–c. 1920)

El Pueblito *see* Corregidora

Elqbiere. Village, northern
Morocco, northwestern
Africa : Les Chênes
(–c. 1959)

El Rio. Barrio, Butuan,
Philippines : Biga
(–1967)

Eluru. Town, eastern India :
Ellore (–1949)

El Vado *see* La Vereda

Elvershagen *see* Lagiewniki

Emamoud. Town, northern
Iran : Shahrud (–1980)

Emilia *see* Emilia-Romagna

Emilia-Romagna. Region,
north-central Italy :
Emilia (–1948)

Emmahaven *see* Telukbajur

Empingham Reservoir *see*
Rutland Water

Encinal *see* Sunnyvale

Encruzilhada *see* Encruzilhada do Sul

Encruzilhada do Sul. City,
southern Brazil, South
America : Encruzilhada
(–1944)

En Gannim *see* Ramat Gan

Engels *see* Pokrovsk

Engelsburg *see* Kalbar

Engelsovo. Urban settle-
ment, Lugansk Oblast,
Ukraine : Shakhty imeni
Engelsa (–c. 1960)

Enham Alamein. Village,
Hampshire, England, UK
: Knights Enham (–1945)

Enkeldoorn *see* Chivhu

Enlung *see* Tientung [Tien-
tung]

Enna. City, central Sicily, Italy : Castrogiovanni
(–1927)

Enrique B. Maga-
lona. Municipality, Ne-
gros Occidental, Philip-
pines : Saravia (–1967)

Enshih. Town, east-central
China : Shihnan (–1912)

Enso *see* Svetogorsk

Entre Ríos. Town, southern
Bolivia, South America :
San Luis (–1906)

Entre Rios *see* (1) Malema;
(2) Rio Brilhante; (3)
Três Rios

Enzeli = Bandar-e Anzali

Epitácio Pessoa *see* Pedro
Avelino

Équateur. Province, northwestern Zaïre, central Africa : Coquilhatville
(1935–47)

Equatoria (1956†). Prov-
ince, southern Sudan :
Mongalla (–1936)

Equatorial
Guinea. Republic, west-
ern Africa : Spanish
Guinea (*1926–68)

Erasmus *see* Bronkhorstspruit

Erastovka *see* Vishnyovoye
(1)

Erdély *see* Transylvania

Erechim. City, southern
Brazil, South America :
Boa Vista (do Erechim)
(*1909–39), José Boni-
fácio (1939–44)

Erechim *see* Getúlio Vargas

Ergfisk *see* Torfelt

Erhyüan. Town, southwest-
ern China : Langkiung
(–1913)

Erice. Town, northwestern

Sicily, Italy : Monte San
Giuliano (–1934)
Erickson. Village, Mani-
toba, Canada : Avesta
(–1908)
Erivan *see* Yerevan
Ersekújvár *see* Nové Zámky
Erzsébetfalva *see* Pestszenterzsébet
Escarabajosa *see* Santa María
del Tiétar
Eschenbach *see* Wolframs-
Eschenbach
Esigodini. Town, southwest-
ern Zimbabwe, southeast-
ern Africa : Essexvale
(–1982)
Eski-Dzhumaya *see* Tŭr-
govishte
Eskije *see* Xanthe
Eskimo Point *see* Arviat
Eslamabad-e Gharb. Town,
western Iran : Shahabad
(–1980)
Esparragosa del Caud-
illo. Village, southwest-
ern Spain : Esparragosa
de Lares (–c.1960)
Esperantina. City, northeast-
ern Brazil, South Amer-
ica : Boa Esperança
(–1944)
Esperanza *see* Cachuela
Esperanza
Espírito Santo *see* Indiaroba
Essaouira. City, southwestern Morocco, northwest-
ern Africa : Mogador
(–1959)
Essexvale *see* Esigodini
Esto-Khaginka *see* Yashalta
Estonia. Republic, central
Europe : Estonian SSR
(1940–90)

Estonian SSR *see* Estonia
Esutoru *see* Uglegorsk (1)
Eucaliptus *see* Tomás Barrón
Euclides da Cunha. City,
eastern Brazil, South
America : Cumbe
(–1939)
Eugenópolis. City, south-
eastern Brazil, South
America : São Manuel
(–1944)
Eva Perón *see* (1) La Pampa;
(2) La Plata
Evaton *see* Residensia
Evensk. Village, Khab-
arovsk Kray, Russia :
Bolshaya Garmanda
(–1951)
Exántheia. Village, Levkás,
Ionian Islands, Greece :
Áno Exántheia
(–1960s)
Exokhé. Village, northern
Greece : Kalývia
Kharádras (–1960s)
Eydtkau *see* Chernyshevskoye
Eydtkuhnen *see* Ch-
ernyshevskoye
Ezaki. Town, southwestern
Honshu, Japan : Ta-
masaki (–1943)
Ezhva. Suburb of Syk-
tyvkar, Komi Autono-
mous Republic, Russia :
Sloboda (–c. 1960)
Ez Zhiliga. Village, north-
western Morocco, north-
western Africa : Christian
(–c. 1959)

Fabian Marcos. Barrio, Ilocos Norte, Philippines :
Lacub (–1968)

Fabrika imeni Krasnoy Armii
i Flota *see* Kras-
noarmeysk (5)
Fachow *see* Fahsien
Fahsien. Town, southeast-
ern China : Fachow
(–1912)
Faire *see* Santo Niño (1)
Fairhaven. Village, New-
foundland, Canada : Fa-
mish Gut (–1940)
Fairview. Village, Alberta,
Canada : Waterhole
(*c.1910–14)
Faisalabad. Town, south-
eastern Pakistan :
Lyallpur (–1979)
Faizully Khodzhayeva, imeni
see Sverdlovsk (1)
Fakel. Urban settlement,
Udmurt Autonomous Re-
public, Russia : Ser-
giyevsky (–c. 1960)
Falkenberg *see* Niemodlin
Falknov *see* Sokolov
Famish Gut *see* Fairhaven
Fangcheng [Fang-cheng].
Town, east-central China
: Yuchow (–1913)
Fanning Island *see* Tabuaeran
Faradofay. Town, southeast-
ern Madagascar, south-
eastern Africa : Fort-
Dauphin (–?), Taolanaro
(?–c. 1979)
Farahal *see* Bab Sebta
Farroupilha. City, southern
Brazil, South America :
Nova Vicenza (–1934)
Fashoda *see* Kodok
Fatshan *see* Namhoi
Faxa *see* Camp Morton
Faya *see* Largeau
Fdérik. Town, north-central

Mauritania, western Af-
rica : Fort Gouraud
(–c. 1960)
Februarie 16, 1933. Suburb
of Bucharest, Romania :
Marele-Voevod-Mihai
(–1948)
Fédala *see* Mohammédia
Federal Capital Territory *see*
Australian Capital Terri-
tory
Feira *see* Luangwa
Felipe Carrillo
Puerto. Town, south-
eastern Mexico, North
America : Santa Cruz de
Bravo (–1935)
Fellin *see* Viljandi
Felshtin *see* Gvardeyskoye
Felsőireg *see* Iregszemcse
Felsőszentgyörgy *see* Jászfel-
sőszentgyörgy
Fencheng [Fen-ch-
eng]. Town, northeast-
ern China : Taiping
(–1914)
Fenchow *see* Fenyang
Fénérive *see* Fenoarivo Atsi-
nanana
Fengcheng [Feng-cheng].
Town, eastern China :
Fenghwang (–1914)
Feng-chieh = Fengkieh
Fengchüan *see* Fengkang
Fenghsien = Fengsien
Fenghwang *see* Fengcheng
[Feng-cheng]
Feng-i = Fengyi
Fengkang. Town, southern
China : Fengchüan (–
1930)
Fengkieh [Feng-chieh].
Town, central China :
Kweichow (–1913)

Fengsien [Feng-hsien].
Town, eastern China :
Nankiao (–1912)
Feng-tien *see* (1) Liaoning; (2)
Shen-yang
Fengyi [Feng-i]. Town,
southwestern China :
Chaochow (–1914)
Fenoarivo Atsinan-
ana. Town, eastern Ma-
dagascar, southeastern
Africa : Fénérive
(–c. 1979)
Fenyang. Town, northeast-
ern China : Fenchow
(–1912)
Ferdinand *see* Mikhailovgrad
Ferdinandov *see* Botev
Fergana. Capital of Fergana
Oblast, Uzbekistan :
Novy Margelan (–1910),
Skobelev (1910–24)
Fernando Po *see* Bioko
Ferreira Gomes. Town,
northern Brazil, South
America : Amapari
(1939–43)
Ferryville *see* Menzel-Bour-
guiba
Festenberg *see* Twardogóra
Fidenza. Town, north-cen-
tral Italy : Borgo San
Donnino (–1927)
Figueira *see* Governador Vala-
dares
Filehne *see* Wieleń
Finale Ligure. Town, north-
western Italy : Finalmar-
ina (–c. 1940)
Finalmarina *see* Finale Ligure
Findley Point *see* Kaniniti
Point
Firdaus. Town, northeast-
ern Iran : Tun (–1920s)

Fischhausen *see* Primorsk (1)
Fishing Lake *see* Rossman
Lake
Fiume *see* Rijeka
Fizuli. Town, Azerbaijan :
Karyagino (–1959)
Flagstaff *see* Siphaqeni
Flatow *see* Złotów
Flers *see* Flers-en-Escrebieux
Flers-en-Escre-
bieux. Suburb of
Douai, northern France :
Flers (–1944)
Fletcher *see* Aurora
Florânia. City, northeastern
Brazil, South America :
Flores (–1944)
Florence Bay *see* Chtimba
Flores *see* (1) Florânia; (2) Ti-
mon
Florissant. City, Missouri,
USA : St. Ferdinand
(–1939)
Fohai. Town, southwestern
China : Menghai (–1929)
Fokino. Town, Bryansk Ob-
last, Russia : Tsementny
(–1964)
Folgares *see* Capelongo
Folgoso de Caurel. Village,
northwestern Spain : Cau-
rel (–c. 1950)
Fondouk *see* Khemis el
Khechna
Fontaine-de-
Vaucluse. Village,
southeastern France :
Vaucluse (–1946)
Foochow [Fuchow, Fu-
chou]. City, southeast-
ern China : Minhow
(1934–43)
Ford *see* East Windsor
Forestburg. Town, Alberta,

Canada : Duxbury
(– 1919)

Forest Park. Village, Illinois, USA : Harlem
(–1907)

Forestville. Town, Quebec, Canada : Sault-au-Cochon (–1941)

Forfarshire *see* Angus

Formosa *see* Ilhabela

Formosa Strait *see* Taiwan Strait

Fort-Aleksandrovsky *see* Fort-Shevchenko

Fortaleza *see* Pedra Azul

Fort Andres Bonifacio. Municipality, Rizal, Philippines : Fort William McKinley (–1905)

Fort Archambault *see* Sarh

Fort Bayard *see* Chan-chiang

Fort-Bayard *see* Siying [Hsiying]

Fort Brabant *see* Tuktoyaktuk

Fort Carcenera *see* Fort Jose Abad Santos

Fort Chimo *see* Kuujjuaq

Fort-Crampel *see* Kaga Bandoro

Fort Crook *see* Offutt Air Force Base

Fort-Dauphin *see* Faradofoy

Fort de Kock *see* Bukittinggi

Fort-de-l'Eau *see* Bordj el Kiffan

Fort de Polignac *see* Illizi

Forte Cameia *see* Lumege

Fort Flatters *see* Bordj Omar Driss

Fort-Foureau *see* Kousseri

Fort George *see* Prince George

Fort Gouraud *see* Fdérik

Fort Hall *see* Muranga

Fort Hertz *see* Putao

Fort Hill *see* Chitipa

Fort Jameson *see* Chipata

Fort Johnston *see* Mangoche

Fort Jose Abad Santos. Barrio, Lanao, Philippines : Fort Carcenera (–1957)

Fort Lamy *see* N'Djamena

Fort-Laperrine *see* Tamanrasset

Fort MacLeod. Town, Alberta, Canada : MacLeod (–1952)

Fort Manning *see* Mchinji

Fort Marion National Monument *see* Castillo de San Marcos National Monument

Fort-National *see* L'Arbaa Naït Irathen

Fort Rosebery *see* Mansa

Fort-Rousset *see* Owando

Fort-Rupert *see* Rupert House

Fort Sandeman *see* Zhob

Fort-Shevchenko. Town, Guryev Oblast, Kazakhstan : Fort-Aleksandrovsky (–1939), Fort Uritskogo (1920s)

Fort Thomas. City, Kentucky, USA : Highlands (–1914)

Fort Trinquet *see* Bir Mogreïn

Fort Uritskogo *see* Fort-Shevchenko

Fort Victoria *see* Masvingo

Fort Walton *see* Fort Walton Beach

Fort Walton Beach. City, Florida, USA : Fort Walton (–1953)

Fort William McKinley *see* Fort Andres Bonifacio

Foucauld *see* Souk Jemaâ Oulad Abbou

Fou-liang = Fowliang

Fou-ling = Fowling

Fouras *see* Fouras-les-Bains

Fouras-les-Bains. Town, western France : Fouras (–1948)

Fou-yang = Fowyang

Fowchow *see* Fowling [Fouling]

Fowliang [Fou-liang]. Town, southeastern China : Kingtehchen [Ching-te-chen] (–1931)

Fowling [Fou-ling]. Town, central China : Fowchow (–1913)

Fowyang [Fou-yang]. Town, eastern China : Yingchow (–1912)

Fraidorf *see* Novosyolovskoye

Francisco Morazán. Department, south-central Honduras, Central America : Tegucigalpa (–1943)

Franco. Barrio, Ilocos Norte, Philippines : Palpalicong (–1969)

Frankenstein (in Schlesien) *see* Ząbkowice Śląskie

Franklin *see* Nutley

Franklin D. Roosevelt Island. Island, East River, New York City, USA : Blackwell's Island (–1921), Welfare Island (1921–73)

Fraserburg Road *see* Leeu-Gamka

Fraserpet *see* Kushalnagar

Fraserville *see* Rivière-du-Loup

Fraserwood. Hamlet, Manitoba, Canada : Kreuzberg (–1918)

Frauenburg *see* Saldus

Frauenstadt *see* Wadowice

Fraustadt *see* Wschowa

Fredrikshald *see* Halden

Fredriksvern *see* Stavern

Freeport *see* Wayne

Freiberg *see* Příbor

Freiburg (in Schlesien) *see* Świebodzice

Freienwalde *see* Chociwel

Frei Paulo. City, northeastern Brazil, South America : São Paulo (–1944)

Freiwaldau *see* Jeseník

French Congo *see* French Equatorial Africa

French Equatorial Africa. French colony (–1958), central Africa : French Congo (–1910)

French Guinea *see* Guinea

French Rocks *see* Pandrapura

French Somaliland *see* Djibouti

French Sudan *see* Mali

French Togoland *see* Togo

Fresnes *see* Fresnes-sur-Escaut

Fresnes-sur-Escaut. Town, northern France : Fresnes (–1941)

Freudenthal *see* Bruntál

Freystadt *see* (1) Kisielice; (2) Kożuchów

Fridenfeld *see* Komsomolskoye (2)

Friedau *see* Ormož

Friedeberg *see* Mirsk

Friedeberg in Neumark *see* Strzelce Krajeńskie

Friedland *see* (1) Mieroszów;
(2) Pravdinsk
Friedrichshain. District of
Berlin, Germany : Horst
Wessel Stadt (1930s–
1945)
Friedrichstadt *see* Jaunjelgava
Frignano *see* Villa di Briano
Frisches Haff *see* Vistula La-
goon
Friuli *see* Udine
Frobisher Bay *see* Iqaluit
Frohenbruck *see* Veselí nad
Lužnicí
Fronteiras. City, northeast-
ern Brazil, South Amer-
ica : Socorro (–1944)
Frunze. Urban settlement,
Osh Oblast, Kirgizia :
Kadamdzhay
(–1937)
Frunze *see* Bishkek
Frunzenskoye. Village, Osh
Oblast, Kirgizia : Pulgan
(–1940)
Frunzensky. Suburb of
Dnepropetrovsk,
Dnepropetrovsk Oblast,
Ukraine : Kamenka
(–c. 1935)
Frunzovka. Urban settle-
ment, Odessa Oblast,
Ukraine : Zakharovka
(–c. 1935)
Fu-chou = Foochow
Fuchow (1) = Foochow; (2)
see Funing
Fuhsien. Town, northeast-
ern China : Wafangtien
(–1931)
Fukiang *see* Kanku
Fukung. Village, southwest-
ern China : Shangpo
(–1935)

Fulford *see* North Miami
Beach
Fulgencio. Barrio, Capiz,
Philippines : Northon
(–1957)
Funan. Town, southern
China : Sinning (–1914)
Funing. Town, southwestern
China : Fuchow (–1927)
Furmanov. Town, Ivanovo
Oblast, Russia : Sereda
(–1941)
Furmanovo. Village, Uralsk
Oblast, Kazakhstan : Slo-
mikhino (–1935)
Fürstenfelde *see* Boleszkowice
Furukamappu *see* Yuzhno-
Kurilsk
Fushih *see* Yenan
Fu-shun. City, northeastern
China : Hsing-jen (1902–
08)
Fuyi *see* Lintseh [Lin-tse]
Fuyü. Town, northeastern
China : Petuna (–1914)
Fuyüan. Town, northeast-
ern China : Suiyüan
(–1929)

Gabaldon. Municipality,
Nueva Ecija, Philippines
: Bitulok (–1953), Sabani
(1953–55)
Gaberones *see* Gaborone
Gablonz *see* Jablonec (nad Ni-
sou)
Gaborone. Capital of
Botswana, southern Af-
rica : Gaberones (–1969)
Gabú (Sara) *see* Nova Lamego
Gaden *see* Zelyony Bor
Gafurov. Town, Leninabad
Oblast, Tajikistan :

Ispisar (–1953), Soveta-
bad (1953–62, 1964–78),
Khodzhent (1962–64)
Gagarin (1). Town, Smolensk
Oblast, Russia : Gzhatsk
(–1968)
Gagarin (2). Town, Syrd-
arya Oblast, Uzbekistan :
Yerzhar (–1974)
Gagarino. Village, Grodno
Oblast, Belorussia : Dro-
chilovo (–1969)
Gago Coutinho *see* Lumbala
Nguimbo
Gaillard Cut. Section of Pan-
ama Canal, Canal Zone,
Panama, Central Amer-
ica : Culebra Cut
(–1913)
Gainash *see* Ainaži
Galane. Village, northeast-
ern Greece : Kromníkos
(–1960s)
Galena Park. City, Texas,
USA : Clinton (–1928)
Galkovsky Rudnik *see* Ar-
tyoma, imeni
Gamelleira do Assuruá *see*
Santo Inácio
Gancheshty *see* Kotovsk (2)
Ganda. Town, western An-
gola, southwestern Africa
: Mariano Machado
(–c. 1979)
Gandzha Guberniya
(1920†). Russia : Yeli-
zavetpol Guberniya
(1868–1918)
Gantiadi. Urban settlement,
Abkhazian Autonomous
Republic, Georgia : Pi-
lenkovo (–1948)
Gapsal *see* Haapsalu
Garampang *see* San Jose (2)

Gardabani. Town, Georgia :
Karaya (–1947)
Gardner Island *see* Nikuma-
roro
Garfield Heights. Suburb of
Cleveland, Ohio, USA :
South Newburgh (*1907–
19)
Gargždai. Town, Lithuania :
Gordž (–1917)
Garmo Peak *see* Communism
Peak
Garson. Village, Manitoba,
Canada : Lyall (*1915–
27)
Gasan-Kuli Nature Reserve
see Krasnovodsk Nature
Reserve
Gaspar Strait *see* Kelasa Strait
Gassen *see* Jasień
Gassino *see* Gassino Torinese
Gassino Torinese. Village,
northwestern Italy :
Gassino (–c. 1936)
Gastello. Urban settlement,
Sakhalin Oblast, Russia :
Nairo (1905–45), Japan
Gata *see* Poona Bayabao
Gatchina. Town, Leningrad
Oblast, Russia : Trotsk
(1923–29), Krasnog-
vardeysk (1929–44)
Gatooma *see* Kadoma
Gatyana. Town, southern
Transkei, southern Af-
rica : Willowvale (–1976)
Gaudencio Antonio
(1). Barrio, Davao del
Norte, Philippines : Pangi
(–1969)
Gaudencio Antonio
(2). Barrio, Mindoro
Oriental, Philippines : Ti-
nalunan (–1969)

Gavinovichi *see* Podgornaya (2)

Gavrilovka *see* Taldy-Kurgan

Gavrilovsky Zavod *see* Druzhkovka

Gaza *see* Klemzig

Gazenpot *see* Aizpute

Gaziantep. City, southern Turkey : Aïntab (–1922)

Gcuwa. Town, southern Transkei, southern Africa : Butterworth (–1976)

Gdańsk. City, northern Poland : Danzig (–1945), Germany

Gdingen *see* Gdynia

Gdyel. Village, northwestern Algeria, northern Africa : Saint-Cloud (–c. 1962)

Gdynia. City, northern Poland : Gdingen (–1939), Germany; Gotenhafen (1939–45), Germany

Geelvink Bay *see* Sarera Bay

Gegechkori *see* Martvili

Gehlenburg *see* Biala (Piska)

Geiranger. Village, western Norway : Maraak [Meraak, Merok] (–1940)

Geistingen *see* Hennef

Gela. Town, southern Sicily, Italy : Terranova di Sicilia (–1928)

Geldenhuis Estate Small Holdings *see* Bedfordview

Geliniátika. Village, southern Greece : Spartináiika (–1960s)

Gemswick. Village, eastern Barbados, West Indies : Penny Hole (–?)

Gene Autry. Town, Oklahoma, USA : Berwyn (–1942)

General Artemio Ricarte. Barrio, Ilocos Norte, Philippines : Nalasin (–1968)

General Câmara. City, southern Brazil, South America : Santo Amaro (–1938)

General Emilio Aguinaldo. Municipality, Cavite, Philippines : Bailen (–1905)

General Enrique Martínez. Town, east-central Uruguay, South America : La Charqueada (–early 1930s)

General Freire *see* Muxaluando

General Machado *see* (1) Camacupa; (2) General Peraza

General Peraza. Town, western Cuba : Lutgardita (–?), General Machado (?–1934)

General Roxas. Barrio, Davao, Philippines : Dacudao (–1957)

General Santos. Municipality, Cotabato, Philippines : Buayan (–1954)

General Tinio. Municipality, Nueva Ecija, Philippines : Payapa (–1957)

General Toshevo. Village, northeastern Bulgaria :

Casim (1913–40), Romania

General Trias. Municipality, Cavite, Philippines : San Francisco de Malabon (–1914), Malabon (1914–?)

General Uriburu *see* Zárate

Genthon. Suburb of St. Vital, Manitoba, Canada : Dufault (–1915)

Georgenswalde *see* Otradnoye

George River *see* Port Nouveau-Québec

Georges Clemenceau *see* Stidia

Georgia. Republic, southeastern Europe : Georgian SSR (*1921–91)

Georgian SSR *see* Georgia

Georgiu-Dezh *see* Liski

Georgiye-Osetinskoye *see* Nazran

Georgouláiika. Village, central Greece : Várnakas (–1960s)

Georgsmarienhütte. Village, northwestern Germany : Georgs Marien Hütte (–1937)

Georgs Marien Hütte *see* Georgsmarienhütte

Geraldton *see* Innisfail

Gerdauen *see* Zheleznodorozhny (1)

Gerlachovka. Mountain, northern Slovakia : Stalin Peak (1949–61)

German New Guinea *see* New Guinea

German Southwest Africa *see* Namibia

Germantown *see* Holbrook

Germiston. Town, Transvaal, South Africa : Elandsfontein Junction (–1904)

Geroyskoye. Village, Kaliningrad Oblast, Russia : Gertlauken (–1946), Germany (–1945)

Gertlauken *see* Geroyskoye

Geryusy *see* Goris

Géryville *see* El Bayadh

Getúlio Vargas. City, southern Brazil, South America : Erechim (–1934)

Gevaram. Settlement, southwestern Israel : Kibbutz Mahar (–1942)

Ghaem Shahr = Qaemshahr

Ghaghara. River, northern India : Gogra (–1966)

Ghana. Republic, western Africa : Gold Coast (–1957)

Ghazaouet. Town, northwestern Algeria, northern Africa : Nemours (–c. 1962)

Ghriss. Village, northwestern Algeria, northern Africa : Thiersville (–c. 1962)

Gibigaan *see* Buenavista

Gigant *see* Kuznetsovsky

Gilbert Islands *see* Kiribati

Gilgenburg *see* Dąbrówno

Gindlicsalád *see* Tengelic

Ginsburg *see* Kaakhka

Girard *see* Woodland Hills

Girgenti *see* Agrigento

Gissar. Urban settlement, Tajikistan : Khanaka (–c. 1960)

Gitschin *see* Jičín

Gizhduvan. Town, Bukhara Oblast, Uzbekistan : Akmal-Abad (c. 1935–37)

Giżycko. Town, northeastern Poland : Lötzen (–1945), Germany

Gladeville see Wise

Gladstone. City, Missouri, USA : Linden (–1952)

Glasgow Junction see Park City

Glatz see Kłodzko

Gleiwitz see Gliwice

Glen Grey see Cacadu

Glistenets see Zalesino

Gliwice. City, southwestern Poland : Gleiwitz (–1945), Germany

Glod see Mirnaya (1)

Glogau see Głogów

Głogów. City, southwestern Poland : Glogau (–1945), Germany

Głogówek. Town, southern Poland : Oberglogau (–1945), Germany

Głubczyce. Town, southern Poland : Leobschütz (–1945), Germany

Glubokaya. Settlement, Sverdlovsk Oblast, Russia : Malomalsk (1933–c. 1965)

Głuchołazy. Town, southern Poland : Ziegenhals (–1945), Germany

Glupiki see Mirnaya (2)

Glypháda. Village, central Greece : Daphnokhórion (–1960s)

Gnadenburg see Vinogradnoye

Gnadenflyur see Pervomayskoye (4)

Gnesen see Gniezno

Gniezno. Town, west-central Poland : Gnesen (–1919, 1939–45), Germany

Gnilyaki see Roshcha

Gnoyev see Vit

Gnoynitsa see Vishnevets (1)

Gobustan. Urban settlement, Azerbaijan : Duvanny (–1972)

Goedgegun see Nhlangano

Gogra see Ghaghara

Gökçe. Urban settlement, Gökceada, Turkey : Imroz (–1973)

Gökçeada. Island. Aegean Sea, Turkey : Imroz Adasi (–1973)

Golaya Snova see Golosnovka

Goldberg see Złotoryja

Gold Coast. City, Queensland, Australia : South Coast Town (–1959)

Gold Coast see Ghana

Goldingen see Kuldiga

Goleniów. City, northwestern Poland : Gollnow (–1945), Germany

Goljam Bratan see Morozov

Gollel see Lavumisa

Gollnow see Goleniów

Golodayevka see (1) Kuybyshevo (2); (2) Pervomayskoye (5)

Golodnaya Step see Gulistan

Golosnovka. Village, Voronezh Oblast, Russia : Golaya Snova (–c. 1938)

Golovnino. Village, Kuril Islands, Sakhalin Oblast,

Russia : Tomari (1905–45), Japan

Golubovsky Rudnik *see* Kirovsk (1)

Golyashi *see* Sosnovy Bor

Goly Karamysh *see* Krasnoarmeysk (1)

Golyshi *see* Vetluzhsky

Golyshmanovo. Urban settlement, Tyumen Oblast, Russia : Katyshka (–1948)

Gombe. Town, northeastern Nigeria, western Africa : Doma (–1913)

Gonobitz *see* Konjic

Go Quao. Town, southern Vietnam : Kien Hung (–c. 1980)

Góra. Town, western Poland : Guhrau (–1945), Germany

Góra Sowia. Mountain, southwestern Poland : Hohe Eule (–1945), Germany

Gordž *see* Gargždai

Goreloye *see* Shumikhinsky

Gorevatka *see* Sovetskaya (3)

Gorgan [Gurgan]. City, northern Iran : Astarabad [Astrabad] (–1930)

Gorgol. District, southern Mauritania, western Africa : Quatrième (–c. 1979)

Goris. Town, Armenia : Geryusy (–1924)

Göritz *see* Górzyca

Görkau *see* Jirkov

Gorky *see* Nizhny Novgorod

Gorky Kray *see* Nizhegorodskaya Oblast

Gorky Oblast *see* Nizhe-gorodskaya Oblast

Gorky-Pavlovy *see* Kaminsky

Gorna Djumaya *see* Blagoevgrad

Gornaya (1). Village, Minsk Oblast, Belorussia : Deryaki (–1964)

Gornaya (2). Village, Gomel Oblast, Belorussia : Kaplitsa (–1964)

Gornji Grad. Village, western Slovenia : Oberburg (–1918), Germany

Gorno-Altay Autonomous Oblast. Altay Kray, Russia : Oyrat Autonomous Oblast (*1922–32), Oyrot Autonomous Oblast (1932–48)

Gorno-Altaysk. Capital of Gorno-Altay Autonomous Oblast, Altay Kray, Russia : Ulala (–1932), Oyrot-Tura (1932–48)

Gornoye *see* Krasny Karachay

Gornozavodsk (1). Town, Sakhalin Oblast, Russia : Naihoro (1905–47), Japan (–1945)

Gornozavodsk (2). Town, Perm Oblast, Russia : Novopashiysky (–1965)

Gorny. Urban settlement, Khabarovsk Kray, Russia : Solnechny (–1965)

Gornyak (1). Town, Donetsk Oblast, Ukraine : Sotsgorodok (–1958)

Gornyak (2). Town, Altay Kray, Russia : Zolotushino (–1946)

Gorodishche. Town, Cherkassy Oblast, Ukraine :

Petrovskogo G.I., imeni
(c. 1935–44)

Gorodok. Town, Lvov Oblast, Ukraine : Gródek Jagielloński (1919–45), Poland

Gorodok *see* Zakamensk

Gorodovikovsk. Town, Kalmyk Autonomous Republic, Russia : Bashanta (–1971)

Gorongosa. Town, central Mozambique, southeastern Africa : Vila Paiva de Andrada (1906–80)

Gorovakha *see* Pervomay (1)

Górowo Iławeckie. Town, northeastern Poland : Landsberg (–1945), Germany

Gorsko-Ivanovskoye *see* Gorskoye

Gorskoye. Town, Lugansk Oblast, Ukraine : Gorsko-Ivanovskoye (–c. 1940)

Goryacheistochnenskaya *see* Goryachevodsky

Goryachevodsky. Urban settlement, Stavropol Kray, Russia : Goryacheistochnenskaya (c. 1940–c. 1957)

Gorzów (Śląski). Town, southern Poland : Landsberg in Oberschlesien (–1945), Germany

Gorzów Wielkopolski. Town, western Poland : Landsberg (an der Warthe) (–1945), Germany

Górzyca. Town, western Poland : Göritz (–1945), Germany

Goskopi *see* Kopeysk

Gostingen *see* Gostyń

Gostinopolye *see* Volkhov

Gostyń. Town, western Poland : Gostingen (1939–45), Germany

Gotenhafen *see* Gdynia

Gotnya *see* Proletarsky (1)

Gottesberg *see* Boguszów

Gottesgab *see* Boží Dar

Gottschee *see* Kočevje

Gottwaldov *see* Zlín

Gotvald *see* Zmiyov

Governador Valadares. City, southeastern Brazil, South America : Figueira (–1939)

Grace McKinley, Mount *see* McKinley, Mount

Gracias *see* Lempira

Graham *see* Bluefield

Graham Land *see* Antarctic Peninsula

Grajos *see* San Juan del Olmo

Grama *see* São Sebastião da Grama

Grande Digue. Village, New Brunswick, Canada : Grandigue (–1944)

Grande Prairie *see* Westwold

Grande Traverse, Montagne de la *see* Edith Cavell, Mount

Grand Falls *see* Churchill Falls

Grandigue *see* Grande Digue

Grand Rapids *see* Wisconsin Rapids

Grantley Adams Airport = (Sir) Grantley Adams Airport

Grassy Mountain *see* Oglethorpe, Mount

Graudenz *see* Grudziądz

Grays Harbor. County,
Washington, USA :
Chehalis (–1915)

Great Whale River *see* Poste
de la Baleine

Grebyonka. Town, Poltava
Oblast, Ukraine : Gre-
byonkovsky (–1959)

Grebyonkovsky *see* Gre-
byonka

Green River *see* Rivière-
Verte

Greenwich Island. Island,
South Shetland Islands,
British Antarctic Terri-
tory : President González
Videla (–1947)

Gregorio del Pi-
lar. Municipality, Ilocos
Sur, Philippines : Con-
cepcion (–1955)

Greifenberg *see* Gryfice

Greifenhagen *see* Gryfino

Greiffenberg *see* Gryfów
Ślaski

Grenfell Rapids *see* Zongo
Rapids

Gretna. City, Louisiana,
USA : Mechanicsham
(–?)

Greylingstad. Town,
Transvaal, South Africa :
Willemsdal (*1913–14)

Gribnoye. Village, Minsk
Oblast, Belorussia :
Khrenovoye (–1964)

Grimm *see* Kamensky

Grishino *see* Krasnoarmeysk
(2)

Grissom Air Force
Base. Indiana, USA :
Bunker Hill Air Force
Base (*1954–68)

Gródek Jagielloński *see* Gorodok

Grodekovo *see* Pogranichny
(2)

Grodków. Town, southwest-
ern Poland : Grottkau
(–1945), Germany

Gromovsky *see* Dubovsky

Gross-Bitesch *see* Velká Bíteš

Grossdale *see* Brookfield

Gross Dirschkeim *see* Donskoye (1)

Grosse Pointe
Woods. Village, Michi-
gan, USA : Lochmoor
(*1926–39)

Grossheidekrug *see* Vzmorye
(1)

Gross Lindenau *see* Ozyorki

Gross-Meseritsch *see* Velké
Meziříčí

Gross Skaisgirren *see* Bolshakovo

Gross Strehlitz *see* Strzelce
(Opolskie)

Gross Wartenberg *see* Syców

Grosulovo *see* Velikaya
Mikhaylovka

Grottau *see* Hrádek nad Nisou

Grottkau *see* Grodków

Grouard. Village, Alberta,
Canada : Lesser Slave
Lake (–1909)

Grover *see* Tiltonsville

Grudziądz. City, north-central Poland : Graudenz
(–1919), Germany

Grukhi *see* Novovyatsk

Grumbkowfelde *see* Pravdino

Grumbkowkeiten *see*
Pravdino

Grünberg *see* Zielona Góra

Grünheide *see* Kaluzhskoye

Gryazliv *see* Borovichi

Gryaznoye *see* Novoye (1)
Gryaznukha *see* Sovetskoye
(1)
Gryfice. Town, northwest-
ern Poland : Greifenberg
(–1945), Germany
Gryfino. Town, northwest-
ern Poland : Greifen-
hagen (–1945), Germany
Gryfów Śląski. Town, south-
western Poland : Greif-
fenberg (–1945), Ger-
many
Guachalla. Town, western
Bolivia, South America :
Ilabaya (–c. 1945)
Guaçuí. City, southeastern
Brazil, South America :
Siqueira Campos
(–1944)
Guaíba. City, southern Bra-
zil, South America :
Pedras Brancas (–c. 1925)
Guapó. City, east-central
Brazil, South America :
Ribeirão (–1944)
Guaporé *see* Rondônia
Guarani *see* Pacajús
Guaraúna. Town, southern
Brazil, South America :
Valinhos (–1944)
Guardafui, Cape *see* Ras Asir
Guastatoya *see* El Progreso
Guben *see* Wilhelm-Pieck-
Stadt Guben
Gubkin. Town, Belgorod
Oblast, Russia : Ko-
robkovo (–1939)
Guchkovo *see* Dedovsk
Gugark. Village, Armenia :
Megrut (–1983)
Guhrau *see* Góra
Guidimaka. District, south-
ern Mauritania, western

Africa : Dixième
(–c. 1979)
Guijá. Town, southern
Mozambique, southeast-
ern Africa : Caniçado
(–1964), Vila Alferes
Chamusca (1964–80)
Guijá *see* Chókué
Guilherme Capelo *see* Ca-
congo
Guimba. Municipality,
Nueva Ecija, Philippines
: San Juan de Guimba
(–1914)
Guinea. Republic, western
Africa : French Guinea
(–1958)
Guinea-Bissau. Republic,
western Africa : Portu-
guese Guinea
(–1973)
Guiratinga. City, western
Brazil, South America :
Santa Rita do Araguaia
(–1939), Lajeado (1939–
43)
Gukasyan *see* Amasiya
Gulbakhor. Urban settle-
ment, Tashkent Oblast,
Uzbekistan : Kirda
(–1977)
Gulbene. Town, Latvia :
Schwanenburg (–1917)
Gulcha. Village, Osh Ob-
last, Kirgizia : Gulcha-
Guzar (–1938)
Gulcha-Guzar *see* Gulcha
Gulistan. Town, Syrdarya
Oblast, Uzbekistan :
Golodnaya Step (–1922),
Mirzachul (1922–61)
Gumbinnen *see* Gusev
Gumuljina *see* Komotine
Gundorovka *see* Donetsk (1)

Gunji *see* Rishabhatirtha
Gunza. Town, western An-
gola, southwestern Africa
: Porto Amboim
(–c. 1976)
Gurgan = Gorgan
Gurkfeld *see* Krško
Gurskoye. Town, Khab-
arovsk Kray, Russia :
Khungari (–1972)
Guruè. Town, north-central
Mozambique, southeast-
ern Africa : Vila Jun-
queiro (1947–80)
Guruwe. Town, northern
Zimbabwe, southeastern
Africa : Sipolilo (–1980),
Chipuriro (1980–82)
Guryevsk. Town, Kalinin-
grad Oblast, Russia :
Neuhausen (–1946), Ger-
many (–1945)
Gusakyan. Village, Arme-
nia : Verin-Gusakyan
(–c. 1960)
Gusev. Town, Kaliningrad
Oblast, Russia : Gumbin-
nen (–1946), Germany
(–1945)
Gusevka *see* Novosibirsk
Gusinoozersk. Town,
Buryat Autonomous Re-
public, Russia : Shakhty
(–1953)
Gussenbakh *see* Linyovo
Guštanj. Village, western
Slovenia : Gutenstein
(–1918), Germany
Gutenstein *see* Guštanj
Guttentag *see* Dobrodzień
Guttstadt *see* Dobre Miasto
Guyana. Republic, northern
South America : British
Guiana (–1966)

Guyman. City, Texas, USA
: Sanford (–1901)
Guyotville *see* Aïn Benian
Guzitsino *see* Krasny Profin-
tern (1)
Gvardeysk. Town, Kalinin-
grad Oblast, Russia :
Tapiau (–1946), Ger-
many (–1945)
Gvardeyskaya. Village,
Vitebsk Oblast, Belorus-
sia : Kukishi (–1964)
Gvardeyskoye. Village,
Khmelnitsky Oblast,
Ukraine : Felshtin
(–1946)
Gwelo *see* Gweru
Gweru. Town, central Zim-
babwe, southeastern Af-
rica : Gwelo (–1981)
Gyandzha. Town, Azer-
baijan : Yelizavetpol
(1804–1918), Kirovabad
(1935–90)
Gymná *see* Akrolímne
Győrszentmárton *see* Pan-
nonhalma
Gýtheion. Town, southern
Greece : Marathonisi
(–?), Turkey
Gzhatsk *see* Gagarin (1)

Haapsalu. Town, Estonia :
Gapsal (–1917)
Haas *see* Camp Morton
Habelschwerdt *see* Bystrzyca
Kłodzka
Hackensack. City, New Jer-
sey, USA : New Barba-
does (–1921)
Haclagan *see* Santo Niño (2)
Had el Brachoua. Village,
northern Morocco, north-

western Africa : (La) Jac-
queline (–c. 1959)
Hadersleben *see* Haderslev
Haderslev. City, southern
Denmark : Hadersleben
(1864–1920), Germany
Hadjadj. Village, northwest-
ern Algeria, northern Af-
rica : Bosquet
(–c. 1962)
Hadjout. Town, northern
Algeria, northern Africa :
Marengo (–c. 1962)
Hadzi Dimitar. Mountain,
central Bulgaria :
Buzuldza (–1967)
Hagía Ánna. Village, cen-
tral Greece : Koúkoura
(–1960s)
Hagía Kyriaké. Village,
northern Greece :
Skoúliare (–1960s)
Hagía Varvára. Village,
southern Greece : Káto
Kollínnai (–1960s)
Hágion Pneúma. Village,
northern Greece : Vez-
nikon (–?), Monoikon (?–
1930s)
Hágios Antónios *see* Hágios
Márkos
Hágios Márkos. Village,
northern Greece : Hágios
Antónios (–1960s)
Hágios Nikólaos. Village,
eastern Greece : Psykhé
(–1960s)
Hágios Nikólaos *see* Kastríon
Hahndorf. Town, South
Australia, Australia :
Ambleside (1918–35)
Haicheng *see* Haiyüan
Haichow *see* Sinhai [Hsin-hai]
Haifeng *see* Wuti

Hailar. City, northeastern
China : Hulun (1910–47)
Hainau *see* Chojnów
Haindorf *see* Hejnice
Haiyang *see* Linyü
Haiyen. Town, northwest-
ern China : Sankiocheng
(–1943)
Haiyüan. Town, north-cen-
tral China : Haicheng
(–1914)
Halden. City, southeastern
Norway : Fredrikshald
(–1928)
Half-Moon Bay *see* Oban
Halfway Village *see* East De-
troit
Hall *see* Solbad Hall in Tirol
Halley. UK research base,
Antarctica : Halley Bay
(–1977)
Halley Bay *see* Halley
Halq-el-Oued. Town, north-
ern Tunisia, northern Af-
rica : La Goulette
(–c. 1958)
Halton City. City, Texas,
USA : Birdville (–1949)
Hamadia. Town, northern
Algeria, northern Africa :
Victor Hugo (–c. 1962)
Hamanaka *see* Shimotsu
Hamilton *see* Trompsburg
Hamilton Falls *see* Kapachira
Falls
Hamilton River *see* Churchill
River
Hammerstein *see* Czarne
Hamônia *see* Ibirama
Hampton *see* Ruth
Hanchow *see* Kwanghan
[Kuang-han]
Hanchung *see* Nancheng (1)
Hansa *see* Corupá

Han-shou = Hanshow
Hanshow [Han-
shou]. Town, south-cen-
tral China : Lungyang
(–1912)
Haňšpach *see* Lipová
Hantsun *see* Hwanghwa [Hu-
ang-hua]
Hanyüan. Town, southern
China : Tsingki
(–1914)
Harare. Capital of Zim-
babwe, southeastern Af-
rica : Salisbury (–1982)
Harbin. City, northeastern
China : Pinkiang (1932–
45), Japan
Hardenberg *see* Neviges
Harding. Hamlet, Mani-
toba, Canada : Parr Sid-
ing (–1904), Earl Gray
(1904–05)
Hardteck *see* Krasnolesye
Harlem *see* Forest Park
Harmanlijska. River, south-
ern Bulgaria : Oludere
(–1967)
Harper *see* Costa Mesa
Harris *see* Westminster
Harrodsville. Town, North
Island, New Zealand :
Otorohanga (–1986)
Hartingsburg *see* Warmbad
Hartley *see* Chegutu
Hasei Nameche. Village,
northwestern Algeria,
northern Africa : Rivoli
(–c. 1962)
Haselberg *see* Krasnoz-
namensk
Hashtpar *see* Talesh
Hau Bon *see* Cheo Reo
Haussonvillers *see* Naciria
Havelock *see* Bulembu

Havlíčkův Brod. Town, cen-
tral Czech Lands :
Německý Brod [Deutsch
Brod] (–1945)
Havre-Saint-Pierre. Village,
Quebec, Canada : Saint-
Pierre-de-la-Pointe-aux-
Esquimaux (–1930)
Haynau *see* Chojnów
Hazendal *see* Sybrand Park
Hazorim *see* Sergunia [Szir-
guni]
Heatherwood *see* Edson
Hebron. City, West Bank,
Jordan : Al-Khalil
(–1950)
Heerwegen *see* Polkowice
Heiligenbeil *see* Mamonovo
Heilsberg *see* Lidzbark War-
miński
Heinrichswalde *see* Slavsk
Heishan. Town, northeast-
ern China : Chenan
(–1914)
Hejnice. Village, northern
Czech Lands : Haindorf
(–1918, 1939–45), Ger-
many
Hellenikón. Village, south-
ern Greece : Koúmares
(–1960s)
Hell-Ville *see* Andoany
Hengchow *see* (1) Henghsien;
(2) Hengyang
Hengfeng. Town, southeast-
ern China : Hingan
(–1914)
Henghsien. Town, southern
China : Hengchow
(–1912)
Hengshan. Town, central
China : Hwaiyüan
(–1914)
Hengyang. City, south-cen-

tral China : Hengchow
(–1912)

Hénin-Beaumont. Town,
northern France : Hénin-
Liétard (–1974)

Hénin-Liétard see Hénin-
Beaumont

Hennef. Village, western
Germany : Geistingen
(–1934)

Hennenman. Town, Orange
Free State, South Africa :
Ventersburgweg (–1927)

Henrique de Carvalho see
Saurimo

Hercegfalva see Mezőfalva

Herculândia. City, south-
eastern Brazil, South
America : Herculânia
(–1944)

Herculânia see (1) Coxim; (2)
Herculândia

Herguijuela de la Sierpe see
Herguijuela del Campo

Herguijuela del
Campo. Village, west-
ern Spain : Herguijuela
de la Sierpe (–c. 1930)

Hermannsbad see Ciechoc-
inek

Hermannstadt see Sibiu

Hermanus. Town, Cape
Province, South Africa :
Hermanuspietersfontein
(–1904)

Hermanuspietersfontein see
Hermanus

Hermsdorf see Sobięcin

Herowabad see Khalkhal

Herrnstadt see Wąsosz

Hesse-Kassel. Province,
western Germany :
Kurhessen (1944–45)

Hexamília. Village, south-

ern Greece : Hexamíllia
(–1960s)

Hexamíllia see Hexamília

Heydebreck see Kędzierzyn

Higashi-kata see Koniya

Higashi-naibuchi see Uglezavodsk

Higashitsuge see Tsuge

Higashi-uji. Town, southern
Honshu, Japan : Uji
(–early 1940s)

Highland Park. Borough,
New Jersey, USA : Rari-
tan (–1905)

Highlands see Fort Thomas

Hilario Valdez (1). Barrio,
Ilocos Norte, Philippines
: Barangay (–1971)

Hilario Valdez (2). Barrio,
Ilocos Norte, Philippines
: Caoyan (–1968)

Hilla see Babil

Hillsboro see Deerfield Beach

Hillsborough Canal Settlement see Belle Glade

Hindenburg see Zabrze

Hingan see (1) Ankang [An-
kang]; (2) Hengfeng

Hingcheng [Hsing-ch-
eng]. Town, northeast-
ern China : Ningyüan
(–1914)

Hinghai [Hsing-hai]. Town,
northwestern China :
Tahopa (–1939)

Hinghwa see Putien [Pu-tien]

Hingi see Anlung

Hingjen [Hsing-jen]. Town,
southern China : Sinch-
eng (–1914)

Hingking see Sinpin [Hsin-pin]

Hingkwo see Yangsin [Yang-
hsin]

Hinglungchen see Mingshui

Hingning *see* Tzehing [Tsu-hsing]

Hinubuan *see* Antipolo

Hirochi *see* Pravda

Hirschberg *see* Jelenia Góra

Hizaori *see* Asaka

Hłuboczek Wielki *see* Veliky Glubochyok

Hlučín. Town, eastern Czech Lands : Hultschin (–1919, 1939–45), Germany

Ho Chi Minh (City). City, southern Vietnam : Saigon (–1976)

Hochow *see* (1) Hochwan [Ho-chuan]; (2) Hohsien; (3) Linsia [Lin-hsia]

Hochstadt *see* Vysoké nad Jizerou

Ho-chuan = Hochwan

Hochwan [Ho-chuan]. Town, central China : Hochow (–1913)

Hockley *see* Levelland

Hodh ech Chargui. District, southeastern Mauritania, western Africa : Première (–c. 1979)

Hodh el Gharbi. District, southern Mauritania, western Africa : Deuxième (–c. 1979)

Hoey's Bridge *see* Moi's Bridge

Hofei. City, eastern China : Lüchow (–1912)

Hofgastein *see* Bad Hofgastein

Hofmeyr. Town, Cape Province, South Africa : Maraisburg (–1911)

Hog Island *see* Paradise Island

Hohe Eule *see* Góra Sowia

Hohenbruck *see* Třebechovice pod Orebem

Hohenelbe *see* Vrchlabí

Hohenfriedeberg *see* Dabromierz

Hohenfurth *see* Vyšší Brod

Hohenmauth *see* Vysoké Mýto

Hohensalza *see* Inowrocław

Hohensalzburg *see* Lunino

Hohenstadt *see* Zábřeh

Hohenstein *see* Olsztynek

Hohsien. Town, eastern China : Hochow (–1912)

Hoihong. Town, southeastern China : Luichow (–1912)

Hokow *see* Yakiang [Ya-chiang]

Holan. Town, northwestern China : Siehkangpao (–1942)

Holbrook. Town, New South Wales, Australia : Germantown (–c. 1918)

Holden. Town, Alberta, Canada : Vermilion Valley (–1907)

Hollandia *see* Jayapura

Holy Cross, Mount of the. Mountain, Colorado, USA : Holy Cross National Monument (1929–50)

Holy Cross National Monument *see* Holy Cross, Mount of the

Homewood. City, Alaska, USA : Edgewood (*1921–26)

Honan *see* Loyang

Hon Quan. Town, southern Vietnam : An Loc (–c. 1980)

Honto *see* Nevelsk
Hoover Dam. Dam, Colo-
rado River, Arizona/Ne-
vada, USA : Boulder
Dam (*1936–47)
Hopeh. Province, northeast-
ern China : Chihli (–1928)
Hoppo. Town, southeastern
China : Limchow (–1912)
Hopwoods Ferry *see* Echuca
Hordaland. County, south-
western Norway : Sondre
Bergenhus (–1918)
Horst Wessel Stadt *see* Fried-
richshain
Hot Springs *see* Truth or Con-
sequences
Houa Khong. Province,
northwestern Laos : Nam
Tha (–1966)
Hradec Králové. City, east-
central Czech Lands : Kö-
niggrätz (–1918, 1939–
45), Germany
Hrádek nad Nisou. Village,
northern Czech Lands :
Grottau (–1918, 1939–
45), Germany
Hranice. Town, eastern
Czech Lands : Mährisch-
Weisskirchen (–1918,
1939–45), Germany
Hsia-ho = Siaho
Hsi-an = Sian
Hsiang-ch'ou *see* Sianghsien
[Hsiang-hsien]
Hsiang-hsien = Sianghsien
Hsiang-yün = Siangyün
Hsia-p'u = Siapu
Hsi-chiang = Sichang
Hsi-chi = Sichi
Hsi-ch'ou = Sichow
Hsi-hsien = Sihsien
Hsin-chin = Sinkin

Hsing-ch'eng = Hingcheng
Hsing-hai = Hinghai
Hsing-jen (1) *see* Fu-shun; (2)
= Hingjen
Hsing-t'ai = Singtai
Hsing-tzu = Singtze
Hsin-hai = Sinhai
Hsin-hsien = Sinhsien
Hsin-pin = Sinpin
Hsin-yang. City, east-cen-
tral China : San-chou
(–1913)
Hsi-shui = Sishui
Hsiu-shui = Siushui
Hsi-ying = Siying
Hsüan-ch'eng = Süancheng
Hsüan-han = Süanhan
Hsüchang [Hsü-
ch'ang]. City, east-cen-
tral China : Hsüchow
(–1913)
Hsü-chou = Süchow
Hsüchow *see* Hsüchang [Hsü-
ch'ang]
Hsün-i = Sünyi
Hsün = k'o = Sünko
Hsü-shui = Süshui
Hsü-yung = Süyung
Hua-an = Hwaan
Hua-hsien = Hwahsien
Huai-an. City, eastern
China : Shan-yang (1912–
14)
Huaicho *see* Puerto Acosta
Huai-ning *see* Anking [An-
ch'ing]
Huai-yang = Hwaiyang
Huai-yin *see* Tsingkiang(pu)
[Ch'ing-chiang(pu)]
Hua-lung = Hwalung
Huambo. City, west-central
Angola, southwestern Af-
rica : Nova Lisboa (1928–
77)

Huang-hua = Hwanghwa
Huang-kang = Hwangkang
Huang-ling = Hwangling
Huang-lung = Hwanglung
Huang-yüan = Hwangyüan
Hua-ning = Hwaning
Huan-jen = Hwanjen
Huan-tai = Hwantai
Hua-ting *see* Sung-chiang
Huauco *see* Sucre
Hubbards. Town, Nova Scotia, Canada : Hubbards
Cove (–1905)
Hubbards Cove *see* Hubbards
Hu-chou *see* Wu-hsing
Huchu. Town, northwestern
China : Weiyüanpu
(–1931)
Hudson Bay. Town, Saskatchewan, Canada :
Hudson Bay Junction
(*1903–46)
Hudson Bay Junction *see*
Hudson Bay
Hueneme *see* Port Hueneme
Hui-chou *see* She-hsien
Hui-chuan = Hweichwan
Hui-min = Hweimin
Hui-nung = Hweinung
Hui-shui = Hweishui
Huitième *see* Dakhlet
Nouâdhibou
Hui-tse = Hweitseh
Hull Island *see* Orona
Hull-Sud *see* Lucerne
Hultschin *see* Hlučín
Hulun *see* Hailar
Huma. Town, northeastern
China : Kuchan (–1914)
Humboldt Bay *see* Kayo Bay
Hummelstadt *see* Lewin
Hummock Hill *see* Whyalla
Hungerburg *see* Narva-Jõesuu
Hungshankiao *see* Linsen

Hungshui *see* Minlo
Huns Valley *see* Polonia
Huntington *see* Shelton
Huntington Beach. City,
California, USA : Shell
Beach (–1901), Pacific
City (1901–?)
Huntington Park. City, California, USA : La Park
(*1900–04)
Hurbanovo. Town, southern
Slovakia : Stará Ďala
(–1948)
Hustopeče. Town, eastern
Czech Lands : Auspitz
(–1918, 1939–45), Germany
Huszt *see* Khust
Hutchinson. Village, Cape
Province, South Africa :
Victoria West Road
(–1901)
Hwaan [Hua-an]. Town,
southeastern China :
Hwafeng (–1928)
Hwachow *see* Hwahsien [Hua-hsien]
Hwafeng *see* Hwaan [Hua-an]
Hwahsien [Hua-hsien]. Town, central
China : Hwachow
(–1913)
Hwaijen *see* Hwanjen [Huan-jen]
Hwaiju *see* Chanhwa [Chan-hua]
Hwaiking *see* Tsinyang [Ch'in-yang]
Hwaining *see* Anking [An-ch'ing]
Hwaiyang [Huai-yang]. Town, east-central China : Chenchow
(–1913)

Hwaiyin *see* Tsingkiang(pu)
[Ching-chiang(-pu)]
Hwaiyüan *see* Hengshan
Hwalung [Hua-lung]. Town,
northwestern China : Pay-
enyungko (–1912),
Payung (1912–28), Payen
(1928–31)
Hwangchow *see* Hwangkang
[Huang-kang]
Hwange. Town, western
Zimbabwe, southeastern
Africa : Wankie (–1982)
Hwanghwa [Huang-
hua]. Town, northeast-
ern China : Hantsun
(–1937), Sinhai (1937–
49)
Hwangkang [Huang-
kang]. Town, east-cen-
tral China : Hwangchow
(–1912)
Hwangling [Huang-
ling]. Town, central
China : Chungpu (–1944)
Hwanglung [Huang-
lung]. Town, central
China : Shihpu (–1941)
Hwangtsun *see* Tahing [Ta-
hsing]
Hwangyüan [Huang-
yüan]. Town, north-
western China : Tangar
(–1912)
Hwaning [Hua-ning]. Town,
southwestern China :
Ningchow (–1913),
Ninghsien (1913–14),
Lihsien (1914–31)
Hwanjen [Huan-
jen]. Town, northeast-
ern China : Hwaijen
(–1914)
Hwantai [Huan-tai]. Town,

eastern China : Sincheng
(–1914)
Hweichow *see* Sihsien [Hsi-
hsien] (1)
Hweichwan [Hui-
chuan]. Town, north-
central China : Kwanpao
(–1944)
Hweilungchen *see* Chitung
[Ch'i-tung]
Hweimin [Hui-min]. Town,
eastern China : Wuting
(–1913)
Hweinung [Hui-
nung]. Town, north-
western China : Paofeng
(–1942)
Hweishui [Hui-shui]. Town,
southern China : Tingfan
(–1940s)
Hweitseh [Hui-tse]. Town,
southwestern China :
Tungchwan (–1929)
Hweitung *see* Kiungtung [Ch'i-
ung-tung]
Hydrómyloi *see* Lydía

Ialbuzi *see* Elbrus
Ian. Town, northeast China
: Lungchüanchen (–1929)
Ibaiti. City, southern Brazil,
South America : Barra
Bonita (–1944)
Ibatuba *see* Soledade de Mi-
nas
Ibiapinópolis *see* Soledade
Ibiraçu. City, southeastern
Brazil, South America :
Pau Gigante (–1944)
Ibirama. City, southeastern
Brazil, South America :
Hamônia (–1944)
Ibirarema. City, southeast-

ern Brazil, South America : Pau d'Alho (–1944)

Ibiúna. City, southeastern Brazil, South America : Una (–1944)

Iboti see Neves Paulista

Icana. Town, northwestern Brazil, South America : São Felipe (–1944)

Icaria. Island, Aegean Sea, Greece : Akhigria (–1913), Turkey

Icaturama see Santa Rosa de Viterbo

Icheng [I-cheng]. Town, east-central China : Tzechung (1944–49)

Ichijo. Town, eastern Shikoku, Japan : Shichijo (–1923)

Ichiki. Town, southern Kyushu, Japan : Nishi-ichiki (–1932)

Ichki(-Grammatikovo) see Sovetsky (1)

I-chou see Lini

Ichow see Lini

I-ch'uan = Ichwan

Ichun [I-ch'un]. Town, southeastern China : Yüanchow (–1912)

Ichwan [I-ch'uan]. Town, east-central China : Nantitien (–1933)

Idenburg Top see Pilimsit, Puncak

Idi Amin Dada, Lake see Edward, Lake

Idlewild see Kennedy

Idlewood see University Heights

Iesolo. Village, northern Italy : Cavazuccherina (–c. 1930)

Ifeng. Town, southeastern China : Sinchang (–1914)

Ighil Izane. Town, northwestern Algeria, northern Africa : Relizane (–c. 1962)

Iglau see Jihlava

Ignatovo see Bolshoye Ignatovo

Iguaçu see (1) Itaetê; (2) Laranjeiras do Sul

Iguaratinga see São Francisco do Maranhão

Iguatama. City, southeastern Brazil, South America : Pôrto Real (–1944)

Igumen see Cherven

Ihsien = Yihsien

Ikawai. Town, South Island, New Zealand : Redcliff (–1935)

Ikeja Province. Province, southwestern Nigeria, western Africa : Colony Province (*1954–67)

Ikramovo see Dzhuma

Ilabaya see Guachalla

Iława. Town, northern Poland : Deutsch Eylau (–1945), Germany

Ilebo. Town, south-central Zaïre, central Africa : Port Francqui (–1972)

Ilek. Village, Orenburg Oblast, Russia : Iletsky Gorodok (–1914)

Ilet see Krasnogorsky

Iletsk see Sol-Iletsk

Iletsky Gorodok see Ilek

Ilhabela. City, southeastern Brazil, South America : Formosa (–1944)

Ili see Kapchagay

Ilim see Shestakovo

(Ilirska) Bistrica. Village,
southwestern Slovenia :
Villa del Nevoso (–1947),
Italy
Iliysk *see* Kapchagay
Ilkenau *see* Olkusz
Illizi. Town, eastern Alge-
ria, northern Africa : Fort
de Polignac (–c. 1962)
Ilmenau *see* (1) Jordanów; (2)
Limanowa
Ilovaysk. Town, Donetsk
Oblast, Ukraine : Ilovay-
skaya (–1938)
Ilovayskaya *see* Ilovaysk
Ilyichyovsk. Town, Nakhi-
chevan Autonomous Re-
public, Azerbaijan : No-
rashen (–1964)
Ilyinsky. Urban settlement,
Sakhalin Oblast, Russia :
Kushunnai (1905–45), Ja-
pan
Iman *see* (1) Bolshaya
Ussurka; (2) Dalnerech-
ensk
Imbert. Town, northern Do-
minican Republic, West
Indies : Bajabonico
(–1925)
Imbuial *see* Bocaiúva do Sul
Imperatora Nikolaya II, Zem-
lya *see* Severnaya Zemlya
Imperatorskaya Gavan *see*
Sovetskaya Gavan
Imperia. Province, north-
western Italy : Port
Maurizio (1860–1923)
Imroz *see* Gökçe
Imroz Adasi *see* Gökçeada
Inabu. Town, central Hon-
shu, Japan : Inatake
(*1930s–early 1940s)
Inchiri. District, western

Mauritania, western Af-
rica : Douzième
(–c. 1979)
Indiaroba. City, northeast-
ern Brazil, South Amer-
ica : Espírito Santo
(–1944)
Indonesia. Republic, south-
eastern Asia : Nether-
lands Indies [Netherlands
East Indies, Dutch East
Indies] (1816–1945),
United States of Indone-
sia (1949–50)
Indrapura *see* Kerintji
Industrial Acres *see* Jacinto
City
Infanta. Municipality,
Quezon, Philippines : Bi-
nangoan de Lampon
(–1902)
Infantes *see* Villanueva de los
Infantes
Ingá *see* Andirá
Ingezi *see* Ngezi
Inghok *see* Yungtai [Yung-tai]
Ingichka. Urban settlement,
Samarkand Oblast,
Uzbekistan : Rudnik In-
gichka (–1959)
Ining *see* Siushui [Hsiu-shui]
Inkermann *see* Oued Rhiou
Innisfail. Town, Queen-
sland, Australia : Ger-
aldton (–1911)
Innokentyevskaya *see* Lenino
(1)
Inowrocław. City, north-
central Poland : Hohen-
salza (–1919), Germany
Insterburg *see* Chernyakhovsk
Interior *see* Interior and La-
buan
Interior and La-

buan. Residency, northern Borneo : Interior (–1946)

Inukjuac. Town, Quebec, Canada : Port Harrison (–1965)

Invermere. City, British Columbia, Canada : Copper City (–1900), Canterbury (1900–12)

Inwood. Village, Manitoba, Canada : Cossette (–1906)

Inyazura see Nyazura

Ionio see Taranto

Ipatovo. Town, Stavropol Kray, Russia : Vinodelnoye (–1930s)

Ipeh [Ipei]. Town, southern China : Anhwa (–1914)

Ipei = Ipeh

Ipek see Péc

Ipiaú. City, eastern Brazil, South America : Rio Novo (–1944)

Ipin. City, south-central China : Süchow [Suifu] (–1912)

Ipixuna. City, northeastern Brazil, South America : São Luís Gonzaga (–1944)

Iqaluit. Settlement, Northwest Territories, Canada : Frobisher Bay (*1942–87)

Iran. Republic, southwestern Asia : Persia (–1935)

Irapiranga see Itaporanga d'Ajuda

Irbitsky Zavod see Krasnogvardeysky

Iregszemcse. Town, west-

central Hungary : Felsőireg (*1938–39)

Ireland. Republic, western Europe : Irish Free State (*1921–37), Eire (1937–49)

Ir Gannim see Bat Yam

Irian Barat see Irian Jaya

Irian Jaya. Western part of New Guinea, Indonesia : Irian Barat [West Irian] (1963–76)

Irish Free State see Ireland

Iriston [†, now joined to Beslan]. Village, North Ossetian Autonomous Oblast, Russia : Tulatovo (–1941)

Is. Urban settlement, Sverdlovsk Oblast, Russia : Sverdlovsky Priisk (–1933)

Isady see Semibratovo

Isayevo-Dedovo see Oktyabrskoye (3)

Ise. Town, southern Honshu, Japan : Ujiyamada (–1955)

Ishan. Town, southern China : Kingyüan (–1913)

Ishanovo see Pioner

Ishley. Village, Chuvash Autonomous Republic, Russia : Ishley-Pokrovskoye (–c. 1960)

Ishley-Pokrovskoye see Ishley

Isiro. Town, northeastern Zaïre, central Africa : Paulis (–1972)

Islam-Terek see Kirovskoye (3)

Isle of Pines [Isla de Pinos] see Isle of Youth [Isla de la Juventud]

Isle of Youth [Isla de la Juventud]. Island, Caribbean Sea, Cuba : Isle of Pines [Isla de Pinos] (–1978)

Ismeli see Oktyabrskoye (4)

Ispica. Town, southeastern Sicily, Italy : Spaccaforno (–1935)

Ispisar see Gafurov

Issyk-Kul. Town, Issyk-Kul Oblast, Kirgizia : Rybachye (–1989)

Istanbul. City, northwestern Turkey : Constantinople (–1930)

Istra (1). Town, Moscow Oblast, Russia : Voskresensk (–1930)

Istra (2). Peninsula, northwestern Croatia : Pola (1919–37), Italy

Itabaiana. City, northeastern Brazil, South America : Tabaiana (1944–48)

Itabira. City, southeastern Brazil, South America : Itabira (de Matto Dentro) (–1944), Presidente Vargas (1944–48)

Itabira (de Matto Dentro) see Itabira

Itaetê. Town, eastern Brazil, South America : Iguaçu (–1944)

Itaguatins. City, north-central Brazil, South America : Santo Antônio da Cachoeira (–1944)

Itajahy do Sul see Rio do Sul

Itamorotinga see Serra Branca

Itapagé. City, northeastern Brazil, South America : São Francisco (–1944)

Itaparica see Petrolândia

Itapecerica see Itapecerica da Serra

Itapecerica da Serra. City, southeastern Brazil, South America : Itapecerica (–1944)

Itapira see Ubaitaba

Itaporanga. City, northeastern Brazil, South America : Misericordia (–1939, 1944–48)

Itaporanga see Itaporanga d'Ajuda

Itaporanga d'Ajuda. City, northeastern Brazil, South America : Itaporanga (–1944), Irapiranga (1944–48)

Itatiaia. Town, southeastern Brazil, South America : Campo Belo (–1943)

Itatupã. Town, northern Brazil, South America : Sacramento (–1943)

Itebej. Village, northern Serbia : Srpski Itebej (–1947)

Itu = Yitu

Ituberá. City, eastern Brazil, South America : Santarém (–1944)

Itumbiara. City, east-central Brazil, South America : Santa Rita (do Paranaíba) (–1944)

Itum Kale see Akhalkhevi

Iúna. City, southeastern Brazil, South America : Rio Pardo (–1944)

Ivailovgrad. City, southeastern Bulgaria : Orta-koi (–1934)

Ivančice. Town, southern Czech Lands : Eiben-

schitz (–1918, 1939–45),
Germany

Ivangorod *see* Deblin

Ivangrad. Town, eastern
Montenegro : Berane
(–1948)

Ivanishchi. Urban settle-
ment, Vladimir Oblast,
Russia : Ukrepleniye
Kommunizma (*early
1920s–1942)

Ivano-Frankovo. Urban settlement, Lvov Oblast,
Ukraine : Yanov (–1941)

Ivano-Frankovsk. Capital of
Ivano-Frankovsk Oblast,
Ukraine : Stanislau
(–1919), Stanisławow
(1919–45), Poland, Stan-
islav (1945–62)

Ivano-Frankovsk Ob-
last. Ukraine : Stanislav
Oblast (*1939–62)

Ivanopol. Urban settlement,
Zhitomir Oblast, Ukraine
: Yanushpol (–1946)

Ivanovka. Urban settle-
ment, Odessa Oblast,
Ukraine : Yanovka
(–1945)

Ivanovo (1). Capital of Ivanovo Oblast, Russia : Ivanovo-Voznesensk
(–1932)

Ivanovo (2). Town, Brest
Oblast, Belorussia : Ya-
nov (–1945)

Ivanovo-Voznesensk *see* Ivanovo (1)

Ivanovskoye *see* Smychka

Ivanski. Village, eastern
Bulgaria : Kopryu-koi
(–?), Zlokuchen (?–1950)

Ivanteyevka. Town,

Moscow Oblast, Russia :
Ivanteyevsky (1928–38)

Ivanteyevsky *see* Ivanteyevka

Ivashchenkovo *see*
Chapayevsk

Ivdel *see* Denezhkin Kamen

IvGRES *see* Komsomolsk (1)

Ivory Coast *see* Côte d'Ivoire

Ivugivic. Town, Quebec,
Canada : Notre-Dame-
d'Ivugivic (–1975)

Ixhuatlán *see* Chapopotla

Izhevsk. Capital of Udmurt
Autonomous Republic,
Russia : Izhevsky Zavod
(–1917), Ustinov (1984–
87)

Izhevsky Zavod *see* Izhevsk

Izhma *see* Sosnogorsk

Izluchistaya *see* Zhovtnevoye
(2)

Izmail Oblast
(1954†). Ukrainian SSR
: Akkerman Oblast
(*1940)

Izobilno-Tishchenskoye *see*
Izobilny

Izobilnoye *see* (1) Izobilny; (2)
Staro-Izobilnoye

Izobilny. Town, Stavropol
Kray, Russia : Izobilno-
Tishchenskoye (–mid-
1930s), Izobilnoye (mid-
1930s–1965)

Izumi-otsu. City, southern
Honshu, Japan : Otsu
(–early 1940s)

Izyaslavl *see* Zaslavl

Izylbash *see* Pristanskoye

Jääski *see* Lesogorsky

Jablonec (nad Nisou). City,
northern Czech Lands :

Gablonz (–1918, 1939–45), Germany

Jablonné v Podještědí. Town, northern Czech Lands : Deutsch Gabel (–1918, 1939–45)

Jaboatão see Japoatã

Jáchymow. Town, western Czech Lands : Joachimsthal (–1918, 1939–45), Germany

Jacinto City. City, Texas, USA : Industrial Acres (–1946)

Jacksonville see Old Hickory

Jacksonville Beach. City, Florida, USA : Ruby Beach (–1925)

Jacobabad District. South-central Pakistan : Upper Sind Frontier District (–?)

Jacobshagen see Dobrzany

Jacqueline, La = (La) Jacqueline

Jacuí see Sobradinho

Jadotville see Likasi

Jagodina see Svetozarevo

Jaguari see Jaguariúna

Jaguariúna. Town, southeastern Brazil, South America : Jaguari (–1944)

Jaguaruna. City, northeastern Brazil, South America : União (–1944)

Jakarta. Capital of Indonesia : Batavia (–1949)

Jakobstadt see Jēkabpils

Jákóhalma see Jászjákóhalma

Jaltenango. Town, southern Mexico, North America : Angel Albino Corzo (–1934)

Jamaica Square see South Floral Park

Jambi see Telanaipura

Jamburg see Kingisepp

Jamestown see Wawa

Jamnagar. Town, western India : Navangar (–1950s)

Janichen see Svoboda

Janików. Village, southwestern Poland : Jankau (–1945), Germany

Jankau see Janików

Jan Kempdorp. Town, Cape Province, South Africa : Andalusia (–1953)

Janské Lázně. Village, northern Czech Lands : Johannisbad (–1918, 1939–45), Germany

Jaochow see Poyang [Po-yang]

Japoatã. City, northeastern Brazil, South America : Jaboatão (–1944)

Jaraguá see Jaraguá do Sol

Jaraguá do Sol. City, southern Brazil, South America : Jaraguá (–1944)

Jarboesville see Lexington Park

Jarlsberg see Vestfold

Jaryczów Nowy see Novy Yarychev

Jasień. Town, western Poland : Gassen (–1945), Germany

Jasło. Town, southeastern Poland : Jessel (1939–45), Germany

Jastrow see Jastrowie

Jastrowie. Town, northwestern Poland : Jastrow (–1945), Germany

Jászalsőszentgyörgy. Town, east-central Hungary :

Alsószentgyörgy
(–1907)
Jászfelsőszentgyörgy.
Town, central Hungary :
Felsőszentgyörgy
(–1911)
Jászjákóhalma. Town, central Hungary : Jákóhalma
(–1928)
Jászkarajenő. Town, central Hungary : Karajenő
(–1901)
Jatobá see Petrolândia
Jauer see Jawor
Jaunjelgava. Town, Latvia :
Friedrichstadt (–1917)
Javier. Municipality, Leyte,
Philippines : Bugho
(–1905)
Jawor. Town, southwestern
Poland : Jauer (–1945),
Germany
Jaya, Puncak : Mountain,
Irian Jaya, Indonesia :
Carstensz Top (–1963),
Sukarno, Puntjak (1963–
69)
Jayapura. Capital of Irian
Jaya, Indonesia : Hollandia (–1963), Sukarnapura
(1963–69)
Jayawijaya, Puncak. Mountain, Irian
Jaya, Indonesia : Oranje
Top (–1963)
Jdiouia. Village, northern
Algeria, northern Africa :
Saint-Aimé (–c. 1962)
Jędrzejów. Town, southcentral Poland : Andreyev (–1919), Russia
Jēkabpils. Town, Latvia :
Jakobstadt (–1917)
Jelenia Góra. City, south-

western Poland : Hirschberg (–1945), Germany
Jelgava. Town, Latvia : Mitava (–1917), Zemgale
(1920–40)
Jema'a Mallam see Kafanchan
Jersey Homesteads see
Roosevelt
Jeseník. Town, northeastern
Czech Lands : Freiwaldau
(–1919, 1939–45), Germany
Jessel see Jasło
Jesselton see Kota Kinabalu
Jeziorany. Town, northeastern Poland : Seeburg
(–1945), Germany
Jičín. Town, northern Czech
Lands : Gitschin (–1918,
1939–45), Germany
Jihlava. City, south-central
Czech Lands : Iglau
(–1918, 1939–45), Germany
Jindřichův Hradec. Town,
southern Czech Lands :
Neuhaus (–1918, 1939–
45), Germany
Jirkov. Town, northwestern
Czech Lands : Görkau
(–1918, 1939–45), Germany
Joaçaba. City, southern Brazil, South America :
Limeira (–1928),
Cruzeiro do Sul (1928–
38), Cruzeiro (1939–43)
Joachimsthal see Jáchymow
João Belo see Xai-Xai
João de Almeida see Chibia
João Pessoa. City, northeastern Brazil, South
America : Paraíba
(–1930)

João Pessoa *see* (1) Eirunepé;
(2) Mimoso do Sul; (3)
Pôrto
Joaquín V. González.
Town, northwestern Ar-
gentina, South America :
Kilómetro 1082 (–?)
Johannes *see* Sovetsky (2)
Johannisbad *see* Janské Lázně
Johannisburg *see* Pisz
John F. Kennedy Interna-
tional Airport = Ken-
nedy
John Martin Reser-
voir.   Colorado, USA :
Caddoa Reservoir
(–1940)
Johnson City.   Village, New
York, USA : Lestershire
(–1910)
Johnstone Lake *see* Old Wives
Lake
Johnston Falls *see* Mambil-
iama Falls
John Wayne.   Airport, Cali-
fornia, USA : Orange
County (–1979)
Jordan (1).   Municipality,
Iloilo, Philippines : Nag-
aba (–1902)
Jordan (2).   Kingdom, south-
western Asia : Transjor-
dan [Transjordania]
(–1946)
Jordânia.   City, southeastern
Brazil, South America :
Palestina (–1944)
Jordanów.   Town, southern
Poland : Ilmenau (1939–
45), Germany
Jose Abad San-
tos.   Municipality,
Davao, Philippines : Tri-
nidad (–1954)

José Batlle y Ordóñez.
Town, southeastern Uru-
guay, South America :
Nico Pérez (–1907)
José Bonifácio *see* Erechim
José de Freitas.   City, north-
eastern Brazil, South
America : Livramento
(–1939)
(José Enrique) Rodó.
Town, southwestern Uru-
guay, South America :
Drable (–1924)
Jose Panganiban *see* Payo
Juan Lacaze.   Town, south-
western Uruguay, South
America : Sauce (–1909)
Juàzeiro *see* Juàzeiro do Norte
Juàzeiro do Norte.   City,
northeastern Brazil,
South America : Juàzeiro
(–1944)
Jubbal.   Town, northern In-
dia : Deorha (–1950s)
Jucás.   City, northeastern
Brazil, South America :
São Mateus (–1944)
Jucheng [Ju-cheng].   Town,
south-central China :
Kweiyang (–1913)
Juchow *see* Linju
Jugohama *see* Okachi
Juicheng [Jui-cheng].   Town,
northeastern China :
Kiangchow (–1912)
Juichow *see* Kaoan
Juliana Top *see* Mandala, Pun-
cak
Junan.   Town, east-central
China : Juning
(–1913)
Jungbunzlau *see* Mladá Bole-
slav
Jung-chiang = Jungkiang

Jungkiang [Jung-chiang].
Town, southern China :
Kuchow (–1913)
Jungwoschitz *see* Mladá
Vožice
Junikabura *see* Tsuchizawa
Juning *see* Junan
Juqueri *see* Mairiporã
Juripiranga. Town, north-
eastern Brazil, South
America : Serrinha
(–1944)
Juventino Rosas. City, cen-
tral Mexico, North Amer-
ica : Santa Cruz (de Gal-
eana) (–1938)
Južni Brod *see* Brod (Make-
donskie)

Kaakhka. Urban settle-
ment, Mary Oblast, Turk-
menistan : Ginsburg
(c. 1920–27)
Kabachishche *see* Zelenodolsk
Kabadian *see* Tartki
Kabakovsk *see* Serov
Kabany *see* Kras-
noarmeyskaya (1)
Kabanye *see* Krasnorech-
enskoye
Kabardin Autonomous Oblast
see Kabardin-Balkar Au-
tonomous Republic
Kabardin Autonomous SSR
see Kabardin-Balkar Au-
tonomous Republic
Kabardin-Balkar Autono-
mous Oblast *see* Kabar-
din-Balkar Autonomous
Republic
Kabardin-Balkar Autono-
mous Republic.
Western Russia : Kabar-
din Autonomous Oblast
(*1921–2), Kabardin-Bal-
kar Autonomous Oblast
(1922–36), Kabardin-Bal-
kar Autonomous SSR
(1936–44, 1957–91), Kab-
ardin Autonomous SSR
(1944–57)
Kabardin-Balkar Autono-
mous SSR *see* Kabardin-
Balkar Autonomous Re-
public
Kabarega Falls. Lake Ed-
ward, Uganda, central
Africa : Murchison Falls
(–1972)
Kabarega National
Park. Western Uganda,
central Africa : Mur-
chison Falls National
Park (*1952–c. 1972)
Kabwe. Town, central Zam-
bia, south-central Africa :
Broken Hill (*1904–65)
Kadamdzhay *see* Frunze
Kademlija *see* Triglav
Kadiak *see* Kodiak
Kadiyevka. Town, Lugansk
Oblast, Ukraine : Sergo
(1937–40), Stakhanov
(1978–91)
Kadnitsy *see* Leninskaya Slo-
boda
Kadoma. Town, central
Zimbabwe, southeastern
Africa : Gatooma (–1980)
Kafanchan. Town, central
Nigeria, western Africa :
Jema'a Mallam (–c. 1927)
Kafiristan *see* Nuristan
Kaga Bandoro. Town, cen-
tral Central African Re-
public, central Africa :
Fort-Crampel (–c. 1979)

Kagan. Town, Bukhara Oblast, Uzbekistan : Novaya Bukhara (–1935)
Kaganovich *see* (1) Novokashirsk; (2) Polesskoye; (3) Sokuluk; (4) Tovarkovsky
Kaganovichabad *see* Kolkhozabad
Kaganovicha, L.M., imeni *see* Popasnaya
Kaganovichevsk *see* Komsomolsk (3)
Kaganovichi pervyye *see* Polesskoye
Kagera. Administrative region, northwestern Tanzania, eastern Africa : West Lake (–1976), Ziwa Magharibi (1976–80)
Kahukura *see* Tikitki
Kaiaua. Town, North Island, New Zealand : New Brighton (–1927)
Kaiba-to *see* Moneron
Kai-chang = Kaikiang
Kaichow *see* (1) Kaiyang [K'ai-yang]; (2) Puyang [P'u-yang]
Kaihwa *see* Wenshan
Kaihwachen *see* Chanye
Kaikiang [K'ai-chiang]. Town, central China : Sinning (–1914)
Kai-Mbaku *see* Bata-Siala
Kainary *see* Dumbraveny
Kaindy. Urban settlement, Kirgizia : Molotovsk (c. 1945–57)
Kainsk *see* Kuybyshev (1)
Kaiser-Wilhelm Canal *see* Kiel Canal
Kaiser-Wilhelmsland *see* North-East New Guinea

Kaiyang [K'ai-yang]. Town, southern China : Kaichow (–1914), Tzekiang (1914–30)
Kaiyüan [K'ai-yüan]. Town, southwestern China : Ami (–1931)
Käkisalmi *see* Priozyorsk
Kakumabetsu *see* Shelekhovo
Kalabak *see* Radomir
Kalachevsky Rudnik *see* Lenina, imeni
Kalai-Mirzabai *see* Kalininabad
Kalai-Vamar *see* Rushan
Kalandula *see* Calandula
Kalata *see* Kirovgrad
Kalatinsky Zavod *see* Kirovgrad
Kalayaan. Municipality, Laguna, Philippines : Longos (–1956)
Kalay-Lyabiob *see* Tadzhikabad
Kalbar. Town, Queensland, Australia : Engelsburg (–c. 1915)
Kalemi. City, eastern Zaïre, central Africa : Albertville (1915–66)
Kalevala. Urban settlement, Karelian Autonomous Republic, Russia : Ukhta (–c. 1960)
Kalimantan. Southern part of Borneo, Indonesia : Dutch Borneo (–1945)
Kalinin. Urban settlement, Tashauz Oblast, Turkmenistan : Porsy (–1935)
Kalinin *see* Tver
Kalininabad. Village, Leninabad Oblast, Tajikistan : Kalai-Mirzabai (–c. 1935)

Kalinina, M.I., imeni.
Urban settlement, Nizhe-
gorodskaya Oblast, Rus-
sia : Kartonnaya Fabrika
(–1938)
Kalinindorf see Kalininskoye
(2)
Kaliningrad (1). Capital of
Kaliningrad Oblast, Rus-
sia : Königsberg (–1946),
Germany
Kaliningrad (2). Town,
Moscow Oblast, Russia :
Podlipki (–1928), Kalin-
insky (1928–38)
Kaliningrad Oblast. Russia :
Königsberg Oblast
(*1946)
Kalinino (1). Village,
Chuvash Autonomous
Republic, Russia : No-
rusovo (–1939)
Kalinino (2). Town, Arme-
nia : Vorontsovka
(–1935)
Kalininsk (1). Town, Don-
etsk Oblast, Ukraine :
Bairak (–c. 1935)
Kalininsk (2). Town, Sara-
tov Oblast, Russia : Bal-
anda (–1962)
Kalininsk see Petrozavodsk
Kalininskaya. Village, Kras-
nodar Kray, Russia : Pop-
ovichskaya (–c. 1960)
Kalininskoye (1). Village,
Kirgizia : Kara-Balty
(–1937)
Kalininskoye (2). Urban set-
tlement, Kherson Oblast,
Ukraine : Seidemenukha
(–c. 1928), Kalinindorf
(c. 1928–44)
Kalininsky see Kaliningrad (2)

Kalinovaya (1). Village,
Vitebsk Oblast, Belorus-
sia : Bloshniki (–1964)
Kalinovaya (2). Village,
Mogilyov Oblast, Belo-
russia : Trebukhi (–1964)
Kalinovka (1). Village, Kaliningrad Oblast, Russia :
Aulowönen (–1938), Ger-
many, Aulenbach (1938–
45), Germany
Kalinovka (2). Urban settle-
ment, Kiev Oblast,
Ukraine : Vasilkov pervy
(–c. 1960)
Kalipetrovo. Town, north-
eastern Bulgaria :
Starčevo (–c. 1967)
Kalisz Pomorski. Town,
northwestern Poland :
Kallies(–1945), Germany
Kalkfontein-Suid see Kar-
asburg
Kallithéa (1). Village, east-
ern Greece : Kalývia
(–1960s)
Kallithéa (2). Village, north-
ern Greece : Kata-
phýgion (–1960s)
Kalmyk Autonomous Oblast
see Kalmyk Autonomous
Republic
Kalmyk Autonomous Repub-
lic. Western Russia :
Kalmyk Autonomous Ob-
last (*1920–35, *1957),
Kalmyk Autonomous
SSR (1935–43†, 1958–
91)
Kalmyk Autonomous SSR see
Kalmyk Autonomous Re-
public
Kalmytsky Bazar see
Privolzhsky

Kalpa. Village, northern India : Chini (–1966)

Kalpákion see Orkhomenós

Kaluzhskoye. Village, Kaliningrad Oblast, Russia : Grünheide (–1945), Germany

Kalyvákia. Village, southern Greece : Xenía (–1960s)

Kalývia see Kallithéa (1)

Kalývia Kharádras see Exokhé

Kama. Urban settlement, Udmurt Autonomous Republic, Russia : Butysh (–1966)

Kamarína see Záloggon

Kamen see Kamen-na-Obi

Kamenets-Podolsk see Kamenets-Podolsky

Kamenets-Podolsky. Town, Khmelnitsky Oblast, Ukraine : Kamenets-Podolsk (–1944)

Kamenets-Podolsky Oblast see Khmelnitsky Oblast

Kamenický Šenov. Town, northwestern Czech Lands : Steinschönau (–1918, 1939–45), Germany

Kamenka. Town, Cherkassy Oblast, Ukraine: Kamenka-Shevchenkovskaya (1930–44)

Kamenka see Frunzensky

Kamenka-Bugskaya. Town, Lvov Oblast, Ukraine : Kamenka-Strumilovskaya (–1944)

Kamenka-Shevchenkovskaya see Kamenka

Kamenka-Strumilovskaya see Kamenka-Bugskaya

Kamen-na-Obi. Town, Altay Kray, Russia : Kamen (–?)

Kamennogorsk. Town, Leningrad Oblast, Russia : Antrea (–1948), Finland (–1940)

Kamensk see Kamensk-Uralsky

Kamenskaya see Kamensk-Shakhtinsky

Kamenskoye see Dneprodzerzhinsk

Kamensk-Shakhtinsky. Town, Rostov Oblast, Russia : Kamenskaya (–1927)

Kamensk-Uralsky. Town, Sverdlovsk Oblast, Russia : Kamensk (–1935)

Kamensky. Urban settlement, Saratov Oblast, Russia : Grimm (–1941)

Kamenz see Kamienec

Kamień (Pomorski). Town, northwestern Poland : Cammin (–1945), Germany

Kamienec. Town, southwestern Poland : Kamenz (–1945), Germany

Kamienna Góra. Town, southwestern Poland : Landeshut (–1945), Germany

Kaminsky. Urban settlement, Ivanovo Oblast, Russia : Gorky-Pavlovy (–1947)

Kami-shikuka see Leonidovo

Kamisianá. Village, western Crete, Greece : Elaión (–1960s)

Kamnik. Village, northern
Slovenia : Stein (–1918),
Germany

Kamo. Town, Armenia :
Nor-Bayazet (–1959)

Kampuchea *see* Cambodia

Kamskoye Ustye. Urban settlement, Tatar Autono-
mous Republic, Russia :
Bogorodskoye
(–1939)

Kamskoy GES, stroiteley *see*
Chaykovsky

Kanai *see* Yingkiang [Ying-
chiang]

Kananga. City, south-cen-
tral Zaïre, central Africa
: Luluabourg (–1966)

Kanash. Town, Chuvash Au-
tonomous Republic, Rus-
sia : Shikhrany
(–1920)

Kan-chou = Kanchow

Kanchow [Kan-chou]. City,
southeastern China :
Kanhsien (1911–49)

Kanchow *see* Changyeh

Kandagach *see* Oktyabrsk (2)

Kanghsien [K'ang-hsien].
Town, north-central
China : Paimawan
(–1928)

Kanglo [K'ang-lo]. Town,
north-central China :
Sintsi (–1930)

Kangting [K'ang-ting].
Town, southwestern
China : Tatsienlu
(–1913)

Kangwane. Homeland,
Transvaal, South Africa :
Swazi (–1977)

Kanhsien *see* Kanchow [Kan-
chou]

Kaniniti Point. Cape, Stewart Island, New Zealand
: Findley Point (–1965)

Kanku. Town, north-central
China : Fukiang (–1928)

Kannan. Town, northeast-
ern China : Kantsingtze
(–1926)

Kanpur. City, northern India : Cawnpore (–1948)

Kanth *see* Katy (Wrocławskie)

Kantsingtze *see* Kannan

Kantyshevo *see* Nartovskoye

Kanukov *see* Privolzhsky

Kaoan. Town, southeastern
China : Juichow (–1912)

Kaochow = Kochow

Kaohiung [Kaohsiung].
City, southern Taiwan :
Takow (1920–45), Japan

Kaohsiung = Kaohiung

Kapachira Falls. Shire
River, Malawi, southeast-
ern Africa : Hamilton
Falls (–c. 1972)

Kapchagay. Town, Alma-
Ata Oblast, Kazakhstan :
Iliysk (–c. 1969), Ili
(c. 1969–c. 1971)

Kaplitsa *see* Gornaya (2)

Kapsukas *see* Marijampolė

Kapuskasing. Town, On-
tario, Canada : MacPher-
son (*1914–17)

Karabagish *see* Sovetabad

Kara-Balty. Urban settle-
ment, Kirgizia : Mikoy-
ana, imeni (?–1937)

Karabalty *see* Kalininskoye (1)

Karabunar *see* Sredets

Karachayevsk. Town, Kara-
chayev-Cherkess Autono-
mous Oblast, Stavropol
Kray, Russia : Mikoyan-

Shakhar (–1944),
Klukhori (1944–57)
Karachukhur *see* Serebrovsky
Kara-Darya *see* Payshanba
Karajenő *see* Jászkarajenő
Kara-Kirgiz Autonomous Oblast *see* Kirgizia
Karaklis. Town, Armenia :
Kirovakan (1935–91)
Karakol *see* Przhevalsk
Karakubstroy *see* Komsomolskoye (3)
Karancslapujtő. Town,
northern Hungary : Bocsárlapujtő (*1928–56)
Karasburg. Village, southern Namibia, southwestern Africa : Kalkfontein-Suid (–1939)
Karasu *see* Voroshilovo
Karasubazar *see* Belogorsk (2)
Karatau. Town, Dhzambul
Oblast, Kazakhstan :
Chulaktau (–1963)
Karaul. Village, Semipalatinsk Oblast, Kazakhstan : Abay
(–c. 1960)
Karavómylos. Village,
Cephalonia, Ionian Islands, Greece : Vlakháta
(–1960s)
Karaya *see* Gardabani
Kardeljevo. Town, southern
Croatia : Ploče (–1949)
Karelian Autonomous Republic. Northwestern Russia : Karelian Autonomous SSR (*1923–40,
1956–91), Karelo-Finnish
SSR (1940–56)
Karelian Autonomous SSR
see Karelian Autonomous
Republic

Karelo-Finnish SSR *see* Karelian Autonomous Republic
Karen *see* Kawthule
Karenni *see* Kayah
Kargalinskoye. Village, Aktyubinsk Oblast, Kazakhstan : Zhilyanka
(–1977)
Kargowa. Town, western
Poland : Unruhstadt
(–1945), Germany
Karítsa. Village, northern
Greece : Díon (–1960s)
Karkeln *see* Mysovka
Karla Libknekhta, imeni
(1). Urban settlement,
Kursk Oblast, Russia :
Peny (–?), Pensky
Sakharny Zavod (?–1930)
Karla Libknekhta, imeni
(2). Suburb of Krivoy
Rog, Dnepropetrovsk
Oblast, Ukraine : Shmakovsky Rudnik
(–c. 1926)
Karla Libknekhta, imeni *see*
Shirokolanovka
Karla Marksa, imeni.
Suburb of Dnepropetrovsk, Dnepropetrovsk
Oblast, Ukraine : Rybalskaya (–1920s)
Karl-Marx-Stadt *see* Chemnitz
Karlo-Marksovo. Urban settlement, Donetsk Oblast,
Ukraine : Sofiyevsky
Rudnik : (–c. 1926)
Karlomarksovsky No. 7/8
Rudnik *see* Shakhta
No. 7/8
Karlovac. City, western
Croatia : Karlstadt (–?)
Karlovac *see* Rankovićevo

Karlovo. City, south-central
Bulgaria : Levskigrad
(1953–62)
Karlovy Vary. Town, west-
ern Czech Lands :
Karlsbad (–1918, 1939–
45), Germany
Karlowitz *see* (1) Sremski Kar-
lovci; (2) Velké Karlovice
Karlsbad *see* Karlovy Vary
Karlsburg *see* Alba Iulia
Karlstadt *see* Karlovac
Karnataka. State, western
India : Mysore (–1973)
Karnobat. Town, southeast-
ern Bulgaria : Polya-
novgrad (1953–62)
Karoro *see* Wharemoa
Karpacz. Town, southwest-
ern Poland : Krum-
mhübel (–1945), Ger-
many
Karpathos. Island, Dode-
canese, Greece : Scar-
panto (1912–47), Italy
Karpilovka *see* Oktyabrsky
(3)
Karsakuwigamak *see* Rutten
Kārsava. Town, Latvia :
Korsovka (–1917)
Karshi. Capital of Kashka-
darya Oblast, Uzbekistan
: Bek-Budi (1926–37)
Kartonnaya Fabrika *see* Kalin-
ina, M.I., imeni
Kartsa *see* Oktyabrskoye (6)
Karudéa. Village, western
Greece : Skoúpa
(–1960s)
Karyagino *see* Fizuli
Kasai (1962†). Province,
south-central Zaïre, cen-
tral Africa : Lusambo
(1935–47)

Kasanga. Town, southwest-
ern Tanzania, eastern Af-
rica : Bismarckburg (–?)
Kaschau *see* Košice
Kasevo *see* Neftekamsk
Kashirinskoye *see*
Oktyabrskoye (3)
Kashirskoye. Village, Kalin-
ingrad Oblast, Russia :
Schaaksvitte (–1945),
Germany
Kashiwabara *see* Severo-
Kurilsk
Kashkatau *see* Sovetskoye (2)
Kashla-koi *see* Zimnitsa
Kašperské Hory. Town,
southwestern Czech
Lands : Bergreichenstein
(–1918, 1939–45), Ger-
many
Kaspiysk. Town, Dagestan
Autonomous Republic,
Russia : Dvigatelstroy
(*1936–47)
Kaspiysky. Town, Kalmyk
Autonomous Republic,
Russia : Lagan (–1944)
Kassa *see* Košice
Kassándra *see* Kassándreia
Kassándreia. Town, north-
ern Greece : Kassándra
(–1960s)
Kastéllion *see* Kíssamos
Kastellorizon. Island, Dode-
canese, Greece : Cas-
telrosso (1923–47), Italy
Kastríon. Village, southern
Greece : Hágios Nikólaos
(–1960s)
Katanga *see* Shaba
Kataoka *see* Boykovo
Kataphýgion *see* Kallithéa (2)
Katavóthra *see* Metamórpho-
sis

Katchiungo. Village, south-central Angola, southwestern Africa : Bela Vista (–c. 1979)

Káto Exántheia see Drymón

Káto Kleitoría see Kleitoría

Káto Kollínnai see Hagía Varvára

Káto Meléa. Village, northern Greece : Meléa (–1960s)

Káto Potamía see Platána

Káto Vardátai see Néon Kríkellon

Katowice. City, southern Poland : Kattowitz (–1922, 1939–45), Germany, Stalinogród (1953–56)

Katscher see Kietrz

Kattowitz see Katowice

Katy (Wrocławskie). Town, southwestern Poland : Kanth (–1945), Germany

Katyk see Shakhtyorsk (2)

Katyshka see Golyshmanovo

Kaufman Peak see Lenin Peak

Kaukehmen see Yasnoye

Kaunas. Town, Lithuania : Kovno (–1917)

Kaunchi see Yangiyul

Kavaklii see Topolovgrad

Kavirondo Gulf see Winam

Kavungo. Town, eastern Angola, southwestern Africa : Nana Candundo (–c. 1975), Caluango (c. 1975–c. 1979)

Kawakami see Sinegorsk

Kawayan. Municipality, Leyte, Philippines : Almeria (–1907)

Kawende see Oakville

Kawthoolei = Kawthule

Kawthule [Kawthoolei]. State, south-central Burma : Karen (*1954–64)

Kayah. State, east-central Myanmar : Karenni (*1947–52)

Kaydanovo see Dzerzhinsk (2)

Kaying see Meihsien

Kayo Bay. Bay, Irian Jaya, Indonesia : Humboldt Bay (–1963)

Kayrakkum. Town, Leninabad Oblast, Tajikistan : Kostakoz (–1944), Chkalovsky (1944–?), Khodzhent (?–1963)

Kazakh Autonomous SSR see Kazakhstan

Kazakh SSR see Kazakhstan

Kazakhstan. Republic, west-central Asia : Kirgiz Autonomous SSR (*1920–25), Kazakh Autonomous SSR (1925–36), Kazakh SSR (1936–91)

Kazakhstan see Aksay

Kazbegi. Urban settlement, Georgia : Stepantsminda (–1921)

Kazgorodok see Kurgaldzhinsky

Kazi-Magomed. Town, Azerbaijan : Adzhibakul (–1939)

Kazincbarcika. Town, northeastern Hungary : Sajókazinc (*1947–48)

Kazinka. Urban settlement, Lipetsk Oblast, Russia : Novaya Zhizn (–c. 1960)

Kearns. Community, Ontario, Canada : Chesterville (*1937–66)

Kędzierzyn. Town, southern
Poland : Heydebreck
(–1945), Germany
Kegulta see Sadovoye
Keksgolm see Priozyorsk
Kelasa Strait. Between
Bangka and Belitung is-
lands, Indonesia : Gaspar
Strait (–?)
Kellomäki see Komarovo
Kells see Ceannanus Mór
Kelomyakki see Komarovo
Kemenongue. Town, east-
central Angola, south-
western Africa : Vila
Bugaco (–c. 1976)
Kempen see Kepno
Kenitra. City, northwestern
Morocco, northwestern
Africa : Port-Lyautey
(*1913–c. 1958)
Kennedy, Cape see Canav-
eral, Cape
Kennedy [John F. Ken-
nedy]. International air-
port, New York City,
USA : Idlewild (–1963)
Kenora. Town, Ontario,
Canada : Rat Portage
(–1905)
Kentani see Centane
Kenya. Republic, eastern
Africa : British East Af-
rica (–1920)
Kephalokhórion. Village,
western Greece : Plagía
(–1960s)
Kephalóvryson see Leukothéa
Kepno. Town, southwestern
Poland : Kempen
(–1945), Germany
Keppel Harbour. Strait,
southern Singapore : New
Harbour (–1900)

Kerbi see Poliny Osipenko,
imeni
Kerensk see Vadinsk
Kerintji. Volcano, west-
central Sumatra, Indone-
sia : Indrapura (–1963)
Kermanshah see Bakhtaran
Kermine see Navoi
Kerr Point see Surville Cliffs
Keshishkend see Yekheg-
nadzor
Kętrzyn. Town, northeast-
ern Poland : Rastenburg
(–1946), Germany
(–1945)
Kettering. City, Ohio, USA
: Van Buren (–1952)
Kexholm see Priozyorsk
Keystone Heights. Town,
Florida, USA : Brooklyn
(–1922)
Khabno(ye) see Polesskoye
Khadima see Kuweit City
Khadyzhensk. Town, Kras-
nodar Kray, Russia :
Khadyzhensky (–1949)
Khadyzhensky see Kha-
dyzhensk
Khakassk see Abakan
Khakulabad see Naryn
Khakurate see Oktyabrsky
(4)
Khakurinokhabl see Shovgen-
ovsky
Khalfaya see North Khartoum
Khalía see Drosía
Khalkhal. Town, northwest-
ern Iran : Herowabad
(–1980)
Khalmer-Sede. Village,
Yamalo-Nenets Autono-
mous Okrug, Tyumen
Oblast, Russia : Ta-
zovskoye (–c. 1930)

Khalturin. Town, Kirov Oblast, Russia : Orlov (–1923)
Khamza. Town, Fergana Oblast, Uzbekistan : Shakhimardan (–c. 1929), Vannovsky (c. 1929–63), Khamzy Khakimzade, imeni (1963–74)
Khamzy Khakimzade, imeni see Khamza
Khanaka see Gissar
Khan Hung see Soc Trang
Khankendy. Capital of Nagorno-Karabakh Autonomous Oblast, Armenia : Stepanakert (1923–91)
Khanlar. Town, Azerbaijan : Yelenendorf (–1938)
Khanty-Mansi Autonomous Okrug. Tyumen Oblast, Russia : Ostyak-Vogul National Okrug (*1930–40)
Khanty-Mansiysk. Capital of Khanty-Mansi Autonomous Okrug, Tyumen Oblast, Russia : Ostyako-Vogulsk (*1931–40)
Kharagouli. Urban settlement, Georgia : Ordzhonikidze (1949–91)
Khargone. District, northern India : West Nimar (–1973)
Kharino see Beregovoy
Khatsapetovka see Uglegorsk (2)
Khavast. Urban settlement, Syrdarya Oblast, Uzbekistan : Ursatyevskaya (–1963)
Khebda see Sovetskoye (3)
Khem-Beldyr see Kyzyl

Khemis el Khechna. Village, northern Algeria, northern Africa : Fondouk (–c. 1962)
Khemis Miliana. Town, northern Algeria, northern Africa : Affreville (–c. 1962)
Khibinogorsk see Kirovsk (2)
Khlevishche see Orekhovichi
Khmelnitsky. Capital of Khmelnitsky Oblast, Ukraine : Proskurov (–1954)
Khmelnitsky Oblast. Ukraine : Kamenets-Podolsky Oblast (*1937–54)
Khmer Republic see Cambodia
Khodavendikyar see Bursa
Khodzhaakhrar see Ulugbek
Khodzha-Arif see Shafirkan
Khodzhent. Capital of Leninabad Oblast, Tajikistan : Leninabad (1936–91)
Khodzhent see (1) Gafurov; (2) Kayrakkum
Khokhulki see Zelyony Log
Kholmsk. Town, Sakhalin Oblast, Russia : Maoka (1905–46), Japan (–1945)
Kholopkovichi see Kolosovo (1)
Khoni. Town, Georgia : Tsulukidze (1936–91)
Khorixas. Town, northeastern Namibia, southwestern Africa : Welwitschia (*1954–74)
Khorly. Village, Kherson Oblast, Ukraine : Port-Khorly (–c. 1960)

Khorramshahr. City, south-
western Iran : Moham-
merah (–1924)
Khortitsa see Verkhnyaya
Khortitsa
Khósepse see Kypséle (1)
Khoshdala see Dzhambay
Khovrino see
Krasnooktyabrsky (1)
Khrapunovo see Vorovskogo,
imeni
Khrenovoye see Gribnoye
Khrompik see Dvurechensk
Khrushchyov see Svetlo-
vodsk
Khrysikós. Village, southern
Greece : Lykoudésion
(–1960s)
Khudeni see Mirnaya (3)
Khulkhuta. Settlement,
Kalmyk Autonomous
Republic, Russia :
Pridorozhnoye
(–c. 1960)
Khungari see Gurskoye
Khust. Town, Transcarpa-
thian Oblast, Ukraine :
Chust (1920–39), Czecho-
slovakia; Huszt (1939–
45), Hungary
Khutor-Mikhaylovsky see
Druzhba (2)
Khuzestan. Province, south-
western Iran : Arabistan
(–1938)
Khvoynaya Polyana. Settle-
ment, Gomel Oblast, Be-
lorussia : Avraamovskaya
(–1964)
Kiachow see Kiahsien [Chia-
hsien]
Kiahsien [Chia-hsien].
Town, central China :
Kiachow (–1913)

Kian [Chi-an]. City, south-
eastern China : Luling
(–1914)
Kiangcheng [Chiang-ch'eng].
Town, southwestern
China : Mangli
(–1929)
Kiangchow see Juicheng [Jui-
ch'eng]
Kiangkow [Chiang-kou].
Town, southern China :
Tungjen (–1913)
Kiangkow see Pingchang
[P'ing-chang]
Kiangling [Chiang-ling].
Town, east-central China
: Kingchow
(–1912)
Kiangna see Yenshan
Kiangning [Chiang-
ning]. Town, eastern
China : Tungshan (–1934)
Kiangning see Nanking
Kiangtu see Yang-chou
Kianly (Tarta) see Tarta
Kiaochow see Kiaohsien
[Chiao-hsien]
Kiaohsien [Chiao-hsien].
Town, eastern China :
Kiaochow
(–1913)
Kiashan [Chia-shan]. Town
eastern China : Sankieh
(–1932)
Kiating see Loshan
Kibbutz Mahar see Gevaram
Kibra see Kuratovo
Kichow see (1) Kichun [Ch'i-
ch'un]; (2) Kihsien [Chi-
hsien]
Kichun [Ch'i-ch'un]. Town,
east-central China :
Kichow (–1912)
Kidmore see Kidmore End

Kidmore End. Village,
Oxfordshire, England,
UK : Kidmore (–1902)
Kiechow *see* Wutu
Kiel Canal. Linking Baltic
Sea and North Sea, north-
western Germany :
Kaiser-Wilhelm Canal
(–c. 1919)
Kienchang [Ch'ien-ch'ang].
Town, northeastern
China : Kienchangying
(–1949)
Kienchang *see* (1) Lingyüan;
(2) Nancheng [Nan-
ch'eng] (2)
Kienchangying *see* Kienchang
[Ch'ien-ch'ang]
Kiencheng [Ch'ien-
ch'eng]. Town, south-
central China : Kienchow
(–1914), Kienhsien
(1913–14)
Kienchow *see* (1) Kiencheng
[Ch'ien-cheng]; (2)
Kienhsien [Ch'ien-hsien];
(3) Kienko [Chien-ko];
(4) Kienyang [Chien-
yang]
Kienho [Chien-ho]. Town,
southern China : Ts-
ingkiang (–1914)
Kienhsien [Ch'ien-
hsien]. Town, central
China : Kienchow
(–1913)
Kienhsien *see* Kiencheng
[Ch'ien-ch'eng]
Kien Hung *see* Go Quao
Kienko [Chien-ko]. Town,
central China : Kienchow
(–1913)
Kienkünchen *see* Yungshow
[Yung-shou]

Kienning [Ch'ien-
ning]. Town, southern
China : Taining (–1945)
Kienning *see* Kienow [Chien-
ou]
Kienow [Chien-ou]. Town,
southeastern China :
Kienning (–1913)
Kienping *see* Langki [Lang-
ch'i]
Kienteh [Chien-te]. Town,
eastern China : Yenchow
(–1914)
Kienyang [Chien-
yang]. Town, central
China : Kienchow
(–1913)
Kietrz. Town, southern Po-
land : Katscher (–1945),
Germany
Kihsien [Chi-hsien]. Town,
northeastern China :
Kichow (–1913)
Kikinda. City, northern Ser-
bia : Velika Kikinda
(–c. 1947)
Kikvidze. Urban settlement,
Volgograd Oblast, Russia
: Preobrazhenskaya
(–1936)
Kilbourn *see* Wisconsin Dells
Kilien [Ch'i-lien]. Town,
northwestern China : Pa-
pao (–1939)
Kiliti *see* Balatonkiliti
Kilómetro 924 *see* Angaco
Norte
Kilómetro 1082 *see* Joaquín V.
González
Kilómetro 1172 *see* Campo
Quijano
Kim. Village, Leninabad
Oblast, Tajikistan : Santo
(–1929)

Kimchaek. City, northeastern North Korea : Sŏnjin (–1952)
Kimovsk. Town, Tula Oblast, Russia : Mikhaylovka (–1952)
Kimpersaysky *see* Batamshinsky
Kinchai [Chin-chai]. Town, eastern China : Kinkiachai (–1933), Lihwang (1933–49)
Kincheloe Air Force Base. Michigan, USA : Kinross Air Force Base (*1941–c. 1959)
Kincheng *see* Yüchung
Kinchow *see* Chinhsien
King Chiang Saen *see* Chiang Saen
Kingchow *see* (1) Kiangling [Chiang-ling]; (2) Kingchwan [Ching-ch'uan]
Kingchwan [Ching-ch'uan]. Town, north-central China : Kingchow (–1913)
Kingfu *see* Sinhsien [Hsinhsien] (1)
King George V National Park *see* Taman Negara National Park
Kingisepp. Town, Leningrad Oblast, Russia : Yamburg [Jamburg] (–1922)
Kingisepp *see* Kuressaare
Kingku [Ching-ku]. Town, southwestern China : Weiyüan (–1914)
King's County *see* Offaly
King's Cross. District of Sydney, New South Wales, Australia : Queen's Cross (–1905)

Kingston *see* Rexton
Kingstown *see* Dun Laoghaire
Kingtai [Ching-t'ai]. Town, north-central China : Talutang (–1934)
Kingtehchen [Ching-te-chen] *see* Fowliang [Fou-liang]
Kingwilliamstown *see* Ballydesmond
Kingyüan [Chingyüan]. Town, eastern China : Yenshan (–1949)
Kingyüan *see* Ishan
Kinho *see* Kinping [Chinp'ing] (1)
Kinhsien *see* Yüchung
Kinkiachai *see* Kinchai [Chinchai]
Kinping [Chin-p'ing] (1). Town, southwestern China : Kinho (–1936)
Kinping [Chin-p'ing] (2). Town, southern China : Liping (–1913)
Kinross Air Force Base *see* Kincheloe Air Force Base
Kinsha [Chin-sha]. Town, southern China : Sinchang (–1932)
Kinshasa. Capital of Zaïre, central Africa : Léopoldville (–1966)
Kintang [Chint'ang]. Village, southern China : Shangyütung (–1932)
Kipling. Town, Saskatchewan, Canada : Kipling Station (–1954)
Kipling Station *see* Kipling
Kipungo *see* Quipungo
Kirchdorf am Haunpold *see* Bruckmühl

Kirchholm *see* Salaspils
Kirda *see* Gulbakhor
Kirgiz Autonomous Oblast *see*
Kirgizia
Kirgiz Autonomous SSR *see*
(1) Kazakhstan; (2) Kir-
gizia
Kirgizia. Republic, central
Asia : Kara-Kirgiz Auton-
omous Oblast (*1924–25),
Kirgiz Autonomous Ob-
last (1925–26), Kirgiz Au-
tonomous SSR (1926–36),
Kirgiz SSR (1936–91)
Kirgiz-Kulak *see* Chirchik
Kirgiz SSR *see* Kirgizia
Kiribati. Island republic,
western Pacific : Gilbert
Islands (–1979)
Kirillovo. Village, Sakhalin
Oblast, Russia : Uryu
(1905–45), Japan
Kirin. City, northeastern
China : Yungki (1929–37)
Kiritimati. Island, Kiribati,
western Pacific : Christ-
mas Island (–1981)
Kirkwood. Town, Cape
Province, South Africa :
Bayville (–1913)
Kirmasti *see* Mustafa Kemal
Paşa
Kirov. Town, Kaluga Ob-
last, Russia : Pesochnya
(–1936)
Kirov *see* Vyatka
Kirova. Bay, Azerbaijan :
Kyzylagach (–c. 1960)
Kirova, imeni *see* (1) Bank;
(2) Besharyk; (3) Kirovo
(1); (4) Kirovsk (3)
Kirovabad *see* (1) Gyandzha;
(2) Pyandzh
Kirovakan *see* Karaklis

Kirovgrad. Town, Sverd-
lovsk Oblast, Russia :
Kalatinsky Zavod
(–1928), Kalata (1928–35)
Kirovo (1). Urban settle-
ment, Donetsk Oblast,
Ukraine : Kirova, imeni
(–c. 1960)
Kirovo (2). Village, Kurgan
Oblast, Russia : Voskre-
senskoye (–1939)
Kirovo *see* (1) Besharyk; (2)
Yelizavetgrad
Kirovo-Chepetsk. Town,
Kirov Oblast, Russia :
Kirovo-Chepetsky
(–1955)
Kirovo-Chepetsky *see* Kirovo-
Chepetsk
Kirovograd *see* Yelizavetgrad
Kirovsk (1). Town, Lugansk
Oblast, Ukraine : Gol-
ubovsky Rudnik (–1944)
Kirovsk (2). Town, Mur-
mansk Oblast, Russia :
Khibinogorsk (*1929–34)
Kirovsk (3). Urban settle-
ment, Donetsk Oblast,
Ukraine : Kirova, imeni
(–c. 1960)
Kirovsk (4). Town, Lenin-
grad Oblast, Russia :
Nevdubstroy (–1953)
Kirovsk (5). Urban settle-
ment, Mogilyov Oblast,
Belorussia : Startsy
(–1939)
Kirovskoye (1). Village, Kir-
gizia : Aleksandrovskoye
(–1937)
Kirovskoye (2). Village,
Chimkent Oblast, Ka-
zakhstan : Bagara
(–c. 1960)

Kirovskoye (3). Urban settlement, Crimean Oblast, Ukraine : Islam-Terek (–1944)

Kirovskoye (4). Village, Sakhalin Oblast, Russia : Rykovskoye (–1937)

Kirovsky (1). Urban settlement, Astrakhan Oblast, Russia : Nikitinskiye Promysly (–1934)

Kirovsky (2). Suburb of Dnepropetrovsk, Dnepropetrovsk Oblast, Ukraine : Obukhovka (–1938)

Kirovsky (3). Urban settlement, Primorsky Kray, Russia : Uspenka (–1939)

Kisangani. City, northeastern Zaïre, central Africa : Stanleyville (–1966)

Kishinyov. Capital of Moldavia : Chişinău (1918–40), Romania

Kishkareny see Lazo

Kishui see Sishui [Hsi-shui]

Kisiaying see Wutung

Kisielice. Town, northeastern Poland : Freystadt (–1919, 1939–45), Germany

Kíssamos. Town, western Crete, Greece : Kastéllion (–1960s)

Kistétény see Budatétény

Kistna see Krishna

Kisumu. City, western Kenya, eastern Africa : Port Florence (–?)

Kisykkamys see Dzhangala

Kita-kozawa see Telnovsky

Kitami. City, eastern Hokkaido, Japan : Nokkeushi (–1942)

Kitchener. City, Ontario, Canada : Berlin (–1916)

Kitikmeot. Administrative region, North West Territories, Canada : Central Arctic (–1982)

Kitose see Chkalovo (2)

Kiuchüan [Chiuchüan]. Town, northcentral China : Suchow (–1913)

Kiungchow see (1) Kiunglai [Ch'iung-lai]; (2) Kiungshan [Ch'iung-shan]

Kiunglai [Ch'iunglai]. Town, central China : Kiungchow (–1913)

Kiungshan [Ch'iungshan]. City, southeastern China : Kiungchow (–1912)

Kiungtung [Ch'iung-tung]. Town, southeastern China : Hweitung (–1914)

Kiupu see Chihteh [Chih-te]

Kiutai [Chiu-t'ai]. Town, northeastern China : Siakiutai (–1947)

Kivu. Province, eastern Zaïre, central Africa : Costermansville (1935–47)

Kiya-Shaltyr see Belogorsk (3)

Kizil-agach see Yelkhovo

Klaipéda. Town, Lithuania : Memel (1918–23, 1941–44), Germany

Klausberg see Mikulczyce

Klausenburg see Cluj

Kléber see Sidi Benyekba

Klein Boetsap see Reivilo

Klein-Liebental see Malodolinskoye

Klein-Schlatten *see* Zlatna

Kleitoría. Village, southern Greece : Káto Kleitoría (–1960s)

Klemzig. District of Adelaide, South Australia, Australia : Gaza (1918–35)

Klimovsk. Town, Moscow Oblast, Russia : Klimovsky (1938–40)

Klimovsky *see* Klimovsk

Kljajićevo. Village, northern Serbia : Krnjaja (–1948)

Kłodzko. Town, southwestern Poland : Glatz (–1945), Germany

Kluczbork. Town, southern Poland : Kreuzburg (in Oberschlesien) (–1945), Germany

Klukhori *see* Karachayevsk

Klyuchevsk. Urban settlement, Sverdlovsk Oblast, Russia : Tyoply Klyuch (*c. 1930–33).

Klyuchevsky. Urban settlement, Chita Oblast, Russia : Klyuchi (–c. 1960)

Klyuchi *see* Klyuchevsky

Klyuchinsky *see* Krasnomaysky

Klyundevka *see* Vishnyovaya (2)

Knights Enham *see* Enham Alamein

Knob Lake *see* Schefferville

Knox. Borough, Pennsylvania, USA : Edenburg (–1933)

Knyaginin *see* Knyaginino

Knyaginino. Urban settlement, Nizhegorodskaya Oblast, Russia : Knyaginin (–1926)

Knyazhitsa *see* Slobozhanka

Koartac. Town, Quebec, Canada : Notre-Dame-de-Koartac (–1965)

Kobarid. Village, western Slovenia : Caporetto (–1947), Italy

Kobbelbude *see* Svetly

Köben (an der Oder) *see* Chobienia

Kobylyanka *see* (1) Rassvetnaya (1); (2) Znamenka (2)

Kočevje. Village, southern Slovenia : Gottschee (–1918), Germany

Kocgiri *see* Zara

Kochow [Kaochow] *see* Mowming

Kochubey. Urban settlement, Dagestan Autonomous Republic, Russia : Chyorny Rynok (–c. 1960)

Kochubeyevskoye. Village, Stavropol Kray, Russia : Olginskoye (–c. 1960)

Kodiak. Island, Alaska, USA : Kadiak (–1901)

Kodok. Town, central Sudan : Fashoda (–1905)

Kohlfurt *see* Węgliniec

Koivisto *see* (1) Bolshoy Beryozovy; (2) Primorsk (2)

Kokankishlak *see* Pakhtaabad

Kokcha *see* Zafarabad (2)

Kokenhausen *see* Koknese

Kokloioí *see* Koukloioí

Koknese. Urban settlement, Latvia : Kokenhausen (–1917)

Koktash *see* Leninsky (2)

Kok-Tash. Urban settlement, Osh Oblast, Kirgizia : Mayli-Su (–c. 1960)
Koktebel *see* Planyorskoye
Kokushkino *see* Lenino-Kokushkino
Kolageran *see* Dzoraget
Kolai *see* Azovskoye
Kolarov. Mountain, western Bulgaria : Belmeken (–1949)
Kolarovgrad *see* Shumen [Šumen]
Kolberg *see* Kołobrzeg
Kolchugino *see* Leninsk-Kuznetsky
Koleno *see* Zalesnaya
Kölesd. Town, southwestern Hungary : Tormáskölesd (*1938–39)
Kolkhozabad. Urban settlement, Khatlon Oblast, Tajikistan : Tugalan (–?), Kaganovichabad (?–1957)
Kolkhozabad *see* Vose
Kolkhoznoye *see* Ulyanovskoye (2)
Koło. Town, central Poland : Warthbrücken (1939–45), Germany
Kołobrzeg. Town, northwestern Poland : Kolberg (–1945), Germany
Kolosjoki *see* Nikel
Kolosovka (1). Village, Omsk Oblast, Russia : Nizhne-Kolosovskoye (–c. 1940)
Kolosovka (2). Village, Minsk Oblast, Belorussia : Pustoy Ugol (–1964)

Kolosovo (1). Village, Vitebsk Oblast, Belorussia : Kholopkovichi (–1964)
Kolosovo (2). Village, Grodno Oblast, Belorussia : Suchki (–1964)
Kolpakovskoye *see* Dzerzhinskoye (1)
Komárom. Town, northwestern Hungary : Komáromújváros (*1919–23)
Komáromújváros *see* Komárom
Komarovo. Urban settlement, Leningrad Oblast, Russia : Kelomyakki [Kellomäki] (–1948), Finland (–1940)
Komavangard *see* Sobinka
Komi Autonomous Oblast *see* Komi Autonomous Republic
Komi Autonomous Republic. Northern Russia : Komi Autonomous Oblast (*1921–36), Komi Autonomous SSR (1936–91)
Komi Autonomous SSR *see* Komi Autonomous Republic
Komintern *see* (1) Marganets; (2) Novoshakhtinsk
Kominterna, imeni. Village, Novgorod Oblast, Russia : Sosninskaya (–c. 1930)
Kominternovskoye. Urban settlement, Odessa Oblast, Ukraine : Antono-Kodintsevo (–1930s)
Kommunar. Urban settlement, Khakass Autonomous Oblast,

Krasnoyarsk Kray, Russia : Bogomdarovanny (–1932)

Kommunarka (1). Village, Grodno Oblast, Belorussia : Laptikha (–1964)

Kommunarka (2). Village, Vitebsk Oblast, Belorussia : Skulovichi (–1964)

Kommunarsk. Town, Lugansk Oblast, Ukraine : Alchevsk (–1931), Voroshilovsk (1931–61)

Kommunizma, Pik = Communism Peak

Komotau see Chomutov

Komotine. City, northeastern Greece : Gumuljina (–1913), Turkey

Kompegádion see Néon Kompegádion

Kompong Som. Town, southern Cambodia : Sihanoukville (–1970)

Komsomolabad. Village, Tajikistan : Pombachi (–c. 1935)

Komsomolsk (1). Town, Ivanovo Oblast, Russia : IvGRES (*1931–50)

Komsomolsk (2). Village, Kaliningrad Oblast, Russia : Löwenhagen (–1946), Germany (–1945)

Komsomolsk (3). Suburb of Chardzhou, Chardzhou Oblast, Turkmenistan : Stary Chardzhuy (–1937), Kaganovichevsk (1937–c. 1957)

Komsomolsk (4). Village, Samarkand Oblast, Uzbekistan : Tailak-Paion (–1939)

Komsomolsk see Komsomolsk-na-Amure

Komsomolskaya. Village, Minsk Oblast, Belorussia : Pukovo (–1964)

Komsomolsk-na-Amure. Town, Khabarovsk Kray, Russia : Permskoye (–1932), Komsomolsk (1932–50)

Komsomolskoye (1). Village, Chuvash Autonomous Republic, Russia : Bolshoy Kosheley (–1939)

Komsomolskoye (2). Village, Saratov Oblast, Russia : Fridenfeld (–1941)

Komsomolskoye (3). Town, Donetsk Oblast, Ukraine : Karakubstroy (–c. 1945)

Komsomolskoye (4). Village, Vinnitsa Oblast, Ukraine : Makhnovka (c. 1935)

Komsomolsky (1). Urban settlement, Kalmyk Autonomous Republic, Russia : Krasny Kamyshanik (–c. 1960)

Komsomolsky (2). Settlement, Arkhangelsk Oblast, Russia : Oktyabrsky (–c. 1960)

Komsomolsky (3). Urban settlement, Tula Oblast, Russia : Oktyabrsky (–c. 1960)

Komsomolsky (4). Urban settlement, Mordovian

Autonomous Republic,
Russia : Zavodskoy
(–c. 1960)
Komsomolsky *see* Chirchik
Konakovo. Town, Tver Ob-
last, Russia : Kuznetsovo
(–1930)
Kondinskoye. Urban settle-
ment, Khanty-Mansi Au-
tonomous Okrug,
Tyumen Oblast, Russia :
Nakhrachi (–c. 1960)
Koneshime *see* Neshime
Kongmoon *see* Sunwui
Königgrätz *see* Hradec
Králové
Königinhof (an der Elbe) *see*
Dvůr Králové (nad La-
bem)
Königsberg *see* (1) Chojna;
(2) Kaliningrad (1)
Königsberg Oblast *see* Kalin-
ingrad Oblast
Königshütte *see* Chorzów
Koniya. Town, Ryukyu Is-
lands, Japan : Higashi-
kata (–1936)
Konjic. Village, south-cen-
tral Bosnia-Herzegovina :
Gonobitz (–1918)
Konradshof *see* Skawina
Konstadt *see* Wołczyn
Konstantinograd *see* Kras-
nograd
Konstantinovsk. Town, Ros-
tov Oblast, Russia : Kon-
stantinovskaya (–1941),
Konstantinovsky (1941–
67)
Konstantinovskaya *see* Kon-
stantinovsk
Konstantinovsky *see* Kon-
stantinovsk

Kontóstablos *see* Arkhaíai
Kleonaí
Konuma *see* Novoaleksan-
drovsk (1)
Kope. Cape, Bioko, Equa-
torial Guinea, western
Africa : Macías Nguema
Bijogo (1973–79)
Kopeysk. Town, Chelyab-
insk Oblast, Russia :
Ugolnyye Kopi (–1917),
Goskopi (1917–28),
Chelyabkopi (1928–33)
Kopryu-koi *see* Ivanski
Korenica *see* Titova Korenica
Korenovsk. Town, Kras-
nodar Kray, Russia :
Korenovskaya (–1961)
Korenovskaya *see* Korenovsk
Kornevo. Village, Kalinin-
grad Oblast, Russia :
Zinten (–1945), Ger-
many
Kornilovichi *see* Udarnaya (1)
Korobkovo *see* Gubkin
Korostovka *see* Borovaya (2)
Korovino *see* Solntsevo
Korsakov. Town, Sakhalin
Oblast, Russia : Mura-
vyovsky (–1905), Oto-
mari (1905–46), Japan
(–1945)
Korsovka *see* Kārsava
Korsun *see* Korsun-Shevche-
novsky
Korsun-Shevch-
enkovsky. Town, Cher-
kassy Oblast, Ukraine :
Korsun (–1944)
Koryavinets *see* Podlesskaya
Koryskhádes. Village, cen-
tral Greece : Kypséle
(–1960s)

Koshan [K'o-shan]. Town, northeastern China : Sanchan (–1915)

Koshu-Kavak see Krumovgrad

Košice. City, eastern Slovakia : Kaschau (–1920, 1939–45), Germany, Kassa (1938–39), Hungary

Kosiorovo see Stanichno-Luganskoye

Kos-Istek see Leninskoye (4)

Köslin see Koszalin

Kosta-Khetagurovo see Nazran

Kostakoz see Kayrakkum

Kostenets see Dimitrovo

Kostrzyn. City, western Poland : Küstrin (–1945), Germany

Koszalin. City, northwestern Poland : Köslin (–1945), Germany

Kotabaru see Dzhezdy

Kota Kinabalu. Capital of Sabah, Malaysia : Jesselton (–1968)

Kotelnikovo (1). Town, Volgograd Oblast, Russia : Kotelnikovskaya (–1929)

Kotelnikovo (2). Village, Leningrad Oblast, Russia : Salyuzi (–1949)

Kotelnikovskaya see Kotelnikovo (1)

Kotikovo. Village, Sakhalin Oblast, Russia : Chirie (1905–45), Japan

Kotor. Town and port, western Montenegro : Cattaro (1941–44), Italy

Kotoura. Town, western Honshu, Japan : Tanokuchi (–1907)

Kotovsk (1). Town, Odessa Oblast, Ukraine : Birzula (–1935)

Kotovsk (2). Town, Moldavia : Gancheshty (–1940), Kotovskoye (1940–65)

Kotovsk (3). Town, Tambov Oblast, Russia : Krasny Boyevik (1930–40)

Kotovskoye see Kotovsk (2)

Kotsyubinskoye. Urban settlement, Kiev Oblast, Ukraine : Berkovets (–1941)

Koty see Sosnovaya (1)

Kotzenau see Chocianów

Koukloioí. Village, western Greece : Kokloioí (–1960s)

Koúkoura see Hagía Anna

Koúmares see Hellenikón

Kousseri. Town, northern Cameroon, western Africa : Fort-Foureau (–1974)

Koutroumpoúkhion see Dáphne

Kovno see Kaunas

Kowary. Town, southwestern Poland : Schmiedeberg (–1945), Germany

Koyiu. Town, southeastern China : Shiuhing (–1912)

Kozhemyaki see Pervomaysky (2)

Kozhevnikovo. Village, Taymyr Autonomous Okrug, Krasnoyarsk Kray, Russia : Nordvik (–1943)

Koźle. Town, southern Poland : Cosel (–1945), Germany

Kozlikha *see* Sitniki
Kozlov *see* Michurinsk
Kozodoi *see* Zaslonovo
Kożuchów. Town, western
Poland : Freystadt
(–1945), Germany
Kózyol *see* Mikhaylo-Kot-
syubinskoye
Krainburg *see* Kranj
Krakau *see* Kraków
Kraków. City, southern Po-
land : Krakau (–1918),
Germany
Kraljevo. Town, central Ser-
bia : Rankovićevo (1949–
c. 1966)
Kranéa Deskátes *see* Kranéa
Elassónos
Kranéa Elassónos. Village,
eastern Greece : Kranéa
Deskátes (–1960s)
Kranj. Village, northern
Slovenia : Krainburg
(–1918), Germany
Kranjska Gora. Village,
northwestern Slovenia :
Kronau (–1918), Ger-
many
Kranz *see* Zelenogradsk
Krapkowice. Town, south-
western Poland : Krap-
pitz (–1945), Germany
Krappitz *see* Krapkowice
Kraskino. Urban settle-
ment, Primorsky Kray,
Russia : Novokiyevskoye
(–?)
Krasnaya Presnya. District
of Moscow, Russia :
Presnya (–1918)
Krasnaya Sloboda. Urban
settlement, Minsk Ob-
last, Belorussia : Vyzna
(–1924)

Krasnaya Sloboda *see*
Krasnoslobodsk
Krásno. Village, western
Czech Lands : Schönfeld
(–1918, 1939–45), Ger-
many
Krasnoarmeysk (1). Town,
Saratov Oblast, Russia :
Goly Karamysh (–1926),
Baltser (1926–42)
Krasnoarmeysk (2). Town,
Donetsk Oblast, Ukraine
: Grishino (–1938)
Krasnoarmeysk (3). Suburb
of Volgograd, Volgograd
Oblast, Russia : Sarepta
(–1920)
Krasnoarmeysk (4). Town,
Kokchetav Oblast, Ka-
zakhstan : Tayncha
(–1962)
Krasnoarmeysk (5). Town,
Moscow Oblast, Russia :
Voznesenskaya Manu-
faktura (–1920s), Fabrika
imeni Krasnoy Armii i
Flota (1920s–1928), Kras-
noarmeysky (1928–47)
Krasnoarmeyskaya (1). Vil-
lage, Minsk Oblast, Belo-
russia : Kabany (–1964)
Krasnoarmeyskaya (2). Vil-
lage, Krasnodar Kray,
Russia : Poltavskaya
(–1930s)
Krasnoarmeyskoye. Vil-
lage, Chuvash Autono-
mous Republic, Russia :
Peredniye Traki (–1939)
Krasnoarmeyskoye *see* Urus-
Martan
Krasnoarmeysky. Settlement,
Rostov Oblast, Russia :
Kuberle (–c. 1960)

Krasnoarmeysky *see* Krasnoarmeysk (5)

Krasnoarmeysky Rudnik *see* Dobropolye

Krasnoberezhye. Village, Gomel Oblast, Belorussia : Zlodin (–1964)

Krasnodar. Capital of Krasnodar Kray, Russia : Yekaterinodar (–1920)

Krasnodon. Town, Lugansk Oblast, Ukraine : Sorokino (*1912–38)

Krasnogorsk (1). Town, Moscow Oblast, Russia : Banki (–1940)

Krasnogorsk (2). Town, Sakhalin Oblast, Russia : Chinnai (1905–47), Japan (–1945)

Krasnogorskoye (1). Village, Udmurt Autonomous Republic, Russia : Baryshnikovo (–1938)

Krasnogorskoye (2). Village, Altay Kray, Russia : Staraya Barda (–c. 1960)

Krasnogorsky. Urban settlement, Mari Autonomous Republic, Russia : Ilet (–1938)

Krasnograd. Town, Kharkov Oblast, Ukraine : Konstantinograd (–1922)

Krasnogrigoryevka *see* Chervonogrigorovka

Krasnogvardeysk. Town, Samarkand Oblast, Uzbekistan : Rostovtsevo (–1930s)

Krasnogvardeysk *see* Gatchina

Krasnogvardeyskoye (1). Urban settlement, Belgorod Oblast, Russia : Biryuch (–early 1920s), Budyonnoye (early 1920s–c. 1960)

Krasnogvardeyskoye (2). Urban settlement, Crimean Oblast, Ukraine : Kurman-Kemelchi (–1945)

Krasnogvardeyskoye (3). Village, Stavropol Kray, Russia : Medvezhye (–1936), Yevdokimovskoye (1936–39), Molotovskoye (1939–57)

Krasnogvardeyskoye (4). Village, Adygey Autonomous Oblast, Krasnodar Kray, Russia : Nikolayevskoye (–c. 1960)

Krasnogvardeysky. Urban settlement, Sverdlovsk Oblast, Russia : Irbitsky Zavod (–1938)

Krasnokokshaysk *see* Yoshkar-Ola

Krasnolesye. Village, Kaliningrad Oblast, Russia : Hardtteck (–1946), Germany (–1945)

Krasnomaysky. Urban settlement, Tver Oblast, Russia : Klyuchinsky (–1940)

Krasnooktyabrsky (1). Suburb of Moscow, Russia : Khovrino (–1928)

Krasnooktyabrsky (2). Urban settlement, Mari Autonomous Republic, Russia : Mitkino (–c. 1960)

Krasnooktyabrsky *see* Shopokov

Krasnoostrovsky. Village, Leningrad Oblast,

Russia : Byorkyo
[Björkö] (–1940), Fin-
land; Byorksky (1940–48)
Krasnorechenskoye.   Urban
settlement, Lugansk Ob-
last, Ukraine : Kabanye
(–1973)
Krasnoslobodsk.   Town, Vol-
gograd Oblast, Russia :
Krasnaya Sloboda
(–1955)
Krasnoturansk.   Village,
Krasnoyarsk Kray,
Russia : Abakanskoye
(–?)
Krasnoturyinsk.   Town,
Sverdlovsk Oblast, Rus-
sia : Turyinskiye Rudniki
(–1944)
Krasnouralsk.   Town,
Sverdlovsk Oblast, Rus-
sia : Uralmedstroy
(*1925–31)
Krasnouralsky Rudnik see No-
voasbest
Krasnovichi.   Village, Mogi-
lyov Oblast, Belorussia :
Volchyi Yamy (–1964)
Krasnovodsk Nature Re-
serve.   Turkmenistan :
Gasan-Kuli Nature
Reserve (*1932– 69)
Krasnoye see (1) Chervonoye
(1); (2) Ulan-Erge
Krasnoye Ekho.   Urban set-
tlement, Vladimir Ob-
last, Russia : No-
vogordino (–1925)
Krasnozavodsk.   Town,
Moscow Oblast, Russia :
Zagorsky (–1940)
Krasnoznamensk.   Town,
Kaliningrad Oblast, Rus-
sia : Lasdehnen (–1938),

Germany; Haselberg
(1938–46) Germany
(–1945)
Krasny see (1) Kyzyl; (2)
Mozhga
Krasny Boyevik see Kotovsk
(3)
Krasny Kamyshanik see Kom-
somolsky (1)
Krasny Karachay.   Village,
Karachayev-Cherkess Au-
tonomous Oblast, Stavro-
pol Kray, Russia : Gor-
noye (–c. 1960)
Krasny Klyuch.   Urban set-
tlement, Bashkir Autono-
mous Republic, Russia :
Bely Klyuch (–?)
Krasny Liman.   Town, Don-
etsk Oblast, Ukraine : Li-
man (–1938)
Krasny Log.   Village, Gomel
Oblast, Belorussia :
Krestovy Log (–1964)
Krasny Luch.   Town, Lu-
gansk Oblast, Ukraine :
Krindachyovka (–1920)
Krasny Mayak.   Urban settle-
ment, Vladimir Oblast,
Russia : Yakunchikov
(–1925)
Krasny Oktyabr.   Urban set-
tlement, Vladimir Ob-
last, Russia :
Voznesensky (–1919)
Krasny Oktyabr see Baran
Krasny Profintern (1).   Sub-
urb of Yenakiyevo, Don-
etsk Oblast, Ukraine :
Guzitsino (–1945)
Krasny Profintern (2).   Ur-
ban settlement, Yaroslavl
Oblast, Russia : Poni-
zovkino (–c. 1926)

Krasny Profintern (3). Urban settlement, Donetsk Oblast, Ukraine : Verovka (–?)

Krasny Steklovar. Urban settlement, Mari Autonomous Republic, Russia : Kuzhery (–1939)

Krasny Sulin. Town, Rostov Oblast, Russia : Sulin (–1926)

Krasny Tekstilshchik. Urban settlement, Saratov Oblast, Russia : Saratovskaya Manufaktura (–1929)

Krasny Tkach. Urban settlement, Moscow Oblast, Russia : Shuvoya (–1935)

Krasny Ural see Uralets

Krasny Vostok. Village, Mogilyov Oblast, Belorussia : Shelomy (–1964)

Krasnyye Baki. Urban settlement, Nizhegorodskaya Oblast, Russia : Baki (–?)

Krasnyye Okny. Urban settlement, Odessa Oblast, Ukraine : Okny (–1920)

Krathiás see Kráthion

Kráthion. Village, southern Greece : Paralía Akrátas [Kráthias] (–1960s)

Kratske see Podchinny

Kreiger see Libau

Kremenets. Town, Ternopol Oblast, Ukraine : Krzemieniec (1921–39), Poland

Kremges see Svetlovodsk

Krenau see Chrzanów

Kresna see Stara Kresna

Krestovy Log see Krasny Log

Kreuz see Krzyż

Kreuzberg see Fraserwood

Kreuzburg see (1) Kluczbork; (2) Krustpils; (3) Slavskoye

Kreuzingen see Bolshakovo

Kribi see Ocean

Krindachyovka see Krasny Luch

Krinichnaya. Village, Vitebsk Oblast, Belorussia : Badyaly (–1964)

Krishna. River, southern India : Kistna (–1966)

Kristiania see Oslo

Kristians see Opland

Kristinopol see Chervonograd

Kritsínion see Taziárkhai

Krivaya Kosa see Sedovo

Krk. Island and village, western Croatia : Veglia (1919–47), Italy

Krn. Mountain, western Slovenia : Nero (–1947), Italy

Krnjaja see Kljajičevo

Królewska Huta see Chorzów

Kromníkos see Galáne

Kronau see Kranjska Gora

Kronstadt see Braşov

Kropotkin (1). Town, Krasnodar Kray, Russia : Romanovsky Khutor (–1921)

Kropotkin (2). Urban settlement, Irkutsk Oblast, Russia : Tikhono-Zadonsky (–1930)

Krosno (Odrzańskie). Town, western Poland : Crossen (–1945), Germany

Krško. Village, southeastern Slovenia : Gurkfeld (–1918), Germany

Kruger National Park. Transvaal, South Africa : Sabi Game Reserve (–1926)
Kruglyakov *see* Oktyabrsky (5)
Krummau *see* Český Krumlov
Krummhübel *see* Karpacz
Krumovgrad. City, southern Bulgaria : Koshu-Kavak (–1934)
Krustpils. Suburb of Jēkabpils, Latvia : Kreuzburg (–1917)
Krylovskaya. Village, Krasnodar Kray, Russia : Yekaterinovskaya (–c. 1960)
Krymsk. Town, Krasnodar Kray, Russia : Krymskaya (–1958)
Krymskaya *see* Krymsk
Krynichka. Village, Minsk Oblast, Belorussia : Pupelichi (–1964)
Krzemieniec *see* Kremenets
Krzyż. Town, west-central Poland : Kreuz (–1945), Germany
Ksar Chellala. Village, northern Algeria, northern Africa : Reïbell (–c. 1962)
Ksar el Boukhari. Town, northern Algeria, northern Africa : Boghari (–c. 1962)
Ksar el Kebir. City, northern Morocco, northwestern Africa : Alcazarquivir (–c. 1959)
Ksar es Souk *see* Ar Rachidiya
Kuang-han = Kwanghan
Kuang-hua = Kwanghwa
Kuang-jao = Kwangjao
Kuang-wu = Kwangwu
Kuan-yün = Kwanyün

Kuberle *see* Krasnoarmeysky
Kuchan *see* Huma
Kuchang [Ku-ch'ang]. Suburb of Kunming, southwestern China : Kwantu (–1945)
Kuchow *see* Jungkiang [Jungchiang]
Kuckerneese *see* Yasnoye
Kuçovë *see* Stalin
Kudara *see* Kudara-Somon
Kudara-Somon. Village, Buryat Autonomous Republic, Russia : Kudara (–1948)
Kudelka *see* Asbest
Kudinovo *see* Elektrougli
Kudirkos-Naumiestis. Town, southwest Lithuania : Vladislavov (–c. 1920)
Kudowa Zdrój. Town, southwestern Poland : Bad Kudowa (–1945), Germany
Kuei-ch'ih = Kweichih
Kuei-chu = Kweichu
Kuei-ping = Kweiping
Kuei-te = Kweiteh
Kühlungsborn. Town, northwestern Germany : Brunshaupten (–1938)
Kuhwa *see* Poshow
Kuito. Town, central Angola, southwestern Africa : Silva Porto (c. 1900– c. 1976), Bié (c. 1976– c. 1979)
Kukarka *see* Sovetsk (1)
Kukishi *see* Gvardeyskaya
Kukkus *see* Privolzhskoye
Kükong. Town, southeastern China : Shiuchow (–1912)

Kukonosy *see* Podlesye
Kükoshakia *see* Kweiteh [Kuei-teh]
Kükow *see* Kungho
Kukshik *see* Pervomaysky (2)
Kulakovtsy *see* Zarechanaya (2)
Kuldiga. Town, Latvia : Goldingen (–1917)
Kulnevo. Village, Vitebsk Oblast, Belorussia : Tserkovishche (–1964)
Kumashkino *see* Kurchum
Kumayri. Town, Armenia : Aleksandropol (1840–1924), Leninakan (1924–90)
Künchow *see* Künhsien [Chün-hsien]
Kunersdorf *see* Kunowice
Kungchang *see* Lungsi [Lung-hsi]
Kungho. Town, northwestern China : Kükow (–1931)
Kungrad. Town, Karakalpak Autonomous Republic, Uzbekistan : Zheleznodorozhny (–1969)
Kungshan. Village, southwestern China : Tala (–1935)
Künhsien [Chün-hsien]. Town, east-central China : Künchow (–1912)
Kunice. Town, northwestern Poland : Kunitz (–1945), Germany
Kunitz *see* Kunice
Kunming [K'un-ming]. City, southwestern China : Yunnan (–1912)

Kunowice. Village, western Poland : Kunersdorf (–1945), Germany
Kuokkala *see* Repino
Kuolayarvi. Village, Murmansk Oblast, Russia : Salla (1937–40)
Kurakhovo. Town, Donetsk Oblast, Ukraine : Kurakhovstroy (–1956)
Kurakhovstroy *see* Kurakhovo
Kuratovo. Village, Komi Autonomous Republic, Russia : Kibra (–c. 1940)
Kurbat. Village, northeastern Bulgaria : Balbunar (–1934)
Kurchaloy. Village, Chechen-Ingush Autonomous Republic, Russia : Chkalovo (–c. 1960)
Kurchum. Village, East Kazakhstan Oblast, Kazakhstan : Kumashkino (–c. 1960)
Kuressaare. Town, Estonia : Arensburg (–1917), Kingisepp (1952–88)
Kurgaldzhinsky. Urban settlement, Tselinograd Oblast, Kazakhstan : Kazgorodok (–1937)
Kurganinsk. Town, Krasnodar Kray, Russia : Kurgannaya (–1961)
Kurgannaya *see* Kurganinsk
Kurganovka. Suburb of Beryozovsky, Kemerovo Oblast, Russia : Zaboyshchik (–1944)
Kurhessen *see* Hesse-Kassel
Kurilsk. Town, Kuril Islands, Sakhalin Oblast,

Russia : Shana (1905–46), Japan (–1945)
Kurisches Haff *see* Kursky Gulf
Kurland *see* Kurzeme
Kurman-Kemelchi *see* Krasnogvardeyskoye (2)
Kursky Gulf. Inlet of Baltic Sea, Lithuania/Kaliningrad Oblast, Russia : Kurisches Haff (–1946), Germany (–1945)
Kursu *see* Salla
Kurzeme. Territory of former Russian province, Latvia : Kurland (–1917), Germany
Kuş Gölü. Island, western Turkey : Manyas Gölü (–1973)
Kushalnagar. Town, southern India : Fraserpet (–1950s)
Kushan. Town, northeastern China : Takushan (–1947)
Kushnarenkovo. Village, Bashkir Autonomous Republic, Russia : Topornino (–1930s)
Kushunnai *see* Ilyinsky
Kusochek *see* Roshchino (1)
Kussen *see* Vesnovo
Küstrin *see* Kostrzyn
Kusye-Aleksandrovsky. Urban settlement, Perm Oblast, Russia : Kusye-Aleksandrovsky Zavod (–1946)
Kusye-Aleksandrovsky Zavod *see* Kusye-Aleksandrovsky
Kut *see* Wasit

Kutaradja *see* Banda Atjeh
Kutuzovka. Village, Minsk Oblast, Belorussia : Drekhcha Panenskaya (–1964)
Kutuzovo. Village, Kaliningrad Oblast, Russia : Schirwindt (–1945), Germany
Kuujjuaq. Village, Quebec, Canada : Fort Chimo (–1965)
Kuvango. Town, southcentral Angola, southwestern Africa : Artur de Paiva (–c. 1975), Cuvango (c. 1975–c. 1979)
Kuweit City. Capital, Kuweit : Khadima (1990)
Kuybyshev (1). Town, Novosibirsk Oblast, Russia : Kainsk (–1935)
Kuybyshev (2). Town, Tatar Autonomous Republic, Russia : Spassk (–1926), Spassk-Tatarsky (1926–35)
Kuybyshev *see* Samara
Kuybysheva, imeni *see* Rishtan
Kuybyshevabad *see* Kuybyshevsky (1)
Kuybyshevka-Vostochnaya *see* Belogorsk (1)
Kuybyshev Kray *see* Samara Oblast
Kuybyshevo (1). Urban settlement, Crimean Oblast, Ukraine : Albat (–1944)
Kuybyshevo (2). Village, Rostov Oblast, Russia : Golodayevka (–c. 1936)

Kuybyshevo (3). Village, Sakhalin Oblast, Russia : Rubetsu (1905–45), Japan

Kuybyshevo (4). Village, Mary Oblast, Turkmenistan : Talkhatan-Baba (–c. 1940)

Kuybyshevo (5). Urban settlement, Zaporozhye Oblast, Ukraine : Tsarekonstantinovka (–c. 1935)

Kuybyshevo *see* Rishtan

Kuybyshev Oblast *see* Samara Oblast

Kuybyshevsky (1). Urban settlement, Khatlon Oblast, Tajikistan : Aral (–c. 1935), Kuybyshevabad (c. 1935–40)

Kuybyshevsky (2). Urban settlement, Kokchetav Oblast, Kazakhstan : Trudovoy (–1969)

Kuybyshevsky Zaton. Urban settlement, Tatar Autonomous Republic, Russia : Spassky Zaton (–1935)

Kuyüan *see* Paoyüan

Kuzhery *see* Krasny Steklovar

Kuznetsk *see* Novokuznetsk

Kuznetsk-Sibirsky *see* Novokuznetsk

Kuznetsovo *see* Konakovo

Kuznetsovsky. Town, Rostov Oblast, Russia : Gigant (*1928–81)

Kvirily *see* Zestafoni

Kwabhaca. Town, northern Transkei, southern Africa : Mount Frere (–1976)

Kwaki *see* Kweichu [Kuei-chu]

Kwangchang *see* Laiyüan

Kwanghan [Kuang-han]. Town, central China : Hanchow (–1913)

Kwanghwa [Kuang-hua]. Town, east-central China : Laohokow [Lao-ho-k'ou] (–1947)

Kwangjao [Kuang-jao]. Town, eastern China : Loan (–1914)

Kwangning *see* Pehchen

Kwangping *see* Yungnien

Kwangsi *see* Lusi [Lu-hsi] (1)

Kwangsin *see* Shangjao

Kwangwu [K'uang-wu]. Town, eastern China : Linghsien (–1949)

Kwanpao *see* Hweichwan [Hui-chuan]

Kwantu *see* Kuchang [Ku-ch'ang]

Kwanyün [Kuan-yün]. Town, eastern China : Panpu (–1912)

Kweichih [Kuei-ch'ih]. Town, eastern China : Chihchow (–1912)

Kweichow *see* (1) Fengkieh [Feng-chieh]; (2) Tzekwei [Tzu-kuei]

Kweichu [Kuei-chu]. Town, southern China : Kwaki (–1930)

Kweihwa *see* (1) Mingki [Ming-ch'i]; (2) Tzeyün [Tzu-yün]

Kweiping [Kuei-ping]. Town, southern China : Sünchow (–1913)

Kweishun *see* Tsingsi [Chinghsi]

Kweiteh [Kuei-teh]. Town, northwestern China : Kükoshakia (–1928)

Kweiyang *see* Jucheng [Ju-ch'eng]
Kwekwe. Town, central Zimbabwe, southeastern Africa : Que Que (*1900–82)
Kwidzyn. Town, northern Poland : Marienwerder (–1919, 1939–45), Germany
Kwilu-Ngongo. Town, western Zaïre, central Africa : Moerbeke (–1972)
Kyaikkami. Town, southwestern Myanmar : Amherst (–?)
Kyakhta. Town, Buryat Autonomous Republic, Russia : Troitskosavsk (–1935)
Kyŏmipo *see* Songnim
Kypséle (1). Village, western Greece : Khósepse (–1960s)
Kypséle (2). Village, northern Greece : Neokhórion (–1960s)
Kypséle *see* (1) Koryskhádes; (2) Kypséle Methánon
Kypséle Methánon. Village, northern Greece : Kypséle (–1960s)
Kyzyl. Capital of Tuva Autonomous Republic, Russia : Belotsarsk (*1914–18), Krasny (1918), Khem-Beldyr (1918–26), Kyzyl-Khoto (1926–?)
Kyzylagach *see* Kirova
Kyzylasker. Suburb of Bishkek, Kirgizia : Chalakazaki (–1944)
Kyzyl-Burun *see* Siazan
Kyzyl-Khoto *see* Kyzyl

Kzyl-Mazar *see* Sovetsky (3)
Kzyl-Orda. Capital of Kzyl-Orda Oblast, Kazakhstan : Ak-Mechet (*1820–53, c. 1920–25), Perovsk (1853–c. 1920)

Laband *see* Łabędy
Łabędy. Town, southern Poland : Laband (–1945), Germany
Labes *see* Łobez
Labiau *see* Polessk
Labinsk. Town, Krasnodar Kray, Russia : Labinskaya (–1947)
Labinskaya *see* Labinsk
Labrador. Municipality, Pangasinan, Philippines : San Isidro Labrador (–1914)
Labrang *see* Siaho [Hsia-ho]
La Calle *see* El-Kala
Laccadive, Minicoy and Amindivi Islands *see* Lakshadweep
La Charqueada *see* General Enrique Martínez
Lachin. Town, Azerbaijan : Abdalyar (–1926)
Lachine *see* La Salle
Lackawanna. City, New York, USA : Limestone Hill (–1909)
La Concepción *see* Riaba
La Cordillera. Department, central Paraguay, South America : Caraguatay (–1944)
Lacub *see* Fabian Marcos
Lada Bay. Inlet, Sunda Strait, Java, Indonesia : Peper Bay (–1963)

Lądek Zdrój. Town, south-
western Poland : Bad
Landeck (–1945), Ger-
many
Ladushkin. Town, Kalinin-
grad Oblast, Russia :
Ludwigsort (–1946), Ger-
many (–1945)
Ladysmith. City, Vancouver
Island, British Columbia,
Canada : Oyster Harbour
(–1901)
La Estrelleta. Province,
western Dominican Re-
public, West Indies : San
Rafael (*1942–65)
Lafayette see Bougaâ
Lafayette National Park see
Acadia National Park
Laflèche. Suburb of Mon-
treal, Quebec, Canada :
Mackayville (–1959)
Lagan see Kaspiysky
Laggan see Lake Louise
Lagiewniki. Town, south-
western Poland : Elver-
shagen (–1945), Ger-
many
Lagona see Laguna Beach
Lagos Airport see Murtala
Muhammad Airport
La Goulette see Halq-el-Oued
Laguna see Padilla
Laguna Beach. City, Califor-
nia, USA : Lagona
(–1904)
Lahij. Town, western
Yemen : Al-Hawtah
(1960s)
Lähn see Wleń
Laibach see Ljubljana
Laichow see Yehsien [Yeh-
hsien]
Laishev see Laishevo

Laishevo. Urban settle-
ment, Tatar Autonomous
Republic, Russia :
Laishev (–c. 1928)
Laiyüan. Town, northeast-
ern China : Kwangchang
(–1914)
Lajeado see Guiratinga
Lake Bogoria. Town, west-
central Kenya, eastern
Africa : Lake Hannington
(–1975)
Lake City. Town, Tennes-
see, USA : Coal Creek
(–1939)
Lake Hannington see Lake
Bogoria
Lake Lanao see Sultan Alonto
Lake Louise. Village, Al-
berta, Canada : Laggan
(–1914)
Lake Oswego. City, Oregon,
USA : Oswego (–1909)
Lake Rudolf see Lake Turkana
Lake Turkana. Town, north-
ern Kenya, eastern Af-
rica : Lake Rudolf
(–1975)
Lake Worth. City, Florida,
USA : Lucerne (–1913)
Lakhdaria. Village, north-
ern Algeria, northern Af-
rica : Palestro (–c. 1962)
Lakiashih see Tungteh [T'ung-
te]
Lakinsk. Town, Vladimir
Oblast, Russia : Lakinsky
(–1969)
Lakinsky see Lakinsk
Lakshadweep. Island terri-
tory, Arabian Sea, India :
Laccadive, Minicoy and
Amindivi Islands (*1956–
73)

Lambèse *see* Tazoult
La Mirada. City, California,
USA : Mirada Hills
(–1960)
Lamoricière *see* Ouled Mi-
moun
Landana *see* Cacongo
Landau *see* Shirokolanovka
Landeck *see* Lędyczek
Landeshut *see* Kamienna
Góra
Landsberg *see* (1) Górowo
Iławeskie; (2) Gorzów
Wielkopolski
Landsberg (an der Warthe)
see Gorzów Wielkopolski
Landsberg in Oberschlesien
see Gorzów (Śląski)
Landsweiler *see* Landsweiler-
Reden
Landsweiler-Reden. Town,
western Germany : Land-
sweiler (–1937)
Lang-ang *see* Santa Theresa
Lang-ch'i = Langki [Lang-
ch'i]
Langchu *see* Ninglang
Langchung. Town, central
China : Paoning (–1913)
Langenbielau *see* Bielawa
Langki [Lang-ch'i]. Town,
eastern China : Kienping
(–1914)
Langkiung *see* Erhyüan
Langshan. Town, northern
China : Yunganpao
(–1942)
Lankao. Town, central
China : Chwanping
(–1913)
Lans *see* Lans-en-Vercors
Lans-en-Vercors. Village,
southeastern France :
Lans (–1947)

Lantsang [Lan-ts'ang].
Town, southwestern
China : Chenpien
(–1914)
Lao-ho-k'ou *see* Kwanghwa
[Kuang-hua]
Laohokow *see* Kwanghwa
[Kuang-hua]
Laois [Leix]. County, cen-
tral Ireland : Queen's
County (–1920)
La Olmeda de las Cebollas *see*
La Olmeda de las Fuentes
La Olmeda de las Fuentes.
Village, central Spain :
La Olmeda de las Cebol-
las (–c. 1960)
Laoyao *see* Lienyün
Laoyatan *see* Yentsing [Yen-
ching]
La Pampa. Province, central
Argentina, South Amer-
ica : Eva Perón (1952–
55)
La Parida *see* (Cerro) Bolívar
La Park *see* Huntington Park
La Plata. City, eastern Ar-
gentina, South America :
Eva Perón (1952–55)
Laptevo *see* Yasnogorsk
Laptev Sea. Arctic Ocean,
northeastern Russia : Nor-
denskjöld Sea (–1913)
Lapti *see* Mayskaya
Laptikha *see* Kommunarka (1)
La Puebla del Río. Village,
southwestern Spain :
Puebla (–c. 1920)
Laragaran *see* Plaridel (1)
Laranjal *see* Laranjal Paulista
Laranjal Paulista. City,
southeastern Brazil, South
America : Laranjal
(–1944)

Laranjeiras *see* (1) Alagoa
Nova; (2) Laranjeiras do
Sul
Laranjeiras do Sul. City,
southern Brazil, South
America : Laranjeiras
(–1944), Iguaçu (1944–
48)
L'Arbaa Naït
Irathen. Town, north-
central Algeria, northern
Africa : Fort-National
(–c. 1962)
Largeau. Town, northern
Chad, north-central
Africa : Faya (–1913)
L'Argentière *see* L'Argen-
tière-la-Bessée
L'Argentière-la-Bessée.
Village, southeastern
France : L'Argentière
(–1941)
Larinsky *see* Never
La Rioja. Province, north-
ern Spain : Logroño
(–1981)
Larkins *see* South Miami
La Salle. Suburb of Mon-
treal, Quebec, Canada :
Lachine (–1912)
Lasdehnen *see* Krasnoz-
namensk
Laško. Village, east-central
Slovenia : Tüffer (–1918),
Germany
Las Mulatas *see* San Blas
Las Palmas. Province, Ca-
nary Islands : Canarias
(–1927)
Laspokhórion *see* Leúke
Las Rosas. Town, southern
Mexico, North America :
Pinola (–1934)

Las Torres de Cotillas. Vil-
lage, southeastern Spain :
Cotillas (–c. 1920)
Las Villas. Province, central
Cuba : Santa Clara
(–1940)
Lászláfalva *see* Szentkirály
Latakia. Governorate,
northwestern Syria :
Alawiya (1920–42)
La Thuile. Village, north-
western Italy : Porta Lit-
toria (c. 1938–45)
Latina (1). City, south-cen-
tral Italy : Littoria
(*1932–47)
Latina (2). Province, south-
central Italy : Littoria
(*1934–47)
La Toma *see* Cuatro de Junio
La Trinidad *see* Villa La Tri-
nidad
La Trinitaria. Town, south-
ern Mexico, North
America : Zapaluta
(–1934)
Latvia. Republic, central
Europe : Latvian SSR
(1940–90)
Latvian SSR *see* Latvia
Lauban *see* Lubań
Lauenburg *see* Lębork
La Unión. Town, eastern
Guatemala, Central
America : Monte Oscuro
(–c. 1920)
Laurahütte *see* Siemianowice
Śląskie
Laurel Hollow. Village,
New York, USA : Laurel-
ton (–1935)
Laurelton *see* Laurel Hollow
Laval *see* Laval-sur-Vologne

Laval-sur-Vologne. Village, eastern France : Laval (–1937)

La Vereda. Village, central Spain : El Vado (–c. 1950)

Lavras see (1) Lavras da Mangabeira; (2) Lavras do Sul

Lavras da Mangabeira. City, northeastern Brazil, South America : Lavras (–1944)

Lavras do Sul. City, southern Brazil, South America : Lavras (–1944)

Lavrentiya. Village, Chukot Autonomous Okrug, Magadan Oblast, Russia : Chukotskaya Kultbaza (–c. 1960)

Lavumisa. Town, southern Swaziland, southern Africa : Gollel (–1970)

Lazarev. Urban settlement, Khabarovsk Kray, Russia : Mys Lazarev (–c. 1960)

Lazdijai. Town, Lithuania : Lozdes (–1917)

Lazo. Village, Moldavia : Kishkareny (–c. 1960)

Lazovsk. Urban settlement, Moldavia : Synzhereya (–c. 1960)

Lbishchensk see Chapayev

Leaksville see Eden

Lebedevka. Health resort, Odessa Oblast, Ukraine : Burnas (–?)

Lebedinovskoye see Voroshilovskoye

Lębork. City, northern Poland : Lauenburg (–1945), Germany

Le Center. Village, Minnesota, USA : Le Sueur Center (–1931)

Łęczyca. Town, central Poland : Lentschütz (1939–45), Germany

Ledengskoye see Babushkina, imeni

Ledo Road see Stilwell Road

Lędyczek. Town, northwestern Poland : Landeck (–1945), Germany

Leeudoringstad. Village, Transvaal, South Africa : Leeudorns Halte (–1906)

Leeudorns Halte see Leeudoringstad

Leeu-Gamka. Town, Cape Province, South Africa : Fraserburg Road (–?)

Leeville see Assiniboia

Leger Corner see Dieppe

Legnica. Town, southwestern Poland : Liegnitz (–1945), Germany

Leipe see Lipno

Leishan. Town, southern China : Tankiang (–1943)

Leix = Laois

Leksura see Lentekhi

Lemberg. Town, Saskatchewan, Canada : Sifton (–1905)

Lemberg see Lvov

Lemeshensky see Orgtrud

Lempira. Department, western Honduras, Central America : Gracias (–1943)

Lemzal see Limbaži

Lençóis see Lençóis Paulista

Lençóis Paulista. City, southeastern Brazil,

South America : Lençóis
(–1944), Ubirama (1944–
48)
L'Enfant-Jésus-de-Sorel *see*
Tracy
Lengwethen *see* Lunino
Lengyeltóti. Town, south-
western Hungary :
Lengyeltótihács (–1907)
Lengyeltótihács *see* Lengyel-
tóti
Lenina, imeni. Suburb of
Krivoy Rog, Dnepropet-
rovsk Oblast, Ukraine :
Kalachevsky Rudnik
(–1926)
Leninabad *see* Khodzhent
Leninakan *see* Kumayri
Lenina, V.I., imeni. Urban
settlement, Ulyanovsk
Oblast, Russia : Ru-
myantsevo (–1938)
Lenin-Dzhol. Village, Osh
Oblast, Kirgizia : Massy
(–?)
Leningrad *see* St. Petersburg
Leningrad Guberniya
(1927†). RSFSR : St.
Petersburg Guberniya
(–1914), Petrograd
Guberniya (1914–24)
Leningradskaya. Village,
Krasnodar Kray, Russia :
Umanskaya (–1930s)
Leningradsky. Urban settle-
ment, Khatlon Oblast,
Tajikistan : Muminabad
(–1973)
Lenin Hills. Section of right
bank of Moskva River,
Moscow, Russia : Spar-
row Hills [Vorobyovy
gory] (–1924)

Lenino (1). Suburb of
Irkutsk, Irkutsk Oblast,
Russia : Innoken-
tyevskaya (–1930s)
Lenino (2). Urban settle-
ment, Crimean Oblast,
Ukraine : Sem Kolodezey
(–1957)
Lenino = Lenino-Dachnoye
Lenino *see* Leninsk-
Kuznetsky
Lenino-Dachnoye [Lenino].
Suburb of Moscow,
Russia : Tsaritsyno-
Dachnoye (–1939)
Leninogorsk. Town, Tatar
Autonomous Republic,
Russia : Novaya
Pismyanka (–1955)
Leninogorsk *see* Ridder
Lenino-Kokushkino. Village,
Tatar Autonomous Re-
public, Russia : Ko-
kushkino (–1964)
Lenin Peak. Mountain, Kir-
gizia/Tajikistan :
Kaufman Peak (–1928)
Leninsk (1). Town, Vol-
gograd Oblast, Russia :
Prishib (–1919)
Leninsk (2). Town, Andi-
zhan Oblast, Uzbekistan :
Assake (–1934, 1935–37),
Zelensk (1934–35)
Leninsk *see* Petrodvorets
Leninskaya Sloboda. Urban
settlement, Nizhe-
gorodskaya Oblast, Rus-
sia : Kadnitsy (–1935)
Leninsk-Kuznetsky. Town,
Kemerovo Oblast,
Russia : Kolchugino
(–1922), Lenino (1922–25)

Leninskoye (1). Village,
Chimkent Oblast,
Kazakhstan :
Alekseyevskoye (–1924)
Leninskoye (2). Urban set-
tlement, Kirov Oblast,
Russia : Bogorodskoye
(–1917), Shabalino
(1917–c. 1940)
Leninskoye (3). Village,
Kustanay Oblast, Ka-
zakhstan : Demyanovka
(–c. 1960)
Leninskoye (4). Village, Ak-
tyubinsk Oblast, Ka-
zakhstan : Kos-Istek
(–c. 1960)
Leninskoye (5). Village,
Uralsk Oblast, Ka-
zakhstan : Masteksay
(–c. 1960)
Leninskoye (6). Village,
Jewish Autonomous Ob-
last, Khabarovsk Kray,
Russia : Mikhailovo-Se-
myonovskoye (–?),
Blyukherovo (?–1939)
Leninskoye (7). Village, Osh
Oblast, Kirgizia : (No-
vaya) Pokrovka (–1937)
Leninsk(-Turkmensky) see
Chardzhou
Leninsky (1). Urban settle-
ment, Tula Oblast, Rus-
sia : Domman-Asfaltovy
Zavod (–1939)
Leninsky (2). Urban settle-
ment, Tajikistan :
Koktash (–c. 1960), Sard-
arova Karakhana, imeni
(c. 1960–70)
Leninsky (3). Urban settle-
ment, Mari Autonomous

Republic, Russia : Mar-
ino (–1941)
Leninsky (4). Urban settle-
ment, Yakut Autono-
mous Republic, Russia :
Nizhnestalinsk (–1962)
Leninsky (5). Urban settle-
ment, Kzyl-Orda Oblast,
Kazakhstan : Zarya
(–c. 1960)
Leninváros. Town, north-
eastern Hungary :
Tiszaszederkény (*1950–
70)
Leninváros see Pestszen-
terzsébet
Lensk. Town, Yakut Auton-
omous Republic, Russia :
Mukhtuya (–1963)
Lentekhi. Urban settle-
ment, Georgia : Leksura
(–1938)
Lentschütz see Łęczyca
Leobschütz see Głubczyce
León see Cotopaxi
Leonidovo. Urban settle-
ment, Sakhalin Oblast,
Russia : Kami-shikuka
(1905–45), Japan
Léopold II, Lake see Mai-
Ndombe, Lake
Leopoldina see (1) Aruaña;
(2) Colônia Leopoldina;
(3) Parnamirim
Léopoldville see Kinshasa
Lepaya = Liepaja
Lermontov. Town, Stavro-
pol Kray, Russia : Ler-
montovsky (–1956)
Lermontovo. Village, Penza
Oblast, Russia : Tark-
hany (–1917)
Lermontovsky see Lermontov

Leschnitz *see* Leśnica

Leselidze. Health resort, Abkhazian Autonomous Republic, Georgia : Yermolovsk (–1944)

Lesínion. Village, central Greece : Palaiokatoúna (–1960s)

Leskhimstroy *see* Severodonetsk

Leslau *see* Włocławek

Leśnica. Town, southern Poland : Leschnitz (–1937), Germany, Bergstadt (1937–45), Germany

Lesnoy *see* (1) Seskar; (2) Umba

Lesogorsk. Town, Sakhalin Oblast, Russia : Nayoshi (1905–46), Japan (–1945)

Lesogorsky. Urban settlement, Leningrad Oblast, Russia : Yaski [Jääski] (–1948), Finland (–1940)

Lesotho. Kingdom, southern Africa : Basutoland (–1966)

Lesovka *see* Ukrainsk

Lesozavodsky *see* Novovyatsk

Lesser Slave Lake *see* Grouard

Lesten *see* Czernina

Lestershire *see* Johnson City

Les Trembles *see* Sidi Hamadouche

Le Sueur Center *see* Le Center

Leszno. City, west-central Poland : Lissa (–1919), Germany

Leubus *see* Lubiąz

Leúke. Village, eastern Greece : Laspokhórion (–1960s)

Leukothéa. Village, western Greece : Kephalóvryson (–1960s)

Leuthen *see* Lutynia

Leutschau *see* Levoča

Levelland. City, Texas, USA : Hockley (*1921–24)

Leverburgh. Village, Western Isles, Scotland, UK : Obbe (–1918)

Leverger *see* Santo Antônio do Leverger

Leverville *see* Lusanga

Levittown *see* Willingboro

Levoča. Town, eastern Slovakia : Leutschau (–1918, 1939–45), Germany

Levski. Mountain, north-central Bulgaria : Ambarica (–c. 1967)

Levskigrad. Town, central Bulgaria : Karlovo (–1953)

Lev Tolstoy. Urban settlement, Lipetsk Oblast, Russia : Astapovo (–1927)

Lewin. Town, southwestern Poland : Hummelstadt (1938–45), Germany

Lewin Brzeski. Town, southwestern Poland : Löwen (–1945), Germany

Lewis. Locality, Manitoba, Canada : Rateau (–1918)

Lewisporte. Town, Newfoundland, Canada : Marshallville (–c. 1900)

Lexington Park. Village, Maryland, USA : Jarboesville (–1950)

Lezhni *see* Bereznitsa (1)

Liangchow *see* Wuwei

Liaocheng [Liao-ch'eng].
Town, north-central
China : Tungchang
(–1913)
Liaochow *see* Tsochüan [Tso-
ch'üan]
Liaohsien *see* Tsochüan [Tso-
ch'üan]
Liaoning. Province, north-
eastern China : Feng-tien
(1903–28)
Liaoyüan *see* Shwangliao
[Shuang-liao]
Libagon. Municipality,
Leyte, Philippines :
Sugod Sur (–1913)
Libau. Hamlet, Manitoba,
Canada : Kreiger (–1906)
Libau *see* Liepaja
Libava *see* Liepaja
Liberec. City, northern
Czech Lands : Reichen-
berg (–1918, 1939–45),
Germany
Libertad (1). Barrio,
Cagayan, Philippines :
Colonia (–1957)
Libertad (2). Barrio, Leyte,
Philippines : Malirong
(–1957)
Libertador *see* Dajabón
Liberty Island. Island, Up-
per New York Bay, New
York City, USA : Bed-
loes Island (–1956)
Libyo. Municipality, Suri-
gao del Norte, Philip-
pines : Albor (–1957)
Licania. City, northeastern
Brazil, South America :
Santana (–1944)
Licheng [Li-cheng]. Town,
eastern China : Wang-
shejenchwang (–1935)

Lichinga. Town, northwest-
ern Mozambique, south-
eastern Africa : Vila
Cabral (–1976)
Lichow *see* Lihsien (1)
Lichtenstein. City, south-
eastern Germany :
Lichtenstein-Callnberg
(–?)
Lichtenstein-Callnberg *see*
Lichtenstein
Li-ch'uan = Lichwan
Lichwan [Li-ch'uan]. Town,
southeastern China :
Sincheng (–1914)
Lidice. Village, Illinois,
USA : Stern Park Gar-
dens (–1942)
Lidzbark Warmiński. Town,
northeastern Poland :
Heilsberg (–1945), Ger-
many
Liebau *see* Lubawka
Liebenau bei Schwiebus *see*
Lubrza
Liebenfelde *see* Zalesye
Liebenthal *see* Lubomierz
Liegnitz *see* Legnica
Lienshan. Village, south-
western China : Chanta
(–1935)
Lienshui. Town, eastern
China : Antung
(–1914)
Lienyün. Town, eastern
China : Laoyao (–1935)
Liepaja [Lepaya]. Town,
Latvia : Libava (–1917),
Libau (1917–18, 1941–
45), Germany
Lievenhof *see* Līvāni
Lifan *see* Lihsien (2)
Lifudzin *see* Rudny
Ligourión *see* Lygoúrion

Lihsien (1). Town, south-central China : Lichow (–1913)

Lihsien (2). Town, central China : Lifan (–1945)

Lihsien see Hwaning [Huaning]

Li-hua = Lihwa

Lihwa [Li-hua]. Town, southern China : Litang (–1913)

Lihwang see Kinchai [Chinchai]

Likasi. City, southeastern Zaïre, central Africa : Jadotville (–1966)

Likhachyovo see Pervomaysky (4)

Likhaya see Likhovskoy

Likhinichi see Rakushevo

Likhovskoy. Urban settlement, Rostov Oblast, Russia : Likhaya (–1930)

Likhvin see Chekalin

Lillo see Puebla de Lillo

Lillooet Lake see Alouette Lake

Liman. Urban settlement, Astrakhan Oblast, Russia : Dolban (–1944)

Liman see Krasny Liman

Limanowa. Town, southern Poland : Ilmenau (1939–45), Germany

Limbaži. Town, Latvia : Lemzal (–1917)

Limbe. Town, southwestern Cameroon, western Africa : Victoria (–1982)

Limbuhan see Pio V. Corpuz

Limchow see Hoppo

Limeira see Joaçaba

Limestone Hill see Lackawanna

Limeville see Aguathuna

Limkong. Town, southeastern China : Shekshing (–1914)

Limoeiro see (1) Limoeiro de Anadia; (2) Limoeiro do Norte

Limoeiro de Anadia. City, northeastern Brazil, South America : Limoeiro (–1944)

Limoeiro do Norte. City, northeastern Brazil, South America : Limoeiro (–1944)

Linchow see Linhsien

Linchüan [Lin-ch'üan]. Town, eastern China : Shenkiu (–1934)

Lincolnwood. Village, Illinois, USA : Tessville (–1935)

Linden. Town, northeastern Guyana, South America : Mackenzie (–1973)

Linden see Gladstone

Linfen. Town, northeastern China : Pingyang (–1912)

Lingchow see Lingwu

Linghsien see Kwangwu [K'uang-wu]

Lingling. Town, south-central China : Yungchow (–1913)

Lingnan see Tsingping [Chingping]

Lingshan see Sansui

Lingwu. Town, northwestern China : Lingchow (–1913)

Lingyüan. Town, northeastern China : Kienchang (–1914), Takow (1914)

Lingyün. Town, southern
China : Szecheng
(–1913)
Linhai. City, eastern China :
Taichow (–1912)
Lin-hsia = Linsia
Linhsien. Town, southeast-
ern China : Linchow
(–1912)
Lini. City, northeastern
China : Ichow [I-chou]
(–1911)
Linju. Town, east-central
China : Juchow (–1913)
Linkiang see (1) Tsingkiang
[Chin-chiang]; (2)
Tungkiang [T'ung-
chiang]
Linkuva. Town, Lithuania :
Lipkovo (–1917)
Linli. Town, south-central
China : Anfu (–1914)
Linlithgow see West Lothian
Linnam. Town, southeast-
ern China : Chaikang
(–1942)
Linsen. Town, southeastern
China : Hungshankiao
(–c. 1945)
Linsia [Lin-hsia]. Town,
north-central China :
Hochow (–1913), Taoho
(1913–28)
Lintan [Lin-t'an]. Town,
north-central China :
Taochow (–1913)
Lintao [Lin-t'ao]. Town,
north-central China :
Titao (–1928)
Lintien. Town, northeastern
China : Tungtsichen
(–1917)
Linton see Delray Beach
Lin-tse = Lintseh

Lintseh [Lin-tse]. Town,
north-central China :
Fuyi (–1913)
Linugos see Magsaysay
Linyovo. Urban settlement,
Volgograd Oblast,
Russia : Gussenbakh
(–1941), Medveditskoye
(1941–c. 1960)
Linyü. Town, northeastern
China : Haiyang
(–1949)
Linyü see Shanhaikwan
Lipiany. Town, northwest-
ern Poland : Lippehne
(–1945), Germany
Liping see Kinping [Chin-
p'ing] (2)
Lipkovo see Linkuva
Lipno. Town, central Po-
land : Leipe (1939–45),
Germany
Lipová. Village, northern
Czech Lands : Haňšpach
(–1947)
Lippehne see Lipiany
Lipras see Villa Ramos
Lishih. Town, northeastern
China : Yungning
(–1912)
Lishui. Town, eastern
China : Chuchow (–1913)
Liskeard see New Liskeard
Liski. Town, Voronezh Ob-
last, Russia : Svoboda
(1928–43), Georgiu-Dezh
(1965–91)
Lispeszentadorján. Town,
western Hungary : Szen-
tadorján (*1937–42)
Lissa see Leszno
Lister og Mandals see Vest
Agder
Litang see Lihwa [Li-hua]

Lithuania. Republic, central Europe : Lithuanian SSR (1940–90)

Lithuanian SSR *see* Lithuania

Litsingtien *see* Nanchao

Little Saskatchewan *see* Minnedosa

Littoria *see* Latina (1), (2)

Litvino *see* Sosnovoborsk

Līvāni. Town, Latvia : Lievenhof (–1917)

Livermore Falls. Town, Maine, USA : East Livermore (–1930)

Livingstone *see* (1) Mosi-oa-Toenja (1)

Livramento *see* (1) José de Freitas; (2) Livramento do Brumado; (3) Nossa Senhora do Livramento

Livramento do Brumado. City, eastern Brazil, South America : Livramento (–1944)

Lizuny *see* Mayskoye (1)

Ljubljana. Capital of Slovenia : Laibach (–1918), Germany

Ljutomer. Village, eastern Slovenia : Luttenberg (–1918), Germany

Llano de Bureba. Village, northern Spain : Solas de Bureba (–c. 1950)

Llanta Apacheta *see* Millares

Loan *see* Kwangjao [Kuangjao]

Loben *see* Lubliniec

Lobethal. Town, South Australia, Australia : Tweedvale (1918–35)

Łobez. Town, northwestern Poland : Labes (–1945), Germany

Lobovsky No. 33/37 Rudnik *see* Shakhta No. 33/37

Lobva. Urban settlement, Sverdlovsk Oblast, Russia : Lobvinsky Zavod (–1928)

Lobvinsky Zavod *see* Lobva

Lochmoor *see* Grosse Pointe Woods

Lockbourne Air Force Base *see* Rickenbacker Air Force Base

Locsin *see* Daraga

Lodi *see* Draâ Esmar

Logroño *see* La Rioja

Loho *see* Lotien

Loire-Atlantique. Department, western France : Loire-Inférieure (–1957)

Loire-Inférieure *see* Loire-Atlantique

Lokot, Cape. Komsomolets Island, Severnaya Zemlya, Krasnoyarsk Kray, Russia : Rozy Lyuksemburg, Cape (*c. 1930–c. 1960)

Lomahasha. Town, northeastern Swaziland, southern Africa : Nomahasha (–1976)

Lomonosov. Town, Leningrad Oblast, Russia : Oranienbaum (–1948)

Londuimbale. Town, west-central Angola, southwestern Africa : Luimbale (–c. 1979)

Longonot. Satellite station, south-central Kenya, eastern Africa : Mount Margaret (–1971)

Longos *see* Kalayaan

Loning. Town, east-central
China : Yungning (–1914)
Loos *see* Loos-en-Gohelle
Loos-en-Gohelle. Town,
northern France : Loos
(–1937)
Lopasnya *see* Chekhov (1)
Lopatino *see* Volzhsk
López de Filippis *see* Mariscal
Estigarribia
Lorraine *see* Baker
Loshan. Town, central
China : Kiating (–1913)
Losino-Ostrovskaya *see* Ba-
bushkin (1)
Losino-Petrovsky. Town,
Moscow Oblast, Russia :
Petrovskaya Sloboda
(–1928)
Loslau *see* Wodzisław Śląski
Lotien. Town, southern
China : Loho (–1930)
Lotu. Town, northwestern
China : Ningpo (–1928)
Lötzen *see* Giżycko
Loubomo. Town, southwest-
ern Congo, west-central
Africa : Dolisie (–1976)
Lough Gowna. Town,
County Cavan, Ireland :
Scrabby (–1950)
Louisbourg. Town, Nova
Scotia, Canada : Louis-
burg (–1966)
Louisburg *see* Louisbourg
Louis-Gentil *see* Youssoufia
Lourenço Marques *see* Maputo
Loutrópolis Methánon.
Town, northern Greece :
Methánon (–1960s)
Löwen *see* Lewin Brzeski
Löwenberg *see* Łwówek Śląski
Löwenhagen *see* Komsomolsk
(2)

Löwenstadt *see* Brzeziny
Löwentin *see* Niegocin
Lower Granville *see* Port
Royal
Loxton. Town, South Aus-
tralia, Australia :
Loxton's Hut (–1907)
Loxton's Hut *see* Loxton
Loya *see* Loyeh
Loyang. City, east-central
China : Honan (–1913)
Loyeh. Town, southern
China : Loya (–1936)
Lozdes *see* Lazdijai
Lozno-Aleksandrovka. Ur-
ban settlement, Lugansk
Oblast, Ukraine :
Aleksandrovka (–mid-
1930s)
Luachimo. Town, northeast-
ern Angola, southwestern
Africa : Portugália
(–c. 1976)
Luan *see* Changchih [Ch'ang-
chih]
Luangwa. Town, southeast-
ern Zambia, south-
central Africa : Feira
(–c. 1982)
Luau. Town, west-central
Angola, southwestern Af-
rica : Bailundo (–1930s),
Vila Teixeira da Silva
(1930s–c. 1976)
Luba. Municipality, Ilocos
Sur, Philippines : Barrit-
Luluno (–1914)
Lubań. Town, southwestern
Poland : Lauban (–1945),
Germany
Lubango. Town, southwest-
ern Angola, southwestern
Africa : Sá da Bandeira
(–c. 1976)

Lubawka. Town, southwestern Poland : Liebau (–1945), Germany

Lüben see Lubin

Lubiąz. Village, southwestern Poland : Leubus (–1945), Germany

Lubin. Town, southwestern Poland : Lüben (–1945), Germany

Lubliniec. Town, southern Poland : Loben (1939–45), Germany

Lubomierz. Town, southwestern Poland : Liebenthal (–1945), Germany

Lubrza. Town, western Poland : Liebenau bei Schwiebus (–1945), Germany

Lubsko. Town, western Poland : Sommerfeld (–1945), Germany

Lubumbashi. City, southeastern Zaïre, central Africa : Élisabethville (*1910–66)

Lucena see New Lucena

Lucerne. Community, Quebec, Canada : Hull-Sud (–1964)

Lucerne see Lake Worth

Luchang see Lushui

Lucheng see Tiensi [T'ien-hsi]

Lu-chou. City, south-central China : Lu-ch'uan (–1912)

Lüchow see (1) Hofei; (2) Luhsien

Lu-chuan see Lu-chou

Lucio Laurel. Barrio, Mindoro Oriental, Philippines : Calamunding (–1969)

Luditz see Žlutice

Ludweiler see Ludweiler-Warndt

Ludweiler-Warndt. Town, western Germany : Ludweiler (–1936)

Ludwigsort see Ladushkin

Ludza. Town, Latvia : Lützin (–1917)

Luena. Town, east-central Angola, southwestern Africa : Luso (–c. 1976)

Lugansk. Capital of Lugansk Oblast, Ukraine : Voroshilovgrad (1935–58, 1970–90)

Lugansk Oblast. Ukraine : Voroshilovgrad Oblast (*1938–58, 1970–90)

Lugovaya (1). Village, Brest Oblast, Belorussia : Durnevichi (–1964)

Lugovaya (2). Village, Vitebsk Oblast, Belorussia : Malaya Dyatel (–1964)

Lugovaya (3). Village, Minsk Oblast, Belorussia : Svinka (–1964)

Lugovaya Proleyka see Primorsk (3)

Luho. Town, southern China : Changku (–1914)

Lu-hsi = Lusi

Luhsien. Town, central China : Luchow (–1913)

Luichow see Hoihong

Luís Correia. City, northeastern Brazil, South America : Amarração (–1939)

Luki see Tzeki [Tz'u-ch'i]

Lukov. Urban settlement, Volyn Oblast, Ukraine : Matseyevo (–1946)

Lukowkiao *see* Wanping [Wan-ping]

Luling *see* Kian [Chi-an]

Luluabourg *see* Kananga

Lulung. Town, northeastern China : Yungping (–1913)

Lumangbayan. Barrio, Batangas, Philippines : Sambat (–1947)

Lumba Bayabao. Municipality, Lanao, Philippines : Maguing (–1956)

Lumbala *see* (1) Lumbala Kaquengue; (2) Lumbala Nguimbo

Lumbala Kaquengue. Village, eastern Angola, southwestern Africa : Lumbala (–c. 1979)

Lumbala Nguimbo. Town, southeastern Angola, southwestern Africa : Gago Coutinho (–c. 1976), Lumbala (c. 1976–c. 1979)

Lumege. Village, east-central Angola, southwestern Africa : Forte Cameia (–c. 1975), Lumeje (c. 1975–c. 1979)

Lumeje *see* Lumege

Luna (1). Municipality, Isabela, Philippines : Antatet (–1951)

Luna (2). Municipality, La Union, Philippines : Namacpacan (–1906)

Lunacharskoye *see* Ordzhonikidze (3)

Lundenburg *see* Břeclav

Lungan *see* Pingwu [P'ing-wu]

Lung-chi = Lungki

Lung-ching = Lungtsin

Lungchow *see* (1) Lunghsien; (2) Lungtsin [Lung-ching]

Lungchüan *see* Suichwan [Sui-ch'uan]

Lungchüanchen *see* Ian

Lung-hsi = Lungsi

Lunghsien. Town, central China : Lungchow (–1913)

Lunghwasze *see* Muchwan [Mu-ch'uan]

Lungki [Lung-ch'i]. Town, southeastern China : Changchow (–1913)

Lungkiang *see* Tsitsihar

Lung-kuan = Lungkwan

Lungkwan [Lung-kuan]. Town, northeastern China : Lungmen (–1914)

Lungmen *see* Lungkwan [Lung-kuan]

Lungping *see* Lungyao

Lungsheng. Town, northern China : Chotzeshan (–1949)

Lungshih *see* Ningkang

Lungsi [Lung-hsi]. Town, north-central China : Kungchang (–1913)

Lungsinhü *see* Yungyün

Lungtsin [Lung-ching]. Town, southern China : Lungchow (–1937)

Lungwusze *see* Tungjen [Tung-jen]

Lungyang *see* Hanshow [Hanshou]

Lungyao. Town, northeastern China : Lungping (–1949)

Luning. Village, southern China : Luningying (–1946)

Luningying *see* Luning

Lunino. Village, Kalinin-
grad Oblast, Russia :
Lengwethen (–1938),
Germany, Hohen-
salzburg (1938–45), Ger-
many
Lunyevka. Urban settle-
ment, Perm Oblast, Rus-
sia : Lunyevskiye Kopi
(–c. 1928)
Lunyevskiye Kopi *see*
Lunyevka
Luperón. Town, northern
Dominican Republic,
West Indies : Blanco
(–1927)
Lupiliche. Town, northwest-
ern Mozambique, south-
eastern Africa : Olivença
(–1980)
Lupin *see* Man-chou-li
Lusambo *see* Kasai
Lusanga. Town, southwest-
ern Zaïre, central Africa :
Leverville (–1972)
Lusavan *see* Charentsavan
Lushan. Town, southern
China : Tsingping (–1914)
Lushui. Village, southwest-
ern China : Luchang
(–1935)
Lüshun = Port Arthur
Lusi [Lu-hsi] (1). Town,
southwestern China :
Kwangsi (–1929)
Lusi [Lu-hsi] (2). Village,
southwestern China :
Mengka (–1935)
Luso *see* Luena
Lutgardita *see* General Peraza
Luting. Town, southern
China : Lutingkao
(–1913)
Lutingkao *see* Luting

Luttenberg *see* Ljutomer
Lutynia. Village, southwest-
ern Poland : Leuthen
(–1945), Germany
Lützin *see* Ludza
Luzhki *see* Chervonoye (2)
Luziânia. City, central Bra-
zil, South America :
Santa Luzia (–1945)
Luzilândia. City, northeast-
ern Brazil, South Amer-
ica : Pôrto Alegre (–1944)
Luzurriaga *see* Valencia
Lvov. Capital of Lvov Ob-
last, Ukraine : Lemberg
(–1919), Germany; Łwów
(1919–44), Poland
Łwów *see* Lvov
Łwówek. Town, western Po-
land : Neustadt (–1945),
Germany
Łwówek Śląski. Town,
southwestern Poland :
Löwenberg (–1945),
Germany
Lyakhovtsy *see* Belogorye
Lyall *see* Garson
Lyallpur *see* Faisalabad
Lyck *see* Ełk
Lydía. Village, northern
Greece : Hydrómyloi
(–1960s)
Lygoúrion. Village, south-
ern Greece : Ligourión
(–1960s)
Lykoudésion *see* Khrysikós
Lykóvryse *see* Lykóvrysis
Lykóvrysis. Village, central
Greece : Lykóvryse
(–1960s)
Lyndhurst. Township, New
Jersey, USA : Union
(–1917)
Lyttelton *see* Verwoerdburg

Lyubinsky. Urban settlement, Omsk Oblast, Russia : Novolyubino (–1947)
Lyudvipol see Sosnovoye
Lyuksemburg see (1) Bolnisi; (2) Rozovka
Lyuksemburgi see Bolnisi
Lyustdorf see Chernomorka

Mabini. Barrio, Davao, Philippines : Doña Alicia (–1954)
Macaloge. Town, northwestern Mozambique, southeastern Africa : Miranda (–1976)
Macapá see Peri Mirim
Macario Adriatico. Barrio, Mindoro Oriental, Philippines : Tubig (–1969)
MacArthur. City, Leyte, Philippines : Ormoc (–1950)
Macatuba. City, southeastern Brazil, South America : Bocaiúva (–1944)
Macaubal. Town, southeastern Brazil, South America : Macaúbas (–1944)
Macaúbas see Macaubal
Ma-chiang = Makiang
Macias. Barrio, Zamboanga, Philippines : Dinokot (–1968)
Macías Nguema Bijogo see (1) Bata; (2) Bioko; (3) Kope
Mackayville see Laflèche
Mackeim see Maków (Mazowiecki)
Mackenzie see Linden
MacLeod see Fort MacLeod
MacMahon see Aïn Touta
MacPherson see Kapuskasing

MacPherson's Point see Douglas Point
Madagascar. Island republic, southeastern Africa : Malagasy Republic (1960–75)
Madeleine, La = (La) Madeleine
Madhya Pradesh. State, central India : Central Provinces (–1947)
Madinat ash-Shab. Town, Yemen : Al-Ittihad (*1959–67)
Madniskhevi see Uchkulan
Madona. Town, Latvia : Birzhi (–1926)
Madras see Tamil Nadu
Madre de Deus see Brejo da Madre de Deus
Mafuteni see Mafutseni
Mafutseni. Town, central Swaziland, southern Africa : Mafuteni (–1976)
Magallanes see Punta Arenas
Magallon see Moises Padilla
Maghnia. Town, northwestern Algeria, northern Africa : Marnia (–c. 1962)
Magoúla. Village, eastern Greece : Phanárion Magoúla (–1960s)
Magsaysay. Municipality, Misamis Oriental, Philippines : Linugos (–1957)
Magu. District, northern Tanzania, eastern Africa : Mwanza (–1974)
Maguing see Lumba Bayabao
Maguntan-hama see Pugachyovo
Maha see Makiang [Ma-chian]
Mahabad. Town, northwestern Iran : Saujbulagh (–1930s)

Mahato. Municipality, Capiz, Philippines : Taft (–1917)

Mährisch-Budwitz see Moravské Budějovice

Mährisch-Kromau see Moravský Krumlov

Mährisch-Schönberg see Šumperk

Mährisch-Trübau see Moravská Třebová

Mährisch-Weisskirchen see Hranice

Mai-Ndombe, Lake. Western Zaïre, central Africa : Léopold II, Lake (–1972)

Mainfranken see Unterfranken

Mairipor. City, southeastern Brazil, South America : Juqueri (–1948)

Maison-Blanche see Dar el Beïda

Maison-Carrée see El-Harrach

Maisonnette. Town, New Brunswick, Canada : Ste. Jeanne d'Arc (–1936)

Major Isidoro. City, northeastern Brazil, South America : Sertãozinho (–1944)

Makanza. Town, northwestern Zaïre, central Africa : Nouvelle Anvers (–1972)

Makarov. Town, Sakhalin Oblast, Russia : Shiritoru (1905–46), Japan (–1945)

Makasar see Ujung Pandang

Makati. Municipality, Rizal, Philippines : San Pedro Macati (–1914)

Makeyevka. Town, Donetsk Oblast, Ukraine : Dmi-triyevsky (–1920), Dmitriyevsk (1920–31)

Makhachkala. Capital of Dagestan Autonomous Republic, Russia : Petrovsk-Port (–1921)

Makhambet. Village, Guryev Oblast, Kazakhstan : Yamankhalinka (–c. 1960)

Makharadze see Ozurgety

Makhnovka see Komsomolskoye (4)

Makiang [Ma-chiang]. Town, southern China : Maha (–1930)

Makin Island see Butaritari

Makinka see Makinsk

Makinsk. Town, Tselinograd Oblast, Kazakhstan : Makinka (*1928–44)

Maków (Mazowiecki). Town, east-central Poland : Mackeim (1939–45), Germany

Ma-kuan = Makwan

Makwan [Ma-kuan]. Town, southwestern China : Anping (–1914)

Malabo. Capital of Equatorial Guinea, western Africa : Santa Isabel (–1973)

Malabon see General Trias

Malabrigo see Puerto Chicama

Malafeyevichi see Vishnya (1)

Malagasy Republic see Madagascar

Malathriá see Díon

Malawi. Republic, southeastern Africa : British Central Africa (Protectorate) (1893–1907), Nyasaland (1891–93, 1907–64)

Malawi, Lake. Malawi/
Mozambique/Tanzania,
southeastern Africa :
Nyasa, Lake (–1965)
Malaya Dyatel see Lugovaya
(2)
Malbork. Town, northern
Poland : Marienburg
(–1945), Germany
Malebo Pool [name used in
Zaïre]. River Congo,
Congo/Zaïre, central
Africa : Stanley Pool
(–1972)
Malema. Town, north-cen-
tral Mozambique, south-
eastern Africa : Entre
Rios (1921–80)
Mali. Republic, northwest-
ern Africa : French Sudan
(*1890–99, 1920–58), Up-
per Senegal and Niger
Territory (1899–1902),
Senegambia and Niger
Territories (1902–04),
Upper Senegal and Niger
Colony (1904–20), Suda-
nese Republic (1958–60)
Malinovoye Ozero. Urban
settlement, Altay Kray,
Russia : Mikhaylovsky
(–c. 1960)
Malirong see Libertad (2)
Mallwen see Mayskoye (2)
Mallwischken see Mayskoye
(2)
Malodolinskoye. Health re-
sort, Odessa Oblast,
Ukraine : Klein-Lieben-
tal (–?)
Malokurilskoye. Village,
Kuril Islands, Sakhalin
Oblast, Russia : Shakotan
(1905–45), Japan

Malomalsk see Glubokaya
Małujowice. Village, south-
western Poland : Moll-
witz (–1945), Germany
Maluko see Manolo Fortich
Malusak see Narra (2)
Malvérnia see Chicualacuala
Maly Taymyr. Island,
Laptev Sea, Krasnoyarsk
Kray, Russia : Tsarevicha
Alekseya (*1913–c. 1918)
Mambiliama Falls. Town,
northwestern Zambia,
south-central Africa :
Johnston Falls (–1976)
Mamonovo. Town, Kalinin-
grad Oblast, Russia :
Heiligenbeil (–1946),
Germany (–1945)
Manawan see Rizal (1)
Man-chou-li. City, northern
China : Lupin (1913–49)
Mandala, Puncak. Moun-
tain, Irian Jaya, Indone-
sia : Juliana Top (–1963)
Mandidzuzure see Chimani-
mani
Mandigos see Manica (1)
Mandrenska see Sredecka
Mangin see El Braya
Mangli see Kiangcheng [Chi-
ang-cheng]
Mangniuyingtze see Tsingping
[Ching-ping]
Mangoche. Town, southern
Malawi, southeastern
Africa : Fort Johnston
(–c. 1966)
Manguaba see Pilar
Mangula see Mhangura
Mangush see Pershotrav-
nevoye (1)
Manica (1). City, west-cen-
tral Mozambique, south-

eastern Africa : Mandigos (–1916), Vila Pery (1916–76)

Manica (2). Province, southwestern Mozambique, southeastern Africa : Vila Pery (–1976)

Manissobal. City, eastern Brazil, South America : Belmonte (–1944)

Mankaiana see Mankayane

Mankayane. Town, western Swaziland, southern Africa : Mankaiana (–1976)

Manning. Town, southeastern China : Wanchow (–1912)

Manolo Fortich. Municipality, Bukidnon, Philippines : Maluko (–1957)

Manra. Island, Kiribati, western Pacific : Sydney Island (–1981)

Mansa. Town, northern Zambia, south-central Africa : Fort Rosebery (–1967)

Manta. City, western Ecuador, South America : San Pablo de Manta (–1965)

Manuel Urbano. Town, western Brazil, South America : Castelo (–1944)

Manyas Gölü see Kuş Göle

Manzini. Town, central Swaziland, southeastern Africa : Bremersdorp (–1960)

Manzovka see Sibirtsevo

Mao. City, northwestern Dominican Republic, West Indies : Valverde (–1959)

Maohsien = Mowhsien

Maoka see Kholmsk

Maomu see Tingsin [Ting-hsin]

Maputo. Capital of Mozambique, southeastern Africa : Lourenço Marques (–1976)

Maraak [Meraak, Merok] see Geiranger

Maraisburg see Hofmeyr

Marandellas see Marondera

Marão. Town, southeastern Mozambique, southeastern Africa : Mau-é-ele (–1980)

Marathonisi see Gýtheion

Marawi. City, Mindanao, Philippines : Dansalan (–?)

Marayskoye see Mostovskoye

Marburg see Maribor

Marchand see Rommani

Marechal Deodoro. City, northeastern Brazil, South America : Alagoas (–1939)

Marechal Floriano see Piranhas

Marele-Voevod-Mihai see Februarie 16, 1933

Marengo see Hadjout

Marganets. Town, Dnepropetrovsk Oblast, Ukraine : Gorodishche (–c. 1926), Komintern (c. 1926–40)

Marganets see Dzhezdy

Marggrabowa see Olecko

Margilan. Town, Fergana Oblast, Uzbekistan : Stary Margilan : (–1907)

Mari. Town, northeastern Brazil, South America : Araçá (–1944)

Mariano Machado *see* Ganda
Mariánské Lázně. Town,
western Czech Lands :
Marienbad (–1918, 1939–
45), Germany
Maria Pereira *see* Mombaça
Maria Rast *see* Ruše
Maria Theresiopel *see* Subot-
ica
Mari Autonomous Oblast *see*
Mari Autonomous Re-
public
Mari Autonomous Republic.
West-central Russia :
Mari Autonomous Oblast
(*1920–36), Mari Auton-
omous SSR (1936–91)
Mari Autonomous SSR *see*
Mari Autonomous Re-
public
Maribor. City, northeastern
Slovenia : Marburg
(–1918), Germany
Maricourt. Town, Quebec,
Canada : Wakeham Bay
(–1967)
Marie Byrd Land *see* Byrd
Land
Marienbad *see* Mariánské Lá-
zně
Marienburg *see* (1) Alūksne;
(2) Malbork
Marienhausen *see* Viljaka
Marienhof *see* Nikitovka
Mariental *see* Sovetskoye (4)
Marienwerder *see* Kwidzyn
Marihatag. Municipality,
Surigao, Philippines :
Oteiza (–1955)
Mariinskoye *see* Maryevka
Mariinsk Water System *see*
Volga-Baltic Waterway
Marijampolė. Town, Lithua-
nia : Kapsukas (1955–89)

Marino *see* Leninsky (3)
Marino Alejandro Selkirk *see*
Robinson Crusoe
Mariscal Estigarribia. Vil-
lage, northern Para-
guay, South America :
López de Filippis
(–1945)
Mariupol. Town, Donetsk
Oblast, Ukraine :
Zhdanov (1948–89)
Marivan. Town, northwest-
ern Iran : Dezh-i-Shahpur
(–1980)
Markhamat. Town, An-
dizhan Oblast, Uzbeki-
stan : Russkoye Selo
(–1974)
Markhlevsk *see* Dovbysh
Märkisch Buchholz. Town,
northeastern Germany :
Wendisch Buchholz
(–1937)
Märkisch Friedland *see* Miros-
kawiec
Markovo. Urban settlement,
Ivanovo Oblast, Russia :
Markovo-Sbornoye
(–1940)
Markovo-Sbornoye *see*
Markovo
Marks. Town, Saratov Ob-
last, Russia : Yekater-
inenshtadt [Baronsk]
(–1920), Marksshtadt
(1920–41)
Marksshtadt *see* Marks
Marneuli. Town, Georgia :
Borchalo (–1964)
Marnia *see* Maghnia
Marondera. Town, east-
central Zimbabwe,
southeastern Africa :
Marandellas (–1982)

Marquês de Valença. City,
southeastern Brazil,
South America : Valença
(–1943)
Marracuene. Town, south-
ern Mozambique, south-
eastern Africa : Vila
Luísa (–1980)
Marruás see Pôrto
Marshallville see Lewisporte
Marshfield see Coos Bay
Martil. Village, northern
Morocco, northwestern
Africa : Rio-Martin
(–c. 1959)
Martimprey-du-Kiss see Ahfir
Martvili. Town, Georgia :
Gegechkori (1939–91)
Martynovka see Bolshaya
Martynovka
Martynovskoye see Bolshaya
Martynovka
Martyshki see Beryozy
Marvão see Castelo do Piauí
Marxwalde see Neu Harden-
berg
Mary. Capital of Mary Ob-
last, Turkmenistan :
Merv (–1937)
Maryborough see Port Laoise
Maryevka. Village, North
Kazakhstan Oblast, Ka-
zakhstan : Mariinskoye
(–1939)
Maryino see Pristen
Más Afuera see Alejandro
Selkirk
Más a Tierra see Robinson
Crusoe
Mashaba see Mashava
Mashava. Village, south-
central Zimbabwe, south-
eastern Africa : Mashaba
(–1982)

Masi. Barrio, Cagayan, Phil-
ippines : Zimigui-
Ziwanan (–1957)
Masimpur see Arunachal
Massa-Carrara. Province,
central Italy : Apuanina
(*1938–45)
Massawa [Mitsiwa]. Admin-
istrative division, Eritrea,
northeastern Ethiopia,
northeastern Africa :
Bassopiano Orientale
(–1941)
Massingire see Morrumbala
Massow see Maszewo
Massy see Lenin-Dzhol
Mastanli see Momchilgrad
Masteksay see Leninskoye (5)
Masulipat(n)am. Town,
southeastern India : Ban-
dar (–1949)
Masvingo. Town, southeast-
ern Zimbabwe, southeast-
ern Africa : Fort Victoria
(–1980), Nyande (1980–
82)
Maszewo. Town, northwest-
ern Poland : Massow
(–1945), Germany
Mata Grande. City, north-
eastern Brazil, South
America : Paulo Affonso
(–1939)
Mataúna see Palmeiras de
Goiás
Mati see President Roxas
Matões see Parnarama
Matrosovo. Village, Kalinin-
grad Oblast, Russia : Ug-
gehnen (–1946), Ger-
many (–1945)
Matseyevo see Lukov
Matsubara see Takahagi
Mau-é-ele see Marão

Mauritania. Republic, northwestern Africa : Trarza (–1903)

Mauritius, Cape *see* Zhelaniya, Cape

Mavabo. Village, northwestern Mozambique, southeastern Africa : Valadim (–1976)

Maxambamba *see* Nova Iguaçu

Maxesibeni. Town, northern Transkei, southern Africa : Mount Aycliff (–1976)

Maxwell *see* Brights Grove

Mayachnaya. Village, Minsk Oblast, Belorussia : Porosyatniki (–1964)

Mayakovsky *see* Bagdadi

Mayak-Salyn *see* Primorskoye (1)

Mayli-Su *see* Kok-Tash

Maymachen *see* Altanbulak

Mayo. Town, Yukon, Canada : Mayo Landing (–1958)

Mayo Landing *see* Mayo

Maysan. Province, eastern Iraq : Amara (–1971)

Maysk (1). Village, Minsk Oblast, Belorussia : Panskoye (–1964)

Maysk (2). Village, Mogilyov Oblast, Belorussia : Pupsa (–1964)

Mayskaya. Village, Gomel Oblast, Belorussia : Lapti (–1964)

Mayskoye (1). Village, Vitebsk Oblast, Belorussia : Lizuny (–1964)

Mayskoye (2). Village, Kaliningrad Oblast, Russia :

Mallwischken (–1938), Germany, Mallwen (1938–46), Germany (–1945)

Mayskoye (3). Village, Gomel Oblast, Belorussia : Shapilovo (–1964)

Mazagan *see* El-Jadida

Mazsalača. Town, Latvia : Salisburg (–1917)

Mažeikiai. Town, Lithuania : Muravyov (1901–17)

Mazoe *see* Mazowe

Mazowe. Village, northern Zimbabwe, southeastern Africa : Mazoe (–1983)

Mbala. Town, northern Zambia, south-central Africa : Abercorn (–1967)

Mbalambala. Town, southern Zimbabwe, southeastern Africa : Balla Balla (–1982)

Mbandaka. Town, northeastern Zaïre, central Africa : Coquilhatville (–1966)

Mbanza Congo. Town, northern Angola, southwestern Africa : São Salvador (do Congo) (–c. 1976)

Mbanza-Ngungu. Town, western Zaïre, central Africa : Thysville (–1966), Songololo (1966–72)

Mberengwa. Village, southern Zimbabwe, southeastern Africa : Belingwe (–1982)

Mbini. River, Río Muni, Equatorial Guinea, western Africa : Río Benito (–1974)

Mbuji-Mayi. City, southern
Zaïre, central Africa :
Bakwanga (–1966)
McHattiesburg see Balfour
Mchinji. Town, west-central
Malawi, southeastern Af-
rica : Fort Manning
(–c. 1966)
McKinley, Mount. Moun-
tain, Antarctica : Grace
McKinley, Mount
(–1967)
Mdiq. Village, northern Mo-
rocco, northwestern Af-
rica : Rincon (–c. 1959)
Mechanicsham see Gretna
Mechtal see Miechowice
Mecseknádasd. Town,
southern Hungary : Pü-
spöknádasd (–1950)
Meddouza. Cape, western
Morocco, northwestern
Africa : Cantin, Cap
(–1970)
Mednogorsk. Town, Oren-
burg Oblast, Russia :
Medny (*1938–39)
Medny see Mednogorsk
Medveditskoye see Linyovo
Medvezhye see Krasnog-
vardeyskoye (3)
Medvode. Village, western
Slovenia : Zwischen-
wässern (–1918), Ger-
many
Meftah. Village, northern
Algeria, northern Africa :
Rivet (–c. 1962)
Megrut see Gugark
Mehlauken see Zalesye
Meihsien. Town, southeast-
ern China : Kaying
(–1912)
Mekhomiya see Razlog

Meknès-La Touraine see
Meknès Saada
Meknès l'Oasis see El Ba-
satine
Meknès-Plaisance see El Men-
zel
Meknès Saada. Village,
northern Morocco, north-
western Africa : Meknès-
La Touraine (–c. 1959)
Melanie Damishana. Vil-
lage, northern Guyana,
South America : Eliza-
beth Hall (–1975)
Meléa see Káto Meléa
Melekess see Dimitrovgrad (2)
Melfort. Town, Saskatche-
wan, Canada : Stoney
Creek (–1904)
Mellah Sidi Brahim. Vil-
lage, northwestern
Morocco, northwestern
Africa : Aviateur-
Lécrivain (–c. 1959)
Melqa el Ouidane. Village,
northern Morocco, north-
western Africa : Camp
Bertaux (–c. 1959)
Melsetter see Chimanimani
Memel see Klaipėda
Mendeleyevsk. Town, Tatar
Autonomous Republic,
Russia : Bondyuzhsky
Zavod (–c.1940), Bon-
dyuzhsky (c. 1920–67)
Ménerville see Thenia
Menghai see Fohai
Mengka see Lusi [Lu-hsi] (2)
Mengkiang see Tsingyü
[Ching-yü]
Mengshan. Town, southern
China : Yungan (–1914)
Mengwang see Ningkiang
[Ning-chiang]

Menongue. Town, south-central Angola, southwestern Africa : Serpa Pinto (–c. 1976)

Menthon see Menthon-Saint-Bernard

Menthon-Saint-Bernard. Village, southeastern France : Menthon (–1943)

Menzeh-Ifrane. Town, north-central Morocco, northwestern Africa : Val d'Ifrane (–c. 1959)

Menzel-Bourguiba. Town, northern Tunisia, northern Africa : Ferryville (–c. 1963)

Meraak see Geiranger

Meriti see São João de Meriti

Merok see Geiranger

Merouana. Village, northeastern Algeria, northern Africa : Corneille (–c. 1962)

Merritt. Town, British Columbia, Canada : The Forks (*1906–11)

Merv see Mary

Mése. Village, northeastern Greece : Pagoúria (–1960s)

Mesembria see Nesebar

Mesemvriya see Nesebar

Meseritz see Międzyrzecz

Meshkhede-Ser see Babolser

Mestia. Village, Georgia : Seti (–c. 1955)

Mestre Caetano. Town, southeastern Brazil, South America : Cuiabá (–1944)

Metamórphosis. Village, southern Greece : Katavóthra (–1960s)

Metangula. Town, northwestern Mozambique, southeastern Africa : Augusto Cardosa (1963–80)

Methánon see Loutrópolis Methánon

Metlika. Village, southern Slovenia : Möttling (–1918), Germany

Meyer's Ferry see Surfer's Paradise

Meylieu-Montrond see Montrond-les-Bains

Mezhdurechensk (1). Town, Kemerovo Oblast, Russia : Olzheras (–1955)

Mezhdurechensk (2). Urban settlement, Samara Oblast, Russia : Perevoloki (–?)

Mezhdurechye see Shali

Mezhevaya Ukta see Sinegorsky

Mezőfalva. Town, west-central Hungary : Hercegfalva (–1951)

Mezőszilas. Town, west-central Hungary : Szilasbalhás (–1942)

Mhangura. Village, northern Zimbabwe, southeastern Africa : Mangula (–1982)

Miami see Mwami

Miami Shores see North Miami

Miami Springs. Town, Florida, USA : Country Club Estates (*1926–30)

Miastko. Town, northwestern Poland : Rummelsburg (–1945), Germany

Michelet see Aïn el Hammam

Miches. Town, east Dominican Republic, West Indies : El Jovero (–1936)

Michurin. Town, southeastern Bulgaria : Vasiliko (–1934), Tsarevo (1934–50)

Michurinsk. Town, Tambov Oblast, Russia : Kozlov (–1932)

Middle Congo see Congo

Middleton see Doonside

Middle Volga Kray see Samara Oblast

Middle Volga Oblast see Samara Oblast

Mid-Western (State) see Bendel

Mid-West Region see Bendel

Miechowice. Town, southern Poland : Mechtal (–1945), Germany

Międzybórz. Town, southwestern Poland : Neumittelwalde (–1945), Germany

Międzylesie. Town, southwestern Poland : Mittelwalde (–1945), Germany

Międzyrzecz. Town, western Poland : Meseritz (–1945), Germany

Międzyzdroje. Town, northwestern Poland : Misdroy (–1945), Germany

Mielau see Mława

Mieroszów. Town, southwestern Poland : Friedland (–1945), Germany

Mies see Stříbro

Miguel Calmon. City, eastern Brazil, South America : Djalma Dutra (1939–44)

Mihidjan see Chittaranjan

Mikasa. Town, west-central Hokkaido, Japan : Mikasayama (–early 1940s)

Mikasayama see Mikasa

Mikhailovgrad. City, northwestern Bulgaria : Ferdinand (–1945)

Mikhailovo-Semyonovskoye see Leninskoye (6)

Mikhalpol see Mikhaylovka

Mikha Tskhakaya see Senaki

Mikhaylo-Kotsyubinskoye. Urban settlement, Chernigov Oblast, Ukraine : Kozyol (–c. 1935)

Mikhaylovka. Village, Khmelnitsky Oblast, Ukraine : Mikhalpol (–1946)

Mikhaylovka see Kimovsk

Mikhaylovsk. Town, Sverdlovsk Oblast, Russia : Mikhaylovsky Zavod (–1942)

Mikhaylovskoye see Shpakovskoye

Mikhaylovsky see Malinovoye Ozero

Mikhaylovsky Zavod see Mikhaylovsk

Mikoyan see Yekhegnadzor

Mikoyana, imeni see Kara-Balty

Mikoyanabad see Tartki

Mikoyan-Shakhar see Karachayevsk

Mikulczyce. Town, southern Poland : Mikultschütz (–1935), Germany, Klausberg (1935–45), Germany

Mikulov. Town, southeastern Czech Lands : Ni-

kolsburg (–1918, 1939–
45), Germany
Mikultschütz *see* Mikulczyce
Mikuriya *see* Shin-mikuriya
Milenino *see* Priupsky
Milevsko. Town, west-cen-
tral Czech Lands : Mühl-
hausen (–1918, 1939–45),
Germany
Milicz. Town, southwestern
Poland : Militsch (–1945),
Germany
Militsch *see* Milicz
Millares. Town, south-
central Bolivia, South
America : Llanta
Apacheta (–1900s)
Millersburg *see* Pierron
Mimoso do Sul. City, south-
eastern Brazil, South
America : João Pessoa
(–1944)
Minami-nayoshi *see* Shebunino
Minami-oji *see* Yasaka
Min-ch'in = Mintsin
Minchow *see* Minhsien
Mindanao and Sulu. Depart-
ment, Philippines : Moro
(–1913)
Mineiros *see* Mineiros do Ti-
etê
Mineiros do Tietê. City,
southeastern Brazil,
South America : Mineiros
(–1944)
Ming-ch'i = Mingki
Mingki [Ming-ch'i]. Town,
southeastern China :
Kweihwa (–1933)
Mingshui. Town, northeast-
ern China : Hinglungchen
(–1929)
Mingshui *see* Changkiu
[Chang-chiu]

Minho. Town, northwestern
China : Chwankow
(–1933)
Minhow *see* Foochow
[Fuchow, Fu-chou]
Minhsien. Town, north-
central China : Minchow
(–1913)
Minlo. Town, north-central
China : Hungshui (–1933)
Minnedosa. River, Mani-
toba, Canada : Little Sas-
katchewan (–1928)
Mintsin [Min-chin]. Town,
north-central China :
Chenfan (–1928)
Minyar. Town, Chelya-
binsk Oblast, Russia :
Minyarsky Zavod
(–c. 1928)
Minyarsky Zavod *see* Minyar
Mirabeau *see* Draâ Ben
Khedda
Mirabel. City, Quebec, Can-
ada : Sainte-Scholastique
(–1973)
Miracatu. City, southeast-
ern Brazil, South Amer-
ica : Prainha (–1944)
Miracema *see* Miracema do
Norte
Miracema do Norte. City,
north-central Brazil,
South America :
Miracema (–1944),
Cherente (1944–48)
Mirada Hills *see* La Mirada
Miraflores *see* Rovira
Miramar *see* El Harhouba
Miranda *see* Macaloge
Mirandópolis. City, south-
eastern Brazil, South
America : Comandante
Arbues (–1944)

Mir-Bashir. Town, Azerbaijan : Terter (–1949)

Mirnaya (1). Village, Minsk Oblast, Belorussia : Glod (–1964)

Mirnaya (2). Village, Mogilyov Oblast, Belorussia : Glupiki (–1964)

Mirnaya (3). Village, Vitebsk Oblast, Belorussia : Khudeni (–1964)

Mirnaya (4). Village, Grodno Oblast, Belorussia : Trebushki (–1964)

Mirnoye (1). Village, Gomel Oblast, Belorussia : Mogilnoye (–1964)

Mirnoye (2). Settlement, Dnepropetrovsk Oblast, Ukraine : Zhyoltyye Vody (–c. 1960)

Mirny. Village, Magadan Oblast, Russia : Stakhanovets (–c. 1960)

Míron. Village, southern Greece : Moíras (–1960s)

Mirosławiec. Town, northwestern Poland : Märkisch Friedland (–1945), Germany

Mirsk. Town, southwestern Poland : Friedeberg (–1945), Germany

Mirzachul see Gulistan

Mirzoyan see Dzhambul

Misamis see Ozamis

Misdroy see Międzyzdroje

Misericordia see Itaporanga

Misery, Mount see Rangoon Heights

Mishih see Ningtung

Mission City. Town, British Columbia, Canada : Mission Junction (–1922)

Mission Junction see Mission City

Mitake see Tsuya

Mitava see Jelgava

Mitkino see Krasnooktyabrsky (2)

Mitrowitz see Sremska Mitrovica

Mitsang [Mi-ts'ang]. Town, northern China : Santaokiao (–1942)

Mitsiwa = Massawa

(Mittel) Schreiberhau see Szklarska Poręba

Mittelwalde see Międzylesie

Mizo Hills see Mizoram

Mizoram. Union territory, northeastern India : Mizo Hills (–1972)

Mizur. Urban settlement, North Ossetian Autonomous Republic, Russia : Mizursky (–1981)

Mizursky see Mizur

Mladá Boleslav. City, northern Czech Lands: Jungbunzlau (–1918, 1939–45), Germany

Mladá Vožice. Town, central Czech Lands : Jungwoschitz (–1918, 1939–45), Germany

Mława. Town, northeastern Poland : Mielau (1939–45), Germany

Mobayembongo. Town, northern Zaïre, central Africa : Banzyville (–1972)

Mobutu Sese Seko, Lake : Zaïre/Uganda, central Africa : Albert, Lake (–1973)

Močâmedes see Namibe

Mocha *see* Chapayevka

Mo-chiang = Mokiang

Mochu *see* Shwangpo [Shu-ang-po]

Modderfontein *see* Niekerk-shoop

Modlin. Village, east-central Poland : Novogeorgiyevsk (1815–1919), Russia

Moerbeke *see* Kwilu-Ngongo

Mogador *see* Essaouira

Mogilnoye *see* Mirnoye (1)

Mohammadia. Town, north-western Algeria, north-ern Africa : Perrégaux (–c. 1962)

Mohammedia. City, north-western Morocco, north-western Africa : Fédala (–c. 1959)

Mohammerah *see* Khorram-shahr

Mohrin *see* Moryń

Moíras *see* Míron

Moi's Bridge. Village, west-ern Kenya, eastern Af-rica : Hoey's Bridge (–1975)

Moises Padilla. Municipal-ity, Negros Occidental, Philippines : Magallon (–1957)

Mokiang [Mo-chiang]. Town, southwestern China : Talang (–1916)

Mokvin *see* Pershotravnevoye (2)

Moldavia. Republic, south-eastern Europe : Molda-vian Autonomous SSR (*1924–40), Moldavian SSR (1940–90)

Moldavian Autonomous SSR *see* Moldavia

Moldavian SSR *see* Moldavia

Mole Hill *see* Mountain

Molière *see* Bordj Bounaama

Molles *see* Carlos Reyles

Mollet *see* San Juan de Mollet

Mollwitz *see* Małujowice

Molodechno. Town, Minsk Oblast, Belorussia : Molodeczno (1919–39), Poland

Molodeczno *see* Molodechno

Molotov *see* (1) Arktichesky; (2) Perm

Molotovabad *see* Uch-Korgon

Molotova, imeni *see* Uch-kupryuk

Molotova, V.M., imeni *see* Oktyabrsky (6)

Molotovo *see* (1) Oktyabrskoye (2); (2) Pristanskoye; (3) Uch-kupryuk

Molotov Oblast *see* Perm Ob-last

Molotov, Peak *see* Moskva, Peak

Molotovsk *see* (1) Kaindy; (2) Nolinsk; (3) Severodvinsk

Molotovskoye *see* Krasnog-vardeyskoye (3)

Molvitino *see* Susanino

Mombaça. City, northeast-ern Brazil, South Amer-ica : Maria Pereira (–1944)

Momchilgrad. City, south-ern Bulgaria : Mastanli (–1934)

Mona. Locality, Manitoba, Canada : Mulvihill (–1930)

Monastir *see* Bitola

Monastyr *see* Sosnovets

Moncha-Guba *see* Mon-chegorsk

Monchegorsk. Town, Murmansk Oblast, Russia :
Moncha-Guba (–1937)

Mönchengladbach. City, western Germany :
München-Gladbach (–1950)

Monda *see* Agnew

Mondino *see* Cheryomushki (1)

Moneron. Island, Sea of Japan, Sakhalin Oblast, Russia : Kaiba-tu (1905–45), Japan

Monfestino in Serra Mazzoni *see* Serramazzoni

Mongalla *see* Equatoria

Monod *see* Sidi Allal Bahraoui

Monoikon *see* Hágion Pneúma

Monroeville. Borough, Pennsylvania, USA : Patton (–1951)

Monsanto *see* Monte Santo de Minas

Monschau. Town, western Germany : Montjoie (–1920s)

Montagnac *see* Remchi

Montagne de la Grande Traverse *see* Edith Cavell, Mount

Montañana *see* Puente de Montañana

Monte Alegre *see* Timbiras

Monte Azul. City, southeastern Brazil, South America : Tremedal (–1939)

Monte Azul *see* Monte Azul Paulista

Monte Azul do Turvo *see* Monte Azul Paulista

Monte Azul Paulista. City, southeastern Brazil,
South America : Monte Azul (–1944), Monte Azul do Turvo (1944–48)

Montebello. City, California, USA : Newmark (–1916), Monterey Park (1916–20)

Montejo de Liceras *see* Montejo de Tiermes

Montejo de Tiermes. Village, north-central Spain : Montejo de Liceras (–c. 1950)

Monteleone di Calabria *see* Vibo Valentia

Montenegro. City, southern Brazil, South America : São João de Montenegro (–1930s)

Monte Nevoso *see* Snežnik

Monte Oscuro *see* La Unión

Monterey Park *see* Montebello

Monterrubio de Demanda. Village, northern Spain : Monterrubio de la Sierra (–c. 1920)

Monterrubio de la Sierra *see* Monterrubio de Demanda

Monte San Giuliano *see* Erice

Monte Santo de Minas. City, southeastern Brazil, South America : Monsanto (1944–48)

Montes de Toledo. Mountain range, south-central Spain : Cordillera Oretana (–c. 1960)

Monte Trujillo *see* Duarte, Pico

Montferri. Village, eastern Spain : Puigtiñós (–c. 1920)

Montgolfier *see* Rahouia

Montgomery *see* Sahiwal

Montjoie *see* Monschau

Montrond-les-Bains. Village,
east-central France :
Meylieu-Montrond
(–1937)

Moodyville *see* North Vancouver

Mook *see* Van Stadensrus

Mórahalom. Town, southeastern Hungary :
Alsóközpont (*1950)

Moravská Třebová. Town,
east-central Czech Lands :
Mährisch-Trübau
(–1918, 1939–45),
Germany

Moravské Budějovice. Town,
southern Czech Lands :
Mährisch-Budwitz
(–1918, 1939–45),
Germany

Moravský Beroun. Town,
eastern Czech Lands :
Bärn (–1918, 1939–45),
Germany

Moravský Krumlov. Town,
southeastern Czech
Lands : Mährisch-
Kromau (–1918, 1939–
45), Germany

Mordovian Autonomous
Oblast *see* Mordovian
Autonomous Republic

Mordovian Autonomous Republic [Mordvinian Autonomous Republic].
West-central Russia :
Mordovian Okrug
(*1928–30), Mordovian
Autonomous Oblast
(1930–34) Mordovian
SSR (1934–91)

Mordovian Okrug *see* Mordovian Autonomous Republic

Mordovian SSR *see* Mordovian
Autonomous Republic

Mordovskaya Bokla *see* Sovetskoye (5)

Mordvinian Autonomous Republic = Mordovian Autonomous Republic

Møre *see* Møre og Romsdal

Møre og Romsdal. County,
western Norway : Romsdal (–1918), Møre (1918–
35)

Moro *see* Mindanao and Sulu

Moron *see* Morong

Morón. City, east-central
Argentina, South America : Seis de Septiembre
(1930–43)

Morong. Municipality, Bataan, Philippines : Moron
(–1955)

Morozov. Mountain, central
Bulgaria : Goljam Bratan
(–1967)

Morozovsk. Town, Rostov
Oblast, Russia :
Morozovskaya (–1941)

Morozovskaya *see* Morozovsk

Morro Grande *see* Baro de
Cocais

Morrumbala. Town, central
Mozambique, southeastern Africa : Massingire
(–1945)

Moryń. Town, northwestern
Poland : Mohrin (–1945),
Germany

Moscow Canal. Linking
Moskva and Volga Rivers, Russia : Moscow-
Volga Canal (*1932–47)

Moscow Oblast. Western Russia : Central Industrial Oblast (*1929)

Moscow-Volga Canal *see* Moscow Canal

Moses Lake. City, Washington, USA : Neppel (*1910–38)

Mosi-oa-Toenja (1). Town, southern Zambia, south-central Africa : Livingstone (–c. 1970)

Mosi-oa-Toenja (2). Province, southern Zambia, south-central Africa : Victoria Falls (–1970)

Moskovsk. Urban settlement, Chardzhou Oblast, Turkmenistan : Buyun-Uzun (–c. 1960)

Moskovsky. Urban settlement, Khatlon Oblast, Tajikistan : Chubek (–c. 1960)

Moskovsky *see* Shakhrikhan

Moskva, Peak. Mountain, northwestern Pamirs, Tajikistan : Molotov, Peak (?–c. 1957), Moskva-Pekin, Peak (c. 1957–?)

Moskva-Pekin, Peak *see* Moskva, Peak

Mosquito Creek *see* Nanton

Mostovskoye. Village, Kurgan Oblast, Russia : Marayskoye (–c. 1960)

Mosty Wielkie *see* Velikiye Mosty

Mosul *see* Ninawa

Motodomari *see* Vostochny

Möttling *see* Metlika

Mouhoun. River, Burkina Faso, western Africa : Volta Noire (–1986)

Mountain. Town, Virginia, USA : Mole Hill (–?)

Mount Ayliff *see* Maxesibeni

Mount Frere *see* Kwabhaca

Mount McKinley National Park *see* Denali National Park

Mount Margaret *see* Longonot

Mount Pearl. Suburb of St. Johns, Newfoundland, Canada : Mount Pearl Park-Glendale (1955–58)

Mount Pearl Park-Glendale *see* Mount Pearl

Mount Shasta (City). Town, California, USA : Sisson (–1925)

Mou-pi'ing = Mowping

Mowchow *see* Mowhsien [Maohsien]

Mowhsien [Maohsien]. Town, central China : Mowchow (–1913)

Mowming. Town, southeastern China : Kochow [Kaochow] (–1912)

Mowping [Mou-p'ing]. Town, eastern China : Ninghai (–1914)

Moyen-Congo *see* Congo

Mozambique. Republic, southeastern Africa : Portuguese East Africa (–1975)

Mozhaysky. Urban settlement, Leningrad Oblast, Russia : Dudergof (–1944), Nagornoye (1944–?)

Mozhga. Town, Udmurt Autonomous Republic, Russia : Syuginsky (–c. 1920), Krasny (c. 1920–26)

Mozirje. Village, western
Slovenia : Prassberg
(–1918), Germany
Mpásion *see* Drosopegé
Mrewa *see* Murewa
Mrkonić-Grad. Village, cen-
tral Bosnia-Herzegovina :
Varcar Vukuf
(–1930s)
Mtepatepa *see* Mutepatepa
Mtoko *see* Mutoko
Mtorashanga *see*
Mutorashanga
Mu-ch'uan = Muchwan
Muchwan [Mu-ch'uan].
Town, central China :
Lunghwasze (–1930)
Muela *see* Villa Rivero
Muende. Town, northwest-
ern Mozambique, south-
eastern Africa : Vila Cal-
das Xavier (–1980)
Muheza. District, northeast-
ern Tanzania, eastern
Africa : Tanga (–1974)
Mühlhausen *see* Milevsko
Muine Bheag. Town, County
Carlow, Ireland : Bage-
nalstown (–?)
Mukden *see* Shen-yang
Mukhtuya *see* Lensk
Mukiaying *see* Sichi [Hsi-chi]
Muli *see* Vysokogorny
Mulungu. Town, northeast-
ern Brazil, South Amer-
ica : Camarazal (1944–48)
Mulvihill *see* Mona
Muminabad *see* Leningrad-
sky
München-Gladbach *see*
Mönchengladbach
Mundelein. Suburb of Chi-
cago, Illinois, USA :
Area (*1909–25)

Mundo Novo. City, south-
eastern Brazil, South
America : Urupês
(1944–?)
Munster *see* Voortrekker-
strand
Münsterberg *see* Ziębice
Muping *see* Paohing [Pao-
hsing]
Muqui. City, southeastern
Brazil, South America :
São João do Muqui
(–1944)
Muranga. Town, south-cen-
tral Kenya, eastern Af-
rica : Fort Hall (–1975)
Murat Bay *see* Ceduna
Muravyov *see* Mažeikiai
Muravyovsky *see* Korsakov
Murchison Falls *see* Kabarega
Falls
Murchison Falls National Park
see Kabarega National
Park
Murewa. Village, eastern
Zimbabwe, southeastern
Africa : Mrewa (–1982)
Murgab. Village, Gorno-
Badakhshan Autono-
mous Oblast, Tajikistan :
Pamirsky Post (–c. 1929)
Murmansk. Capital of Mur-
mansk Oblast, Russia :
Romanov-na-Murmane
(–1917)
Murotozaki. Town, south-
ern Shikoku, Japan :
Tsuro (–1929)
Murphy's Station *see* Sun-
nyvale
Murtala Muhammad Air-
port. Southwestern Ni-
geria, western Africa :
Lagos Airport (–1977)

Musala. Mountain, south-
western Bulgaria : Stalin,
Peak (1949–?)
Muscat and Oman *see* Oman
Mussolinia di Sardegna *see*
Arborea
Mustafa Kemal Paşa. Town,
northwestern Turkey :
Kirmasti (-?)
Mustayevka *see* Mustayevo
Mustayevo. Village,
Orenburg Oblast, Russia
: Mustayevka (–c. 1940)
Mutare. Town, eastern Zim-
babwe, southeastern Af-
rica : Umtali (–1982)
Mutepatepa. Village, north-
ern Zimbabwe, southeast-
ern Africa : Mtepatepa
(–1983)
Mutoko. Village, northeast-
ern Zimbabwe, southeast-
ern Africa : Mtoko
(–1982)
Mutorashanga. Village,
northern Zimbabwe,
southeastern Africa :
Mtorashanga (–1982)
Mutum. City, southeastern
Brazil, South America :
São Manuel do Mutum
(–1939)
Muxaluando. Town, south-
ern Angola, southwestern
Africa : General Freire
(–c. 1976)
Muyupampa *see* Vaca
Guzmán
Muzhichi *see* Pervomayskoye
(6)
Muzhichok *see* Ozyornaya (1)
Muztor *see* Toktogul
Mvuma. Village, central
Zimbabwe, southeastern

Africa : Umvuma
(*1902–82)
Mvurwi. Village, northern
Zimbabwe, southeastern
Africa : Umvukwes
(–1983)
Mwami. Village, northwest-
ern Zimbabwe, southeast-
ern Africa : Miami
(–1983)
Mwanza *see* Magu
Mwenezi. Village, southern
Zimbabwe, southeastern
Africa : Nuanetsi (–1982)
Myanmar. Republic, south-
eastern Asia : Burma
(–1989)
Mýlos *see* Smértos
Mymensingh. City, central
Bangladesh : Nasirabad
(-?)
Myrtiá. Village, central
Crete, Greece : Várvaron
(–1960s)
Mys Lazarev *see* Lazarev
Myślibórz. Town, north-
western Poland : Soldin
(–1945), Germany
Mysłowice. Town, southern
Poland : Myslowitz
(–1922), Germany
Myslowitz *see* Mysłowice
Mysore *see* Karnataka
Mysovka. Village, Kalinin-
grad Oblast, Russia :
Karkeln (–1945), Ger-
many
Mysovsk *see* Babushkin (2)
Mzizima *see* Dar es Salaam

Naberezhnaya. Village,
Brest Oblast, Belorussia :
Vonki (–1971)

Naberezhnyye Chelny.
Town, Tatar Autono-
mous Republic, Russia :
Chelny (–1930),
Brezhnev (1982–88)
Nabresina *see* Aurisina
Naciria. Village, northern
Algeria, northern Africa :
Haussonvillers (–c.
1962)
Nadezhdinzk *see* Serov
Nadezhdinsky Priisk *see*
Aprelsk
Nadezhdinsky Zavod *see* Serov
Nadterechnaya. Village,
Chechen-Ingush Autono-
mous Republic, Russia :
Nizhny Naur (–1944)
Naga. Municipality, Camar-
ines Norte, Philippines :
Nueva Caceres (–1914)
Nagaba *see* Jordon (1)
Nagahama *see* Ozyorsky
Nagaland. State, northeast-
ern India : Naga Hills
(–1963)
Nag Hills *see* Nagaland
Nagibovo. Village, Jewish
Autonomous Oblast,
Khabarovsk Kray,
Russia : Stalinsk (?–1961)
Nagornoye *see* Mozhaysky
Nagpartian *see* Burgos (1)
Nagykapos *see* Velké Ka-
pušány
Nagyszombat *see* Trnava
Nagyvárad *see* Oradea
Naibo *see* Dobroye
Naibuchi *see* Nayba
Naihoro *see* Gornozavodsk (1)
Nairo *see* Gastello
Nakanbe. River, Burkina
Faso, western Africa :
Volta Blanche (–1986)
Nakel *see* Nakło

Nakhodka. Bay, Primorsky
Kray, Russia : Amerika
(–1974)
Nakhrachi *see* Kondinskoye
Nakło (nad Notecią). Town,
north-central Poland : Na-
kel (1939–45), Germany
Nalasin *see* General Artemio
Ricarte
Naldrug *see* Osmanabad
Namacpacan *see* Luna (2)
Namhoi. City, southeastern
China : Fatshan (–1912)
Namibe. Town and province,
southwestern Angola,
southwestern Africa :
Moçâmedes (–1982)
Namibia. Republic, south-
western Africa : German
Southwest Africa
(–1915), South West
Africa (1915–68)
Namp'o. City, western
North Korea : Chin-
namp'o (–1947)
Namslau *see* Namysłow
Nam Tha *see* Houa Khong
Namysłow. Town, south-
western Poland :
Namslau (–1945),
Germany
Nana Candundo *see* Kavungo
Nanan *see* (1) Shwangpo [Shu-
ang-po]; (2) Tayü
Nanchao. Town, east-cen-
tral China : Litsingtien
(–c. 1947)
Nancheng (1). Town, cen-
tral China : Hanchung
(–1913)
Nancheng [Nan-ch'eng] (2).
Town, southeastern
China : Kienchang
(–c. 1912)

Nan-chiao = Nankiao

Nanchow *see* Nanhisen

Nanchung [Nan-chung].
Town, central China :
Shunking (–1913)

Nanhsien. Town, south-central China : Nanchow
(–1913)

Nankang *see* Singtze [Hsing-tzu]

Nankiao [Nan-chiao]. Town,
southwestern China :
Wufu (–1934)

Nankiao *see* Fengsien [Feng-hsien]

Nanking. City, east-central
China : Chiang-ning
[Kiangning] (–1911)

Nanlung *see* Anlung

Nanning. City, southeastern
China : Yungning (1913–
45)

Nanping [Nan-ping]. City,
southeastern China : Yen-ping [Yen-ping] (–1913)

Nantitien *see* Ichwan
[I-ch'uan]

Nanton. Town, Alberta,
Canada : Mosquito Creek
(–1902)

Napo *see* Tienyang [Tien-yang]

Narbada *see* Narmada

Narimanabad. Urban settlement, Azerbaijan : Sara-Ostrov (–c. 1960)

Narimanov (1). Town,
Tashkent Oblast, Uzbekistan : Bektemir (–1981)

Narimanov (2). Urban settlement, Astrakhan Oblast, Russia : Nizhnev-olzhsk (–1984)

Narimanova, imeni *see* Bank

Narmada. River, central India : Narbada (–1966)

Narra (1). Barrio, Mindoro
Oriental, Philippines :
Batingan (–1969)

Narra (2). Barrio, Mindoro
Oriental, Philippines :
Malusak (–1969)

Nartkala. Town, Kabardin-Balkarian Autonomous
Republic, Russia : Dok-shukino (–1967)

Nartovskoye. Village, North
Ossetian Autonomous
Republic, Russia : Kanty-shevo (–1944)

Narva-Jõesuu. Urban settlement, Estonia : Hunger-burg (–1917)

Naryan-Mar. Capital of
Nenets Autonomous
Okrug, Arkhangelsk
Oblast, Russia : Be-loshchelye (–1933),
Dzerzhinskogo, imeni
(1933–35)

Naryn. Village, Andizhan
Oblast, Uzbekistan :
Khakulabad (–c. 1935)

Naryn Oblast (1988†). Kirgiz SSR : Tyan-Shan Oblast (*1939–62)

Nasirabad *see* Mymensingh

Natividade *see* Natividade da
Serra

Natividade da Serra. City,
southeastern Brazil,
South America : Na-tividade (–1944)

Naugard *see* Nowogard

Naumburg am Queis *see* Nowogrodziec

Navabad. Urban settlement,
Tajikistan : Shulmak

(–1959), Novabad (1959–
c. 1980)
Navan. Town, County
Meath, Ireland : An
Uaimh (c. 1930–71)
Navangar *see* Jamnagar
Navarredonda de Gredos.
Village, east-central
Spain : Navarredonda de
la Sierra (–1969)
Navarredonda de la Sierra *see*
Navarredonda de Gredos
Navoi. Town, Bukhara Ob-
last, Uzbekistan : Ker-
mine (–1958)
Navozy *see* Oreshnitsa
Nayarit. State, west-central
Mexico, North America :
Tepic (–1917)
Nayba. River, Sakhalin Ob-
last, Russia : Naibuchi
(1905–45), Japan
Nayoshi *see* Lesogorsk
Nayung. Town, southern
China : Tatuchang
(–1932)
Nazaré *see* Nazaré da Mata
Nazaré da Mata. City,
northeastern Brazil,
South America : Nazaré
(–1944)
Nazimovo *see* Putyatin
Nazinon. River, Burkina
Faso, western Africa :
Volta Rouge (–1986)
Nazran. Town, Chechen-
Ingush Autonomous
Republic, Russia :
Georgiye-Osetinskoye
(–1944), Kosta-
Khetagurovo (1944–
67)
Nazyvayevsk. Town, Omsk
Oblast, Russia : Sibirsky

(*1910–c. 1935), Novon-
azyvayevka (c. 1935–56)
Ndalatando. Town, north-
western Angola, south-
western Africa : Salazar
(1930s–c. 1976)
N'Djamena. Capital of
Chad, north-central
Africa : Fort Lamy
(*1900–73)
Néa Ekklesoúla. Village,
southern Greece : Ekkle-
soúla (–1960s)
Néai Vrysoúlai. Village,
southern Greece :
Vrysoúlai (–1960s)
Néa Kóme *see* Pontolívadon
Néa Philadélpheia. Vil-
lage, northern Greece :
Philadelphianá (–1960s)
Nedenes *see* Aust-Agder
Neftechala *see* 26 Bakinskikh
Komissarov, imeni
Neftegorsk. Urban settle-
ment, Sakhalin Oblast,
Russia : Vostok (–1970)
Neftekamsk. Town, Bashkir
Autonomous Republic,
Russia : Kasevo (–1963)
Nefteyugansk. Town,
Khanty-Mansi Autono-
mous Okrug, Tyumen
Oblast, Russia : Ust-
Balyk (–1967)
Neidenburg *see* Nidzica
Neisse *see* Nysa
Nekrasovo. Village, Mogi-
lyov Oblast, Belorussia :
Tsarevsk (–1964)
Nekrasovskoye. Urban set-
tlement, Yaroslavl Ob-
last, Russia : Bolshiye
Soli (–1938)
Nelepovsky *see* Artyomovo

Nelson-Miramichi. Town,
New Brunswick, Canada :
South Nelson (–1968)
Neman. Town, Kaliningrad
Oblast, Russia : Ragnit
(–1946), Germany (–1945)
Německý Brod see Havlíčkův
Brod
Németbóly see Bóly
Nemours see Ghazaouet
Neokhórion see Kypséele (2)
Néon Kompegádion. Vil-
lage, southern Greece :
Kompegádion (–1960s)
Néon Kríkellon. Village,
central Greece : Káto
Vardátai (–1960s)
Neppel see Moses Lake
Nero see Krn
Nesebar. City, eastern Bul-
garia : Mesemvriya
[Mesembria] (–1934)
Neshime. Town, southern
Kyushu, Japan : Kone-
shime (–1943)
Nesísta Néas Helládos see Ro-
daugé
Nesterov (1). Town, Kalinin-
grad Oblast, Russia :
Stallupönen (–1938), Ger-
many, Ebenrode (1938–
46), Germany (–1945)
Nesterov (2). Town, Lvov
Oblast, Ukraine :
Zholkev (–1941), Poland;
Zholkva (1941–51)
Nesvetevich see Proletarsk (2)
Netherlands East Indies see
Indonesia
Netherlands Indies see Indo-
nesia
Neu-Bentschen see Zbąszynek
Neuenberg (an der Elbe) see
Nymburk

Neu Hardenberg. Town,
eastern Germany :
Marxwalde (1949–90)
Neuhäusel see Nové Zámky
Neuhausen see Guryevsk
Neukirch see Timiryazevo
Neukuhren see Pionersky
Neu-Langenburg see Tukuyu
Neumarkt see (1) Nowy Targ;
(2) Środa Śląska
Neumarktl see Tržič
Neu-Mecklenburg see New
Ireland
Neumittelwalde see Między-
bórz
Neumyvaki see Orekhovskaya
Neu-Pommern see New Britain
Neusalz (an der Oder) see
Nowa Sól
Neu-Sandec see Nowy Sącz
Neu Sandez see Nowy Sącz
Neusatz see Novi Sad
Neusohl see Banská Bystrica
Neustadt see (1) Lwówek; (2)
Prudnik; (3) Wejherowo
Neustadt an der Hardt see
Neustadt (an der Wein-
strasse)
Neustadt (an der Weinstrasse).
City, western Germany :
Neustadt an der Hardt
(–1936, 1945–50)
Neustädtel see Nowe Mias-
teczko
Neustädtl see Novo Mesto
Neustettin see Szczecinek
Neutitschein see Nový Jičín
Neuvième see Tagant
Neuwedell see Drawno
Nevbily see Zaborovtsy
Nevdubstroy see Kirovsk (4)
Nevelsk. Town, Sakhalin
Oblast, Russia : Honto
(1905–46), Japan (–1945)

Never. Urban settlement, Amur Oblast, Russia : Larinsky (*1907–?)

Neves see Neves Paulista

Neves Paulista. City, southeastern Brazil, South America : Neves (–1944), Iboti (1944–48)

Neviges. Town, northwestern Germany : Hardenberg (–1935)

Nevskoye. Village, Kaliningrad Oblast, Russia : Pilupönen (–1938), Germany; Schlossbach (1935–45), Germany

(New) Anzac-on-Sea see Peacehaven

New Ayuquitan see Amlan

New Barbadoes see Hackensack

New Berlin see North Canton

Newbridge see Droichead Nua

New Brighton see Kaiaua

New Britain. Island, Bismarck Archipelago, Papua New Guinea : New Pomerania [Neu-Pommern] (1884–1920)

(New) Brookland see West Columbia

New Butler see Butler

Newcastle. Town, Natal, South Africa : Viljoensdorp (1899–1900)

New Denmark. Town, New Brunswick, Canada : Salmonhurst (–1962)

New Guinea. Part of Papua New Guinea : German New Guinea (1884–1920)

New Harbour see Keppel Harbour

New Hebrides see Vanuatu

New Ireland. Island, Bismarck Archipelago, Papua New Guinea : New Mecklenburg [Neu-Mecklenburg] (1884–1920)

New Liskeard. Town, Ontario, Canada : Liskeard (–1903)

New Lucena. Municipality, Iloilo, Philippines : Lucena (–1955)

Newmark see Montebello

New Mecklenburg see New Ireland

New Pomerania see New Britain

New Smyrna see New Smyrna Beach

New Smyrna Beach. City, Florida, USA : New Smyrna (–1937)

Newtown see Newtownshandrum

Newtownbarry see Bunclody

Newtownshandrum. Town, County Cork, Ireland : Newtown (–1971)

Ney-Valter see Sverdlovo

Neyvo-Rudyanka. Urban settlement, Sverdlovsk Oblast, Russia : Neyvo-Rudyansky Zavod (–1928)

Neyvo-Rudyansky Zavod see Neyvo-Rudyanka

Nezametny see Aldan

Ngaliema, Mount : Mountain, Zaïre/Uganda, east-central Africa : Stanley, Mount (–1972)

Ngezi. Village, central Zimbabwe, southeastern Africa : Ingezi (–1983)

Ngiva *see* Ondjiva
Nguema Biyogo *see* Ekuku
Ngunza-Kabolu *see* Sumbe
Ngwa. Town, southeastern
China : Onliu (–1941)
Nhlangano. Town, south-
western Swaziland, south-
ern Africa : Goedgegun
(–c. 1970)
Niagara *see* Niagara-on-the-
Lake
Niagara-on-the-Lake. Town,
Ontario, Canada :
Niagara (–1906)
Niangsiang *see* Chungyang
Niassa. Province, northwest-
ern Mozambique, south-
eastern Africa : Vila
Cabral (*1945–46), Lago
(1946–54)
Nicholas II Land *see* Sever-
naya Zemlya
Nico Pérez *see* José Batlle y
Ordóñez
Nidaros *see* Trondheim
Nidzica. Town, northeast-
ern Poland : Neidenburg
(–1945), Germany
Niegocin. Lake, northeast-
ern Poland : Löwentin
(–1945), Germany
Niekerkshoop. Village,
Cape Province, South
Africa : Modderfontein
(–1902)
Niemcza. Town, southwest-
ern Poland : Nimptsch
(–1945), Germany
Niemodlin. Town, south-
western Poland : Falken-
berg (–1945), Germany
Niger (1). Republic, northwestern Africa : Zinder
(1900–10)

Niger (2) (*1908). Province,
west-central Nigeria,
western Africa : Nupe
(1918–26)
Niislel Khureheh *see* Ulan
Bator
Niitoi *see* Novoye (2)
Nikel. Urban settlement,
Murmansk Oblast,
Russia : Kolosjoki
(*c. 1935–44), Finland
Nikitinskiye Promysly *see*
Kirovsky (1)
Nikitovka. Village, Kalinin-
grad Oblast, Russia :
Marienhof (–1945),
Germany
Nikolainkaupunki *see* Vaasa
Nikolaistad *see* Vaasa
Nikolayevsk. Town, Vol-
gograd Oblast, Russia :
Nikolayevsky (1936–
67)
Nikolayevsk *see* (1) Ni-
kolayevsk-na-Amure; (2)
Pugachyov
Nikolayevsk-na-Amure.
Town, Khabarovsk Kray,
Russia : Nikolayevsk
(–1926)
Nikolayevskoye *see* Krasnog-
vardeyskoye (4)
Nikolayevsky *see* Nikolayevsk
Nikolsburg *see* Mikulov
Nikolsk. Town, Penza Ob-
last, Russia : Nikolskaya
Pestravka (–1954)
Nikolsk *see* Ussuriysk
Nikolskaya Pestravka *see*
Nikolsk
Nikolskoye *see* Sheksna
Nikolsk-Ussuriysky *see* Us-
suriysk
Nikolsky Khutor *see* Sursk

Nikópolis. Village, western Greece : Smyrtoúla (–1960s)

Nikumaroro. Island, Kiribati, western Pacific : Gardner Island (–1981)

Niles Center *see* Skokie

Nimptsch *see* Niemcza

Ninawa. Province, northwestern Iraq : Mosul (–1971)

Ninety Mile Beach *see* Eighty Mile Beach

Ningcheng [Ning-ch'eng]. Town, northeastern China : Siaochengtze (–1947)

Ning-chiang = Ningkiang

Ningchow *see* (1) Hwaning [Hua-ning]; (2) Ninghsien

Ningerh. Town, southwestern China : Puerh (–1914)

Ninghai *see* Mowping [Mouping]

Ninghsien. Town, south-central China : Ningchow (–1913)

Ninghsien *see* (1) Hwaning [Hua-ning]; (2) Ningpo

Ningkang. Town, southeastern China : Lungshih (–1934)

Ningkiang [Ning-chiang]. Village, southwestern China : Mengwang (–1935)

Ningkwo *see* Süancheng [Hsüan-cheng]

Ninglang. Village, southwestern China : Langchu (–1936)

Ningnan. Town, southern China : Pisha (–1930)

Ningpo. City, eastern China : Ninghsien (1911–49)

Ningpo *see* Lotu

Ningsho = Ningso

Ningsia *see* Yinchwan [Yinch'uan]

Ningso [Ningshuo]. Town, northwestern China : Siaopapao (–1942)

Ningting. Town, north-central China : Taitsesze (–1919)

Ningtsing *see* Chenhwa [Chenhua]

Ningtung. Village, southern China : Mishih (–1938)

Ningyüan *see* (1) Hingcheng [Hsing-cheng]; (2) Sichang [Hsi-chang]; (3) Wushan

Ninomiya. Town, central Honshu, Japan : Azuma (–1935)

Niquelândia. City, east-central Brazil, South America : São José do Tocantins (–1944)

Nishi-ichiki *see* Ichiki

Nísia Floresta. City, eastern Brazil, South America : Papari (–1948)

Nivenskoye. Village, Kaliningrad Oblast, Russia : Wittenberg (–1946), Germany (–1945)

Nizhegorodskaya Oblast [Nizhny Novgorod Oblast]. East-central Russia : (*1929), Nizhegorodsky Kray [Nizhny Novgorod Kray] (1929–32), Gorky Kray (1932–36), Gorky Oblast (1936–90)

Nizhegorodsky Kray *see* Nizhegorodskaya Oblast

Nizhnegniloye *see* Sosnovka

Nizhnegorsky. Urban settlement, Crimean Oblast, Ukraine : Seitler (–1944)
Nizhne-Kolosovskoye *see* Kolosovka (1)
Nizhnesaldinsky Zavod *see* Nizhnyaya Salda
Nizhne-Saraninsky *see* Sarana
Nizhneserginsky Zavod *see* Nizhniye Sergi
Nizhnestalinsk *see* Leninsky (4)
Nizhnetroitsky. Town, Bashkir Autonomous Republic, Russia : Nizhnetroitsky Zavod (–1928)
Nizhnetroitsky Zavod *see* Nizhnetroitsky
Nizhneufaleysky Zavod *see* Nizhny Ufaley
Nizhniye Kresty *see* Chersky
Nizhniye Sergi. Town, Sverdlovsk Oblast, Russia : Nizhneserginsky Zavod (–c. 1928)
Nizhniye Ustriki *see* Ustrzyki Dolne
Nizhny Agdzhakend *see* Shaumyanovsk
Nizhnyaya *see* Ust-Bagaryak
Nizhnyaya Akhtala *see* Akhtala
Nizhnyaya Dobrinka *see* Dobrinka
Nizhnyaya Salda. Town, Sverdlovsk Oblast, Russia : Nizhnesaldinsky Zavod (–?)
Nizhnyaya Tura. Town, Sverdlovsk Oblast, Russia : Nizhneturinsky Zavod (–1929)
Nizhny Naur *see* Nadterechnaya

Nizhny Novgorod. Capital of Nizhegorodskaya Oblast, Russia : Gorky (1932–90)
Nizhny Novgorod Kray *see* Nizhegorodskaya Oblast
Nizhny Novgorod Oblast = Nizhegorodskaya Oblast
Nizhny Ufaley. Urban settlement, Chelyabinsk Oblast, Russia : Nizhneufaleysky Zavod (–1928)
Nizovye. Village, Kaliningrad Oblast, Russia : Waldau (–1945), Germany
Nkai *see* Nkayi
Nkayi. Village, central Zimbabwe, southeastern Africa : Nkai (–1982)
Noda *see* Chekhov (2)
Nogaysk *see* Primorskoye (2)
Noginsk. Town, Moscow Oblast, Russia : Bogorodsk (–1930)
Nógrádverőce *see* Veróce
Nokia. Town, southwestern Finland : Pohjois-Pirkkala (–1938)
Nokkeushi *see* Kitami
Nolinsk. Town, Kirov Oblast, Russia : Molotovsk (1940–57)
Nomahasha *see* Lomahasha
Norak *see* Nurek
Norashen *see* Ilyichyovsk
Nor-Bayazet *see* Kamo
Nordenskjöld Sea *see* Laptev Sea
Nordre Bergenhus *see* Sogn og Fjordane
Nordre Trondhjem *see* Nord-Trondelag

Nord-Trondelag. County, central Norway : Nordre Trondhjem (–1918)

Nordvik see Kozhevnikovo

Nor-Kharberd. Urban settlement, Armenia : Nor-Kyank (–c. 1960)

Nor-Kyank see Nor-Kharberd

Norris Lake = Norris Reservoir

Norris Reservoir [Norris Lake]. Lake, Tennessee, USA : Clinch-Powell Reservoir (*1936–?)

North Bedfordshire. Administrative district, Bedfordshire, England, UK : Bedford (*1973–76)

North Borneo see Sabah

North Canton. City, Ohio, USA : New Berlin (–1918)

North Caucasus Kray see Stavropol Kray

North East Frontier Agency see Arunachal Pradesh

North-East New Guinea. Region of New Guinea, Papua New Guinea : Kaiser-Wilhelmsland (1884–1920)

Northern Rhodesia see Zambia

North Field see Andersen Air Force Base

North Greenfield see West Allis

North Khartoum. Town, central Sudan, northeastern Africa : Khalfaya (–1903)

North Las Vegas. Suburb of Las Vegas, Nevada, USA : Vegas Verde (*early 1920s–1932)

North Little Rock. City, Arkansas, USA : Argenta (–1901)

North Miami. Suburb of Miami, Florida, USA : Miami Shores (1926–36)

North Miami Beach. City, Florida, USA : Fulford (–1926)

Northon see Fulgencio

North Ossetian Autonomous Oblast see North Ossetian Autonomous Republic

North Ossetian Autonomous Republic. Western Russia : North Ossetian Autonomous Oblast (*1924–36), North Ossetian Autonomous SSR (1936–91)

North Ossetian Autonomous SSR see North Ossetian Autonomous Republic

North Solomon Islands. Province, Papua New Guinea : Bougainville (–1979)

North Union see Shaker Heights

North Vancouver. City, British Columbia, Canada : Moodyville (–1902)

North-Western Provinces and Oudh see Uttar Pradesh

North Yakima see Yakima

Norusovo see Kalinino (1)

Nossa Senhora do Livramento. City, northeastern Brazil, South America : Livramento (–1943), São José dos Cocais (1944–48)

Nosy Boraha. Island, eastern Madagascar, south-

eastern Africa : Sainte-
Marie (–c. 1979)
Notre-Dame-de-Koarta *see*
Koartac
Notre-Dame-de-Lorette *see*
Ancienne-Lorette
Notre-Dame-d'Ivugivic *see*
Ivugivic
Nottaway *see* Senneterre
Nouadhibou. Town, north-
western Mauritania, west-
ern Africa : Port-Étienne
(–c. 1965)
Nouveau Comptoir. Town,
Quebec, Canada : Paint
Hills (–1967)
Nouvelle Anvers *see* Makanza
Novabad *see* Navabad
Nova Dantzig *see* Cambé
Nova Era. City, southeast-
ern Brazil, South Amer-
ica : São José da Lagoa
(–1930s), Presidente
Vargas (1930s–1944)
Nova Fontesvila *see* Vila
Machado
Nova-Freixo. City, north-
central Mozambique,
southeastern Africa :
Cuamba (–1942)
Nova Goa *see* Panaji
Nova Iguaçu. Suburb of Rio
de Janeiro, southeastern
Brazil, South America :
Maxambamba (–?)
Nova Lamego. Village,
northeastern Guinea-
Bissau, western Africa :
Gabú (Sara) (–1948)
Nova Lisboa *see* Huambo
Nova Prata. City, southern
Brazil, South America :
Prata (–1944)
Nova Sintra *see* Catabola

Nova Vicenza *see* Farroupilha
Novaya *see* Novokruchininsky
Novaya Aleksandriya *see* Pu-
ławy
Novaya Bukhara *see* Kagan
Novaya Eushta *see* Timirya-
zevsky
Novaya Lyala. Town,
Sverdlovsk Oblast,
Russia : Novolyalinsky
Zavod (–c. 1928)
Novaya Pismyanka *see* Lenin-
ogorsk
(Novaya) Pokrovka *see* Len-
inskoye (7)
Novaya Tarya *see* Rybachy (1)
Novaya Zhizn *see* Kazinka
Nové Zámky. Town, south-
ern Slovakia : Neuhäusel
(–1918), Germany;
Ersekújvár (1938–45),
Hungary
Novgradets *see* Suvorovo (1)
Noviki (1). Village, Vitebsk
Oblast, Belorussia : Beda
(–1964)
Noviki (2). Village, Mogi-
lyov Oblast, Belorussia :
Bolvanovka (–1964)
Novi Kricim *see* Stamboliyski
Novi Pazar. Town, south-
western Serbia : Yeni-
Pazar (–1913), Turkey
Novi Sad. City, northern
Serbia : Neusatz (–1918),
Germany
Novoaleksandrovsk (1). Vil-
lage, Sakhalin Oblast,
Russia : Konuma (1905–
45), Japan
Novoaleksandrovsk (2).
Town, Stavropol Kray,
Russia : Novoaleksan-
drovskaya (–1971)

Novoaleksandrovsk *see*
Zarasai
Novoaleksandrovskaya *see*
Novoaleksandrovsk (2)
Novoaltaysk. Town, Altay
Kray, Russia : Chesno-
kovka (–1962)
Novoanninskaya *see* Novoan-
ninsky
Novoanninsky. Town, Vol-
gograd Oblast, Russia :
Novoanninskaya
(–c. 1939)
Novoasbest. Urban settle-
ment, Sverdlovsk Oblast,
Russia : Krasnouralsky
Rudnik (–1933)
Novoazovsk. Town, Don-
etsk Oblast, Ukraine :
Novonikolayevka
(–c. 1935), Budyonnovka
(c. 1935–66)
Novobureysky. Urban set-
tlement, Amur Oblast,
Russia : Bureya-Pristan
(–c. 1960)
Novocheremshansk. Urban
settlement, Ulyanovsk
Oblast, Russia : Stary
Salavan (–c. 1960)
Novodvinsk. Town, Ark-
hangelsk Oblast, Russia :
Pervomaysky (–1977)
Novoekonomicheskoye *see*
Dimitrov
Novogeorgiyevsk *see* Modlin
Novogordino *see* Krasnoye
Ekho
Novograd-Volynsk *see*
Novograd-Volynsky
Novograd-Volynsky. Town,
Zhitomir Oblast,
Ukraine : Novograd-
Volynsk (–c. 1928)

Novogroznensky. Urban set-
tlement, Chechen-Ingush
Autonomous Republic,
Russia : Oisungur (–1944)
Novokashirsk. Suburb of
Kashira, Moscow Oblast,
Russia : Ternovsky
(–1932), Ternovsk (1932–
c. 1935), Kaganovich
(c. 1935–c. 1957)
Novokiyevskoye *see* Kraskino
Novokocherdyk *see* Tselin-
noye (1)
Novokruchininsky. Urban
settlement, Chita Oblast,
Russia : Novaya
(–c. 1960)
Novokubansk. Town, Kras-
nodar Kray, Russia :
Novokubansky (–1966)
Novokubansky *see* Novoku-
bansk
Novokuznetsk. Town, Keme-
rovo Oblast, Russia :
Kuznetsk(-Sibirsky)
(–1931), Stalinsk (1932–
61)
Novolakskoye. Village, Dag-
estan Autonomous Re-
public, Russia : Yaryksu-
Aukh (–1944)
Novolyalinsky Zavod *see* Novaya Lyala
Novolyubino *see* Lyubinsky
Novo-Mariinsk *see* Anadyr
Novo Mesto. Village, southeastern Slovenia : Neu-
städtl (–1918), Germany
Novomoskovsk. Town, Tula
Oblast, Russia : Bobriki
(–1934), Stalinogorsk
(1934–61)
Novonazyvayevka *see* Nazyvayevsk

Novonikolayevka *see* No-
voazovsk
Novo-Nikolayevka *see*
Chkalovo (3)
Novonikolayevsk *see* Novosi-
birsk
Novoorsk. Urban settle-
ment, Orenburg Oblast,
Russia : Novoorskaya
(–c. 1935)
Novoorskaya *see* Novoorsk
Novopashiysky *see* Gor-
nozavodsk (2)
Novopavlovsk. Town,
Stavropol Kray, Russia :
Novopavlovskaya
(–1981)
Novopavlovskaya *see* No-
vopavlovsk
Novo Redondo *see* Sumbe
Novoselskoye *see* Achkhoy-
Martan
Novoshakhtinsk. Town,
Rostov Oblast, Russia :
Tretyego Internatsionala,
imeni (1920s), Komintern
(1929–39)
Novosibirsk. Capital of No-
vosibirsk Oblast, Russia :
Gusevka (–1903), Novon-
ikolayevsk (1903–25)
Novosineglazovsky. Urban
settlement, Chelyabinsk
Oblast, Russia : Sinegla-
zovo (–c. 1960)
Novo-Starobinsk *see* Soli-
gorsk
Novostroyevo. Village,
Kaliningrad Oblast,
Russia : Trempen
(–1946), Germany
(–1945)
Novosyolovskoye. Urban
settlement, Crimean Ob-

last, Ukraine : Fraidorf
(–1944)
Novo-Troitskoye *see* (1)
Baley; (2) Sokuluk
Novourgench *see* Urgench
Novovyatsk. Town, Kirov
Oblast, Russia : Grukhi
(–1939), Lesozavodsky
(1939–55)
Novoye (1). Village, Vitebsk
Oblast, Belorussia :
Gryaznoye (–1964)
Novoye (2). Village,
Sakhalin Oblast, Russia :
Niitoi (1905–45), Japan
Novy Afon. Urban settle-
ment, Abkhazian
Autonomous Republic,
Georgia : Psirtskha
(–1948), Akhali-Afoni
(1948–c. 1965)
Nový Bor. Town, northern
Czech Lands : Bor u Čes-
ké Lípy (–1946)
Novy Donbass *see* Dimitrov
Nový Jičín. Town, eastern
Czech Lands :
Neutitschein (–1918,
1939–45), Germany
Novy Karachay. Urban set-
tlement, Karachayev-
Cherkess Autonomous
Oblast, Stavropol Kray,
Russia : Pravoberezhnoye
(–c. 1960)
Novy Margelan *see* Fergana
Novy Yarychev. Urban set-
tlement, Lvov Oblast,
Ukraine : Jaryczów Nowy
(–1940), Poland
Novyye Aldy *see* Chernore-
chye
Novyye Petushki *see* Petushki
Novy Zay *see* Zainsk

Nowa Sól. Town, western
Poland : Neusalz (an der
Oder) (–1945), Germany
Nowawes *see* Babelsberg
Nowe Miasteczko. Town,
western Poland : Neu-
städtel (–1945), Germany
Nowogard. Town, north-
western Poland : Naugard
(–1945), Germany
Nowogrodziec. Town,
southwestern Poland
: Naumburg am Queis
(–1945), Germany
Noworadomsk *see* Radomsko
Nowy Sącz. City, southern
Poland : Neu-Sandec
(–1919), Germany, Neu
Sandez (1939–45),
Germany
Nowy Targ. Town, southern
Poland : Neumarkt
(–1914), Germany
Nozhay-Yurt. Village,
Chechen-Ingush Autono-
mous Republic, Russia :
Andalaly (1944–c. 1960)
Nsanje. City, southern
Malawi, southeastern
Africa : Port Herald
(–c. 1964)
Nsiom Fumu. Town, west-
ern Zaïre, central Africa :
Vista (–1972)
Nuanetsi *see* Mwenezi
Nueva Caceres *see* Naga
Nueva Valencia *see* Valencia
Nukha *see* Sheki
Nukus *see* Pristansky
Nuling *see* Sultan Kudarat
Numancia de la Sagra.
Village, south-central
Spain : Azaña
(–c. 1940)

Numancin *see* Del Carmen
Nupe *see* Niger (2)
Nurabad. Town, Samarkand
Oblast, Uzbekistan :
Sovetabad (–1983)
Nurek. Town, Khatlon Ob-
last, Tajikistan : Norak
(–1937)
Nuristan. District, eastern
Afghanistan : Kafiristan
(–c. 1900)
Nutley. Town, New Jersey,
USA : Franklin (–1902)
Nyagan. Town, Khanty-
Mansi Autonomous
Okrug, Tyumen Oblast,
Russia : Nyakh (–1985)
Nyahururu. Town, west-
central Kenya, eastern
Africa : Thomson's Falls
(–1975)
Nyakh *see* Nyagan
Nyanda. Town, central Zim-
babwe, southeastern
Africa : Fort Victoria
(–1982)
Nyando *see* Roosevelttown
Nyasa, Lake *see* Malawi, Lake
Nyasaland *see* Malawi
Nyazura. Village, eastern
Zimbabwe, southeastern
Africa : Inyazura (–1982)
Nyírbakta *see* Baktalórántháza
Nymburk. Town, north-
central Czech Lands :
Neuenburg (an der Elbe)
(–1918, 1939–45),
Germany
Nysa. City, southern Poland :
Neisse (–1945), Germany
Nzeto. Town, northwestern
Angola, southwestern
Africa : Ambrizete
(–c. 1979)

Oak Bluffs. Town, Massachusetts, USA : Cottage City (–1907)
Oakville. Village, Manitoba, Canada : Kawende (–1939)
Oban. Township, Stewart Island, New Zealand : Half-Moon Bay (–early 1940s)
Obbe *see* Leverburgh
Obdorsk *see* Salekhard
Obedovo *see* Oktyabrsky (7)
Oberburg *see* Gornji Grad
Oberdonau *see* Upper Austria
Oberdorf *see* Remennikovo
Oberglogau *see* Głogówek
Oberlaibach *see* Vrhnika
Obernigk *see* Oborniki Śląskie
Oberösterreich = Upper Austria
Oberpahlen *see* Põltsamaa
Obiralovka *see* Zheleznodorozhny (2)
Oborniki Śląskie. Town, southwestern Poland : Obernigk (–1945), Germany
Obruchevo *see* Ulyanovo (2)
Obukhovka *see* Kirovsky (2)
Ocean. Administrative division, western Cameroon, western Africa : Kribi (–1974)
Ocean (Island) *see* Banaba
Ocean Ridge. Town, Florida, USA : Boynton Beach (*1931–37)
Ocean View *see* Albany
Ocheng [O-ch'eng]. Town, east-central China : Showchang (–1914)
Ochyor. Town, Perm Oblast, Russia : Ochyorsky Zavod (–1929)

Ochyorsky Zavod *see* Ochyor
Oco *see* San Jose (3)
O'Connor. Province, southern Bolivia, South America : Salinas (–1906)
October Revolution Island = Oktyabrskoy Revolyutsii, Ostrov
Ödenburg *see* Sopron
Odenpe *see* Otepää
Odesskaya *see* Rozy Lyuksemburg
Oebisfelde. Town, eastern Germany : Oebisfelde-Kaltendorf (–1938)
Oebisfelde-Kaltendorf *see* Oebisfelde
Oels (in Schlesien) *see* Oleśnica
Offaly. County, east-central Ireland : King's County (–1920)
Offutt Air Force Base. Nebraska, USA : Fort Crook (–1924)
Oglethorpe, Mount. Mountain, Georgia, USA : Grassy Mountain (–1929)
Ogloblya *see* Slavyanka
Ogre. Town, Latvia : Oger (–1917)
Oger *see* Ogre
Oguni. Town, northern Honshu, Japan : Ogunimoto (–late 1930s)
Oguni-moto *see* Oguni
O'Higgins Land *see* Antarctic Peninsula
Ohlau *see* Oława
Oisungur *see* Novogroznensky
Oka *see* Aiga
Okachi. Town, northern Honshu, Japan : Jugohama (–late 1930s)

Okny *see* Krasnyye Okny

Oko *see* Yasnomorsky

Okonek. Town, northwestern Poland : Ratzebuhr (–1945), Germany

Oktemberyan. Town, Armenia : Sardarabad (–1932)

Oktyabrsk (1). Village, Khatlon Oblast, Tajikistan : Chichka (–?)

Oktyabrsk (2). Town, Aktyubinsk Oblast, Kazakhstan : Kandagach (–1967)

Oktyabrskoye (1). Urban settlement, Crimean Oblast, Ukraine : Biyuk-Onlar (–1944)

Oktyabrskoye (2). Village, Lipetsk Oblast, Russia : Dryazgi (–1948), Molotovo (1948–57)

Oktyabrskoye (3). Village, Orenburg Oblast, Russia : Isayevo-Dedovo (–1923), Kashirinskoye (1923–37)

Oktyabrskoye (4). Village, Chuvash Autonomous Republic, Russia : Ismeli (–1939)

Oktyabrskoye (5). Urban settlement, Khanty-Mansi Autonomous Okrug, Tyumen Oblast, Russia : Kondinskoye (–1963)

Oktyabrskoye (6). Village, North Ossetian Autonomous Republic, Russia : Sholkhi (–1944), Kartsa (1944–c. 1960)

Oktyabrskoye *see* Zhovtn-evoye (1)

Oktyabrskoy Revolyutsii, imeni. Suburb of Krivoy Rog, Dnepropetrovsk Oblast, Ukraine : Rostkovsky Rudnik (–c. 1926)

Oktyabrskoy Revolyutsii, Ostrov [October Revolution Island]. Island, Severnaya Zemlya, Arctic Ocean, Taymyr Autonomous Okrug, Krasnoyarsk Kray, Russia : Tsarevicha Alekseya, Ostrov [Tsarevich Alexei Island] (*1913–26)

Oktyabrsky (1). Urban settlement, Kostroma Oblast, Russia : Brantovka (–1939)

Oktyabrsky (2). Urban settlement, Perm Oblast, Russia : Chad (–c. 1960)

Oktyabrsky (3). Urban settlement, Gomel Oblast, Belorussia : Karpilovka (–c. 1960)

Oktyabrsky (4). Village, Adygey Autonomous Oblast, Krasnodar Kray, Russia : Khakurate (–1938), Takhtamukay (1938–c. 1960)

Oktyabrsky (5). Urban settlement, Volgograd Oblast, Russia : Kruglyakov (–c. 1960)

Oktyabrsky (6). Urban settlement, Nizhegorodskaya Oblast, Russia : Molotova V.M., imeni (?–1957)

Oktyabrsky (7). Urban settlement, Ivanovo Oblast, Russia : Obedovo (–1941)

Oktyabrsky (8). Urban settlement, Ryazan Oblast, Russia : Sapronovo (–1927)

Oktyabrsky (9). Urban settlement, Belgorod Oblast, Russia : Voskresenovka (–?), Mikoyanovka (?–1957)

Oktyabrsky *see* Komsomolsky (2), (3)

Oława. City, southwestern Poland : Ohlau (–1945), Germany

Olbia. Town, northeastern Sardinia, Italy : Terranova Pausania (–1939)

Old Ayuquitan *see* Ayuquitan

Old Calabar *see* Calabar

Old Glory. Town, Texas, USA : Brandenburg (–1917)

Old Hickory. Village, Tennessee, USA : Jacksonville (–1923)

Old Wives Lake. Lake, Saskatchewan, Canada : Johnstone Lake (–1953)

Olecko. Town, northeastern Poland : Marggrabowa (–1928), Germany; Treuburg (1928–45), Germany

Olenegorsk. Town, Murmansk Oblast, Russia : Olenya (–1957)

Olenya *see* Olenegorsk

Oleskow *see* Tolstoi

Oleśnica. City, southwestern Poland : Oels (in Schlesien) (–1945), Germany

Oleśno. Town, southern Poland : Rosenberg (–1945), Germany

Olginskoye *see* Kochubeyevskoye

Olita *see* Alitus

Olivença *see* Lupiliche

Olkhovskaya. Village, Vitebsk Oblast, Belorussia : Zabuldychino (–1964)

Olkhovsky *see* Artyomovsk (2)

Olkusz. Town, southern Poland : Ilkenau (1939–45), Germany

Ollila *see* Solnechnoye

Olmütz *see* Olomouc

Olomouc. City, eastern Czech Lands : Olmütz (–1918, 1939–45), Germany

Olsztyn. City, northeastern Poland : Allenstein (–1945), Germany

Olsztynek. Town, northeastern Poland : Hohenstein (–1945), Germany

Oludere *see* Harmanlijska

Olviopol *see* Pervomaysk (1)

Olzheras *see* Mezhdurechensk (1)

Oma. Town, northern Honshu, Japan : Ooku (–early 1940s)

Oman. Sultanate, southeastern Arabia : Muscat and Oman (–1970)

Omchak. Urban settlement, Magadan Oblast, Russia : Timoshenko, imeni (–c. 1960)

Omurtag. City, east-central Bulgaria : Osman Pazar (–1934)

Ondjiva. Town, southern
Angola, southwestern
Africa : Pereira de Eça
(–c. 1976), Ngiva (c.
1976–c. 1979)
Onikšty see Anikšiai
Onliu see Ngwa
Onzième see Tiris Zemmour
Ooku see Oma
Opatija. Town, western
Croatia : Abbazia (1919–
45), Italy
Opava. City, northeastern
Czech Lands : Troppau
(–1918, 1939–45),
Germany
Ophir, Mount see Talakmau,
Mount
Opland. County, south-
central Norway : Kris-
tians (–1918)
Opole. City, southern Po-
land : Oppeln (–1945),
Germany
Oppekaln see Ape
Oppeln see Opole
Oradea. City, northwestern
Romania : Nagyvárad
(–1919, 1940–45),
Hungary
Orange County see John
Wayne
Orange Free State. Prov-
ince, east-central South
Africa : Orange River
Colony (1900–10)
Orange River Colony see
Orange Free State
Oranienbaum see
Lomonosov
Oranje Top see Jayawijaya,
Puncak
Orany see Varena

Oraşul Stalin see Braşov
Orchard Park. Village, New
York, USA : East Ham-
burg (–1934)
Ordzhonikidze (1). Urban
settlement, Dnepropet-
rovsk Oblast, Ukraine :
Aleksandrovka (–1939)
Ordzhonikidze (2). Village,
Kustanay Oblast, Ka-
zakhstan : Denisovka
(–c. 1960)
Ordzhonikidze (3). Suburb
of Tashkent, Tashkent
Oblast, Uzbekistan : Lu-
nacharskoye (–c. 1935)
Ordzhonikidze see (1) Khara-
gouli; (2) Vladikavkaz;
(3) Yenakiyevo
Ordzhonikidzeabad. Town,
Tajikistan : Yangibazar
(–1936)
Ordzhonikidzegrad see
Bezhitsa
Ordzhonikidze Kray see
Stavropol Kray
Ordzhonikidzevskaya. Vil-
lage, Chechen-Ingush
Autonomous Republic,
Russia : Sleptsovskaya
(–1939)
Orekhi-Vydritsa see
Orekhovsk
Orekhovichi. Village,
Vitebsk Oblast, Belorus-
sia : Khlevishche (–1964)
Orekhovsk. Urban settle-
ment, Vitebsk Oblast,
Belorussia : Orekhi-
Vydritsa (–1946)
Orekhovskaya. Village,
Minsk Oblast, Belorus-
sia : Neumyvaki (–1964)

Orenburg. Capital of Orenburg Oblast, Russia : Chkalov (1938–57)

Orenburg Oblast (*1934). Central Russia : Chkalov Oblast (1938–57)

Oreshenka. Village, Vitebsk Oblast, Belorussia : Popovka (–1964)

Oreshnitsa. Village, Minsk Oblast, Belorussia : Navozy (–1964)

Orgeyev. Town, Moldavia : Orhei (1918–40, 1941–44), Romania

Orgtrud. Urban settlement, Vladimir Oblast, Russia : Lemeshensky (1927–c. 1940)

Orhei see Orgeyev

Oriente. Province, eastern Cuba : Santiago (de Cuba) (–1905)

Orizona. City, east-central Brazil, South America : Campo Formoso (–1944)

Orkhaniye see Botevgrad

Orkhonomenós. Village, southern Greece : Kalpákion (–1960s)

Orléansville see El-Asnam

Orlov see Khalturin

Orlovo. Village, Sakhalin Oblast, Russia : Ushiro (1905–45), Japan

Ormoc see MacArthur

Ormond see Ormond Beach

Ormond Beach. City, Florida, USA : Ormond (–1949)

Ormož. Village, eastern Slovenia : Friedau (–1918), Germany

Orona. Island, Kiribati, western Pacific : Hull Island (–1981)

Orta-koi see Ivailovgrad

Ortelsburg see Sczcytno

Ortona. Town, south-central Italy : Ortona a Mare (c. 1938–47)

Ortona a Mare see Ortona

Orūmīyeh = Urmia

Orzysz. Town, northeastern Poland : Arys (–1945), Germany

Oshan. Town, southwestern China : Siwo (–1929)

Oshmyany. Town, Grodno Oblast, Belorussia : Oszmiana (1921–45), Poland

Osipenko see Berdyansk

Oslo. Capital of Norway : Christiania (1624–1877), Kristiania (1877–1924)

Osmalenik see Udarnaya (2)

Osmanabad. District, south-central India : Naldrug (–c. 1920)

Osman-Kasayevo. Village, Mogilyov Oblast, Belorussia : Sermyazhenka (–1964)

Osman Pazar see Omurtag

Ośno. Town, western Poland : Drossen (–1945), Germany

Ossersee see Zarasai

Ossining. Village, New York, USA : Sing Sing (–1901)

Ostenburg see Pultusk

Osterode (in Ostpreussen) see Ostróda

Österreich ober der Ems see Upper Austria

Østfold. County, southeastern Norway : Smaalenene (–1918)

Ostróda. City, northeastern Poland : Osterode (in Ostpreussen) (–1945), Germany

Ostrołęka. Town, northeastern Poland : Scharfenwiese (1939–45), Germany

Ostrovskoye. Urban settlement, Kostroma Oblast, Russia : Semyonovskoye (–1956)

Ostrów (Wielkopolski). City, west-central Poland : Ostrowo (–1918), Germany

Ostrowo see Ostrów (Wielkopolski)

Ostyako-Vogulsk see Khanty-Mansiysk

Ostyak-Vogul National Okrug see Khanty-Mansi Autonomous Okrug

Oswego see Lake Oswego

Oświęcim. Town, southern Poland : Auschwitz (–1918, 1939–45), Germany

Osy-kolyosy see Slavino

Oszmiana see Oshmyany

Otani see Sokol

Otdykh see Zhukovsky

Oteiza see Marihatag

Otepää. Town, Estonia : Odenpe (–1917)

Otiai see Dolinsk

Otmuchów. Town, southern Poland : Ottmachau (–1945), Germany

Otomari see Korsakov

Otorohanga see Harrodsville

Otpor see Zabaykalsk

Otradnoye. Health resort, Kaliningrad Oblast, Russia : Georgenswalde (–1945), Germany

Otradnoye see Otradny

Otradny. Town, Samara Oblast, Russia : Otradnoye (–1956)

Otrogovo see Stepnoye

Otsu see Izumi-otsu

Ottmachau see Otmuchów

Otvazhnoye see Zhigulyovsk

Otvazhny see Zhigulyovsk

Ouachita National Forest. Arkansas/Oklahoma, USA : Arkansas National Forest (*1907–26)

Oued Eddahab. Province, southern Western Sahara, northwestern Africa : Río de Oro (–1976), Tiris el Gharbia (1976–78)

Oued el Abtal. Village, northwestern Algeria, northern Africa : Uzès-le-Duc (–c. 1962)

Oued Rhiou. Village, northern Algeria, northern Africa : Inkermann (–c. 1962)

Ouiatchouan see Val-Jalbert

Ouled Mimoun. Village, northwestern Algeria, northern Africa : Lamoricière (–c. 1962)

Ouled Moussa. Town, northern Algeria, northern Africa : Saint-Pierre-Saint-Paul (–c. 1962)

Oulmes(-les-Thermes). Town, northwestern Morocco, northwestern Africa : Tarmilate (1971–?)

Oulx *see* Ulzio
Ovechki *see* Sosnovtsy
Owando. Town, central
    Congo, central Africa :
    Fort-Rousset (–1977)
Oyen. Town, Alberta, Can-
    ada : Bishopburg (–1912)
Oyrat Autonomous Oblast *see*
    Gorno-Altay Autono-
    mous Oblast
Oyrot Autonomous Oblast *see*
    Gorno-Altay Autono-
    mous Oblast
Oyrot-Tura *see* Gorno-Altaysk
Oyster Harbour *see* Ladysmith
Ozamis. City, Mindanao,
    Philippines : Misamis
    (–1940s)
Oznachennoye *see* Sayan-
    ogorsk
Ozurgety. Town, Georgia :
    Makharadze (1934–91)
Ozyorki. Village, Kalinin-
    grad Oblast, Russia :
    Gross Lindenau (–1946),
    Germany (–1945)
Ozyornaya (1). Village,
    Mogilyov Oblast, Belo-
    russia : Muzhichok
    (–1964)
Ozyornaya (2). Village,
    Vitebsk Oblast, Belorus-
    sia : Popova Luka (–1964)
Ozyornoye. Village, Saratov
    Oblast, Russia : Dura-
    sovka (–c. 1960)
Ozyorsk. Town, Kalinin-
    grad Oblast, Russia :
    Darkehmen (–1938),
    Germany; Angerapp
    (1938–46), Germany
    (–1945)
Ozyorsky. Urban settle-
    ment, Sakhalin Oblast,

Russia : Nagahama
    (1905–45), Japan

Paan. Town, southern
    China : Batang (–1913)
Pabrade. Town, Lithuania :
    Podbrodze (–1917)
Pacajús. City, northeastern
    Brazil, South America :
    Guarani (–1944)
Pachai *see* Tanchai
Pachow *see* (1) Pachung; (2)
    Pahsien
Pachung. Town, central
    China : Pachow (–1913)
Paciencia. Barrio, Panay,
    Philippines : Taguimtim
    (–1957)
Pacific City *see* Huntington
    Beach
Pacific Range *see* Western
    Test Range
Paczków. Town, south-
    western Poland :
    Patschkau (–1945),
    Germany
Padali *see* Amursk
Paderno. Village, northern
    Italy : Paderno Ossolaro
    (–1950)
Paderno Ossolaro *see* Paderno
Padilla. Town, south-central
    Bolivia, South America :
    Laguna (–1900s)
Padre Las Casas. Town,
    southwestern Dominican
    Republic, West Indies :
    Túbano (–1928)
Padre Miguelinho *see* Santo
    Antônio (1)
Pagalu. Island, Equatorial
    Guinea, western Africa :
    Annobón (–1973)

Pagayawan. Municipality, Lanao del Sur, Philippines : Tatarikan (–1914)

Pagoúria see Mése

Pahlavi Dezh see Aq Qaleh

Pahlevi see Bandar-e Anzali

Pahsien. Town, northeastern China : Pachow (–1913)

Paide. Town, Estonia : Weisenstein (–1917)

Paimawan see Kanghsien [Kang-hsien]

Paint Hills see Nouveau Comptoir

Paishambe see Payshanba

Paituk see Vose

Paiva Couceiro see Quipungo

Paiyentsing see Yenfeng

Paiyintailai see Tungliao [Tung-liao]

Pakhtaabad. Town, Andizhan Oblast, Uzbekistan : Kokankishlak (–1975)

Pakhtakor. Town, Syrdarya Oblast, Uzbekistan : Ziyautdin (–1937), Binokor (1971–74)

Pakiachen see Tsingyüan [Ching-yüan]

Paklay see Sayaboury

Palaiá Halónia see Petrálona

Palaikatoúna see Lesínion

Palandoc see Ramon Magsaysay

Palau de Montagut see San Jaime de Llierca

Palau de Plegamáns. Village, northeastern Spain : Palausolitar (–c. 1940)

Palausolitar see Palau de Plegamáns

Palawan. Island, southwestern Philippines : Paragua (*1902–05)

Paldiski. Town, Estonia : Baltiysky (Port) (–1917)

Palestina see Jordânia

Palestro see Lakhdaria

Palikao see Tighennif

Palma see (1) Coreaú; (2) Parań

Palmeira see Palmeira das Missões

Palmeira das Missões. City, southern Brazil, South America : Palmeira (–1944)

Palmeirais. City, northeastern Brazil, South America : Belém (–1944)

Palmeiras see (1) Palmeiras de Goiás; (2) Santa Cruz das Palmeiras

Palmeiras de Goiás. City, central Brazil, South America : Palmeiras (–1944), Mataúna (1944–48)

Palmer Peninsula see Antarctic Peninsula

Palmerston see Darwin

Palmnicken see Yantarny

Palmyras see Santos Dumont

Palpalicong see Franco

Pama see Wankang

Pamirsky Post see Murgab

Pamyati 13 Bortsov. Urban settlement, Krasnoyarsk Kray, Russia : Znamensky (–?)

Panagía see Askraía

Panaji. Town, western India : Nova Goa (–1961)

Panapaan see Pedro Espiritu

Panchow *see* Panhsien [P'an-hsien]

Pandrapura. Town, southern India : French Rocks (–1950s)

Panfilov. Town, Taldy-Kurgan Oblast, Kazakhstan : Dzharkent (–1942)

Panfilovskoye. Village, Kirgizia : Staro-Nikolayevskoye (–1942)

Panghü *see* Pingchih [P'ing-chih]

Pangi *see* Gaudencio Antonio (1)

Panhsien [P'an-hsien]. Town, southern China : Panchow (–1913)

Pannonhalma. Town, northwestern Hungary : Győrszentmárton (–1965)

Panpu *see* Kwanyün [Kuan-yün]

Panskoye *see* Maysk (1)

Pantaleímon. Village, northern Greece : Platamón (–1960s)

Paoan *see* Chihtan

Pao-ch'ing *see* Shao-yang

Paofeng *see* Hweinung [Hui-nung]

Paohing [Pao-hsing]. Town, southern China : Muping (–1929)

Pao-hsing = Paohing

Paoning *see* Langchung

Paoshan. Town, southwestern China : Yungchang (–1914)

Paosintsi *see* Sihsien [Hsi-hsien] (2)

Pao-ting. City, northeastern China : Tsingyüan [Ching-yüan] (–1958)

Paoyüan. Town, northeastern China : Kuyüan (–1950)

Papao *see* Kilien [Ch'i-lien]

Papari *see* Nísia Floresta

Papendorp *see* Woodstock

Paracales *see* Paracelis

Paracelis. Municipality, Mountain Province, Philippines : Paracales (–1966)

Paradise Island. Northeast of New Providence Island, Bahamas, West Indies : Hog Island (–c. 1960)

Paragua *see* Palawan

Paraguaçu *see* Paraguaçu Paulista

Paraguaçu Paulista. City, southeastern Brazil, South America : Paraguaçu (–1944), Araguaçu (1944–48)

Paraíba *see* João Pessoa

Paralía Akrátas *see* Kráthion

Paran. City, southern Brazil, South America : Palma (–1944)

Paranaíba. City, western Brazil, South America : Santana do Paranaíba (–1939)

Paraprástaina *see* Proástion

Parati *see* Araquari

Paratinga. City, eastern Brazil, South America : Rio Branco (–1944)

Parchwitz *see* Prochowice

Parco *see* (1) Altofonte; (2) Sinclair

Pardubice. Town, north-
central Czech Lands :
Pardubitz (–1918, 1939–
45), Germany
Pardubitz *see* Pardubice
Paredón *see* Anzaldo
Parizhskaya Kommuna.
Suburb of Kommunarsk,
Lugansk Oblast,
Ukraine : Seleznevsky
Rudnik (–1926)
Parkań *see* Štúrovo
Park City. Town, Kentucky,
USA : Glasgow Junction
(–1938)
Parnamirim. City, northeast-
ern Brazil, South Amer-
ica : Leopoldina (–1944)
Parnarama. City, north-
eastern Brazil, South
America : São José dos
Matões (–1944), Matões
(1944–48)
Pärnu. Town, Estonia :
Pernov (–1917)
Parreiras *see* Caldas
Parroquia de Besalú *see* San
Ferreol
Parr Siding *see* Harding
Parshevichi *see* Berezovichi
Partizanka. Village, Minsk
Oblast, Belorussia :
Zhabovka (–1964)
Partizanovka. Village,
Grodno Oblast, Belorus-
sia : Pleshki (–1964)
Partizansk. Town, Primor-
sky Kray, Russia : Su-
chansky Rudnik (–1932),
Suchan (1932–72)
Partizanskaya (1). Village,
Gomel Oblast, Belorus-
sia : Avraamovskaya
(–1964)

Partizanskaya (2). Village,
Grodno Oblast, Belorus-
sia : Puzovichi (–1964)
Partizanskaya (3). River,
Primorsky Kray, Russia :
Suchan (–1972)
Partizanskaya (4). Village,
Vitebsk Oblast, Belorus-
sia : Zhirospyory (–1964)
Partizánske. Town, west-
central Slovakia :
Šimonovany (–1947),
Batovany (1947–49)
Partizanskoye. Village,
Krasnoyarsk Kray, Rus-
sia : Perovo (–1930s)
Partizanskoye *see* Prokhlad-
noye
Partizany (1). Village,
Gomel Oblast, Belorus-
sia : Siporovka (–1964)
Partizany (2). Village,
Vitebsk Oblast, Belorus-
sia : Torbinka (–1964)
Pârvomay. City, south-cen-
tral Bulgaria : Bori-
sovgrad (–1944)
Pasarel Dam *see* Stalin Dam
Pashalu *see* Azizbekov
Pashiya. Urban settlement,
Perm Oblast, Russia :
Arkhangelo-Pashisky
Zavod (–1929)
Pashmakli *see* Smolyan
Pašićevo *see* Zmajevo
Pasłęk. Town, northeastern
Poland : Preussisch
Holland (–1945),
Germany
Passenheim *see* Pasym
Pasym. Town, northeastern
Poland : Passenheim
(–1945), Germany
Patos *see* Patos de Minas

Patos de Minas. City, south-
eastern Brazil, South
America : Patos (–1944)
Patriarsheye *see* Donskoye (2)
Patschkau *see* Paczków
Patton *see* Monroeville
Pau d'Alho *see* Ibirarema
Pau Gigante *see* Ibiraçu
Paulis *see* Isiro
Paulista *see* Paulistana
Paulistana. City, northeast-
ern Brazil, South Amer-
ica : Paulista (–1944)
Paulo Affonso *see* Mata
Grande
Pavlogradskiye Khutora per-
vyye *see* Vishnyovoye (2)
Pavlovka *see* Bogatoye
Pavlovo. Village, Grodno
Oblast, Belorussia :
Puzovichi (–1964)
Pavlovsk. Town, Leningrad
Oblast, Russia : Slutsk
(1918–44)
Payapa *see* General Tinio
Payen *see* Hwalung [Hua-
lung]
Payenyungko *see* Hwalung
[Hua-lung]
Payne Bay *see* Bellin
Payo. Municipality, Catan-
duanes, Philippines :
Jose Panganiban (–1957)
Payo Obispo *see* Chetumal
Payshanba. Village, Samar-
kand Oblast, Uzbekistan
: Paishambe (–c. 1935),
Kara-Darya (c. 1935–c.
1960)
Payung *see* Hwalung [Hua-
lung]
Pazardžik. City, southwest-
ern Bulgaria : Tatar-Paz-
ardžik (–1934)

Peacehaven. Town, East
Sussex, England, UK :
(New) Anzac-on-Sea
(*1916–19)
Peć. Town, southwestern
Serbia : Ipek (–1913),
Turkey
Pechenga. Urban settle-
ment, Murmansk Oblast,
Russia : Petsamo (1920–
44), Finland
Pechory. Town, Pskov Ob-
last, Russia : Petseri
(1920–45)
Pedra Azul. City, southeast-
ern Brazil, South Amer-
ica : Fortaleza (–1944)
Pedras Brancas *see* Guaíba
Pedro Avelino. City, north-
eastern Brazil, South
America : Epitácio Pes-
soa (–1948)
Pedro Espiritu. Barrio, Cav-
ite, Philippines : Pana-
paan (–1969)
Pehchen. Town, northeast-
ern China : Kwangning
(–1914)
Pehchwan [Pei-chuan].
Town, central China :
Shihchwan (–1914)
Pehtatung *see* Weiyüan
Peichow *see* Pihsien [P'ei-
hsien]
Pei-ch'uan = Pehchwan
Peifeng *see* Sian [Hsi-an]
(2)
P'ei-hsien = Pihsien
Peiping [Pei-p'ing] *see* Peking
[Beijing]
Peking [Beijing]. Capital of
China : Peiping [Pei-
p'ing] (1928–49)
Peklevskaya *see* Troitsky

Pełczyce. Town, western Poland : Bernstein (–1945), Germany
Pelten see Piltene
Pemba. City, northeastern Mozambique, southeastern Africa : Porto Amélia (–1976)
Pemberton Spur see Pritchard
Pengan [P'eng-an]. Town, central China : Pengchow (–1913)
Pengchow see Pengan [P'eng-an]
Penglai [P'eng-lai]. Town, eastern China : Tengchow (–1913)
Peninsular Malaysia. Administrative territory, Malaysia : West Malaysia (–1970s)
Penn see Penn Hills
Penn Hills. Township, Pennsylvania, USA : Penn (–1958)
Penny Hole see Gemswick
Pensky Sakharny Zavod see Karla Libknekhta, imeni (1)
Penthièvre see Aïn Berda
Pentyukhi see Vysochany (1)
Peny see Karla Libknekhta, imeni (1)
Peper Bay see Lada Bay
Peravia. Province, southern Dominican Republic, West Indies : Trujillo Valdéz (*1944–61)
Perdigão. Town, southeastern Brazil, South America : Saúde (–1944)
Perdizes see Videira
Peredelki see Borovshchina (1)

Peredniye Traki see Krasnoarmeyskoye
Peremozhets. Village, Minsk Oblast, Belorussia : Smorkovo (–1964)
Peremyshl see Przemyśl
Pereira d'Eça see Ondjiva
Perevoloki see Mezhdurechensk (2)
Perevoz. Urban settlement, Nizhegorodskaya Oblast, Russia : Pyansky Perevoz (–c. 1960)
Pereyaslav see Pereyaslav-Khmelnitsky
Pereyaslav-Khmelnitsky. Town, Kiev Oblast, Ukraine : Pereyaslav (–1943)
Perigotville see Aïn el Kebira
Peri Mirim. City, northeastern Brazil, South America : Macapá (–1944)
Perkhayly see Zarechnaya (3)
Perm. Capital of Perm Oblast, Russia : Molotov (1940–57)
Perm Oblast. East-central Russia : Molotov Oblast (*1940–57)
Permskoye see Komsomolsk-na-Amure
Pernik. Town, western Bulgaria : Dimitrovo (1949–62)
Pernov see Pärnu
Perovo see Partizanskoye
Perovsk see Kzyl-Orda
Perparim see Pogradec
Perrégaux see Mohammadia
Pershotravenka see Terny
Pershotravensk. Town, Dnepropetrovsk Oblast,

Ukraine :
Shakhtyorskoye
(–c. 1960), Per-
shotravnevoye (c. 1960–
66)
Pershotravnevoye (1). Ur-
ban settlement, Donetsk
Oblast, Ukraine : Man-
gush (–1946)
Pershotravnevoye (2). Ur-
ban settlement, Rovno
Oblast, Ukraine : Mokvin
(–c. 1960)
Pershotravnevoye see Per-
shotravensk
Persia see Iran
Pervomay (1). Village,
Gomel Oblast, Belorus-
sia : Gorovakha (–1964)
Pervomay (2). Village,
Minsk Oblast, Belorussia
: Plevaki (–1964)
Pervomaysk (1). Town, Ni-
kolayev Oblast, Ukraine :
Olviopol (–1920)
Pervomaysk (2). Town,
Lugansk Oblast, Ukraine
: Petromaryevka (–1920)
Pervomaysk (3). Village,
Vitebsk Oblast, Belorus-
sia : Svinoye (–1964)
Pervomaysk (4). Town, Niz-
hegorodskaya Oblast,
Russia : Tashino (–1951)
Pervomaysk (5). Village,
Minsk Oblast, Belorussia
: Zhivoglodovichi (–1964)
Pervomayskoye (1). Village,
Brest Oblast, Belorussia :
Bluden (–1964)
Pervomayskoye (2). Village,
Chuvash Autonomous
Republic, Russia : Bol-
shiye Arabuzy (–1939)

Pervomayskoye (3). Urban
settlement, Crimean Ob-
last, Ukraine : Dzurchi
(–1944)
Pervomayskoye (4). Village,
Saratov Oblast, Russia :
Gnadenflyur (–1941)
Pervomayskoye (5). Village,
Rostov Oblast, Russia :
Golodayevka (–1940)
Pervomayskoye (6). Village,
Chechen-Ingush Autono-
mous Republic, Russia :
Muzhichi (–1944)
Pervomayskoye (7). Village,
Tomsk Oblast, Russia :
Pyshkino-Troitskoye
(–c. 1960)
Pervomayskoye (8). Village,
Altay Kray, Russia :
Srednekrayushkino
(–c. 1960)
Pervomaysky (1). Urban set-
tlement, Tambov Oblast,
Russia : Bogoyav-
lenskoye (–c. 1960)
Pervomaysky (2). Urban set-
tlement, Samara Oblast,
Russia : Kozhemyaki
(–c. 1960)
Pervomaysky (3). Suburb of
Sterlitamak, Bashkir Au-
tonomous Republic, Rus-
sia : Kukshik (–1943)
Pervomaysky (4). Urban set-
tlement, Kharkov Oblast,
Ukraine : Likhachyovo
(–c. 1960)
Pervomaysky (5). Suburb of
Slobodskoy, Kirov Ob-
last, Russia : Spas (–1938)
Pervomaysky see (1) Ak-Suu;
(2) Novodvinsk; (3)
Podlesny

Pervouralsk. Town,
Sverdlovsk Oblast, Russia : Vasilyevsko-Shaytansky (–1920), Shaytansky Zavod (1920–28), Pervouralsky (1928–33)
Pervouralsky see Pervouralsk
Pervy Severny see Severny
Pescado see Villa Serrano
Peschanoye see Yashkul
Pesochnya see Kirov
Pesterszébet see Pestszenterszébet
Pestovo see Zavolzhye
Pestszenterzsébet. Suburb of Budapest, Hungary : Erzsébetfalva (–1919), Leninváros (1919–24), Pesterszébet (1924–32)
Pestszentimre. Suburb of Budapest, Hungary : Soroksárpéteri (*1930–31)
Pestújhely. Suburb of Budapest, Hungary : Széchenyitelep (*1909–10)
Peterborough. Town, South Australia, Australia : Petersburg (–1917)
Peterborough see Wilmer
Petergof see Petrodvorets
Peterhof see Petrodvorets
Petersburg see Peterborough
Petitjean see Sidi Kacem
Petrálona. Village, western Greece : Palaiá Halónia (–1960s)
Petra Stuchki, imeni see Stuchka
Petroaleksandrovsk see Turtkul
Petrodvorets. Town, Leningrad Oblast, Russia : Leninsk (1930s), Petergof [Peterhof] (1930s–1944)

Petro-Golenishchevo see Dolinovskoye
Petrograd see St. Petersburg
Petrograd Guberniya see Leningrad Guberniya
Petrokrepost. Town, Leningrad Oblast, Russia : Shlisselburg [Schlüsselburg] (–1944)
Petrolândia. City, northeastern Brazil, South America : Jatobá (–1939), Itaparica (1939–43)
Petromaryevka see Pervomaysk (2)
Petropavlovsk-Kamchatsky. Capital of Kamchatka Oblast, Russia : Petropavlovsky port (–1924)
Petropavlovsky see Severouralsk
Petropavlovsky port see Petropavlovsk-Kamchatsky
Petroverovka see Zhovten (1)
Petrovgrad see Zrenjanin
Petrovskaya Sloboda see Losino-Petrovsky
Petrovskogo G.I., imeni see Gorodishche
Petrovskoye. Town, Lugansk Oblast, Ukraine : Shterovsky (–1920)
Petrovskoye see Svetlograd
Petrovsk-Port see Makhachkala
Petrovsky Zavod see Petrovsk-Zabaykalsky
Petrovsk-Zabaykalsky. Town, Chita Oblast, Russia : Petrovsky Zavod (–1926)
Petrozavodsk. Capital of Karelian Autonomous

Republic, Russia : Kalininsk (1930s)

Petsamo see Pechenga

Petseri see Pechory

Petukhovo. Town, Kurgan Oblast, Russia : Yudino (–1944)

Petuna see Fuye

Petushki. Town, Vladimir Oblast, Russia : Novyye Petushki (–1965)

Phanárion Magoúla see Magoúla

Philadelphianá see Néa Philadélpheia

Philippeville see Skikda

Philipstown see Daingean

Phoenix Island see Rawaki

Phou-Khao-Khuai. Mountain resort, eastern Laos : Ritaville (–1967)

Phu Cuong see Thu Dau Mot

Phu Vinh see Tra Vinh

Piat. City, eastern Brazil, South America : Anchieta (–1944)

Pi-chiang = Pikiang

Picos see Colinas

Piedras Negras. City, northern Mexico, North America : Ciudad Porfirio Díaz (1888–c. 1911)

Piekar see Piekary (Śląskie)

Piekary (Śląskie). City, southern Poland : Piekar (–1945)

Pierrefonds. City, Quebec, Canada : Sainte-Geneviève (–1958)

Pierron. Village, Illinois, USA : Millersburg (–1939)

Pietole see Virgilio

Pihsien [P'ei-hsien]. Town, eastern China : Peichow (–1912)

Pik 20 let VLKSM see Pobedy, Pik

Pikiang [Pi-chiang]. Village, southwestern China : Yingpankai (–1934)

Piła. Town, northwestern Poland : Schneidemühl (–1945), Germany

Pilar. City, northeastern Brazil, South America : Manguaba (1944–48)

Pilar see Pilar do Sul

Pilar do Sul. City, southeastern Brazil, South America : Pilar (–1944)

Pilawa. Town, southwestern Poland : Beilau (–1945), Germany

Pilenkovo see Gantiadi

Pilimsit, Puncak. Mountain, Irian Jaya, Indonesia : Idenburg Top (–1963)

Piliscsév. Town, northern Hungary : Csév (–1954)

Pillau see Baltiysk

Pillkallen see Dobrovolsk

Pillupönen see Nevskoye

Piloto Juan Fernandez see Alejandro Selkirk

Pilsen see (1) Pilzno; (2) Plzeň

Piltene. Town, Latvia : Pelten (–1917)

Pilzno. Town, southeastern Poland : Pilsen (1939–45), Germany

Pinchow see (1) Pinhsien (1), (2); (2) Pinyang

Pinellas see Pinellas Park

Pinellas Park. City, Florida, USA : Pinellas (–1911)

Pingchang [P'ing-ch'ang].
Town, central China :
Kiangkow (–1944)
Pingchih [P'ing-chih].
Town, southern China :
Panghü (–1936)
Pingfan *see* Yungteng
Pingmei *see* Tsungkiang
[Ts'ung-chiang]
Pingpien [P'ing-pien].
Town, southwestern
China : Tsingpien (–1933)
Pingtang [P'ing-t'ang].
Town, southern China :
Tungchow (–1942)
Pingtichüan *see* Tsining
[Chi-ning]
Pingtung [P'ing-tung]. Town,
southern Taiwan : Akow
(–1920)
Pingwu [P'ing-wu]. Town,
central China : Lungan
(–1913)
Pingyang *see* Linfen
Pingyüan *see* Chihkin [Chih-
chin]
Pinhsien (1). Town, central
China : Pinchow (–1913)
Pinhsien (2). Town,
eastern China :
Pinchow (–1913)
Pinkiang *see* Harbin
Pinola *see* Las Rosas
Pinyang. Town, southern
China : Pinchow
(–1912)
Pioner. Suburb of
Kemerovo, Kemerovo
Oblast, Russia : Ishanovo
(–1936)
Pionersky. Town, Kalinin-
grad Oblast, Russia :
Neukuhren (–1946),
Germany (–1945)

Pio V. Corpuz. Municipality,
Masbate, Philippines :
Limbuhan (–1954)
Piperno *see* Priverno
Piracanjuba. City, central
Brazil, South America :
Pouso Alto (–1944)
Piraí *see* Piraí do Sul
Piraí do Sul. City, southern
Brazil, South America :
Piraí (–1944), Piraí Mirim
(1944–48)
Piraí Mirim *see* Piraí do Sul
Pirajaí *see* Cabrália Paulista
Piranhas. City, northeastern
Brazil, South America :
Marechal Floriano
(1939–48)
Pirapora *see* Pirapora do Bom
Jesus
Pirapora do Bom Jesus.
Town, southeastern
Brazil, South America :
Pirapora (–1944)
Piraquara. City, southern
Brazil, South America :
Deodoro (–c. 1935)
Pirchevan *see* Zangelan
Pirogovsky. Urban settle-
ment, Moscow Oblast,
Russia : Proletarskaya
Pobeda (c. 1918–28)
Pisha *see* Ningnan
Pishpek *see* Bishkek
Pistianá. Village, western
Greece : Pistianá Néas
Helládos (–1960s)
Pistianá Néas Helládos *see*
Pistianá
Pisyuta *see* Zalesskaya
Pisz. Town, northeastern
Poland : Johannisburg
(–1945), Germany
Pitschen *see* Byczyna

Pittsburg. City, California,
USA : Black Diamond
(–1911)

Pittsworth. Town, Queen-
sland, Australia : Beauaraba (–1915)

Pitzewo *see* Sinkin [Hsin-chin]

Pitzthal *see* Sankt Leonhard
(im Pitztal)

Piyüan *see* Tangho [Tang-ho]

Plagiá *see* Kephalokhórion

Planyorskoye. Urban settlement, Crimean Oblast,
Ukraine : Koktebel
(–1944)

Plaridel (1). Municipality,
Misamis, Philippines :
Laragaran (–1914)

Plaridel (2). Municipality,
Bulacan, Philippines :
Quingua (–1936)

Plaridel *see* Calamba

Platamón. Village, northern
Greece : Stathmós
(–1960s)

Platamón *see* Pantaleímon

Platána. Village, Euboea,
eastern Greece : Káto
Potamiá (–1960s)

Platános. Village, western
Greece : Akhoúria
Vavouríou (–1960s)

Plathe *see* Płoty

Platt National Park. Oklahoma, USA : Sulphur
Springs National Reserva-
tion (*1902–06)

Plavsk. Town, Tula Oblast,
Russia : Sergiyevskoye
(–1949)

Playa de Cabra *see* Playa de
Santa María

Playa de Santa María. Village, eastern Spain :

Playa de Cabra
(–c. 1960)

Plazigaz *see* Yasen

Pleasureville *see* South Pleasureville

Plekhovo *see* Zalesovtsy

Pleshivtsy *see* Zelyonaya (1)

Pleshki *see* Partizanovka (1)

Pleskau *see* Pskov

Plevaki *see* Pervomay (2)

Ploče *see* Kardeljevo

Płock. City, central Poland :
Plotsk (–1921), Russia,
Schröttersburg (1939–
45), Germany

Plöhnen *see* Płońsk

Plokhino *see* Ulyanovsk (3)

Płońsk. Town, east-central
Poland : Plöhnen (1939–
45), Germany

Ploskoye *see* Stanovoye

Plotsk *see* Płock

Płoty. Town, northwestern
Poland : Plathe (–1945),
Germany

Plzeň. City, western Czech
Lands : Pilsen (–1918,
1939–45), Germany

Poai. Town, north-central
China : Tsinghwa (–1929)

Pobedinsky *see* Zarechny

Pobednaya (1). Village,
Mogilyov Oblast, Belo-
russia : Polzukhi (–1964)

Pobednaya (2). Village,
Minsk Oblast, Belorussia :
Rakoyedovshchina
(–1964)

Pobednaya (3). Village, Gomel Oblast, Belorussia :
Stary Folvarok (–1964)

Pobedy, Pik. Russian name
of Tomur Feng, moun-
tain, western China/east-

ern Kirgizia : Pik 20 let
VLKSM (*1938–43)
Pochow see Pohsien
Poções. City, eastern Brazil,
South America : Djalma
Dutra (1944–48)
Podbrodze see Pabrade
Podchinny. Settlement, Vol-
gograd Oblast, Russia :
Kratske (–1941)
Poddannyye see Cheryomush-
ki (2)
Podgorica see Titograd
Podgornaya (1). Village,
Grodno Oblast, Belorus-
sia : Bloshno (–1964)
Podgornaya (2). Village,
Brest Oblast, Belorussia :
Gavinovichi (–1964)
Podlesnaya. Village, Minsk
Oblast, Belorussia :
Telyatki (–1964)
Podlesnoye. Village, Sara-
tov Oblast, Russia : Un-
tervalden (–1941)
Podlesny. Urban settlement,
Tula Oblast, Russia : Per-
vomaysky (–c. 1960)
Podlesskaya. Village, Mogi-
lyov Oblast, Belorussia :
Koryavinets (–1964)
Podlesye. Village, Vitebsk
Oblast, Belorussia :
Kukonosy (–1964)
Podlipki see Kaliningrad (2)
Podmokly. Town, north-
western Czech Lands :
Bodenbach (–1918, 1939–
45), Germany
Podonki see Znamenka (3)
Podrassolay see Vishnya (2)
Pofadder. Town, Cape Prov-
ince, South Africa :
Theronsville (1917–36)

Pogradec. Town, southeast-
ern Albania : Perparim
(1939–43), Italy
Pogranichny (1). Urban set-
tlement, Grodno Oblast,
Belorussia : Berestovitsa
(–1978)
Pogranichny (2). Urban set-
tlement, Primorsky Kray,
Russia : Grodekovo
(–1958)
Pohjois-Pirkkala see Nokia
Pohsien. Town, eastern
China : Pochow (–1912)
Pokrovka see (1) Leninskoye
(7); (2) Priamursky
Pokrovsk. Town, Saratov
Oblast, Russia :
Pokrovskaya Sloboda
(–1914), Engels (1931–
91)
Pokrovskaya Sloboda see
Pokrovsk
Pokrovskoye see (1)
Priazovskoye; (2)
Velikooktyabrsky
Pola see Istra (2)
Polanica Zdrój. Town,
southwestern Poland :
Bad Altheide (–1945),
Germany
Polanów. Town, northwest-
ern Poland : Pollnow
(–1945), Germany
Połczyn Zdrój. Town, north-
western Poland : Bad
Polzin (–1945), Germany
Polenovo. Country estate
and art museum, Tula
Oblast, Russia : Borok
(–1931)
Polessk. Town, Kaliningrad
Oblast, Russia : Labiau (–
1946), Germany (–1945)

Polesskoye. Urban settlement, Kiev Oblast, Ukraine : Khabno(ye) (–c. 1935), Kaganovich (c. 1935–c. 1940), Kaganovichi pervyye (c. 1940–57)

Polevskoy. Town, Sverdlovsk Oblast, Russia : Polevskoy Zavod (–1928)

Polevskoy Zavod see Polevskoy

Police. Suburb of Szczecin, northwestern Poland : Pölitz (–1945), Germany

Poliny Osipenko, imeni. Village, Khabarovsk Kray, Russia : Kerbi (–1939)

Pölitz see Police

Polkowice. Town, western Poland : Polkwitz (–1938), Germany; Heerwegen (1938–45), Germany

Polkwitz see Polkowice

Pollnow see Polanów

Pologi. Town, Zaporozhye Oblast, Ukraine : Chubarovka (c. 1928–39)

Polonia. Settlement, Manitoba, Canada : Huns Valley (–1921)

Polovinka see (1) Ugleuralsky; (2) Umaltinsky

Poltavka see Bashtanka

Poltavskaya see Krasnoarmeyskaya (2)

Poltoratsk see Ashkhabad

Põltsamaa. Town, central Estonia : Oberpahlen (–c. 1920)

Poludeno see Poludino

Poludino. Village, North Kazakhstan Oblast, Kazakhstan : Poludeno (–1937)

Polyanovgrad see Karnobat

Polyarny. Town, Murmansk Oblast, Russia : Aleksandrovsk (–1930s)

Polzukhi see Pobednaya (1)

Pomabamba see Azurduy

Pomba see Rio Pomba

Pombachi see Komsomolabad

Pomoriye. City, eastern Bulgaria : Ankhialo (–1934)

Pompei. Town, southern Italy : Valle de Pompei (–1928)

Pond Inlet. Settlement, Baffin Island, Northwest Territories, Canada : Ponds Bay (–1951)

Ponds Bay see Pond Inlet

Ponizovkino see Krasny Profintern (2)

Ponoka. Town, Alberta, Canada : Siding No. 14 (–1904)

Pont-du-Chéliff see Sidi Bel Atar

Ponthierville see Ubundi

Pontolívadon. Village, northern Greece : Néa Kóme (–1960s)

Poona Bayabao. Municipality, Lanao, Philippines : Gata (–1956)

Popasnaya. Town, Lugansk Oblast, Ukraine : Kaganovicha, L.M., imeni (1938–43)

Poplar Head see Dothan

Popova Luka see Ozyornaya (2)

Popovichskaya *see* Kalin-
inskaya
Popovka *see* Oreshenka
Porcupine *see* Porcupine
Plain
Porcupine Plain. Town,
Saskatchewan, Canada :
Porcupine (–1929)
Porechye *see* Demidov
Poronaysk. Town, Sakhalin
Oblast, Russia : Shikuka
(1905–46), Japan
Porosyatniki *see* Mayachnaya
Porozhsky. Urban settle-
ment, Irkutsk Oblast,
Russia : Bratsk
(–c. 1960)
Porrette Terme. Town,
north-central Italy :
Bagni della Porretta
(–c. 1931)
Porsy *see* Kalinin
Porta Littoria *see* La Thuile
Port Arthur [Lüshun]. City,
northeastern China :
Ryojun (1905–45), Japan
Port-Cartier. Town, Que-
bec, Canada : Shelter Bay
(*1918–1962)
Port Durnford *see* Bur Gao
Port Étienne *see* Nouadhibou
Port Florence *see* Kisumu
Port Francqui *see* Ilebo
Port Gueydon *see* Azetfoun
Port Harrison *see* Inukjuak
Port Herald *see* Nsanje
Port Hueneme. City, Cali-
fornia, USA : Hueneme
(–1940)
Port Kelang. Town, south-
western Malaya, Malay-
sia : Port Swettenham
(–1971)
Port-Khorly *see* Khorly

Port Laoise. Town, County
Laois, Ireland : Marybor-
ough (–1920)
Port-Lyautey *see* Kenitra
Port Nouveau-Québec.
Town, Quebec, Canada :
George River (–1967)
Pôrto. City, northeastern
Brazil, South America :
Marruás (–1930s), João
Pessoa (1930s–1944)
Pôrto Alegre *see* Luzilândia
Porto Amboim *see* Gunza
Porto Amélia *see* Pemba
Porto Azzurro. Town, Elba,
central Italy : Porto Lon-
gone (–1949)
Porto Longone *see* Porto
Azzurro
Porto Maurizio *see* Imperia
Pôrto Real *see* Iguatama
Porto Rico *see* Puerto Rico
Port Radium. Village, North-
west Territories, Canada :
Cameron Bay (–1937)
Port Royal. Community,
Nova Scotia, Canada :
Lower Granville (–1949)
Port St. Johns *see* Umzim-
vubu
Port Stanley. Capital of
Falkland Islands, south-
ern Atlantic : Puerto
Argentino (1982), Puerto
Rivero (1982)
Port Swettenham *see* Port
Kelang
Portugália *see* Luachimo
Portuguese East Africa *see*
Mozambique
Portuguese Guinea *see*
Guinea-Bissau
Portuguese Timor *see* Timor
Timur

Portuguese West Africa *see*
Angola
Posen *see* Poznań
Poshow. Town, southern
China : Yungning
(–1915), Kuhwa (1915–
33)
Possedimenti Italiani dell'
Egeo *see* Dodecanese
Poste de la Baleine. Town,
Quebec, Canada : Great
Whale River (–1967)
Postojna. Town, western
Slovenia : Postumia
(–1947), Italy
Postumia *see* Postojna
Pouso Alto *see* Piracanjuba
Powell. City, Wyoming,
USA : Camp Coulter
(*1906–09)
Power House *see* Drayton
Valley
Poyang [P'o-yang]. Town,
southeastern China :
Jaochow (–1912)
Poyo del Cid. Village, east-
ern Spain : El Poyo
(–1962)
Pozharskoye. Village, Pri-
morsky Kray, Russia :
Tikhonovka (–1939)
Poznań. City, western
Poland : Posen (–1919,
1939–45), Germany
Prabuty. Town, northeast-
ern Poland : Riesenburg
(–1919, 1939–45),
Germany
Praia da Condúcia. Village,
eastern Mozambique,
southeastern Africa :
Choca (–1971)
Prainha *see* Miracatu
Prassberg *see* Mozirje

Prata *see* Nova Prata
Prausnitz *see* Prusice
Praust *see* Pruszcz (Gdański)
Pravda. Urban settlement,
Sakhalin Oblast, Russia :
Hirochi (1905–46), Japan
(–1945)
Pravdino. Village, Kalinin-
grad Oblast, Russia :
Grumbkowfelde
(–c. 1930), Germany,
Grumbkowkeiten
(c. 1930–45), Germany
Pravdinsk. Town, Kalinin-
grad Oblast, Russia :
Friedland (–1946),
Germany (–1945)
Pravoberezhnoye *see* Novy
Karachay
Predgornoye. Village,
Chechen-Ingush Autono-
mous Republic, Russia :
Staryye Atagi (–1944)
Première *see* Hodh ech Char-
gui
Preobrazhenskaya *see*
Kikvidze
Presidencia da la Plaza.
Town, northern Argen-
tina, South America :
Presidente de la Plaza
(-early 1940s)
Presidente de la Plaza *see*
Presidencia de la Plaza
Presidente Dutra. City,
northeastern Brazil,
South America : Curador
(–1948)
Presidente Juán Perón *see*
Chaco
Presidente Marques *see*
Abunã
Presidente Vargas *see* (1)
Itabira; (2) Nova Era

President González Videla *see*
Greenwich
Island
President Roxas. Barrio,
Leyte, Philippines : Mati
(–1957)
Presnya *see* Krasnaya Presnya
Pressburg *see* Bratislava
Preussisch Eylau *see* Bagra-
tionovsk
Preussisch Friedland *see*
Debrzno
Preussisch Holland *see* Paslek
Preussisch Stargard *see* Star-
ogard (Gdański)
Priamursky. Urban settle-
ment, Jewish Autono-
mous Oblast, Khab-
arovsk Kray, Russia :
Pokrovka (–c. 1960)
Priargunsk. Urban settle-
ment, Chita Oblast,
Russia : Tsurukhaytuy
(–1962)
Priazovskoye. Urban settle-
ment, Zaporozhye
Oblast, Ukraine :
Pokrovskoye (–c. 1935)
Pribalkhash *see* Balkhash
Příbor. Town, eastern Czech
Lands : Freiberg (–1919,
1939–45), Germany
Pridnestrovskoye. Village,
Moldavia : Vertyuzhany
(–c. 1960)
Pridorozhnoye *see* Khulkhuta
Prikumsk *see* Budyonnovsk
Primkenau *see* Przemków
Primorsk (1). Town, Kalin-
ingrad Oblast, Russia :
Fischhausen (–1946),
Germany (–1945)
Primorsk (2). Town, Lenin-
grad Oblast, Russia :

Björkö (–1918), Sweden;
Koivisto (1918–49),
Finland (–1940)
Primorsk (3). Urban settle-
ment, Volgograd Oblast,
Russia : Lugovaya
Proleyka (–c. 1960)
Primorskoye (1). Village,
Crimean Oblast,
Ukraine : Mayak-Salyn
(–1944)
Primorskoye (2). Urban set-
tlement, Zaporozhye Ob-
last, Ukraine : Nogaysk
(–c. 1960)
Primorskoye (3). Urban set-
tlement, Donetsk Oblast,
Ukraine : Sartana (–1946)
Primorsky. Urban settle-
ment, Primorsky Kray,
Russia : Ust-Mongunay
(–c. 1960)
Primorye. Village, Minsk
Oblast, Belorussia :
Skulovka (–1964)
Prince George. City, British
Columbia, Canada : Fort
George (–1915)
Principele-Nicolae *see* De-
cemvrie 30, 1947
Prinkipo *see* Büyükada
Prins Hendrik Top *see* Yamin,
Puncak
Priozyorsk. Town, Lenin-
grad Oblast, Russia :
Keksgolm [Kexholm,
Käkisalmi] (–1948),
Finland (–1940)
Prishib *see* Leninsk (1)
Pristanskoye. Village, Omsk
Oblast, Russia : Izylbash
(–?), Molotovo (?–1957)
Pristansky. Urban settle-
ment, Karakalpak Auton-

omous Republic, Uzbekistan : Nukus (–c. 1960)
Pristen. Urban settlement, Kursk Oblast, Russia : Maryino (–c. 1960)
Pritchard. Town, British Columbia, Canada : Pemberton Spur (–1911)
Priupsky. Urban settlement, Tula Oblast, Russia : Milenino (–c. 1960)
Priverno. Town, south-central Italy : Piperno (–1928)
Privolzhsk. Town, Ivanovo Oblast, Russia : Yakovlevskoye (–1941)
Privolzhskoye. Village, Saratov Oblast, Russia : Kukkus (–1941)
Privolzhsky. Suburb of Astrakhan, Astrakhan Oblast, Russia : Kalmytsky Bazar (–1936), Kanukov (1936–44)
Proástion. Village, eastern Greece : Paraprástaina (–1960s)
Prochowice. Town, southwestern Poland : Parchwitz (–1945), Germany
Proctor. Village, Minnesota, USA : Proctorknott (–1939)
Proctorknott see Proctor
Prokhladnoye. Village, Crimean Oblast, Ukraine : Partizanskoye (–c. 1960)
Proletarsk (1). Urban settlement, Leninabad Oblast, Tajikistan : Dragomirovo (–?)
Proletarsk (2). Suburb of Lisichansk, Lugansk

Oblast, Ukraine : Nesvetevich (–?)
Proletarsk (3). Town, Rostov Oblast, Russia : Proletarskaya (–1970)
Proletarskaya see Proletarsk (3)
Proletarskaya Pobeda see Pirogovsky
Proletarsky (1). Urban settlement, Belgorod Oblast, Russia : Gotnya (–?)
Proletarsky (2). Urban settlement, Moscow Oblast, Russia : Proletary (–1928)
Proletary see Proletarsky (2)
Promyshlennovsky. Urban settlement, Kemerovo Oblast, Russia : Bolshaya Promyshlenka (–c. 1960)
Promzino see Surskoye
Propoysk see Slavgorod
Proskurov see Khmelnitsky
Prossnitz see Prostějov
Prostějov. City, east-central Czech Lands : Prossnitz (–1918, 1939–45), Germany
Prudnik. City, southwestern Poland : Neustadt (–1945), Germany
Prusice. Town, southwestern Poland : Prausnitz (–1945), Germany
Pruszcz (Gdański). Town, northern Poland : Praust (–1945), Germany
Przemków. Town, western Poland : Primkenau (–1945), Germany
Przemyśl. Town, southeastern Poland : Peremyshl

(1939–40), USSR [on
right bank of San River];
Deutsch Przemysl (1939–
40), Germany [on left
bank]
Przhevalsk. Capital of Issyk-
Kul Oblast, Kirgizia :
Karakol (*1869–89,
1921–39)
Przhevalskoye. Village,
Smolensk Oblast, Russia :
Sloboda (–c. 1960)
Psedakh *see* Alanskoye
Psirtskha *see* Novy Afon
Pskov. Capital of Pskov
Oblast, Russia : Pleskau
(1941–44), Germany
Psyché *see* Hagíos Nikólaos
Puchow *see* (1) Puhsien
[P'u-hsien]; (2) Yüngtsi
[Yüng-chi]
Pudjut Point. Cape, north-
western Java, Indonesia :
Saint Nicholas Point
(–1963)
Puebla *see* La Puebla del
Río
Puebla de Don Fadrique *see*
Villa de Don Fadrique
Puebla de la Mujer Muerta *see*
Puebla de la Sierra
Puebla de la Sierra. Village,
central Spain : Puebla
de la Mujer Muerta
(–c. 1940)
Puebla de Lillo. Village,
northwestern Spain :
Lillo (–c. 1920)
Pueblo de la Capilla *see* Sauce
del Yí
Pueblo Viejo *see* Villa Canales
Puente de Montañana. Vil-
lage, northeastern Spain :
Montañana (–c. 1960)

Puerh *see* Ningerh
Puerto Acosta. Town, west-
ern Bolivia, South Amer-
ica : Huaicho (–1908)
Puerto Aguirre *see* Puerto
Iguazú
Puerto Argentino *see* Port
Stanley
Puerto Chicama. Town,
northwestern Peru, South
America : Malabrigo
(–1920)
Puerto de Cabras *see* Puerto
del Rosario
Puerto de Castilla. Village,
east-central Spain : Casas
del Puerto de Tornavacas
(–c. 1940)
Puerto del Rosario. Village,
Gran Canaria, Canary Is-
lands : Puerto de Cabras
(–c. 1960)
Puerto de San Juan *see* Puerto
Lápice
Puerto de Son. Village,
northwestern Spain : Son
(–c. 1950)
Puerto Iguazú. Village,
northeastern Argentina,
South America : Puerto
Aguirre (–1940s)
Puerto Lápice. Village,
south-central Spain :
Puerto de San Juan
(–c. 1930)
Puerto México *see* Coatzacoal-
cos
Puerto Pérez. Town, west-
ern Bolivia, South Amer-
ica : Chililaya (–1900)
Puerto Rico. Island com-
monwealth, West Indies :
Porto Rico (–1932)
Puerto Rivero *see* Port Stanley

Puerto Sandino. Town, western Nicaragua, Central America : Puerto Somoza (–1980)

Puerto-Seguro. Village, western Spain : Barba de Puerco (–c. 1960)

Puerto Somoza *see* Puerto Sandino

Pugachyov. Town, Saratov Oblast, Russia : Nikolayevsk (–1918)

Pugachyovo. Village, Sakhalin Oblast, Russia : Maguntan-hama (1905–45), Japan

Puhsien [P'u-hsien]. Town, north-central China : Puchow (–1913)

Puigtiñós *see* Montferri

Pukova *see* Komsomolskaya

Pulau Blakang Mati *see* Sentosa

Puławy. Town, eastern Poland : Novaya Aleksandriya (–c. 1914), Russia

Pulgan *see* Frunzenskoye

Pulin *see* Chervonoarmeysk (1)

Pułtusk. Town, east-central Poland : Ostenburg (1939–45), Germany

Pungarabato *see* Altamirano

Punta Arenas. City, southern Chile, South America : Magallanes (1927–37)

Punyü. Town, southeastern China : Shikyu (–1946)

Punyü *see* Canton

Pupelichi *see* Krynichka

Pupsa *see* Maysk (2)

Pushkin. Town, Leningrad Oblast, Russia : Tsarskoye Selo (–1918), Detskoye Selo (1918–37)

Pushkino (1). Village, Kaliningrad Oblast, Russia : Dosmahlen (–1946), Germany, (–1945)

Pushkino (2). Village, Saratov Oblast, Russia : Urbakh (–1941)

Püspöknádasd *see* Mecseknádasd

Pustoy Ugol *see* Kolosovka (2)

Pustynka *see* Svetlaya Roshcha

Putao. Government post, northern Myanmar : Fort Hertz (–?)

Putien [P'u-t'ien]. Town, southeastern China : Hinghwa (–1913)

Putyatin. Urban settlement, Putyatin island, Primorsky Kray, Russia : Nazimovo (c. 1947–c. 1960)

Puyang [P'u-yang]. Town, north-central China : Kaichow (–1913)

Puziki *see* (1) Borovshchina (2); (2) Safonovo

Puzol *see* Tugaoen

Puzovichi *see* (1) Partizanskaya (2); (2) Pavlovo

Pwani. Administrative region, eastern Tanzania, eastern Africa : Coast (–1976)

Pyandzh. Town, Khatlon Oblast, Tajikistan : Saray Komar (–1931), Baumanabad (1931–36), Kirovabad (1936–63)

Pyandzh *see* Dusti

Pyansky Perevoz *see* Perevoz

Pyany Les *see* Sosnovaya (2)

Pyarnu = Pärnu
Pyatikhatka *see* Pyatikhatki
Pyatikhatki. Town, Dnepro-
petrovsk Oblast,
Ukraine : Pyatikhatka
(–1944)
Pyrénées-Atlantiques. Depart-
ment, southwestern
France : Basses-Pyrénées
(–1969)
Pyshkino-Troitskoye *see* Per-
vomayskoye (7)
Pyshma *see* Verkhnyaya
Pyshma
Pyshminsky Zavod *see* Staro-
pyshminsk
Pytalovo. Town, Pskov Ob-
last, Russia : Abrene
(1920–45)

Qa'emshahr [Ghaem Shahr].
Town, northern Iran :
Shahi (–1980)
Qahremanshar *see* Bakhta-
ran
Qomisheh. Town, central
Iran : Shahreza (–1980)
Quan Long *see* Ca Mau
Quatrième *see* Gorgol
Quebec West *see* Vanier (2)
Queen Elizabeth National
Park *see* Ruwenzori Na-
tional Park
Queen's County *see* Laois
Queen's Cross *see* King's Cross
Queenstown *see* Cóbh
Que Que *see* Kwekwe
Quezon. Province, Luzon,
Philippines : Tayabas
(–1946)
Quingua *see* Plaridel (2)
Quintanilla de Abajo *see*
Quintanilla de Onésimo

Quintanilla de Onésimo. Village, north-central Spain :
Quintanilla de Abajo
(–c. 1950)
Quipungo. Town, southwestern Angola, southwestern
Africa : Paiva Couceiro
(–c. 1975), Kipungo
(c. 1975–c. 1979)
Quitexe *see* Dange
Qytet Stalin = Stalin

Raahe. Town, western Fin-
land : Brahestad (–?)
Rača. Town, south-central
Poland : Ratibor (–1945),
Germany
Racibórz. Town, south-
central Poland : Ratibor
(–1945), Germany
Račisdorf *see* Rača
Radeče. Village, western
Slovenia : Ratschach
(–1918), Germany
Radishchevo (1). Village,
Ulyanovsk Oblast,
Russia : Dvoryanskaya
Tereshka (–1918)
Radishchevo (2). Village,
Penza Oblast, Russia :
Verkhneye Ablyazovo
(–?)
Radków. Town, southwest-
ern Poland : Wünsch-
elburg (–1945), Germany
Radmannsdorf *see* Radovl-
jica
Radomir. Mountain, south-
western Bulgaria : Kala-
bak (–1967)
Radomsko. Town, south-
central Poland : Nowora-
domsk (–1914)

Radovitsky. Urban settle-
ment, Moscow Oblast,
Russia : Tsentralny
(–c. 1960)
Radovljica. Village, north-
western Slovenia : Rad-
mannsdorf (–1918), Ger-
many
Radzivilov see Cher-
vonoarmeysk (2)
Radzivilovichi see Dzerzhinsk
(3)
Ragnit see Neman
Ragusa see Dubrovnik
Rahouia. Village, northern
Algeria, northern Africa :
Montgolfier (–c. 1962)
Rainbow City. Town, Pan-
ama Canal Zone, Central
America : Silver City (–?)
Raivola see Roshchino (2)
Rajaori. District, northern
India : Riasi (–c. 1948)
Rajasthan. State, northwest-
ern India : Rajputana
(1818–1950)
Rajhenburg. Village, west-
ern Slovenia : Reichen-
burg (–1918), Germany
Rajputana see Rajasthan
Rakhmanovka. Urban settle-
ment, Dnepropetrovsk
Oblast, Ukraine : Alek-
sandrov Dar (–c. 1960)
Rakoyedovshchina see
Pobednaya (2)
Rakushevo. Village, Mogi-
lyov Oblast, Belorussia :
Likhinichi (–1967)
Rakvere. Town, Estonia :
Wesenberg (–1917)
Ramat Gan. City, west-
central Israel : En Gan-
nim (*1920–c. 1921)

Ramon Magsaysay. Barrio,
Zamboanga del Norte,
Philippines : Palandoc
(–1968)
Randolph see Brea
Ranenburg see Chaplygin
Rangoon see Yangon
Rangoon Heights. Moun-
tain, North Island, New
Zealand : Misery, Mount
(–1966)
Rankovićevo. Village, west-
ern Slovenia : Karlovac
(–1947)
Rankovićevo see Kraljevo
Rantomari see Yablochny
Raritan see (1) Edison; (2)
Highland Park
Ras Asir. Cape, northeast-
ern Somalia, eastern Af-
rica : Guardafui (–?)
Ras el Ma. Town, north-
western Algeria, north-
ern Africa : Bedeau
(–c. 1962)
Ras el Oued. Village, north-
eastern Algeria, northern
Africa : Tocqueville
(–c. 1962)
Ras Kebdana. Village,
northwestern Morocco,
northwestern Africa :
Cabo-Agua (–c. 1959)
Rassvet. Village, Vitebsk
Oblast, Belorussia : Cher-
tovshchina (–1964)
Rassvetnaya (1). Village,
Gomel Oblast, Belorus-
sia : Kobylyanka (–1964)
Rassvetnaya (2). Village,
Minsk Oblast, Belorussia
: Tsitskovichi (–1964)
Rastenburg see Kętrzyn
Rastorguyevo see Vidnoye

Rastyapino *see* Dzerzhinsk
(1)
Rateau *see* Lewis
Ráth Luirc.   Town, County
Cork, Ireland : Charle-
ville (–1939)
Ratibor *see* Racibórz
Rat Portage *see* Kenora
Ratschach *see* Radeče
Ratzebuhr *see* Okonek
Rauschen *see* Svetlogorsk
(1)
Rautenberg *see* Uzlovoye
Rautu *see* Sosnovo
Rawaki.   Island, Kiribati,
western Pacific : Phoenix
Island (–1981)
Rawicz.   Town, west-central
Poland : Rawitsch (1939–
45), Germany
Rawitsch *see* Rawicz
Razdan (1).   Town, Arme-
nia : Akhta (–1959)
Razdan (2).   Settlement, Ar-
menia : Ulukhanlu (–?),
Zangibasar (?–1964)
Razdolnaya.   Village,
Vitebsk Oblast, Belorus-
sia : Bezdelichi (–1964)
Razdolnoye.   Urban settle-
ment, Crimean Oblast,
Ukraine : Ak-Sheikh
(–1944)
Razino.   Village, Kalinin-
grad Oblast, Russia :
Doristhal (–1945), Ger-
many
Razlog.   City, southwestern
Bulgaria : Mekhomiya
(–1925), Turkey
Recz.   Town, northwestern
Poland : Reetz (–1945),
Germany
Redcliff *see* Ikawai

Redenção *see* Redenção da
Serra
Redenção da Serra.   City,
southeastern Brazil,
South America : Re-
denção (–1944)
Red Jacket *see* Calumet
Red Oak.   City, Iowa, USA :
Red Oak Junction
(–1901)
Red Oak Junction *see* Red
Oak
Reetz *see* Recz
Regar *see* Tursunzade
Regele Carol II *see* Suvorovo
(2)
Regele Mihai I *see* Suvorovo
(2)
Regenwalde *see* Resko
Reïbell *see* Ksar Chellala
Reichenau *see* (1) Bogatynia;
(2) Rychnov nad
Kněžnou
Reichenau (bei Gablonz) *see*
Rychnov
Reichenbach *see* Dzierżoniów
Reichenberg *see* Liberec
Reichenburg *see* Rajhenburg
Reichenstein *see* Złoty Stok
Reichshof *see* Rzeszów
Reichstadt *see* Zákupy
Reifnig *see* Ribnica (na
Pohorju)
Reivilo.   Town, Cape Prov-
ince, South Africa : Klein
Boetsap (*1917–27)
Relizane *see* Ighil Izane
Remchi.   Village, northwest-
ern Algeria, northern Af-
rica : Montagnac
(–c. 1962)
Remennikovo.   Village, Vol-
gograd Oblast, Russia :
Oberdorf (–1941)

Renault *see* Sidi M'Hamed
Ben Ali
Repelen-Baerl *see* Rheinkamp
Repino. Urban settlement,
Leningrad Oblast, Rus-
sia : Kuokkala (–1948),
Finland (–1940)
Reppen *see* Rzepin
Rerik. Town, northeastern
Germany : Alt Gaarz
(–1938)
Reriutaba. City, northeast-
ern Brazil, South Amer-
ica : Santa Cruz (–1944)
Residensia. Township,
Transvaal, South Africa :
Evaton (*1904–62)
Resko. Town, northwestern
Poland : Regenwalde
(–1945), Germany
Resulayn *see* Ceylanpinar
Reszel. Town, northeastern
Poland : Rössel (–1945),
Germany
Reutov. Town, Moscow Ob-
last, Russia : Reutovo
(–1940)
Reutovo *see* Reutov
Revel *see* Tallinn
Rexton. Town, New Brun-
swick, Canada : Kingston
(–1901)
Rezā'īyeh *see* Urmia
Rezekne. Town, Latvia :
Rezhitsa (–1917)
Rezhitsa *see* Rezekne
Rheinkamp. City, western
Germany : Repelen-
Baerl (–?)
Rhodesia *see* Zimbabwe
Riaba. Town, Bioko, Equa-
torial Guinea,
western Africa : La Con-
cepción (–1974)

Riachão *see* Riachão do Dan-
tas
Riachão do Dantas. City,
northeastern Brazil,
South America : Riachão
(–1944)
Riasi *see* Rajaori
Ribas do Rio Pardo. City,
western Brazil, South
America : Rio Pardo
(–1944)
Ribeirão *see* Guapó
Ribnica (na Pohorju). Vil-
lage, south-central Slov-
enia : Reifnig (–1918),
Germany
Rickenbacker Air Force
Base. Ohio, USA :
Lockbourne Air Force
Base (*1942–74)
Ridder. Town, East Ka-
zakhstan Oblast, Ka-
zakhstan : Leninogorsk
(1941–91)
Riesenburg *see* Prabuty
Riggládes *see* Áno Leukímme
Rijeka. City, western
Croatia : Fiume (1924–
45), Italy
Rimske Toplice. Village,
western Slovenia : Römer-
bad (–1918), Germany
Rincon *see* Mdiq
Río Benito *see* Mbini
Rio Bonito *see* (1) Caiapônia;
(2) Tangará
Río Branco. Town, north-
eastern Uruguay, South
America : Artigas
(–1909)
Rio Branco *see* (1) Arcoverde;
(2) Paratinga; (3) Ro-
raima; (4) Visconde do
Rio Branco

Rio Brilhante. City, western Brazil, South America : Entre Rios (–1943), Caiuás (1944–48)

Rio da Dúvida *see* Roosevelt, Rio

Rio das Flores. City, southeastern Brazil, South America : Santa Teresa (–1943)

Río de Oro *see* Oued Eddahab

Rio do Sul. City, southern Brazil, South America : Bela Aliança (*1903–?), Itajahy do Sul (?–?)

Rio-Martin *see* Martil

Rio Novo *see* Ipiaú

Rio Pardo *see* (1) Iúna; (2) Ribas do Rio Pardo; (3) Rio Pardo de Minas

Rio Pardo de Minas. City, southeastern Brazil, South America : Rio Pardo (–1944)

Rio Pomba. City, southeastern Brazil, South America : Pomba (–1948)

Rio Prêto *see* São José do Rio Prêto

Río Seco *see* Villa de María

Rippin *see* Rypin

Rishabhatirtha. Town, central India : Gunji (–1950s)

Rishtan. Town, Fergana Oblast, Uzbekistan : Kuybysheva, imeni (1937– c. 1940), Kuybyshevo (c. 1940–77)

Ritaville *see* Phou-Khao-Khuai

Ritlyab *see* Sayasan

Riva *see* Riva-del-Garda

Riva-del-Garda. Town, northeastern Italy : Riva (–1971)

Riversdale *see* Albertinia

Rivet *see* Meftah

Riviera *see* Riviera Beach

Riviera Beach. City, Florida, USA : Riviera (–1940)

Rivière-du-Loup. City, Quebec, Canada : Fraserville (–1919)

Rivière-Verte. Town, New Brunswick, Canada : Green River (–1935)

Rivoli *see* Hasei Nameche

Rizal (1). Municipality, Cagayan, Philippines : Manawan (–1914)

Rizal (2). Barrio, Sorsogon, Philippines : Tublijon (–1914)

Roberts Heights *see* Voortrekkerhoogte

Robert Williams *see* Caála

Robinson Crusoe. Island, Juan Fernández group, Chile, South America : Más a Tierra (–1962), Marino Alejandro Selkirk (1962–66)

Roçadas *see* Xangongo

Rock Springs. Village, Wisconsin, USA : Ableman (–1947)

Rocky Bay *see* Carmanville

Roda *see* Stadroda

Rodaugé. Village, western Greece : Nesísta Néas Helládos (–1960s)

Rodó = (José Enrique) Rodó

Rogaland. County, southwestern Norway : Stavanger (–1918)

Rogaška Slatina. Village,
eastern Slovenia : Ro-
hitsch-Sauerbrunn
(–1918), Germany
Rohitsch-Sauerbrunn see Ro-
gaška Slatina
Rolândia. City, southern
Brazil, South America :
Caviúna (1944–48)
Romanov see Dzerzhinsk (4)
Romanov-Borisoglebsk see
Tutayev
Romanovka see Bessarabka
Romanov-na-Murmane see
Murmansk
Romanovsky Khutor see Kro-
potkin (1)
Römerbad see Rimske Toplice
Romit. Village, Tajikistan :
Uramit (–c. 1935)
Rommani. Town, northwest-
ern Morocco, northwest-
ern Africa : Marchand
(–c. 1958)
Romsdal see Møre og Romsdal
Rondônia. Territory, west-
ern Brazil, South Amer-
ica : Guaporé (*1943–
56)
Ronne Ice Shelf. Territory,
Antarctica : Edith Ronne
Land (*1948–?)
Roosevelt. Borough, New
Jersey, USA : Jersey
Homesteads (*1933–
c. 1940)
Roosevelt see Carteret
Roosevelt, Rio. River, west-
central Brazil, South
America : Rio da Dúvida
(–1914)
Roosevelttown. Town, New
York, USA : Nyando
(–1934)

Roraima. State, northern
Brazil, South America :
Rio Branco (*1943–62)
Rosário see (1) Rosário do
Catete; (2) Rosário do
Sul
Rosário do Catete. City,
northeastern Brazil,
South America : Rosário
(–1944)
Rosário do Sul. City, south-
ern Brazil, South Amer-
ica : Rosário (–1944)
Rose-Marie see Ech Chiahna
Rosenberg see (1) Oleśno; (2)
Susz
Roshcha. Village, Vitebsk
Oblast, Belorussia : Gni-
lyaki (–1964)
Roshchino (1). Village,
Gomel Oblast, Belorus-
sia : Kusochek (–1964)
Roshchino (2). Urban settle-
ment, Leningrad Oblast,
Russia : Raivola (–1948),
Finland (–1940)
Roshchino (3). Village,
Vitebsk Oblast, Belorus-
sia : Zvyagi (–1964)
Rössel see Reszel
Rossitten see Rybachy (2)
Rossman Lake. Lake, Mani-
toba, Canada : Fishing
Lake (–1967)
Rossony. Urban settlement,
Vitebsk Oblast, Belorus-
sia : Stanislavovo
(–c. 1940)
Rostkovsky Rudnik see
Oktyabrskoy Revolyutsii,
imeni
Rostovtsevo see Krasnog-
vardeysk
Rot-Front see Dobropolye

Rouffach *see* Ebn Ziad
Rovigno (d'Istria) *see* Ro-
vinj
Rovinj.   Town, western
Croatia : Rovigno (d'Is-
tria) (–?), Italy
Rovira.   Town, west-central
Colombia, South Amer-
ica : Miraflores (–1930)
Rovno.   City, Rovno Oblast,
Ukraine : Równe (1920–
39), Poland
Rovnoye.   Urban settle-
ment, Saratov Oblast,
Russia : Zelman (–1941)
Równe *see* Rovno
Roxas.   City, Capiz, Philip-
pines : Capiz (–?)
Roycroft *see* Rycroft
Rozenburg *see* Rozovka
Rozhdestvenskaya *see* (1)
Dzerzhinskoye (2); (2)
Sivashskoye
Rozovka.   Urban settlement,
Zaporozhye Oblast,
Ukraine : Rozenburg
(–c. 1935), Lyuksemburg
(c. 1935–41)
Rozy Lyuksemburg.   Village,
Gomel Oblast, Belorus-
sia : Odesskaya (–1919)
Rozy Lyuksemburg, Cape *see*
Lokot, Cape
Ruanda *see* Rwanda
Rubetsu *see* Kuybyshevo (3)
Rubezhnaya *see* Rubezhnoye
Rubezhnoye.   Town, Lu-
gansk Oblast, Ukraine :
Rubezhnaya (–c. 1940)
Ruby Beach *see* Jacksonville
Beach
Rudaka *see* Aniva
Rudnaya Pristan.   Urban
settlement, Primorsky

Kray, Russia : Tetyukhe-
Pristan (–1972)
Rudnichny.   Urban settle-
ment, Sverdlovsk Oblast,
Russia : Auerbakhovsky
Rudnik (–1933)
Rudnik imeni Shvartsa *see*
Zhyoltyye Vody
Rudnik Ingichka *see* Ingichka
Rudny.   Urban settlement,
Primorsky Kray, Russia :
Lifudzin (–1972)
Rukhlovo *see* Skovorodino
Rummelsburg *see* Miastko
Rumyantsevo *see* Lenina,
V.I., imeni
Rupert House.   Village,
Quebec, Canada :
Fort-Rupert (–?)
Ruše.   Village, northern
Slovenia : Maria Rast
(–1918), Germany
Rushan.   Settlement, Gorno-
Badakhshan Autono-
mous Oblast, Tajikistan :
Kalai-Vamar (–c. 1935)
Russia.   Republic, Europe/
Asia : Russian Soviet
Federal Socialist Repub-
lic [RSFSR; popularly,
Russia] (*1922–90)
Russia *see* Commonwealth of
Independent States
Russkoye Selo *see* Markhamat
Rust *see* El Cerrito
Ruth.   Town, North Carolina,
USA : Hampton (–1939)
Ruth, Mount.   Mountain,
Antarctica : Ruth Black,
Mount (*1934–67)
Ruth Black, Mount *see* Ruth,
Mount
Ruthenia *see* Transcarpathian
Oblast

Rutland Water. Reservoir, Leicestershire, England, UK : Empingham Reservoir (*1971–76)
Rutten. Lake, Manitoba, Canada : Karsakuwigamak (–1972)
Ruwenzori National Park. Southwestern Uganda, eastern Africa : Queen Elizabeth National Park (*1952– c. 1975)
Rwanda. Republic, east-central Africa : Ruanda (–1962)
Rybachy (1). Urban settlement, Kamchatka Oblast, Russia : Novaya Tarya (–c. 1960)
Rybachy (2). Settlement, Kaliningrad Oblast, Russia : Rossitten (–1946), Germany (–1945)
Rybachye see Issyk-Kul
Rybalskaya see Karla Marksa, imeni
Rybinsk. Town, Yaroslavl Oblast, Russia : Shcherbakov (1946–57), Andropov (1984–89)
Rychnov. Village, northern Czech Lands : Reichenau (bei Gablonz) (–1918, 1939–45), Germany
Rychnov nad Kněžnou. Town, northeastern Czech Lands : Reichenau (–1918, 1939–45), Germany
Rycroft. Town, Alberta, Canada : Spirit River (–1920), Roycroft (1920–33)
Rykovo see Yenakiyevo
Rykovskoye see Kirovskoye (4)
Ryojun see Port Arthur
Rypin. Town, north-central Poland : Rippin (1939–45), Germany
Rzepin. Town, western Poland : Reppen (–1945), Germany
Rzeszów. City, southeastern Poland : Reichshof (1939–45), Germany

Sa'adiyeh. Town, northwestern Iran : Soltaniyeh (–1980)
Saar (in Mähren) see Žd'ár
Saarlauten see Saarlouis
Saarlouis. City, western Germany : Saarlautern (1936–45)
Saaz see Žatec
Sabah. State, eastern Malaysia : North Borneo (–1963)
Sabaneta see Santiago Rodríguez
Sabani see Gabaldon
Sabi Game Reserve see Kruger National Park
Sablino see Ulyanovka
Sabra. Village, northwestern Algeria, northern Africa : Turenne (–c. 1962)
Saby see Bogatyye Saby
Sacramento see Itatupā
Sacré-Coeur-de-Jésus. Community, Quebec, Canada : Dolbeau (–1900)

Sá da Bandeira *see* Lubango
Sadovoye. Village, Astra-
khan Oblast, Russia :
Kegulta (–1944)
Šafárikovo. Town, eastern
Slovakia : Tornala
(–1949)
Safonovo. Village, Mogi-
lyov Oblast, Belorussia :
Puziki (–1964)
Sagan *see* Żagań
Sagbayan. Municipality,
Bohol, Philippines :
Borja (–1957)
Saglouc. Village, Quebec,
Canada : Sugluk
(–1975)
Sahiwal. City, northeastern
Pakistan : Montgomery
(–?)
Saigon *see* Ho Chi Minh (City)
Saint-Aimé *see* Jdiouia
Saint-Alban *see* Saint-Alban-
Leysse
Saint-Alban-Leysse. Com-
mune, southeastern
France : Saint-Alban
(–1946)
Saint-Arnaud *see* El Eulma
St. Augustin *see* Anatsogno
Saint-Barthélemy-le-Plain.
Village, southern France :
Saint-Barthélemy-le-Plein
(–1939)
Saint-Barthélemy-le-Plein *see*
Saint-Barthélemy-le-
Plain
Saint-Bon *see* Saint-Bon-Tar-
entaise
Saint-Bon-Tarentaise. Vil-
lage, southeastern
France : Saint-Bon
(–1941)
Saint-Briac *see* Saint-Briac-
sur-Mer
Saint-Briac-sur-Mer. Village,
western France : Saint-
Briac (–1939)
Saint-Cloud *see* Gdyel
Saint-Dalmas-de-Tende.
Village, southeastern
France : San Dalmazzo di
Tenda (–1947), Italy
Saint-Denis(-du-Sig) *see* Sig
Sainte-Geneviève *see* Pierre-
fonds
Ste. Jeanne d'Arc *see* Maison-
nette
Sainte-Marie *see* Nosy Boraha
Sainte-Rose-du-Dégelé *see*
Dégelis
Sainte-Scholastique *see* Mira-
bel
Saint-Étienne *see* Saint-
Étienne-lès-Remiremont
Saint-Étienne-lès-Remire-
mont. Village, south-
eastern France : Saint-
Étienne (–1937)
Saint-Eugène *see* Bologhine
St. Ferdinand *see* Florissant
Saint-Gérard. Village, Que-
bec, Canada : Weedon
Lake (–1905)
Saint-Jean-de-Fédala *see* El-
louizia
Saint-Joseph-d'Alma *see*
Alma
Saint-Joseph-de-Chambly *see*
Carignan
Saint-Léonard. Suburb of
Montreal, Quebec, Can-
ada : Saint-Léonard-de-
Port-Maurice (–1962)
Saint-Léonard-de-Port-Mau-
rice *see* Saint-Léonard
Saint-Leu *see* Bettioua
Saint-Louis *see* Boufatis

Saint-Lucien *see* Zahana
Saint-Macaire *see* Saint-
Macaire-en-Mauges
Saint-Macaire-en-Mauges.
Town, western France :
Saint-Macaire
(–1939)
St. Marks *see* Cofimvaba
Saint Nicholas Point *see*
Pudjut Point
Saint Paul. Town, Alberta,
Canada : Saint Paul de
Métis (*1912–36)
Saint Paul de Métis *see* Saint
Paul
St. Petersburg [Sankt-Peter-
burg]. Capital of Lenin-
grad Oblast, Russia : Pet-
rograd (1914–24), Lenin-
grad (1924–91)
St. Petersburg Guberniya *see*
Leningrad Guberniya
Saint-Pierre-de-la-Pointe-aux-
Esquimaux *see* Havre-
Saint-Pierre
Saint-Pierre-du-Lac *see* Val-
Brillant
Saint-Pierre-Saint-Paul *see*
Ouled Moussa
St. Quentin. Town, New
Brunswick, Canada : An-
derson Siding (–1920)
St. Thomas *see* Charlotte
Amalie
St. Vincent, Cap *see* Anka-
boa, Tanjona
Sakaehama *see* Starodubskoye
Sakiz-Adasi *see* Chios
Salacgriva. Town, Latvia :
Salisy (–1917)
Salaspils. Urban settlement,
Latvia : Kirchholm
(–1917)
Salazar *see* Ndalatando

Salcedo. Municipality, Ilo-
cos Sur, Philippines :
Bauguen (–1957)
Saldus. Town, Latvia :
Frauenburg (–1917)
Salegard *see* Salekhard
Salekhard. Capital of
Yamal-Nenets Autono-
mous Okrug, Tyumen
Oblast, Russia : Obdorsk
(–1933), Salegard (1933–
38)
Salinas *see* (1) O'Connor; (2)
Salinópolis
Salinópolis. City, northern
Brazil, South America :
Salinas (–1944)
Salisburg *see* Mazsalača
Salisbury *see* Harare
Salisy *see* Salacgriva
Salla. Commune, northeast-
ern Finland : Kursu
(–1940)
Salla *see* Kuolayarvi
Salmas. Town, northwest-
ern Iran : Shahpur
(–1980)
Salmon Cove *see* Avondale
Salmonhurst *see* New Den-
mark
Salonika *see* Thessaloniki
Salop *see* Shropshire
Salsk. Town, Rostov Oblast,
Russia : Torgovaya
(–1926)
Salvacion (1). Barrio,
Leyte, Phillipines :
Cogon-Bingkay (–1957)
Salvacion (2). Barrio, Pala-
wan, Philippines : Tapul
(–1957)
Salyuzi *see* Kotelnikovo (2)
Salzburgen *see* Château-
Salins

Salzgitter. City, northern Germany : Watenstadt-Salzgitter (–1951)

Sama. Settlement, Sverdlovsk Oblast, Russia : Severnaya Sama (–c. 1960)

Samar. Province, eastern Philippines : Western Samar (–1969)

Samara. Capital of Samara Oblast, Russia : Kuybyshev (1935–91)

Samara Oblast. East-central Russia : Srednevolzhskaya Oblast [Middle Volga Oblast] (*1928–29), Srednevolzhsky Kray [Middle Volga Kray] (1929–35), Kuybyshev Kray (1935–36), Kuybyshev Oblast (1936–91)

Samarkandsky see Temirtau

Sambat see Lumangbayan

Samos. Island, Aegean Sea, Greece : Susam-Adasi (–1913), Turkey

Samothrace. Island, Aegean Sea, Greece : Semadrek (–1913), Turkey

Samsonovo see Amu-Darya

Samtredi see Samtredia

Samtredia. Town, Georgia : Samtredi (–1936)

San Angel see Silvestre Domingo

San Antonio. Barrio, Mindoro Oriental, Philippines : Dalagan (–1969)

San Antonio (de Cortés). Town, west-central Honduras, Central America : Talpetate (–early 1930s)

San Bartolomé see Venustiano Carranza

San-Beyse see Choybalsan

San Blas. Island group, northeastern Panama, Central America : Las Mulatas (–1979)

San Carlos see Butuka-Luba

Sanchan see Koshan [K'o-shan]

San-chou see Hsin-yang

Sanchursk. Urban settlement, Kirov Oblast, Russia : Tsaryovo-Sanchursk (–1918)

San Cristóbal. Province, south-central Dominican Republic, West Indies : Trujillo (*1935–61)

San Cristóbal de Trabancos. Village, east-central Spain : Cebolla de Trabancos (–c. 1960)

San Dalmazzo di Tenda see Saint-Dalmas-de-Tende

San Daniele del Carso see Štanjel na Krasu

Sandanski. City, southwestern Bulgaria : Sveti Vrach (–1949)

Sandino. International airport, Managua, Nicaragua, Central America : De Las Mercedes (–1980)

San Eugenio see Artigas

San Ferreol. Village, northeastern Spain : Parroquia de Besalú (–c. 1930)

Sanford see Guyman

San Francisco (1). Municipality, Surigao del Norte, Philippines : Anao-aon (–1911)

San Francisco (2). Municipality, Quezon, Philippines : Aurora (–1967)

San Francisco de Malabon *see* General Trias

San Gabriel. Barrio, Quezon, Philippines : Tubog (–1957)

San Giuliano Terme. Town, central Italy : Bagni San Giuliano (–1935)

Sango. Town, southeastern Zimbabwe, southeastern Africa : Vila Salazar (*1955–82)

Sangorodok *see* Ust-Vorkuta

Sangpiling *see* Tingsiang

Sanho *see* Santu

San Isidoro *see* Torrecilla sobre Alesanco

San Isidro. Barrio, Ilocos Norte, Philippines : Batuli (–1969)

San Isidro *see* Ureña

San Isidro de Potot *see* Burgos (2)

San Isidro Labrador *see* Labrador

Sanitary and Ship Canal. Linking southern branch of Chicago and Des Plaines Rivers, Illinois, USA : Chicago Drainage Canal (*1900–1930)

San Jacinto *see* Catigbian

San Jaime de Llierca. Village, northeastern Spain : Palau de Montagut (–c. 1930)

San Jose (1). Municipality, Romblon, Philippines : Carabao Island (–1905)

San Jose (2). Barrio, La Union, Philippines : Garampang (–1957)

San Jose (3). Barrio, Catanduanes, Philippines : Oco (–1969)

San Jose Sur *see* Santo Niño (3)

San Juan. Province, west-central Dominican Republic, West Indies : Benefactor (*1938–61)

San Juan Bautista *see* Villahermosa

San Juan de Bocboc *see* San Juan de Bolbok

San Juan de Bolbok. Municipality, Batangas, Philippines : San Juan de Bocboc (–1914)

San Juan de Guimba *see* Guimba

San Juan del Olmo. Village, east-central Spain : Grajos (–c. 1960)

San Juan de Mollet. Village, northeastern Spain : Mollet (–c. 1920)

San Juan de Villa Hermosa *see* Villahermosa

San Julián de Vallfogona. Village, northeastern Spain : Vallfogona (–1961)

Sankieh *see* Kiashan [Chiashan]

Sankiocheng *see* Haiyen

Sankioh *see* Santu

Sankt Leonhard *see* Bad Sankt Leonhard im Lavanttale

Sankt Leonhard (im Pitztal). Village, western Austria : Pitzthal (–1935)

Sankt Marein *see* Šmarje (pri Jelšah)

Sankt-Peterburg = St. Petersburg

San Luis *see* (1) Entre Ríos; (2) Sevilla

San Magro *see* Santiago (1)

San Manuel. Municipality, Isabela, Philippines : Callang (–1905)

San Martín *see* Tarapoto

San Martín de Tous. Village, northeastern Spain : Tous (–c. 1920)

San Martín Land *see* Antarctic Peninsula

San Miguel *see* (1) Diez y Ocho de Julio; (2) Sarrat

San Nicolás de Buenos Aires. Town, central Mexico, North America : (San Nicolás) Malpaís (–1941)

(San Nicolás) Malpaís *see* San Nicolás de Buenos Aires

San Pablo del Monte *see* Villa (General) Vicente Guerrero

San Pablo de Manta *see* Manta

San Pedro. Municipality, Laguna, Philippines : San Pedro Tunasan (–1914)

San Pedro Macati *see* Makati

San Pedro Remate *see* Bella Vista

San Pedro Tunasan *see* San Pedro

San Rafael *see* La Estrelleta

San Roque. Barrio, Leyte, Philippines : Curba (–1957)

San Sadurní de Noya. Village, northeastern Spain :

San Saturnino de Noya (–c. 1960)

San Saturnino de Noya *see* San Sadurní de Noya

Sanshui *see* Sünyi [Hsün-i]

Sansui. Town, southern China : Angshui (–1913), Lingshan (1926–31)

Santa Bárbara *see* Santa Bárbara d'Oeste

Santa Bárbara d'Oeste. City, southeastern Brazil, South America : Santa Bárbara (–1944)

Santa Clara *see* Las Villas

Santa Comba *see* Waku Cungo

Santa Cruz *see* (1) Aracruz; (2) Reriutaba; (3) Santa Cruz do Sul

Santa Cruz das Palmeiras. City, southeastern Brazil, South America : Palmeiras (–1944)

Santa Cruz de Bravo *see* Felipe Carrillo Puerto

Santa Cruz (de Galeana) *see* Juventino Rosas

Santa Cruz de Malabon *see* Tanza

Santa Cruz de Tenerife. Province, Canary Islands : Canarias (–1927)

Santa Cruz do Sul. City, southern Brazil, South America : Santa Cruz (–1944)

Santa Eulalia *see* Camembe

Santa Isabel *see* Malabo

Santa Luzia *see* Luziânia

Santa Maria. Barrio, Mindoro Occidental, Philippines : Bulbugan (–1969)

Santa María de Barbará. Village, northeastern Spain : Barbará (–c. 1920)

Santa María del Tiétar. Village, east-central Spain : Escarabajosa (–c. 1960)

Santa Maria do Araguaia see Araguacema

Santa Monica. Municipality, Surigao del Norte, Philippines : Sapao (–1967)

Santana see (1) Licania; (2) Uruaçu

Santana de Tinonganine. Village, southern Mozambique, southeastern Africa : Tinonganine (–1963)

Santana do Paranaíba see Paranaíba

Santaokiao see Mitsang [Mits'ang]

Santarém see Ituberá

Santa Rita do Araguaia see Guiratinga

Santa Rita (do Paranaíba) see Itumbiara

Santa Rosa see (1) Bella Unión; (2) Santa Rosa do Viterbo; (3) Santo Tomas

Santa Rosa do Viterbo. City, southeastern Brazil, South America : Santa Rosa (–1944), Icaturama (1944–48)

Santa Teresa see Rio das Flores

Santa Theresa. Barrio, Mindoro Oriental, Philippines : Lang-ang (–1969)

Santiago (1). Barrio, Ilocos Norte, Philippines : San Magro (–1968)

Santiago (2). City, southern Brazil, South America :

Santiago do Boqueiro (–1938)

Santiago de Alcántara. Village, western Spain : Santiago de Carbajo (–c. 1960)

Santiago de Carbajo see Santiago de Alcántara

Santiago (de Cuba) see Oriente

Santiago do Boqueiro see Santiago (2)

Santiago Rodríguez. Town, northwestern Dominican Republic, West Indies : Sabaneta (–1936)

Santiváñez. Town, central Bolivia, South America : Caraza (–1900s)

Santo see Kim

Santo Amaro see (1) General Câmara; (2) Santo Amaro da Imperatriz; (3) Santo Amaro das Brotas

Santo Amaro da Imperatriz. Town, southern Brazil, South America : Santo Amaro (–1944), Cambirela (1944–48)

Santo Amaro das Brotas. City, northeastern Brazil, South America : Santo Amaro (–1944)

Santo Antônio (1). City, northeastern Brazil, South America : Padre Miguelinho (1944–48)

Santo Antônio (2). City, southern Brazil, South America : Santo Antônio da Patrulha (–1938)

Santo Antônio see Santo Antônio do Leverger

Santo Antônio da Cachoeira
see Itaguatins
Santo Antônio da Patrulha *see*
Santo Antônio (2)
Santo Antônio de Balsas *see*
Balsas
Santo Antônio do Leverger.
City, western Brazil,
South America : Santo
Antônio do Rio Abaixo
(–1939), Santo Antônio
(1939–43), Leverger
(1944–48)
Santo Antônio do Rio Abaixo
see Santo Antônio do
Leverger
Santo Antônio do Zaïre *see*
Soya
Santo Domingo. Capital of
Dominican Republic,
West Indies : Ciudad
Trujillo (1936–61)
Santo Inácio. City, eastern
Brazil, South America :
Gamelleira do Assuruá
(–?), Assuruá (?–
1939)
Santo Niño (1). Municipality,
Cagayan, Philippines :
Faire (1914–69)
Santo Niño (2). Barrio,
Leyte, Philippines. Hacla-
gan (–1950)
Santo Niño (3). Barrio,
Bohol, Philippines : San
Jose Sur (–1968)
Santos Dumont. City, south-
eastern Brazil, South
America : Palmyras
(–1930s)
Santo Tomas. Barrio, Iloilo,
Philippines : Santa Rosa
(–1957)
Santo Tomas *see* Arcangel

Santu. Town, southern
China : Sankioh (–?),
Sanho (?–1942)
Sanyen *see* Wucheng [Wu-
ch'eng]
São Benedito *see* Benedi-
tinos
São Bento *see* (1) São Bento
do Sul; (2) São Bento do
Una
São Bento do Sul. City,
southern Brazil, South
America : São Bento
(–1944), Serra Alta
(1944–48)
São Bento do Una. City,
northeastern Brazil,
South America : São
Bento (–1944)
São Felipe *see* Icana
São Felippe *see* Eirunepé
São Francisco *see* (1) Itapagé;
(2) São Francisco do
Conde; (3) São Francisco
do Maranho; (4) São
Francisco do Sul
São Francisco do Conde.
City, eastern Brazil,
South America : São
Francisco (–1944)
São Francisco do Maranho.
City, northeastern Brazil,
South America : São
Francisco (–1944),
Iguaratinga (1944–48)
São Francisco do Sul. City,
southern Brazil, South
America : São Francisco
(–1944)
São Gonçalo *see* (1) Arari-
pina; (2) São Gonçalo dos
Campos
São Gonçalo dos Campos.
City, eastern Brazil,

South America : São
Gonçalo
(–1944)
São João da Bocâina *see* Bo-
câina
São João de Camaquã *see*
Camaquã
São João de Meriti. Suburb
of Rio de Janeiro, south-
eastern Brazil, South
America : Meriti
(–1944)
São João de Montenegro *see*
Montenegro
São João do Muqui *see* Muqui
São Joaquim *see* São Joaquim
da Barra
São Joaquim da Barra. City,
southeastern Brazil,
South America : São Joa-
quim (–1944)
São José da Lagoa *see* Nova
Era
São José do Campestre.
City, northeastern Brazil,
South America : Cam-
pestre (–1944)
São José do Rio Prêto. City,
southeastern Brazil,
South America : Rio
Prêto (–1944)
São José dos Cocais *see* Nossa
Senhora do Livramento
São José dos Matões *see* Par-
narama
São José do Tocantins *see*
Niquelândia
São Lourenço *see* São
Lourenço da Mata
São Lourenço da Mata.
City, northeastern Brazil,
South America : São
Lourenço (–1944)
São Luís. City, northeastern

Brazil, South America :
São Luíz do Maranhão
(–?)
São Luís Gonzaga *see* Ipixuna
São Luíz de Cáceres *see*
Cáceres
São Luíz do Maranho *see* São
Luís
São Manuel *see* Eugenópolis
São Manuel do Mutum *see*
Mutum
São Mateus *see* (1) Jucás; (2)
São Mateus do Sul
São Mateus do Sul. City,
southern Brazil, South
America : São Mateus
(–1943)
São Miguel *see* São Miguel das
Matas
São Miguel das Matas. City,
eastern Brazil, South
America : São Miguel
(–1944)
São Nicolau *see* Bentiaba
São Paolo *see* Frei Paulo
São Pedro *see* São Pedro do
Sul
São Pedro (do Cariry) *see*
Caririaçu
São Pedro do Sul. City,
southern Brazil, South
America : São Pedro
(–1944)
São Roque *see* São Roque do
Paraguaçu
São Roque do Paraguaçu.
Town, eastern Brazil,
South America : São Ro-
que (–1944)
São Salvador (do Congo) *see*
Mbanza Congo
São Sebastião *see* São Sebas-
tião do Passé
São Sebastião da Grama.

City, southeastern Brazil,
South America : Grama
(–1948)
São Sebastião do Passé. City,
eastern Brazil, South
America : São Sebastião
(–1944)
São Vicente *see* Araguatins
Sapao *see* Santa Monica
Sapé *see* Sapeaçu
Sapeaçu. Town, eastern Bra-
zil, South America : Sapé
(–1944)
Sapronovo *see* Oktyabrsky (8)
Sarana. Urban settlement,
Sverdlovsk Oblast, Rus-
sia : Nizhne-Saraninsky
(–1933)
Saranovo *see* Septemvri
Sara-Ostrov *see* Narimana-
bad
Saratovskaya Manufaktura
see Krasny Tekstilshchik
Saravia *see* Enrique B. Maga-
lona
Saray Komar *see* Pyandzh
Sarbinowo. Village, western
Poland : Zorndorf
(–1945), Germany
Sardarabad *see* Oktemberyan
Sardarova Karakhana, imeni
see Leninsky (2)
Sarepta *see* Krasnoarmeysk (3)
Sarera Bay. Bay, northern
Irian Jaya, Indonesia :
Geelvink Bay (–1963)
Sar Eskand Khan *see* Azaran
Sarh. Town, southern Chad,
central Africa : Fort
Archambault (–1974)
Sarrat. Municipality, Ilocos
Norte, Philippines : San
Miguel (–1914)
Sars. Urban settlement,

Perm Oblast, Russia :
Sarsinsky Zavod (–1939)
Sarsinsky Zavod *see* Sars
Sartana *see* Primorskoye (3)
Sasmaka *see* Valdemārpils
Sasmakken *see* Valdemārpils
Sauce *see* Juan Lacaze
Sauce del Yí. Town, south-
central Uruguay, South
America : Pueblo de la
Capilla (–1924)
Saúde *see* Perdigo
Saujbulagh *see* Mahabad
Sault-au-Cochon *see* Forest-
ville
Saurimo. Town, northeast-
ern Angola, southwestern
Africa : Henrique de Car-
valho (–c. 1976)
Sawmill *see* Concepcion
Sayaboury. Town, north-
western Laos : Paklay
(–1946), Thailand (1941–
46)
Sayanogorsk. Town, Kha-
kass Autonomous Oblast,
Krasnoyarsk Kray, Rus-
sia : Oznachennoye
(–1975)
Sayasan. Village, Chechen-
Ingush Autonomous Re-
public, Russia : Ritlyab
(1944–c. 1960)
Saybrook *see* Deep River
Saybusch *see* Żywiec
Sazanovka *see* Ananyevo
Sazonovo. Urban settle-
ment, Vologda Oblast,
Russia : Belyye Kresty
(–1947)
Scarpanto *see* Karpathos
Schaaksvitte *see* Kashirs-
koye
Scharfenwiese *see* Ostrołęka

Schässburg see Sighişoara
Schatzlar see Žacléř
Schefferville. Town, Que-
bec, Canada : Knob Lake
(*1950–55)
Schemnitz see Banská
Štiavnica
Schieratz see Sieradz
Schippenbeil see Sępopol
Schirwindt see Kutuzovo
Schivelbein see Świdwin
Schlawa see Sława
Schlesiersee see Sława
Schlettstadt see Sélestat
Schlichtingsheim see Szlichtyn-
gowa
Schlochau see Człuchów
Schloppe see Człopa
Schlossbach see Nevskoye
Schlossberg see Dobrovolsk
Schlüsselburg see Petrokre-
post
Schmiedeberg see Kowary
Schneidemühl see Piła
Schömberg see Chelmsko
Śląskie
Schönau see Świerzawa
Schönberg see Sulików
Schöneck see Skarszewy
Schönfeld see Krásno
Schönlanke see Trzcianka
Schönstein see Šoštanj
Schreckenstein see Střekov
Schreiberhau see Szklarska
Poręba
Schröttersburg see Płock
Schwanenburg see Gulbene
Schwarzheide. Town,
eastern Germany :
Zschornegosda (–1936)
Schweidnitz see Świdnica
Schwerin see Skwierzyna
Schwiebus see Świebodzin

Scottsdale. Town, Tasma-
nia, Australia : Ellesmere
(–1906)
Scrabby see Lough Gowna
Seabra see Tarauacá
Seawell Airport see (Sir)
Grantley Adams Air-
port
Sechenevo. Village, Nizhe-
gorodskaya Oblast, Rus-
sia : Tyoply Stan (–1945)
Seckenburg see Zapovednoye
Sedova, G. Ya., imeni see
Sedovo
Sedovo. Urban settlement,
Donetsk Oblast,
(–1941), Sedova, G. Ya.,
imeni (1941–c. 1960)
Seeburg see Jeziorany
Seelowitz see Židlochovice
Segaon see Sevagram
Segeberg see Bad Segeberg
Segewold see Sigulda
Sehb Dheb. Village, north-
western Morocco, north-
western Africa : Val d'Or
(–c. 1959)
Sehb Sidi ben Aïssa. Village,
northwestern Morocco,
northwestern Africa : La
Madeleine (–c. 1959)
Seidemenukha see Kalin-
inskoye (2)
Seine-Inférieure see Seine-
Maritime
Seine-Maritime. Depart-
ment, northern France :
Seine-Inférieure (–1955)
Seis de Septiembre see Morón
Seitler see Nizhnegorsky
Sélestat. Town, northeast-
ern France : Schlettstadt
(1870–1918), Germany

Seleznevsky Rudnik *see* Par-
izhskaya Kommuna
Selukwe *see* Shurugwi
Semadrek *see* Samothrace
Semibratovo. Urban settle-
ment, Yaroslavl Oblast,
Russia : Isady (–1948)
Seminole. City, Oklahoma,
USA : Tidmore (–1906)
Semirechensk Guberniya *see*
Dzhetysuy Guberniya
Sem Kolodezey *see* Lenino (2)
Semyonovka *see* Arsenyev
Semyonovskoye *see* (1)
Bereznik; (2) Ostrovsky
Senaki. Town, Georgia :
Mikha Tskhakaya (1933–
76), Tskhakaya (1976–91)
Senegambia and Niger Terri-
tories *see* Mali
Senftenberg *see* Žamberk
Senhor do Bonfim. City,
eastern Brazil, South
America : Bonfim
(–1944)
Senneterre. Town, Quebec,
Canada : Nottaway
(*1914–18)
Sentosa. Island, southern
Singapore : Pulau
Blakang Mati (–1970)
Sępolno (Kraińskie). Town,
northwestern Poland :
Zempelburg (–1945),
Germany
Sępopol. Village, northeast-
ern Poland : Schippenbeil
(–1945), Germany
Septemvri. Village, west-
central Bulgaria : Sara-
novo (–1950)
Septième *see* Adrar
Sept-Îles. City, Quebec,

Canada : Seven Islands
(–1951)
Serafimovich. Town, Volgo-
grad Oblast, Russia : Ust-
Medveditskaya (–1933)
Serdán *see* (Ciudad) Serdán
Serdobol *see* Sortavala
Serebrovsky. Urban settle-
ment, Azerbaijan : Kara-
chukhur (–c. 1960)
Serebryanyye Prudy. Urban
settlement, Moscow Ob-
last, Russia : Sergiyevy
Prudy (–c. 1928)
Sereda *see* Furmanov
Sergiopol *see* Ayaguz
Sergiyev *see* Sergiyev Posad
Sergiyev Posad. Town, Mos-
cow Oblast, Russia : Ser-
giyev (–1930), Zagorsk
(1930–91)
Sergiyevskoye *see* Plavsk
Sergiyevsky *see* Fakel
Sergiyevy Prudy *see* Serebry-
anyye Prudy
Sergo *see* Kadiyevka
Sergunia [Szirguni]. Urban
settlement, northeastern
Israel : Hazorim (*1939–
48)
Sermyazhenka *see* Osman-
Kasayevo
Serov. Town, Sverdlovsk Ob-
last, Russia : Nadezhdin-
sky Zavod (–1926), Na-
dezhdinsk (1926–34,
1937–39), Kabakovsk
(1934–37)
Serpa Pinto *see* Menongue
Serra Alta *see* São Bento do
Sul
Serra Branca. City, eastern
Brazil, South America :

Itamorotinga (1944–48)

Sérrai. City, northern Greece : Siroz (–1913), Turkey

Serramazzoni. Village, north-central Italy : Monfestino in Serra Mazzoni (–1948)

Serra Negra *see* Serra Negra do Norte

Serra Negra do Norte. City, northeastern Brazil, South America : Serra Negra (–1944)

Serra Talhada. City, northeastern Brazil, South America : Villa Bella (–1939)

Serravalle Libarna. Village, northern Italy : Serravalle Scrivia (–early 1930s)

Serravalle Scrivia *see* Serravalle Libarna

Serrinha *see* Juripiranga

Sertânia. City, northeastern Brazil, South America : Alagoa de Baixo (–1944)

Sertozinho *see* Major Isidoro

Seskar. Island, Gulf of Finland, Baltic Sea, Leningrad Oblast, Russia : Lesnoy (–c. 1960)

Seto(-kanayama) *see* Shirahama

Sevagram. Town, central India : Segaon (*1936–40)

Sevan. Town, Armenia : Yelenovka (–c. 1935)

Seven Islands *see* Sept-Îles

Severnaya Sama *see* Sama

Severnaya Zemlya. Archipelago, Arctic Ocean, Taymyr Autonomous Okrug, Krasnoyarsk Kray, Russia : Zemlya Imperatora Nikolaya II [Nicholas II Land] (*1913–26)

Severnoye. Village, Orenburg Oblast, Russia : Sok-Karmala (–c. 1960)

Severny. Urban settlement, Sverdlovsk Oblast, Russia : Pervy Severny (–c. 1960)

Severny Suchan *see* Uglekamensk

Severodonetsk. Town, Lugansk Oblast, Ukraine : Leskhimstroy (*1934–58)

Severodvinsk. Town, Arkhangelsk Oblast, Russia : Sudostroy (*c. 1918–38), Molotovsk (1938–57)

Severokavkavsky Kray *see* Stravropol Kray

Severo-Kurilsk. Town, Kuril Islands, Sakhalin Oblast, Russia : Kashiwabara (1908–45), Japan

Severomorsk. Town, Murmansk Oblast, Russia : Vayenga (–1951)

Severouralsk. Town, Sverdlovsk Oblast, Russia : Petropavlovsky (–1944)

Seversk. Town, Donetsk Oblast, Ukraine : Yama (–1973)

Sevilla. City, western Colombia, South America : San Luis (*1903–14)

Sevlyush *see* Vinogradov

Sewell *see* Camp Hughes

Shaarikhan *see* Shakhrikhan

Shaba.   Province, southern
  Zaïre, central Africa :
  Elisabethville (1935–47),
  Katanga (1947–72)
Shabalino *see* Leninskoye (2)
Shabani *see* Zvishavane
Shabbaz *see* Biruni
Shafirkan.   Village, Bukhara
  Oblast, Uzbekistan :
  Khodzha-Arif (-c. 1935),
  Bauman (c. 1935–37)
Shagali *see* Vaagni
Shahabad *see* Eslamabad-e
  Gharb
Shahi.   Town, northern
  Iran : Aliabad (-mid–
  1930s)
Shahi *see* Qa'emshahr
  [Ghaem Shahr]
Shaho(chen) *see* An-shan
Shah Pasand *see* Azadshah
Shahpur *see* (1) Bandar-e
  Khomeyni; (2) Salmas
Shahreza *see* Qomisheh
Shahrud *see* Emamoud
Shahsavar *see* Tonekabon
Shaker Heights.   Suburb of
  Cleveland, Ohio,
  USA : North Union
  (-1900s)
Shakhimardan *see* Khamza
Shakhrikhan.   Town, Andi-
  zhan Oblast, Uzbekistan :
  Shaarikhan (-1937), Stal-
  ina, imeni (1937–c. 1940),
  Stalino (c. 1940–61),
  Moskovsky (1961–70)
Shakhta No. 7/8.   Town, Lu-
  gansk Oblast, Ukraine :
  Karlomarksovsky No. 7/8
  Rudnik (-?)
Shakhta No. 33/37.   Town,
  Lugansk Oblast,
  Ukraine : Lobovsky No.

33/38 Rudnik (-?)
Shakhty.   Town, Rostov
  Oblast, Russia : Aleksan-
  drovsk-Grushevsky
  (-1920)
Shakhty imeni Engelsa *see*
  Engelsovo
Shakhtyorsk (1).   Town,
  Sakhalin Oblast, Russia :
  Toro (1905–47), Japan
  (-1945)
Shakhtyorsk (2).   Town,
  Donetsk Oblast,
  Ukraine; Zapadno-
  Gruppsky (-1945), Katyk
  (1945–53)
Shakhtyorskoye *see* Per-
  shotravensk
Shakotan *see* Malokurilskoye
Shali.   Village, Chechen-
  Ingush Autonomous
  Republic, Russia :
  Mezhdurechye (1944–
  c. 1960)
Shamkhor.   Town, Azerbai-
  jan : Annenfeld [Annino]
  (1928–37)
Shana *see* Kurilsk
Shangchih.   Town, north-
  western China : Wuchuho
  (-1927), Chuho (1927–
  49)
Shangchow *see* Shanghsien
Shanghsien.   Town, central
  China : Shangchow
  (-1913)
Shangi.   Town, northeastern
  China : Tatskingkow
  (-1935)
Shangjao.   Town, southeast-
  ern China : Kwangsin
  (-1912)
Shangpo *see* Fukung
Shangri-La *see* Camp David

Shangtsichang *see* Suileng
Shangyütung *see* Kintang
[Chin-t'ang]
Shanhaikwan. City, north-
eastern China : Lunyü
(1912–49)
Shani *see* Taosha [T-ao-sha]
Shan-yang *see* Huai-an
Shao-yang. City, southeast-
ern China : Pao-ch'ing
(–1912)
Shapilovo *see* Mayskoye (3)
Shargun. Town, Surkhan-
darya Oblast, Uzbeki-
stan : Takchiyan
(–1973)
Sharklauk *see* Druzhba (2)
Sharypovo. Town, Krasno-
yarsk Kray, Russia :
Chernenko (1985–88)
Shatilki *see* Svetlogorsk (2)
Shatoy *see* Sovetskoye (6)
Shatura. Town, Moscow Ob-
last, Russia : Shaturtorf
(*1923–28)
Shaturtorf *see* Shatura
Shaumyan *see* Shaumyani
Shaumyani. Urban settle-
ment, Georgia : Shulav-
ery (–1925), Shaumyan
(1925–36)
Shaumyanovsk. Urban set-
tlement, Azerbaijan :
Nizhny Agdzhakend
(–1938)
Shavli *see* Šiauliai
Shaydan *see* Asht
Shaygino. Urban settle-
ment, Nizhegorodskaya
Oblast, Russia : Ton-
shayevo (–c. 1960)
Shaytansky Zavod *see* Perv-
ouralsk
Shcherbakov *see* Rybinsk

Shcherbinovka *see* Dzerzhinsk
(5)
Shchors. Town, Chernigov
Oblast, Ukraine : Snovsk
(–1935)
Shchorsk. Urban settle-
ment, Dnepropetrovsk
Oblast, Ukraine : Bozhe-
darovka (–c. 1940)
Shchuchinsk. Town, Kok-
chetav Oblast, Kazakh-
stan : Shchuchye (–1939)
Shchuchye *see* Shchuchinsk
Shebunino. Urban settle-
ment, Sakhalin Oblast,
Russia : Minami-nayoshi
(1905–46), Japan (–1945)
She-hsien. City, eastern
China : Hui-chou (–1912)
Sheki. Town, Azerbaijan :
Nukha (–1968)
Shekshing *see* Limkong
Sheksna. Urban settlement,
Vologda Oblast, Russia :
Nikolskoye (–c. 1960)
Shelekhovo. Village, Kuril
Islands, Sakhalin Oblast,
Russia : Kakumabetsu
(1905–46), Japan (–1945)
Shell Beach *see* Huntington
Beach
Shelomy *see* Krasny Vostok
Shelter Bay *see* Port-Cartier
Shelton. City, Connecticut,
USA : Huntington (–
1919)
Shelyakino *see* Sovetskoye (7)
Shenchow *see* (1) Shenhsien;
(2) Yüanling
Shenhsien. Town, northeast-
ern China : Shenchow
(–1913)
Shenkiu *see* Linchüan [Lin-
ch'üan]

Shen-yang. City, northeast-
ern China : Mukden
(1625–1912, 1945–49),
Fengt'ien (1931–45)
Shestakovo. Urban settle-
ment, Irkutsk Oblast,
Russia : Ilim (–c. 1960)
Shevchenko *see* (1) Aktau; (2)
Vita
Shevchenkovo *see* Dolinskaya
Shibetoro *see* Slavnoye
Shichijo *see* Ichijo
Shih-chia-chuang = Shihkia-
chwang
Shichü [Shih-ch'ü]. Town,
southern China : Shihshu
(–1912)
Shihchwan *see* Pehchwan [Pei-
ch'uan]
Shihkiachwang [Shih-chia-
chuang]. City, north-
eastern China : Shihmen
(1947–49)
Shihmen *see* (1) Shihkiach-
wang [Shih-chia-chuang];
(2) Tsungteh
Shihnan *see* Enshih
Shihpu *see* Hwanglung [Hu-
ang-lung]
Shihshu *see* Shihchü [Shih-
ch'ü]
Shihwei. Town, northeast-
ern China : Chilalin
(–1920)
Shikhirdany *see* Chkalovskoye
(1)
Shikhrany *see* Kanash
Shikirlikitai *see* Suvorovo (2)
Shikiu *see* Punyü
Shikuka *see* Poronaysk
Shimba *see* Dachnoye
Shimotsu. Town, southern
Honshu, Japan :
Hamanaka (–1938)

Shimo-yoshida. Town,
southern Honshu, Japan :
Yoshida (–1928)
Shin-mikuriya. Town, west-
ern Kyushu, Japan :
Mikuriya (–1943)
Shirahama. Town, southern
Honshu, Japan :
Seto(-kanayama) (–early
1940s)
Shiraura *see* Vzmorye (2)
Shiritoru *see* Makarov
Shirley City *see* Woodburn
(City)
Shirokolanovka. Village, No-
kolayev Oblast, Ukraine :
Landau (–c. 1935), Karla
Libknekhta, imeni
(c. 1935–45)
Shiuchow *see* Kükong
Shiuhing *see* Koyiu
Shlisselburg *see* Petrokrepost
Shmakovsky Rudnik *see* Karla
Libknekhta, imeni (2)
Shokalsky. Island, Kara
Sea, Tyumen Oblast,
Russia : Agnessa (–1926)
Sholdaneshty. Urban settle-
ment, Moldavia :
Chernenko (1985–88)
Sholkhi *see* Oktyabrskoye (6)
Shopa *see* Vysochany (2)
Shoping *see* Yuyü
Shopokov. Town, Kirgizia :
Krasnooktyabrsky
(*1939–85)
Shorewood. Village, Wis-
consin, USA : East Mil-
waukee (–1917)
Shovgenovsky. Village,
Adygey Autonomous Ob-
last, Krasnodar Kray,
Russia : Khakurinokhabl
(–c. 1960)

Showchang *see* Ocheng [O-ch'eng]

Showchow *see* Showhsien

Showhsien. Town, eastern China : Showchow (–1912)

Shpakovskoye. Village, Stavropol Kray, Russia : Mikhaylovskoye (–c. 1960)

Shropshire. County, westcentral England, UK : Salop (1974–80)

Shterovsky *see* Petrovskoye

Shuang-liao = Shwangliao

Shuang-po = Shwangpo

Shulan. Town, northeastern China : Chaoyangchwan (–1910)

Shulavery *see* Shaumyani

Shulmak *see* Navabad

Shumanay. Village, Karakalpak Autonomous Republic, Uzbekistan : Taza-Bazar (–1950)

Shumatovo *see* Sovetskoye (8)

Shumen [Šumen]. Province (*1949–1987†) and its capital, northeastern Bulgaria : Kolarovgrad (1950–65)

Shumikhinsky. Urban settlement, Perm Oblast, Russia : Goreloye (–c. 1960)

Shunking *see* Nanchung [Nanch'ung]

Shunteh *see* Singtai [Hsingt'ai]

Shuragat. Village, Dagestan Autonomous Republic, Russia : Alleroi (–1945)

Shurala. Village, Sverdlovsk Oblast, Russia : Shuralinksy Zavod (–c. 1930)

Shurugwi. Village, central Zimbabwe, southeastern Africa : Selukwe (–1982)

Shuvoya *see* Krasny Tkach

Shwangliao [Suang-liao]. Town, northeastern China : Liaoyüan (–1949)

Shwangliuchen *see* Taonan [T'ao-nan]

Shwangpo [Shuang-po]. Town, southwestern China : Nanan (–1913), Mochu (1913–29)

Siaho [Hsia-ho]. Town, north-central China : Labrang (–1928)

Siakiutai *see* Kiutai [Ciu-t'ai]

Siali *see* Timgnan

Siam *see* Thailand

Sian [Hsi-an] (1). City, northwestern China : Changan (1913–32), Siking (1932–43)

Sian [Hsi-an] (2). City, northeastern China : Peifeng (1947–49)

Sianghsien [Hsiang-hsien]. Town, southern China : Hsiang-ch'ou (–1912)

Siangkow *see* Wulung

Siangÿn [Hsiang-yün]. Town, southwestern China : Yunnan (–1929)

Sianów. Town, northwestern Poland : Zanow (–1945), Germany

Siaochengtze *see* Ningcheng [Ning-ch'eng]

Siaopapao *see* Ningso [Ningshuo]

Siaoyi *see* Tsoshui

Siapu [Hsia-p'u]. Town, southeastern China : Funing (–1913)

Šiauliai. Town, Lithuania :
Shavli (–1920)
Siazan. Town, Azerbaijan :
Kyzyl-Burun (–1954)
Sibirsky see Nazyvayevsk
Sibirtsevo. Urban settle-
ment, Primorsky Kray,
Russia : Manzovka
(–1972)
Sibiu. City, central Roma-
nia : Hermannstadt
(–1918), Germany
Sichang [Hsi-chang]. Town,
southern China :
Ningyüan (–1913)
Sichelberg see Sierpc
Sichi [Hsi-chi]. Town, north-
central China : Mukiay-
ing (–1941)
Sichow [Hsi-ch'ou]. Town,
southwestern China :
Sisakai (–1929)
Sichow see Sihsien [Hsi-hsien]
(3)
Sidi Ali. Village, northwestern Algeria, northern Af-
rica : Cassaigne (–c. 1962)
Sidi Allal Bahraoui. Village,
northwestern Morocco,
northwestern Africa :
Monod (–c. 1959)
Sidi Bel Atar. Village,
northwestern Algeria,
northern Africa : Pont-
du-Chéliff (–c. 1962)
Sidi Benyekba. Village,
northwestern Algeria,
northern Africa : Kléber
(–c. 1962)
Sidi el Abed. Village, northwestern Morocco, north-
western Africa : Plage des
Contrebandiers (–c. 1959)
Sidi Hamadouche. Village,

northwestern Algeria,
northern Africa : Les
Trembles (–c. 1962)
Sidi Kacem. Town, north-
western Morocco, north-
western Africa : Petitjean
(–c. 1959)
Sidi M'Hamed Ben Ali. Vil-
lage, northern Algeria,
northern Africa : Renault
(–c. 1962)
Siding No. 14 see Ponoka
Siehkangpao see Holan
Siemianowice Śląskie. City,
south-central Poland :
Laurahütte (1939–45),
Germany
Sieradz. Town, central
Poland : Schieratz (1939–
45), Germany
Sieraków. Town, central
Poland : Zirke (1939–45),
Germany
Sierpc. Town, north-central
Poland : Sichelberg (1939–
45), Germany
Sierra Morena. Mountain
range, southern Spain :
Cordillera Mariánica
(–c. 1960)
Sieur de Monts National Mon-
ument see Acadia Na-
tional Park
Sifton see Lemberg
Sig. Town, northwesten Al-
geria, northern Africa :
Saint-Denis(-du-Sig)
(–c. 1962)
Sighişoara. City, central
Romania : Schässburg
(–c. 1918), Germany
Signakh see Signakhi
Signakhi. Town, Georgia :
Signakh (–1936)

Sigulda. Town, Latvia :
Segewold (–1917)
Sihanoukville *see* Kompong
Som
Sihsien [Hsi-hsien] (1).
Town, eastern China :
Hweichow (–1912)
Sihsien [Hsi-hsien] (2).
Town, east-central China :
Paosintsi (–1935)
Sihsien [Hsi-hsien] (3).
Town, northeastern
China : Sichow (–1912)
Siking *see* Sian [Hsi-an] (1)
Silberberg *see* Srebrna Góra
Silikow *see* Tulan
Sillein *see* Žilina
Silva Jardim. City, south-
eastern Brazil, South
America : Capivari
(–1943)
Silvania. City, central
Brazil, South America :
Bonfim (–1944)
Silva Porto *see* Kuito
Silver City *see* Rainbow City
Silvestre Domingo. Barrio,
Pangasinan, Philippines :
San Angel (–1972)
Sim. Town, Chelyabinsk
Oblast, Russia : Simsky
Zavod (–c. 1928)
Simão Dias. City, northeast-
ern Brazil, South Amer-
ica : Anápolis (–1944)
Simbirsk *see* Ulyanovsk
Simbirsk Guberniya *see* Ulya-
novsk Guberniya
Šimanovsky *see* Partizánske
Simsky Zavod *see* Sim
Sinancha *see* Cheremshan
Sinchang *see* (1) Ifeng; (2)
Kinsha [Chin-sha]
Sincheng *see* (1) Hingjen

[Hsing-jen]; (2) Hwantai
[Huan-t'ai]; (3) Lichwan
[Li-ch'uan]
Sinchow *see* Sinhsien [Hsin-
hsien] (2)
Sinchu *see* Taoyüan [T'ao-
yüan]
Sinclair. Town, Wyoming,
USA : Parco (–1943)
Sinebryukhi *see* Bereznyaki
Sinegorsk. Urban settle-
ment, Sakhalin Oblast,
Russia : Kawakami
(-tanzan) (1905–45),
Japan
Sinegorsky. Urban settle-
ment, Sverdlovsk Oblast,
Russia : Mezhevaya Utka
(–1963)
Sinelnikovo. Town, Dnepro-
petrovsk Oblast,
Ukraine : Tovarishcha
Khatayevicha, imeni
(mid-1930s)
Sing Sing *see* Ossining
Singtai [Hsing-t'ai]. Town,
northeastern China :
Shunteh (–1912)
Singtze [Hsing-tzu]. Town,
southeastern China :
Nankang (–1912)
Sinhai [Hsin-hai]. City, east-
ern China : Haichow
(–1912), Tunghai (1912–
49)
Sinhai *see* Hwanghwa [Huang-
hua]
Sinho *see* Changpeh
Sinhsien [Hsin-hsien] (1).
Town, east-central China :
Kingfu (–1949)
Sinhsien [Hsin-hsien] (2).
Town, northeastern
China : Sinchow (–1912)

Sining *see* Yangyuan
Sinkin [Hsin-chin]. Town,
   northeastern China :
   Pitzewo (–1949)
Sinning *see* (1) Funan; (2)
   Kaikiang [K'ai-chiang]
Sinoya *see* Chinhoyi
Sinpin [Hsin-pin]. Town,
   northeastern China :
   Hingking (–1929)
Sinsing *see* Yüki
Sintsi *see* Kanglo [K'ang-lo]
Siphaqeni. Town, northeast-
   ern Transkei, southern
   Africa : Flagstaff (–1976)
Sipolilo *see* Guruwe
Sipon(d)zh *see* Bartang
Siporovka *see* Partizany (1)
Siqueira Campos *see* Guaçui
(Sir) Grantley Adams Airport.
   Barbados, West Indies :
   Seawell Airport (–1976)
Siroz *see* Serrai
Sisakai *see* Sichow [Hsi-ch'ou]
Sishui [Hsi-shui]. Town,
   east-central China :
   Kishui (–1933)
Sisqueira Campos. City,
   southern Brazil, South
   America : Colonia
   Mineira (–c. 1935)
Sisson *see* Mount Shasta (City)
Sistema Central. Mountain
   range, west-central Spain :
   Cordillera Capetónica
   (–c. 1960)
Siteki. Town, eastern Swa-
   ziland, southern Africa :
   Stegi (–1976)
Sitio Rawrawang *see* Don
   Mariano
Sitniki. Urban settlement,
   Nizhegorodskaya Oblast,
   Russia : Kozlikha (–1946)

Siuna *see* Yüki
Siushui [Hsiu-shui]. Town,
   southeastern China :
   Ining (–1912)
Sivashskoye. Urban settle-
   ment, Kherson Oblast,
   Ukraine : Rozhd-
   estvenskoye (–c. 1935)
Siwo *see* Oshan
Sixième *see* Trarza
Siyen *see* Tzeyüan [Tzu-yüan]
Siying [Hsi-ying]. Town,
   southeastern China :
   Fort-Bayard (1898–1945)
Skala (nad Zbruczem) *see*
   Skala-Podolskaya
Skala-Podolskaya. Urban
   settlement, Ternopol
   Oblast, Ukraine : Skala
   (nad Zbruczem) (–1940),
   Poland
Skarszewy. Town, northern
   Poland : Schöneck (–
   1945), Germany.
Skawina. Town, southern
   Poland : Konradshof
   (1939–45), Germany
Skhematárion. Village, cen-
   tral Greece : Sk-
   himatárion (–1960s)
Skhimatárion *see* Skhe-
   matárion
Skikda. City, northeastern
   Algeria, northern Africa :
   Philippeville (–c. 1962)
Skit *see* Divnogorsk
Skobelev *see* Fergana
Škofja Loka. Village, west-
   ern Slovenia : Bischoflack
   (–1918), Germany
Skokie. Suburb of Chicago,
   Illinois, USA : Niles
   Center (–1940)
Skopje = Skoplje

Skoplje [Skopje]. City, Capital of Macedonia : Üsküb (–1913), Turkey
Skotovataya see Verkhnetoretskoye
Skoúliare see Hagia Kyriaké
Skoúpa see Karudéa
Skovorodino. Town, Amur Oblast, Russia : Rukhlovo (–1948)
Skulovichi see Kommunarka (2)
Skulovka see Primorye
Skuratovsky. Urban settlement, Tula Oblast, Russia : Yuzhny (–1948)
Skwierzyna. Town, western Poland : Schwerin (–1945), Germany
Slatina Radenci. Village, western Slovenia : Bad Radein (–1918), Germany
Slavgorod. Town, Mogilyov Oblast, Belorussia : Propoysk (–1945)
Slavino. Village, Mogilyov Oblast, Belorussia : Osy-Kolyosy (–1964)
Slavjanka. Mountain, southwestern Bulgaria : Ali Butus (–1967)
Slavkov. Town, southeastern Czech Lands : Austerlitz (–1918, 1939–45), Germany
Slavnoye. Village, Kuril Islands, Sakhalin Oblast, Russia : Shibetoro (1905–45), Japan
Slavsk. Town, Kaliningrad Oblast, Russia : Heinrichswalde (–1946), Germany (–1945)

Slavskoye. Village, Kaliningrad Oblast, Russia : Kreuzberg (–1945), Germany
Slavyanka. Village, Mogilyov Oblast, Belorussia : Ogloblya (–1964)
Slavyanogorsk. Town, Donetsk Oblast, Ukraine : Bannovsky (–1964)
Slavyanskaya see Slavyansk-na-Kubani
Slavyansk-na-Kubani. Town, Krasnodar Kray, Russia : Slavyanskaya (–1958)
Slawa. Town, western Poland : Schlawa (–1937), Germany; Schlesiersee (1937–45), Germany
Slawentzitz see Sławięcice
Sławięcice. Village, southern Poland : Slawentzitz (–c. 1935), Germany, Ehrenforst (c. 1935–45), Germany
Sleptsovskaya see Ordzhonikidzevskaya
Sleptsy see Znamenka (4)
Sloboda see (1) Ezhva; (2) Przhevalskoye
Slobozhanka. Village, Gomel Oblast, Belorussia : Knyazhitsa (–1964)
Slobozhany. Village, Brest Oblast, Belorussia : Bovdilovtsy (–1964)
Slomikhino see Firmanovo
Slovenj Gradec. Village, northern Slovenia : Windischgraz (–1918), Germany
(Slovenska) Bistrica. Village, eastern Slovenia :

Windisch-Feistritz
(–1918), Germany

Słupsk. Town, northwestern
Poland : Stolp (–1945),
Germany

Slutsk see Pavlovsk

Smaalenene see Østfold

Smaldeel see Theunissen

Šmarje (pri Jelšah). Village,
western Slovenia : Sankt
Marien (–1918), Ger-
many

Smértos. Village, western
Greece : Mýlos (–1960s)

Smirnovo. Urban settle-
ment, North Kazakhstan
Oblast, Kazakhstan :
Smirnovsky (–1973)

Smirnovsky see Smirnovo

Smolyan. City, southern
Bulgaria : Pashmakli
(–1934)

Smorkovo see Peremozhets

Smychka. Suburb of Mos-
cow, Moscow Oblast,
Russia : Ivanovskoye
(–1929)

Smyrtóula see Nikópolis

Snegurovka see Tetiyev

Snežnik. Mountain, south-
ern Slovenia : Monte
Nevoso (–1947), Italy

Śniardwy. Lake, northeastern Poland : Spirding
(–1945), Germany

Snovsk see Schors

Sobięcin. Town, southwestern Poland : Hermsdorf
(–1945), Germany

Sobinka. Town, Vladimir
Oblast, Russia :
Komavangard (early
1920s)

Sobótka. Town, southwest-

ern Poland : Zobten
(–1945), Germany

Sobradinho. City, southern
Brazil, South America :
Jacui (–1938)

Socoro see Fronteiras

Soc Trang. City, southern
Vietnam : Khan Hung
(–c. 1980)

Sofala. Province, southeastern Mozambique, south-
eastern Africa : Beira
(–1976)

Sofiyevka see Volnyansk

Sofiyevsky Rudnik see Karla
Marksa, imeni

Sogn og Fjordane. County,
southwestern Norway :
Nordre Bergenhus
(–1918)

Sohrau see Zory

Sok-Karmala see Severnoye

Sokol. Urban settlement,
Sakhalin Oblast, Rus-
sia : Otani (1905–45),
Japan

Sokolov. Town, northwest-
ern Czech Lands :
Falknov (nad Ohři)
(–1948)

Sokuluk. Village, Kirgizia :
Novo-Troitskoye (–1937),
Kaganovich (1937–57)

Solas de Bureba see Llano de
Bureba

Solbad Hall in Tirol. City,
western Austria : Hall
(–1938)

Soldatskoye see Soldatsky

Soldatsky. Town, Tashkent
Oblast, Uzbekistan :
Yangi-Bazar (–c. 1930),
Soldatskoye (c. 1930–c.
1960)

Soldin *see* Myślibórz

Soledade. City, northeastern Brazil, South America : Ibiapinópolis (1944–48)

Soledade *see* Soledade de Minas

Soledade de Minas. City, southeastern Brazil, South America : Soledade (–1944), Ibatuba (1944–48)

Soligorsk. Town, Minsk Oblast, Belorussia : Novo-Starobinsk (*1958–59)

Sol-Iletsk. Town, Orenburg Oblast, Russia : Iletsk (–1945)

Solnechnoye. Urban settlement, Leningrad Oblast, Russia : Ollila (–1948), Finland (–1940)

Solnechny *see* Gorny

Solntsevo. Urban settlement, Kursk Oblast, Russia : Korovino (–c. 1960)

Solonópole. City, northeastern Brazil, South America : Cachoeira (–1944)

Soltaniyeh *see* Sa'adiyeh

Solun. Town, northeastern China : Solunshan (–1917)

Solunshan *see* Solun

Solzavod. Village, Evenki Autonomous Okrug, Krasnoyarsk Kray, Russia : Bachinsky (–?), Stalino (?–c. 1961)

Somabhula. Village, central Zimbabwe, southeastern Africa : Somabula (–1982)

Somabula *see* Somabhula

Someitsun *see* Tehjung

Sommerfeld *see* Lubsko

Son *see* (1) Puerto de Son; (2) Sonsky

Søndre Bergenhus *see* Hordaland

Søndre Trondhjem *see* Sør-Trøndelag

Songjin *see* Kinmch'aek

Songnim. City, western North Korea : Kyŏmipo (1910–45), Japan

Songolo *see* Mbanza-Ngungu

Sonsky. Urban settlement, Khakass Autonomous Oblast, Krasnoyarsk Kray, Russia : Son (–1940)

Soochow [Su-chou]. City, eastern China : Wuhsien (1912–49)

Sopot *see* Vazovgrad

Sopron. City, western Hungary : Ödenburg (–1921), Germany

Soroca *see* Soroki

Sorochinsk. Town, Orenburg Oblast, Russia : Sorochinskoye (c. 1935)

Sorochinskoye *see* Sorochinsk

Soroka *see* Belomorsk

Soroki. Town, Moldavia : Soroca (1918–40, 1941–44), Romania

Sorokino *see* Krasnodon

Soroksárpéteri *see* Pestszentimre

Sorsk. Town, Khakass Autonomous Oblast, Krasnoyarsk Kray, Russia : Dzerzhinsky (–c. 1960)

Sortavala. Town, Karelian Autonomous Republic, Russia : Serdobol (–1918)

Sør-Trøndelag. County, central Norway : Søndre Trondhjem (–1918)

Sosninskaya *see* Kominterna, imeni

Sosnogorsk. Town, Komi Autonomous Republic, Russia : Izhma (–1957)

Sosnovaya (1). Village, Mogilyov Oblast, Belorussia : Koty (–1964)

Sosnovaya (2). Village, Vitebsk Oblast, Belorussia : Pyany Les (–1964)

Sosnovaya (3). Village, Brest Oblast, Belorussia : Zherebilovichi (–1964)

Sosnovets. Village, Gomel Oblast, Belorussia : Monastyr (–1964)

Sosnovichi. Village, Brest Oblast, Belorussia : Beskhlebichi (–1964)

Sosnovka. Village, Kursk Oblast, Russia : Nizhnegniloye (–c. 1960)

Sosnovo. Settlement, Leningrad Oblast, Russia : Rautu (–1948), Finland (–1940)

Sosnovoborsk. Urban settlement, Penza Oblast, Russia : Litvino (–1940)

Sosnovoye. Urban settlement, Rovno Oblast, Ukraine : Lyudvipol (–1946)

Sosnovtsy. Village, Grodno Oblast, Belorussia : Ovechki (–1964)

Sosnovy Bor. Village, Vitebsk Oblast, Belorussia : Golyashi (–1964)

Sosnowiec. City, southern Poland : Sosnowitz (1939–45), Germany

Sosnowitz *see* Sosnowiec

Šoštanj. Village, northern Slovenia : Schönstein (–1918), Germany

Sosva. Urban settlement, Sverdlovsk Oblast, Russia : Sosvinsky Zavod (–1938)

Sosvinsky Zavod *see* Sosva

Soto del Real. Village, central Spain : Chozas de la Sierra (–c. 1950)

Sotsgorodok *see* Gornyak (1)

Souk el Arba de l'Oued Beth. Village, northwestern Morocco, northwestern Africa : Camp-Bataille (–c. 1959)

Souk Eltnine. Village, northwestern Morocco, northwestern Africa : Valgravé (–c. 1959)

Souk Jemaâ Oulad Abbou. Village, northwestern Morocco, northwestern Africa : Foucauld (–c. 1959)

Souk Tleta Loulad. Village, northwestern Morocco, northwestern Africa : Venet-Ville (–c. 1959)

Soure *see* Caucaia

Sour el Ghozlane. Town, northern Algeria, northern Africa : Aumale (–c. 1962)

Sousa de Lara *see* Bocoio

South Africa Republic *see* Transvaal

South Auckland *see* Churchill

South Coast Town *see* Gold Coast

South-Eastern Oblast *see* Stavropol Kray

Southern Rhodesia *see* Zimbabwe

Southern Yemen *see* Yemen

South Floral Park. Village,
New York, USA :
Jamaica Square (–1931)

South Kazakhstan Oblast *see*
Chimkent Oblast

South Miami. Suburb of
Miami, Florida, USA :
Larkins (–1926)

South Nelson *see* Nelson-
Miramichi

South Newburgh *see* Garfield
Heights

South Pleasureville. Town,
Kentucky, USA : Pleas-
ureville (–1930s)

South West Africa *see* Namibia

Sovetabad. Town, Andizhan
Oblast, Uzbekistan : Kar-
abagish (–1972)

Sovetabad *see* (1) Gafurov;
(2) Nurabad

Sovetsk (1). Town, Kirov
Oblast, Russia : Kukarka
(–1937)

Sovetsk (2). Town, Kaliningrad Oblast, Russia :
Tilsit (–1946), Germany
(–1945)

Sovetskaya (1). Village,
Gomel Oblast, Belorus-
sia : Amerika (–1964)

Sovetskaya (2). Village,
Rostov Oblast, Russia :
Chernyshevskaya
(–c. 1960)

Sovetskaya (3). Village, Mogilyov Oblast, Belorussia :
Gorevatka (–1964)

Sovetskaya (4). Village,
Krasnodar Kray, Russia :
Urupskaya (–?)

Sovetskaya (5). Village,

Vitebsk Oblast, Belorus-
sia : Yudenichi (–1964)

Sovetskaya Gavan. Town,
Khabarovsk Kray,
Russia : Imperatorskaya
Gavan (*1914–c. 1920)

Sovetskoye (1). Village,
Altay Kray, Russia :
Gryaznukha (–c. 1960)

Sovetskoye (2). Urban settlement, Kabardin-Bal-
kar Autonomous Repub-
lic, Russia : Kashkatau
(–1944)

Sovetskoye (3). Village,
Dagestan Autonomous
Republic, Russia :
Khebda (–c. 1960)

Sovetskoye (4). Village,
Saratov Oblast, Russia :
Mariental (–1941)

Sovetskoye (5). Village,
Orenburg Oblast, Russia :
Mordovskaya Bokla
(–c. 1960)

Sovetskoye (6). Village,
Chechen-Ingush Autono-
mous Republic, Russia :
Shatoy (–1944)

Sovetskoye (7). Village,
Belgorod Oblast, Russia :
Shelyakino (–c. 1960)

Sovetskoye (8). Village,
Chuvash Autonomous
Republic, Russia :
Shumatovo (–1939)

Sovetskoye (9). Urban
settlement, Kalmyk
Autonomous Republic,
Russia : Sukhotinskaya
(–c. 1960)

Sovetskoye *see* Zelenokumsk

Sovetsky (1). Urban settlement, Crimean Oblast,

Ukraine : Ichki(–Gram-matikovo) (–1944)
Sovetsky (2). Urban settle-ment, Leningrad Oblast, Russia : Johannes (–1948), Finland (–1940)
Sovetsky (3). Urban settle-ment, Khatlon Oblast, Tajikistan : Kzyl-Mazar (–c. 1960)
Soviet Union *see* Common-wealth of Independent States
Soya. Town, northwestern Angola, southwestern Africa : Santo Antônio do Zaïre (–c. 1979)
Soylan *see* Azizbekov
Spaccaforno *see* Ispica
Spadafora. Village, north-eastern Sicily, Italy : Spadafora San Martino (–1937)
Spadafora San Martino *see* Spadafora
Spanish Guinea *see* Equatorial Guinea
Spanish Sahara *see* Western Sahara
Sparling *see* Camrose
Sparrow Hills *see* Lenin Hills
Spartináiika *see* Geliniátika
Spas *see* Pervomaysky (5)
Spassk *see* (1) Bednodemya-novsk; (2) Kuybyshev (2); (3) Spassk-Dalny; (4) Spassk-Ryazansky
Spassk-Dalny. Town, Primorsky Kray, Russia : Spasskoye (–1917), Spassk (1917–29)
Spasskoye *see* Spassk-Dalny
Spassk-Ryazansky. Town,

Ryazan Oblast, Russia : Spassk (–1929)
Spassk-Tatarsky *see* Kuy-byshev (2)
Spassky Zaton *see* Kuybyshevsky Zaton
Spáta *see* Spáta-Loútsa
Spáta-Loútsa. Town, cen-tral Greece : Spáta (–1960s)
Spirding *see* Śniardwy
Spirit River *see* Rycroft
Spitak. Town, Armenia : Amamlu (–1948)
Spitsevka. Village, Stavro-pol Kray, Russia : Spit-sevskoye (–c. 1940)
Spitsevskoye *see* Spitsevka
Spokane. City, Washington, USA : Spokane Falls (–1900)
Spokane Falls *see* Spokane
Springfield *see* Winterton
Spring Forest *see* Willow Springs
Sprottau *see* Szprotawa
Sproule *see* Ebor
Spyaglitsa *see* Svetilovichi
Srebrna Góra. Town, south-western Poland : Silberberg (–1945), Germany
Sredecka. River, southeast-ern Bulgaria : Man-drenska (–1967)
Sredets. Village, southeast-ern Bulgaria : Karabunar (–1934)
Srednekrayushkino *see* Per-vomayskoye (8)
Srednevolzhskaya Oblast *see* Samara Oblast
Srednevolzhsky Kray *see* Sam-ara Oblast

Srednyaya Nyukzha. Village, Amur Oblast, Russia : Blyukherovsk (late 1930s)

Sremska Mitrovica. Town, northern Serbia : Mitrowitz (–1918), Germany

Sremski Karlovci. Town, northern Serbia : Karlowitz (–1918), Germany

Srikakulam. Town, southeastern India : Chicacole (–1950s)

Sri Lanka. Island republic, Indian Ocean : Ceylon (–1972)

Środa Śląska. Town, southwestern Poland : Neumarkt (–1945), Germany

Srpski Itebej *see* Itebej

Ssu-hai = Szehai

Ssu-hsien = Szehsien

Ssu-yang = Szeyang

Stadroda. Town, westcentral Germany : Roda (–1922)

Stakhanov *see* Kadiyevka

Stakhanovets *see* Mirny

Stakhanovo *see* (1) Zhovten (2); (2) Zhukovsky

Stalin [Qytet Stalin]. City, south-central Albania : Kuçovë (–1950)

Stalin *see* (1) Braşov; (2) Donetsk (2); (3) Varna

Stalina, imeni *see* Shakhrikhan

Stalinabad *see* Dushanbe

Stalin Dam. Iskar River, western Bulgaria : Pasarel Dam (–1951)

Stalindorf *see* Zhovtnevoye (2)

Stalingrad *see* Volgograd

Stalingrad Guberniya (1928†). USSR : Tsaritsyn Guberniya (*1919–25)

Stalingrad Kray *see* Volgograd Oblast

Stalingrad Oblast *see* Volgograd Oblast

Staliniri *see* Tskhinvali

Stalino *see* (1) Donetsk (2); (2) Shakhrikhan; (3) Solzavod

Stalinogorsk *see* Novomoskovsk

Stalinogród *see* Katowice

Stalino Oblast *see* Donetsk Oblast

Stalin Peak *see* (1) Communism Peak; (2) Gerlachovka; (3) Musala

Stalinsk *see* (1) Nagibovo; (2) Novokuznetsk

Stalinskoye *see* (1) Belovodskoye; (2) Zhovtnevoye (2)

Stalinsky *see* Bolshevo

Stallupönen *see* Nesterov (1)

Stamboliyski. Town, southern Bulgaria : Novi Kricim (–1980)

Stanichno-Luganskoye. Urban settlement, Lugansk Oblast, Ukraine : Kosiorovo (mid-1930s)

Stanimaka *see* Asenovgrad

Stanislau *see* Ivano-Frankovsk

Stanislav *see* Ivano-Frankovsk

Stanislav Oblast *see* Ivano-Frankovsk Oblast

Stanislavovo *see* Rossony

Stanisławów *see* Ivano-Frankovsk

Štanjel na Krasu. Village, western Slovenia : San Daniele del Carso (–1947), Italy

Stanke Dimitrov. Town, southwestern Bulgaria :

Dupnitsa (–1949), Marek (1949–c. 1960)

Stanley, Mount see Ngaliema, Mount

Stanley Falls see Boyoma Falls

Stanley Pool see Malebo Pool

Stanleyville see (1) Eastern Province; (2) Kisangani

Stann Creek see Dungriga

Stannum see Stanthorpe

Stanovoye. Village, Lipetsk Oblast, Russia : Ploskoye (–1984)

Stanthorpe. Town, Queensland, Australia : Stannum (–1902)

Stantsiya-Leninabad see Gafurov

Stantsiya-Regar see Tursunzade

Stantsiya-Yakkabag see Yakkabag

Stará Ďala see Hurbanovo

Stara Kresna. Town, southwestern Bulgaria : Kresna (–1980)

Staraya Barda see Krasnogorskoye (2)

Staraya Bukhara see Bukhara

Starčevo see Kalipetrovo

Stargard (in Pommern) see Stargard Szczeciński

Stargard Szczeciński. City, northwestern Poland : Stargard (in Pommern) (–1945), Germany

Stari Bečej see Bečej

Starobachaty. Urban settlement, Kemerovo Oblast, Russia : Bachaty (–c. 1960)

Starodubskoye. Village,

Sakhalin Oblast, Russia : Sakaehama (1905–45), Japan

Starogard (Gdański). Town, northern Poland : Preussisch Stargard (–1945), Germany

Staro-Izobilnoye. Village, Stavropol Kray, Russia : Izobilnoye (–1930s)

Staromaryevka. Village, Stavropol Kray, Russia : Starymaryevskoye (–c. 1940)

Staromaryevskoye see Staromaryevka

Staromlinovka. Village, Donetsk Oblast, Ukraine : Stary Kermenchik (–1946)

Staro-Nikolayevskoye see Panfilovskoye

Staropyshminsk. Urban settlement, Sverdlovsk Oblast, Russia : Pyshminsky Zavod (–1943)

Staroutkinsk. Urban settlement, Sverdlovsk Oblast, Russia : Utkinsky Zavod (–1933)

(Staroye) Drozhzhanoye. Village, Tatar Autonomous Republic, Russia : Drozhzhanoye (–c. 1940)

Startsevichi see Znamya

Startsy see Kirovsk (5)

Stary Chardzhuy see Komsomolsk (3)

Stary Dashev see Dashev

Stary Folvarok see Pobednaya (3)

Stary Kermenchik see Staromlinovka

Stary Margilan see Margilan

Stary Salavan *see* Novocheremshansk

Staryye Atagi *see* Predgornoye

Stathmós *see* Platamón

Staurodrómion. Village, southern Greece : Xerokhórion (–1960s)

Stavanger *see* Rogaland

Stavern. City, southeastern Norway : Fredriksvern (–1929)

Stavropol. Capital of Stavropol Kray, Russia : Voroshilovsk (1935–43)

Stavropol *see* Tolyatti

Stavropol Kray. Southeastern Russia : South-Eastern Oblast (*1924), Severokavkazsky Kray [North Caucasus Kray] (1924–37), Ordzhonikidze Kray (1937–43)

Stębark. Town, northeastern Poland : Tannenberg (–1945), Germany

Stegi *see* Siteki

Stegman *see* Artesia

Stein *see* Kamnik

Steinschönau *see* Kamenický Šenov

Stepanakert *see* Khankendy

Stepanavan. Town, Armenia : Dzhalal-Ogly (–1924)

Stepantsminda *see* Kazbegi

Stephenson *see* Crosby

Stepnoy *see* Elista

Stepnoye. Urban settlement, Saratov Oblast, Russia : Otrogovo (–c. 1960)

Stern Park Gardens *see* Lidice

Stettin *see* Szczecin

Stettler. Town, Alberta, Canada : Blumenau (–1906)

Stidia. Village, northwestern Algeria, northern Africa : Georges Clemenceau (–c. 1962)

Stilwell Road (1945†). Military highway, India/China : Ledo Road (*1942–45)

Stolp *see* Slupsk

Stolpmünde *see* Ustka

Stonefort. Village, Illinois, USA : Bolton (–1934)

Stoney Creek *see* Melfort

Strassburg *see* Aiud

Strehlen *see* Strzelin

Střekov. Town, southern Slovakia : Schreckenstein (–1918, 1939–45), Germany

Stříbro. Town, western Czech Lands : Mies (–1918, 1939–45), Germany

Striegau *see* Strzegom

Strýme. Village, northeastern Greece : Strýmne (–1960s)

Strýmne *see* Strýme

Strzegom. City, southwestern Poland : Striegau (–1945), Germany

Strzelce Krajeńskie. Town, western Poland : Friedeberg in Neumark (–1945), Germany

Strzelce (Opolskie). Town, southwestern Poland : Gross Strehlitz (–1945), Germany

Strzelin. City, southwestern Poland : Strehlen (–1945), Germany

Stuart *see* Alice Springs

Štubnianske Teplice *see* Turčianske Teplice

Stuchka. Town, Latvia :
Petra Stuchki, imeni
(*1961–67)
Stuhm see Sztum
Stupino. Town, Moscow
Oblast, Russia :
Elektrovoz (*c. 1935–
38)
Štúrovo. Town, southern
Slovakia : Parkań (–1949)
Stutthof see Sztutowo
Süancheng [Hsüan-cheng].
City, eastern China :
Ningkwo (–1912)
Süanhan [Hsüan-han].
Town, central China :
Tungsiang (–1914)
Subotica. City, northern Ser-
bia : (Maria-)Theresiopel
(–1918), Germany
Suchan. Town, northwest-
ern Poland : Zachan
(–1945), Germany
Suchan see (1) Partizansk; (2)
Partizanskaya (3)
Suchansky Rudnik see Parti-
zansk
Suchki see Kolosovo (2)
Su-chou = Soochow
Süchow [Hsü-chou]. City,
eastern China : Tungshan
(1912–45)
Suchow see Ipin
Süchow see (1) Kiuchüan
[Chiu-chüan]; (2) Suhsien
Sucre. City, northwestern
Peru, South America :
Huauco (–1940)
Sudanese Republic see Mali
Sudauen see Suwałki
Sudostroy see Severodvinsk
Sufikishlak see Akhunbabayev
Sug-Aksy see Sut-Khol
Sugluc see Saglouc

Sugod. Municipality, Leyte,
Philippines : Sugod Norte
(–1913)
Sugod Norte see Sugod
Sugod Sur see Libagon
Suhaile Arabi. Barrio, Zam-
boanga del Norte, Philip-
pines : Bucana (–1969)
Suhsien. Town, eastern
China : Suchow (–1912)
Sui-chiang = Suikiang
Suichow see Suihsien (1), (2)
Sui-chuan = Suichwan
Suichwan [Sui-chuan].
Town, southeastern Chi-
na : Lungchüan (–1914)
Suifu see Ipin
Suihsien (1). Town, east-
central China : Suichow
(–1913)
Suihsien (2). Town, east-
central China : Suichow
(–1912)
Suikiang [Sui-chiang]. Town,
southwestern China :
Tsingkiang (–1914)
Suileng. Town, northeastern
China : Shangtsichang
(–1915)
Suiting see Tahsien
Suiyüan see Fuyüan
Sukarnapura see Jayapura
Sukarno, Puntjak see Jaya,
Puncak
Sukhotinskaya see Sovetskoye
(9)
Sukhum see Sukhumi
Sukhumi. Capital of
Abkhazian Autonomous
Republic, Georgia :
Sukhum (–1935)
Sulawesi. Island, Greater
Sundas, Indonesia :
Celebes (–1945)

Sulechów. Town, western Poland : Züllichau (–1945), Germany

Sulęcin. Town, western Poland : Zielenzig (–1945), Germany

Sulików. Town, southwestern Poland : Schönberg (–1945), Germany

Sulimov see Cherkessk

Sulin see Krasny Sulin

Sulphur Springs National Reservation see Platt National Park

Sultanabad see Arak

Sultan Alonto. Municipality, Lanao del Sur, Philippines : Lake Lanao (–1905)

Sultan Kudarat. Municipality, Cotabato, Philippines : Nuling (–1969)

Sumbawanga. District, western Tanzania, eastern Africa : Ufipa (–1974)

Sumbe. Town, western Angola, southwestern Africa : Novo Redondo (–1975), Ngunza-Kabolu (1975–81)

Šumen = Shumen

Šumperk. Town, eastern Czech Lands : Mährisch-Schönberg (–1918, 1939–45), Germany

Sünchow see Kweiping [Kueiping]

Sunfung. Town, southeastern China : Chongning (–1914)

Sung-chiang. City, eastern China : Hua-t'ing (1912–13)

Sünko [Hsün-ko]. Town, northeastern China : Chike (–1949)

Sunning see Toishan

Sunnyvale. City, California, USA : Murphy's Station (–?), Encinal (?–1912)

Sunwui. Town, southeastern China : Kongmoon (–1931)

Sünyi [Hsün-yi]. Town, central China : Sanshui (–1914)

Suram see Surami

Surami. Urban settlement, Georgia : Suram (–1936)

Surendranagar. Town, western India : Wadhwan (–1950s)

Surfer's Paradise. Beach, Southport, Queensland, Australia : Meyer's Ferry (–1920s)

Surinam. Republic, northeastern South America : Dutch Guiana (–1954)

Sursk. Town, Penza Oblast, Russia : Nikolsky Khutor (–1953)

Surskoye. Urban settlement, Ulyanovsk Oblast, Russia : Promzino (–c. 1930)

Surveyors Bay see Whalers Bay

Surville Cliffs. Cape, North Island, New Zealand : Kerr Point (–1966)

Susam-Adasi see Samos

Susanino. Urban settlement, Kostroma Oblast, Russia : Molvitino (–1938)

Süshui [Hsü-shui]. Town, northeastern China : Ansu (–1914)

Susz. Town, northeastern
Poland : Rosenberg
(–1919), Germany
Sut-Khol. Village, Tuva Au-
tonomous Republic, Rus-
sia : Sug-Aksy (–c. 1960)
Suvorovo (1). Village, east-
ern Bulgaria : Novgradets
(–1950)
Suvorovo (2). Urban settle-
ment, Odessa Oblast,
Ukraine : Shikirlikitai
(–c. 1930), Regele Carol
II (c. 1930–40), Romania,
Regele Mihai I (1941–
44), Romania
Suwałki. Town, northeast-
ern Poland : Sudauen
(1941–45), Germany
Suyetikha see Biryusinsk
Süyung [Hsü-yung]. Town,
central China : Yungning
(–1913)
Svárov. Town, western
Czech Lands : Tanvald
(–1949)
Sverdlova, imeni see
Sverdlovsk (2)
Sverdlovo. Village, Saratov
Oblast, Russia : Ney-
Valter (–1941)
Sverdlovo see Sverdlovsky
Sverdlovsk (1). Village,
Bukhara Oblast, Uzbeki-
stan : Dzhandar
(–c. 1935), Faizully
Khodzhayeva, imeni
c. 1935–37)
Sverdlovsk (2). Town,
Lugansk Oblast,
Ukraine : Sverdlova,
imeni (*1930s–1938)
Sverdlovsk see Yekaterinburg
Sverdlovsky. Urban settle-

ment, Moscow Oblast,
Russia : Sverdlovo
(–1928)
Sverdlovsky Priisk see Is
Sveti Ivan Zelina see Zelina
Svetilovichi. Village,
Grodno Oblast, Belorus-
sia : Spyaglitsa (–1964)
Sveti Vrach see Sandanski
Svetlaya Roshcha. Village,
Gomel Oblast, Belorus-
sia : Pustynka (–1964)
Svetlogorsk (1). Town, Ka-
liningrad Oblast, Russia :
Rauschen (–1946), Ger-
many (–1945)
Svetlogorsk (2). Town,
Gomel Oblast, Belorus-
sia : Shatilki (–1961)
Svetlograd. Town, Stavro-
pol Kray, Russia :
Petrovskoye (–1965)
Svetlovodsk. Town, Kiro-
vograd Oblast, Ukraine :
Khrushchyov (?–1961),
Kremges (1961–69)
Svetloye see Svetly
Svetly. Town, Kaliningrad
Oblast, Russia :
Kobbelbude (–1945),
Germany, Svetloye
(1945–55)
Svetogorsk. Town, Lenin-
grad Oblast, Russia :
Enso (–1948), Finland
(–1940)
Svetozarevo. Town, central
Serbia : Jagodina (–1946)
Svinka see Lugovaya (3)
Svinoye see Pervomaysk (3)
Svitavy. Town, southeastern
Czech Lands : Zwittau
(–1918, 1939–45),
Germany

Svoboda. Village, Kaliningrad Oblast, Russia : Janichen (–1946), Germany (–1945)
Svoboda *see* Liski
Svobodny. Town, Amur Oblast, Russia : Alekseyevsk (*1912–17)
Svyatogorovsky Rudnik *see* Dobropolye
Svyatoy Krest *see* Budyonnovsk
Swazi *see* Kangwane
Świdnica. City, southwestern Poland : Schweidnitz (–1945), Germany
Świdwin. Town, northwestern Poland : Schivelbein (–1945), Germany
Świebodzice. Town, southwestern Poland : Freiburg (in Schlesien) (–1945), Germany
Świebodzin. Town, western Poland : Schiebus (–1945), Germany
Swieradów Zdrój. Town, southwestern Poland : Bad Flinsberg (–1945), Germany
Świerzawa. Town, southwestern Poland : Schönau (–1945), Germany
Swiftcurrent Creek. River, Saskatchewan, Canada : Swiftcurrent River (–1970)
Swiftcurrent River *see* Swiftcurrent Creek
Swinemünde *see* Świnoujście
Świnoujście. City, northwestern Poland : Swinemünde (–1945), Germany

Sybrand Park. Suburb of Cape Town, Cape of Good Hope, South Africa : Hazendal (–1959)
Syców. Town, southwestern Poland : Gross Wartenberg (–1945), Germany
Sydney Island *see* Manra
Sykás Hypátes. Village, central Greece : Sykéa Hypátes (–1960s)
Sykéa Hypátes *see* Sykás Hypátes
Syktyvkar. Capital of Komi Autonomous Republic, Russia : Ust-Sysolsk (–1930)
Synzhereya *see* Lazovsk
Syrdarya. Town, Syrdarya Oblast, Uzbekistan : Syrnovorossiysk (–1947), Syrdaryinsky (1947–c. 1960)
Syrdaryinsky *see* Syrdarya
Syrnovorossiysk *see* Syrdarya
Syuginsky *see* Mozhga
Szczawno Zdrój. Town, southwestern Poland : Bad Salzbrunn (–1945), Germany
Szczecin. City, northwestern Poland : Stettin (–1945), Germany
Szczecinek. Town, northwestern Poland : Neustettin (–1938, 1939–45), Germany
Szczytno. Town, northeastern Poland : Ortelsburg (–1945), Germany

Szecheng *see* Lingyün
Széchenyitelep *see* Pestújhely
Szechow *see* (1) Szehsien
[Ssu-hsien]; (2) Tsenkung
[Ts'en-kung]
Szehai [Ssu-hai]. Town,
northeastern China :
Szehaipao (–1950)
Szehaipo *see* Szehai [Ssu-hai]
Szehsien [Ssu-hsien]. Town,
eastern China : Szechow
(–1912)
Szehsien *see* Tsenkung [Ts'en-
kung]
Szentadorján *see* Lispeszenta-
dorján
Szentimre *see* Tiszaszen-
timre
Szentkirály. Village, central
Hungary : Lászláfalva
(–1987)
Szewczenko *see* Vita
Szeyang [Ssu-yang]. Town,
eastern China : Taoyüan
(–1914)
Szilasbalhás *see* Mezőszilas
Szirguni = Sergunia
Szklarska Poręba. Town,
southwestern Poland :
(Mittel) Schreiberhau
(–1945), Germany
Szlichtyngowa. Town,
western Poland :
Schlichtingsheim (–1945),
Germany
Szprotawa. Town, south-
western Poland : Sprottau
(–1945), Germany
Sztálinváros *see* Dunaújvá-
ros
Sztum. Town, northern
Poland : Stuhm (–1919,
1939–45), Germany
Sztutowo. Town, northwest-
ern Poland : Stutthof
(–1945), Germany

Tabaiana *see* Itabaiana
Tabuaeran. Island, Kiribati,
western Pacific : Fanning
Island (–1981)
Tachangtze *see* Tsinglung
[Ching-lung]
Tacopaya *see* Zudañez
Tadzhikabad. Village,
Tajikistan : Kalay-
Lyabiob (–1949)
Tadzhik Autonomous SSR *see*
Tajikistan
Tadzhik SSR *see* Tajikistan
Taerhhu *see* Yenkiang [Yen-
chiang]
Tafangshen *see* Tehhwei
[Te-hui]
Taft *see* Mahato
Tagant. District, south-
central Mauritania, west-
ern Africa : Neuvième
(–c. 1979)
Tagdempt. City, northern
Algeria, northern Africa :
Tiaret (–c. 1962)
Taguimtim *see* Paciencia
Tahing [Ta-hsing]. Town,
northeastern China :
Hwangtsun (–1928)
Tahopa *see* Hinghai [Hsing-
hai]
Tahsien. Town, central
China : Suiting
(–1913)
Ta-hsing = Tahing
Tai-chiang = Taikiang
Taichow *see* (1) Linhai; (2)
Taihsien [T'ai-hsien]
Taiei *see* Ugolny
Taihei *see* Udarny

Taihsien [T'ai-hsien]. Town, northeastern China : Taichow (–1912)

Taikiang [Tai-chiang]. Town, southern China : Taikung (–1942)

Taikung see Taikiang [T'ai-chiang]

Tailak-Paion see Komsomolsk (4)

Taining see Kienning [Ch'ien-ning]

Taiping see (1) Fencheng [Fen-ch'eng]; (2) Tsungshan [Ch'ung-shan]; (3) Wanyüan; (4) Wenling; (5) Yangchung

Taitsesze see Ningting

Taiwan Strait. Between China and Taiwan : Formosa Strait (–1984)

Taiyüan [Tai-yüan]. City, northeastern China : Yangkü (1912–47)

Taiyüan see Chinyüan

Tajikistan. Republic, central Asia : Tadzhik Autonomous SSR (*1924–29), Tadzhik SSR (1929–91)

Takahagi. Town, central Honshu, Japan : Matsubara (–1937)

Takaki see Yamato

Takchiyan see Shargun

Takhtamukay see Oktyabrsky (4)

Takow see (1) Kaohiung [Kaohsiung]; (2) Lingyüan

Takushan see Kushan

Tala see Kungshan

Talai. Town, northeastern China : Choerhcheng (–1913)

Talakmau, Mount. Mountain, Sumatra, Indonesia : Ophir, Mount (–c. 1966)

Talang see Mokiang [Mo-chiang]

Talas. Town, Kirgizia : Dmitriyevskoye (–1937)

Taldom. Town, Moscow Oblast, Russia : Leninsk (1918–29)

Taldy-Kurgan. Capital of Taldy-Kurgan Oblast, Kazakhstan : Gavrilovka (–1920)

Talesh. Town, northwestern Iran : Hashtpar (–1980)

Talin. Urban settlement, Armenia : Verin-Talin (–1978)

Talitsa. Town, Sverdlovsk Oblast, Russia : Talitsky Zavod (–c. 1928)

Talitsky Zavod see Talitsa

Talkhatan-Baba see Kuybyshevo (4)

Tallinn. Capital of Estonia : Revel (–1917)

Talpaki. Village, Kaliningrad Oblast, Russia : Taplacken (–1945), Germany

Talpetate see San Antonio (de Cortés)

Talutang see Kingtai [Chint'ai]

Taman Negara National Park. Malay Peninsula, Malaysia : King George V National Park (*1938–?)

Tamanrasset. Town, southern Algeria, northern Africa : Fort-Laperrine (–c. 1962)

Tamasaki see Ezaki

Tamatave *see* Toamasina

Tamil Nadu. State, southern India : Madras (–1969)

Tanchai. Town, southern China : Pachai (–1941)

Tanchow *see* Tanhsien

Tanga *see* Muheza

Tanganyika. Republic [uniting with Zanzibar (1964†) to form Tanzania], eastern Africa : German East Africa (–1920)

Tangar *see* Hwangyüan [Huang-yüan]

Tangará. City, southern Brazil, South America : Rio Bonito (–1944)

T'ang-chia-kuan = Tangkiakwan

Tangho [T'ang-ho]. Town, east-central China : Tanghsien (–1914), Piyüan (1914–23)

Tanghsien *see* Tangho [T'ang-ho]

Tangkiakwan [Tang-chia-kuan]. Town, southeastern China : Chungshan (1930–34)

Tanhsien. Town, southeastern China : Tanchow (–1912)

Taning *see* Wuki [Wu-ch'i]

Tankiang *see* Leishan

Tannenberg *see* Stębark

Tannu-Tuva *see* Tuva Autonomous Republic

Tanokuchi *see* Kotoura

Tan-t'u *see* Chen-chiang

Tantung. Town, northeastern China : Antung (–1965)

Tantura *see* Dor

Tanvald *see* Svárov

Tanza. Municipality, Cavite, Philippines : Santa Cruz de Malabon (–1914)

Taoan [T'ao-an]. Town, northeastern China : Tsingan (–1914)

Taochen. Town, southern China : Tukichang (–1932)

Taochow *see* (1) Lintan [Lin-t'an]; (2) Taohsien

Taofu. Town, southern China : Taowu (–1913)

Taoho *see* Linsia [Lin-hsia]

Taohsien. Town, south-central China : Taochow (–1913)

Taolanaro *see* Faradofay

Taonan [T'ao-nan]. Town, northeastern China : Shwangliuchen (–1905)

Taosha [T'ao-sha]. Town, north-central China : Shani (–1914)

Taowu *see* Taofu

Taoyüan [T'ao-yüan]. Town, northern Taiwan : Sinchu (1945–50)

Taoyüan *see* Szeyang [Ssuyang]

Taperoá. City, northeastern Brazil, South America : Batalhão (1944–48)

Tapiau *see* Gvardeysk

Taplacken *see* Talpaki

Tapul *see* Salvacion (2)

Taquari *see* Taquarituba

Taquarituba. Town, southeastern Brazil, South America : Taquari (–1944)

Taraka *see* Tayozhny

Taranovskoye. Village, Kustanay Oblast,

Kazakhstan : Viktorovka (–c. 1960)

Taranto (*1923). Province, southern Italy : Ionio (c. 1937–51)

Tarapoto. City, north-central Peru, South America : San Martín (1940–47)

Tarauacá. City, western Brazil, South America : Seabra (–1944)

Tarfaya. Town, southwestern Morocco, northwestern Africa : Cabo Yubi [Cape Juby] [Villa Bens] (1950–58)

Targovište. City, eastern Bulgaria : Yeski Dzhumaya (–1909)

Tarkhany see Lermontovo

Tarmilate see Oulmes(-les-Thermes)

Târnàveni. Town, central Romania : Dicio-sânmartin (–1930)

Tarnopol see Ternopol

Tarnopol Oblast see Ternopol Oblast

Tarnowitz see Tarnowskie Góry

Tarnowskie Góry. Town, southern Poland : Tarnowitz (–1921), Germany

Tarquinia. Town, central Italy : Corneto (Tarquinia) (–1922)

Tarta. Settlement, Krasnovodsk Oblast, Turkmenistan : Kianly (Tarta) (c. 1945–c. 1960)

Tartki. Village, Tajikistan : Kabadian (–c. 1935), Mikoyanabad (c. 1935–57)

Tartu. Town, Estonia : Yuryev (1030–1224, 1893–1919)

Tashetai see Anpeh [Anpei]

Tashino see Pervomaysk (4)

Tata. Town, northern Hungary : Tatatóváros (*1938–39)

Tatar Autonomous Republic. West-central Russia : Tatar Autonomous SSR (*1920–91)

Tatar Autonomous SSR see Tatar Autonomous Republic

Tatarikan see Pagayawan

Tatar Pazardžik see Pazardžik

Tatatóváros see Tata

Tatsienlu see Kangting [K'ang-ting]

Tatsingkow see Shangi

Tatuchang see Nayung

Tatung see Tungho [T'ung-ho]

Taus see Domažlice

Tayabas see Quezon

Tay Bac. Region, northeastern Vietnam : Thai Meo (*1955–62)

Tayncha see Krasnoarmeysk (4)

Tayozhny. Urban settlement, Krasnoyarsk Kray, Russia : Taraka (–c. 1960)

Tayü. Town, southeastern China : Nanan (–1912)

Tayung. Town, south-central China : Yungting (–1914)

Taza-Bazar see Shumanay

Taza-Kala see Telmansk

Taziárkhai. Village, eastern Greece : Kritsínion (–1960s)

Tazoult. Town, northeastern Algeria, northern Africa : Lambèse (–c. 1962)

Tazovskoye see Khalmer-Sede

Tazuruhama. Town, central Honshu, Japan : Wakura (–1934)

Tbilisi. Capital of Georgia : Tiflis (–1936)

Tbilisskaya. Village, Krasnodar Kray, Russia : Tiflisskaya (–1936)

Tchikala-Tcholohanga. Village, central Angola, southwest Africa : Vila Nova (–c. 1979)

Tczew. City, northern Poland : Dirschau (–1919), Germany

Te-chiang = Tehkiang

Te-ch'in = Tehtsin

Te-chou = Tehchow

Tegucigalpa see Francisco Morazán

Tehchow [Te-chou]. City, eastern China : Tehsien (1913–49)

Tehhwei [Te-hui]. Town, northeastern China : Tafangshen (–1910)

Tehjung [Te-jung]. Town, southern China : Someitsun (–1913)

Tehkiang [Te-chiang]. Town, southern China : Anhwa (–1914)

Tehko [Te-ko]. Town, southern China : Tehwa (–1914)

Tehsien see Tehchow [Te-chou]

Tehtsin [Te-ch'in]. Village, southwestern China : Atentze (–1935)

Te-hui = Tehhwei

Tehwa see Tehko [Teh-ko]

Teian see Anlu

Teixeira da Silva see Bailundo

Teixeira de Sousa see Luau

Teixeira Pinto. Village, western Guinea-Bissau : Canchungo (–1948)

Te-jung = Tehjung

Te-ko = Tehko

Telanaipura. Town, southeastern Sumatra, Indonesia : Jambi (–c. 1966)

Telemark. County, southeastern Norway : Bratsberg (–1918)

Telford. Town, Shropshire, England, UK : Dawley (*1963–68)

Telmansk. Urban settlement, Tashauz Oblast, Turkmenistan : Taza-Kala (–1938)

Telnovsky. Urban settlement, Sakhalin Oblast, Russia : Kita-kozawa (1905–47), Japan (–1945)

Telukbajur. Town, western Sumatra, Indonesia : Emmahaven (–c. 1966)

Telyatki see Podlesnaya

Temir-Khan-Shura see Buynaksk

Temirtau. Town, Karaganda Oblast, Kazakhstan : Samarkandsky (*1934–45)

Tempelburg see Czaplinek

Tenda see Tende

Tende. Village, southeastern France : Tenda (–1947), Italy

Tengchow see (1) Penglai [P'eng-lai]; (2) Tenghsien

Tengchung [T'eng-ch'ung].
Town, southwestern
China : Tengyüeh (–1913)
Tenge. Urban settlement,
Guryev Oblast, Ka-
zakhstan : Uzen (–1977)
Tengelic . Town, west-
central Hungary :
Gindlicsalád (–1931)
Tenghsien. Town, east-
central China : Tengchow
(–1913)
Tengi-Kharam see Dekhkana-
bad
Tengyüeh see Tengchung
[Teng-chung]
T'en-hsi = Tiensi
Teniente Bullaín. Town,
western Bolivia, South
America : Dalence
(–early 1940s)
Tepic see Nayarit
Teplice nad Metují. Town,
northern Czech Lands :
Wekelsdorf (–1918,
1939–45), Germany
Teplice(-Šanov). City,
northwestern Czech
Lands : Teplitz(-
Schönau) (–1918, 1939–
45), Germany
Teplitz(-Schönau) see Tep-
lice(-Šanov)
Teploozyorsk. Urban settle-
ment, Jewish Autono-
mous Oblast, Khab-
arovsk Kray, Russia :
Tyoploye Ozero
(–c. 1960)
Teraina. Island, Kiribati,
western Pacific : Wash-
ington Island (–1981)
Terebovlya. Town, Ter-
nopol Oblast, Ukraine :

Trembowla (–1945),
Poland
Terezín. Town, northwest-
ern Czech Lands : There-
sienstadt (–1918, 1939–
45), Germany
Terijoki see Zelenogorsk
Ternopol. Capital of Ter-
nopol Oblast, Ukraine :
Tarnopol (1919–44),
Poland (–1939)
Ternopol Oblast. Western
Ukraine : Tarnopol
Oblast (*1939–44)
Ternovsk see Novokashirsk
Ternovskoye see Trunovskoye
Ternovsky see Novokashirsk
Terny. Town, Dnepropet-
rovsk Oblast, Ukraine :
Pershotravenka (–c. 1960)
Terpilovichi see Zelenets (1)
Terranova di Sicilia see Gela
Terranova Pausania see Olbia
Terter see Mir-Bashir
Tervel. Village, northeast-
ern Bulgaria : Curt-Bunar
(1913–40), Romania
Teschen see Český Těšín
Tessville see Lincolnwood
Teterboro. Borough, New
Jersey, USA : Bendix
(1937–43)
Tetiyev. Town, Kiev Oblast,
Ukraine : Snegurovka
(–c. 1960)
Tetri-Tskaro. Town, Geor-
gia : Agbulakhi (–1940)
Tetschen see Děčín
Tetyukhe see Dalnegorsk
Tetyukhe-Pristan see
Rudnaya Pristan
Teuchezhsk. Town, Kras-
nodar Kray, Russia :
Adygeysk (–1976)

Tezebazar. Urban settlement, Tashauz Oblast, Turkmenistan : Andreyevsk (–c. 1960)

Thailand. Kingdom, southeastern Asia : Siam (–1939, 1945–48)

Thai Meo *see* Tay Bac

The Dalles *see* City of the Dalles

The Forks *see* Merritt

Thenia. Town, northern Algeria, northern Africa : Ménerville (–c. 1962)

Theodore Roosevelt Island. Island, Potomac River, Washington, DC, USA : Analostan Island (–?)

Theresienstadt *see* Terezín

Therma *see* Eagle Nest

Theronsville *see* Pofadder

Thessaloníki. City, northern Greece : Salonika (–1912), Turkey

Theunissen. Town, Orange Free State, South Africa : Smaldeel (–1909)

Thiersville *see* Ghriss

Thionville. Town, northeastern France : Diedenhofen (1870–1919), Germany

Thomson's Falls *see* Nyahururu

Thorens *see* Thorens-Glières

Thorens-Glières. Village, southeastern France : Thorens (–1947)

Thorn *see* Toruń

Thu Dau Mot. Town, southern Vietnam : Phu Cuong (–c. 1980)

Thule *see* Dundas

Thurston Island. Island, Antarctica : Thurston Peninsula (?–1961)

Thurston Peninsula *see* Thurston Island

Thysville *see* Mbanza-Ngungu

Tiaret *see* Tagdempt

Tidmore *see* Seminole

Tiehli [Tieh-li]. Town, northeastern China : Tiehshanpao (–1915)

Tiehshanpao *see* Tiehli [Tieh-li]

Tien-hsi = Tiensi

Tienpao [T'ien-pao]. Town, southern China : Chenan (–1913)

Tien-shui. City, north-central China : Chin-chou (–1912)

Tiensi [T'ien-hsi]. Town, southern China : Lucheng (–1936)

Tientung [T'ien-tung]. Town, southern China : Enlung (–1936)

Tienyang [T'ien-yang]. Town, southern China : Napo (–1936)

Tiflis *see* Tbilisi

Tiflisskaya *see* Tbilisskaya

Tighennif. Town, northwestern Algeria, northern Africa : Palikao (–c. 1962)

Tighina *see* Bendery

Tikhonkaya *see* Birobidzhan

Tikhonovka *see* Pozharskoye

Tikhono-Zadonsky *see* Kropotkin (2)

Tikitki. Town, North Island, New Zealand : Kahukura (–1940)

Tiligulo-Berezanka *see* Berezanka

Tillsonburg. Town, Ontario, Canada : Tilsonburg (–1902)

Tilsit *see* Sovetsk (2)

Tilsonburg *see* Tillsonburg

Tiltonsville. Village, Ohio, USA : Grover (–1930)

Timashyovsk. Town, Krasnodar Kray, Russia : Timashyovskaya (–1966)

Timashyovskaya *see* Timashyovsk

Timbiras. City, northeastern Brazil, South America : Monte Alegre (–1944)

Timerhi. Settlement, northern Guyana, South America : Atkinson Field (–1968)

Timiryazevo. Village, Kaliningrad Oblast, Russia : Neukirch (–1945), Germany

Timiryazevsky. Town, Tomsk Oblast, Russia : Novaya Eushta (–1940)

Timon. City, northeastern Brazil, South America : Flores (–1944)

Timor Timur. Province, eastern Timor, Indonesia : Portuguese Timor (–1976)

Timoshenko, imeni *see* Omchak

Tinalunan *see* Gaudencio Antonio (2)

Tingchow *see* (1) Changting [Ch'ang-t'ing]; (2) Tinghsien

Tingfan *see* Hweishui [Hui-shui]

Ting-hsi = Tingsi

Ting-hsiang = Tingsiang

Tinghsien. Town, northeastern China : Tingchow (–1913)

Ting-hsin = Tingsin

Tingnan. Town, southeastern China : Siali (–1928)

Tingsi [Ting-hsi]. Town, north-central China : Anting (–1914)

Tingsiang [Ting-hsiang]. Town, southern China : Sangpiling (–1913)

Tingsin [Ting-hsin]. Town, north-central China : Maomu (–1928)

Tingyüan *see* (1) Chenpa; (2) Wusheng

Tinonganine *see* Santana de Tinonganine

Tiris el Gharbia *see* Oued Eddahab

Tiris Zemmour. District, northwestern Mauritania, western Africa : Onzième (–c. 1979)

Tirschtiegel *see* Trzciel

Tissemsilt. Town, northern Algeria, northern Africa : Vialar (–c. 1962)

Tiszaszederkény *see* Leninváros

Tiszaszentimre. Town, east-central Hungary : Szentimre (–1902)

Tiszavasvári. Town, northeastern Hungary : Bűdszentmihály (1941–46, 1950–52)

Titao *see* Lintao [Lin-tao]

Titograd. Capital of Montenegro : Podgorica (–1952)

Titova Korenica. Village, western Slovenia : Korenica (–c. 1945)

Titovo Užice. Town, west-central Serbia : Užice (–1946)

Titov Veles. Town, central
Macedonia : Veles
(–1952)
Tjolotjo see Tsholotsho
Tłuste see Tolstoye
Toamasina. Town, eastern
Madagascar, southeast-
ern Africa : Tamatave
(–c. 1979)
Tobias Barreto. City, north-
eastern Brazil, South
America : Campos
(–1944)
Tobolsk Guberniya see
Tyumen Guberniya
Tocantinópolis. City, north-
central Brazil, South
America : Boa Vista
(–1944)
Tocqueville see Ras el Oued
Togo. Republic, western
Africa : French Togoland
(*1920–60)
Toishan. Town, southeastern
China : Sunning (–1914)
Tokmak (1). Town, Kirgizia :
Bolshoy Tokmak (–1927)
Tokmak (2). Town, Zapo-
rozhye Oblast, Ukraine :
Bolshoy Tokmak (–1963)
Toktogul. Urban settle-
ment, Osh Oblast, Kir-
gizia : Akchi-Karasu
(–1940), Muztor (1940–
c. 1960)
Tolbukhin. Town, northeast-
ern Bulgaria : Bazarjik
(–1913), Bazargic (1913–
40), Romania, Dobrič
(1940–49)
Tolbukhino. Village, Ya-
roslavl Oblast, Russia :
Davydkovo (–1950)
Tolkemit see Tolmicko

Tolmicko. Town, northern
Poland : Tolkemit
(–1945), Germany
Tolochin. Town, Vitebsk
Oblast, Belorussia :
Tolochino (–c. 1940)
Tolochino see Tolochin
Tolstoi. Hamlet, Manitoba,
Canada : Oleskow
(–1905)
Tolstoye. Urban settle-
ment, Ternopol Oblast,
Ukraine : Tluste (–1944),
Poland
Tolyatti. Town, Samara Ob-
last, Russia : Stavropol
(–1964)
Tomaniivi, Mount. Moun-
tain, Viti Levu, Fiji :
Victoria, Mount (–?)
Tomari. Town, Sakhalin Ob-
last, Russia : Tomarioru
(1905–47), Japan (–1945)
Tomari see Golovnino
Tomarikishi see Vakhrushev
Tomarioru see Tomari
Tomás Barrón. Village,
western Bolivia, South
America : Eucaliptus
(–early 1940s)
Tomislavgrad see Duvno
Tomur Feng. Chinese name
of Pik Pobedy, mountain,
northwestern China/
southeastern Kirgizia :
Sheng-li Feng (–1977)
Tonder. City, southern Den-
mark : Tondern (–1920),
Germany
Tondern see Tonder
Tonekabon. Town, northern
Iran : Shahsavar (–1980)
Tongyòng see Ch'ungmu
Tonshayevo see Shaygino

Topolovgrad. City, south-
eastern Bulgaria : Kavak-
lii (–1934)
Topornino see Kushnar-
enkovo
Torbinka see Partizany (2)
Torez. Town, Donetsk
Oblast, Ukraine :
Chistyakovo (–1964)
Torfelt. Oilfield, North Sea,
Norway : Ergfisk (–1971)
Torgovaya see Salsk
Tormáskölesd see Kölesd
Tornala see Šafárikovo
Toro see Shakhtyorsk (1)
Torrecilla sobre Alesanco.
Village, northern Spain :
San Isidoro (–c. 1950)
Toruń. City, north-central
Poland : Thorn (1793–
1807, 1815–1918, 1939–
45), Germany
Toscanella see Tuscania
Tourane see Da Nang
Tous see San Martín de Tous
Tovarishcha Khatayevicha,
imeni see Sinelnikovo
Tovarkovsky. Urban settle-
ment, Tula Oblast, Rus-
sia : Kaganovich (?–1957)
Toyohara see Yuzhno-Sakhal-
insk
Trachenberg see Żmigród
Tracy. Town, Quebec, Can-
ada : L'Enfant-Jésus-de-
Sorel (–1954)
Trakai. Town, Lithuania :
Troki (–1917)
Transcarpathian Oblast
[Zakarpatskaya Ob-
last]. Western Ukraine :
Ruthenia (1920–46)
Transcaspian Oblast see Turk-
menistan

Transjordan(ia) see Jordan (2)
Transvaal. Province, north-
ern South Africa : South
Africa Republic (1884–
1900)
Transylvania. Region, north-
western Romania :
Erdély (1867–1918),
Hungary
Trarza. District, southwest-
ern Mauritania, western
Africa : Sixième (–c. 1979)
Trarza see Mauritania
Tra Vinh. Town, southern
Vietnam : Phu Vinh
(–c. 1980)
Třebechovice pod Orebem.
Town, east-central Czech
Lands : Hohenbruck
(–1918, 1939–45),
Germany
Třebíč. Town, southern
Czech Lands : Trebitsch
(–1918, 1939–45),
Germany
Trebitsch see Třebíč
Trebnitz see Trzebnica
Třeboň. Town, southern
Czech Lands : Wittingau
(–1918, 1939–45), Ger-
many
Trebukhi see Kalinovaya (2)
Trebushki see Mirnaya (4)
Trembovla see Terebovlya
Tremedal see Monte Azul
Trempen see Novostroyevo
Trentino-Alto Adige. Re-
gion, northern Italy : Ven-
ezia Tridentina (1919–47)
Treptow (an der Rega) see
Trzebiatów
Treptow (an der Tollense) see
Altentreptow
Treputikha see Bereznitsa (2)

Tungsiang *see* Süanhan
[Hsüan-han]

T'ung-te = Tungteh

Tungteh [T'ung-te]. Town,
northwestern China :
Lakiashih (–1913)

Tungtsichen *see* Lintien

Tupaceretã *see* Tupanciretã

Tupanciretã. City, southern
Brazil, South America :
Tupaceretã (–1938)

Tura. Capital of Evenki
Autonomous Okrug,
Krasnoyarsk Kray, Rus-
sia : Turinskaya Kultbaza
(c. 1920–38)

Turčianske Teplice. Town,
central Slovakia : Štubnianske Teplice (–1945)

Turenne *see* Sabra

Tùrgovishte. Town, north-
eastern Bulgaria : Eski-
Dzhumaya (–1934)

Turinskaya Kultbaza *see* Tura

Türkeh. Island, Sea of Marmara, Turkey : Avşar
(–1973)

Turkmenistan. Republic,
west-central Asia : Tran-
scaspian Oblast [Zakas-
piyskaya Oblast] (–1921),
Turkmen Oblast (1921–
24), Turkmen SSR (1924–
91)

Turkmen Oblast *see* Turkmenistan

Turkmen SSR *see* Turkmenistan

Tŭrnovo *see* Veliko-Tŭrnovo

Tursunzade. Town, Tajiki-
stan : Stantsiya-Regar
(–1952), Regar (1952–78)

Turtkul. Town, Karakalpak
Autonomous Republic,

Uzbekistan : Petroa-
leksandrovsk (–1920)

Turtucaia *see* Tutrakan

Turyinskiye Rudniki *see*
Krasnoturyinsk

Tuscania. Town, central Italy : Toscanella (–1911)

Tushan *see* Tsinglung [Ching-
lung]

Tusket Wedge *see* Wedgeport

Tutayev. Town, Yaroslavl
Oblast, Russia : Roma-
nov-Borisoglebsk (–1918)

Tutrakan. City, northeastern Bulgaria : Turtucaia
(1913–40), Romania

Tütz *see* Tuczno

Tuva Autonomous Oblast *see*
Tuva Autonomous Re-
public

Tuva Autonomous Repub-
lic. Southern Russia :
Uriankhai (–1921), Outer
Mongolia; Tannu-Tuva
(1921–26), Tuva People's
Republic (1926–44),
Tuva Autonomous Ob-
last (1944–61), Tuva Au-
tonomous SSR (1961–91)

Tuva Autonomous SSR *see*
Tuva Autonomous Re-
public

Tuvalu. Island state, southwestern Pacific : Ellice Islands (–1975)

Tuva People's Republic *see*
Tuva Autonomous Re-
public

Tver. Capital, Tver Oblast,
Russia : Kalinin (1931–
90)

Tver Oblast. Northwestern
Russia : Kalinin Oblast
(*1935–91)

Twardogóra. Town, south-
western Poland : Festen-
berg (–1945), Germany
Tweedvale see Lobethal
Tyan-Shan Oblast see Naryn
Oblast
Tyatino. Village, Kuril Is-
lands, Sakhalin Oblast,
Russia : Chinomiji (1905–
46), Japan (–1945)
Tyazhin see Tyazhinsky
Tyazhinsky. Urban settle-
ment, Kemerovo Oblast,
Russia : Tyazhin
(–c. 1960)
Tymovskoye. Urban settle-
ment, Sakhalin Oblast,
Russia : Derbinskoye
(–1949)
Tynda. Town, Amur Oblast,
Russia : Tyndinsky
(–1975)
Tyndinsky see Tynda
Tyoploye Ozero see Te-
ploozyorsk
Tyoply Klyuch see Klyuchevsk
Tyoply Stan see Sechenovo
Typhloséllion see Drosok-
hórion
Tyumen Guberniya (1923†).
USSR : Tobolsk Guber-
niya (–1919)
Tyuriseva see Ushkovo
Tzechow see (1) Tzechung
[Tsu-chung]; (2) Tzehsien
[Tz'u-hsien]
Tzechung [Tzu-chung].
Town, central China :
Tzechow (–1913)
Tzehing [Tzu-hsing]. Town,
south-central China :
Hingning (–1914)
Tzehsien [Tzu-hsien].
Town, northeastern

China : Tzechow
(–1913)
Tzekam. Town, southeastern
China : Wingon (–1914)
Tzeki [Tz'u-ch'i]. Town,
southeastern China : Luki
(–1914)
Tzekiang see Kaiyang [K'ai-
yang]
Tzekwei [Tzu-kuei]. Town,
east-central China :
Kweichow (–1912)
Tzeyang [Tzu-yang]. Town,
eastern China : Yenchow
(–1913)
Tzeyüan [Tzu-yüan]. Town,
southern China : Siyen (–
1936)
Tzeyun [Tzu-yun]. Town,
southern China :
Kweihwa (–1913)
Tz'u-ch'i = Tzeki
Tzu-chung = Tzechung
Tz'u-hsien = Tzehsien
Tzu-hsing = Tzehing
Tzu-kuei = Tzekwei
Tzu-yang = Tzeyang
Tzu-yüan = Tzeyüan
Tzu-yun = Tzeyun

Uaco Congo see Waku Kungo
Ubaíra. City, eastern Brazil,
South America : Areia
(–1944)
Ubaitaba. City, eastern Bra-
zil, South America :
Itapira (–1944)
Ubanghi Shari see Central Af-
rican Republic
Ubirama see Lençóis Paulista
Ubundi. Town, northeast-
ern Zaïre, central Africa :
Ponthierville (–1966)

Uch-Korgon. Village, Osh Oblast, Kirgizia : Molotovabad (1938–57)

Uchkulan. Village, Karachayev-Cherkess Autonomous Oblast, Stavropol Kray, Russia : Madniskhevi (–c. 1960)

Uchkupryuk. Village, Fergana Oblast, Uzbekistan : Molotova, imeni (1937–40), Molotovo (1940–57)

Udarnaya (1). Village, Vitebsk Oblast, Belorussia : Kornilovichi (–1964)

Udarnaya (2). Village, Gomel Oblast, Belorussia : Osmalenik (–1964)

Udarny. Town, Sakhalin Oblast, Russia : Taihei (1905–45), Japan

Udd see Chkalov

Udine. Province, northeastern Italy : Friuli (1923–c. 1945)

Udmurt Autonomous Oblast see Udmurt Autonomous Republic

Udmurt Autonomous Republic. West-central Russia : Votyak Autonomous Oblast (*1920–32), Udmurt Autonomous Oblast (1932–34), Udmurt Autonomous SSR (1934–91)

Udmurt Autonomous SSR see Udmurt Autonomous Republic

Ufipa see Sumbawanga

Uggehnen see Matrosovo

Uglegorsk (1). Town, Sakhalin Oblast, Russia : Esutoru (1905–47), Japan (–1945)

Uglegorsk (2). Town, Donetsk Oblast, Ukraine : Khatsapetovka (–1958)

Uglekamensk. Urban settlement, Primorsky Kray, Russia : Severny Suchan (–1972)

Ugleuralsky. Urban settlement, Perm Oblast, Russia : Polovinka (*1928–51)

Uglezavodsk. Urban settlement, Sakhalin Oblast, Russia : Higashi-naibuchi (1905–45), Japan

Ugodsky Zavod see Zhukovo

Ugolny. Urban settlement, Sakhalin Oblast, Russia : Taiei (1905–45), Japan

Ugolny see Beringovsky

Ugolnyye Kopi see Kopeysk

Uherské Hradiště. Town, southeastern Czech Lands : Ungarisch-Hradisch (–1918, 1939–45), Germany

Uherský Brod. Town, southeastern Czech Lands : Ungarisch Brod (–1918, 1939–45), Germany

Uherský Ostroh. Town, southeastern Czech Lands : Ungarisch Ostra (–1918, 1939–45), Germany

Uige. Town, northwestern Angola, southwestern Africa : Vila Marechal Carmona (–c. 1979)

Ujazd. Town, southern Poland : Bischofstal (–1945), Germany

Uji see Higashi-uji

Ujiyamada see Ise

Ujung Pandang. City, south-
western Sulawesi, Indone-
sia : Makasar (–c. 1970)
Ukhta. Town, Komi Auton-
omous Republic, Russia :
Chibyu (*1931–43)
Ukhta see Kalevala
Ukmerge. Town, Lithuania :
Vilkomir (–1917)
Ukraine. Republic, south-
eastern Europe : Ukrain-
ian SSR (*1917–91)
Ukrainian SSR see Ukraine
Ukrainsk. Town, Donetsk
Oblast, Ukraine : Le-
sovka (–1963)
Ukrepleniye Kommunizma
see Ivanishchi
Uku. Village, western An-
gola, southwest Africa :
Vila Nova do Seles
(–c. 1979)
Ulaanbaatar = Ulan Bator
Ulala see Gorno-Altaysk
Ulan Bator [Ulaanbaatar].
Capital of Mongolia :
Urga (–1911), Niislel
Khureheh (1911–24)
Ulan-Erge. Settlement,
Kalmyk Autonomous Re-
public, Russia : Krasnoye
(1944–57)
Ulan Hoto. City, northeast-
ern China :
Wangyehmiao (–1949)
Ulanovka see Ulanovsky
Ulanovsky. Urban settle-
ment, Tula Oblast,
Russia : Ulanovka
(–1948)
Ulan-Ude. Capital of
Buryat Autonomous Re-
public, Russia : Verkh-
neudinsk (–1934)

Ulonguè. Town, northwest-
ern Mozambique, south-
eastern Africa : Vila
Coutinho (*c. 1909–80)
Ulugbek. Village, Samar-
kand Oblast, Uzbekistan :
Khodzhaakhrar (–c. 1960)
Ulukhanlu see Razdan (2)
Ulyanovka. Urban settle-
ment, Leningrad Oblast,
Russia : Sablino (–1922)
Ulyanovo (1). Village, Ka-
liningrad Oblast, Russia :
Breitenstein (–1946),
Germany (–1945)
Ulyanovo (2). Town, Syrd-
arya Oblast, Uzbekistan :
Obruchevo (–1974)
Ulyanovo (3). Village,
Kaluga Oblast, Russia :
Plokhino (–1938)
Ulyanovsk. Capital of Ulya-
novsk Oblast, Russia :
Simbirsk (–1924)
Ulyanovsk Guberniya (1928†).
USSR : Simbirsk Guber-
niya (–1924)
Ulyanovskoye (1). Village,
Sakhalin Oblast, Russia :
Dorokawa (1905–45),
Japan
Ulyanovskoye (2). Village,
Karaganda Oblast, Ka-
zakhstan : Kolkhoznoye
(–c. 1960)
Ulzio. Village, northwestern
Italy : Oulx (–1937)
Umaltinsky. Village, Khab-
arovsk Kray, Russia :
Polovinka (–1942)
Umba. Urban settlement,
Murmansk Oblast, Rus-
sia : Lesnoy (–c. 1960)
Umtali see Mutare

Umupuia. Settlement,
North Island, New
Zealand : Duders Beach
(–1971)
Umvukwes *see* Mvurwi
Umvuma *see* Mvuma
Umzimvubu. Town, eastern
Transkei, southern Af-
rica : Port St. Johns
(–1976)
Una *see* Ibiúna
Undur Khan. Town, east-
central Mongolia : Tset-
sen Khan (–1931)
Ungarisch Brod *see* Uherský
Brod
Ungarisch Hradisch *see* Uher-
ské Hradiště
Ungarisch Ostra *see* Uherský
Ostroh
Ungvár *see* Uzhgorod
União *see* (1) Jaguaruna; (2)
União dos Palmares
União dos Palmares. City,
northeastern Brazil,
South America : União
(–1944)
Union *see* Lyndhurst
Union Jack. Community,
Saskatchewan, Canada :
Vérendrye (–1928)
Union of Free Sovereign Re-
publics *see* Common-
wealth of Independent
States
Union of Sovereign States *see*
Commonwealth of Inde-
pendent States
Union of Soviet Socialist Re-
publics *see* Common-
wealth of Independent
States
United Arab Emirates.
Federal state, eastern

Arabian Peninsula : Tru-
cial States (–1971)
United Arab Republic *see*
Arab Republic of Egypt
United Provinces (of Agra
and Oudh) *see* Uttar
Pradesh
United States of Brazil *see*
Brazil
University Heights. Suburb
of Cleveland, Ohio,
USA : Idlewood (*1908–
25)
Unruhstadt *see* Kargowa
Unterdrauburg *see* Dravograd
Unterfranken. Administra-
tive district, southwestern
Germany : Mainfranken
(1938–45)
Untervalden *see* Podlesnoye
Upper Austria [Oberöster-
reich]. State, northeast-
ern Austria : Österreich
ober der Ems (–1918),
Oberdonau (1938–45)
Upper Senegal and Niger Col-
ony *see* Mali
Upper Senegal and Niger Ter-
ritory *see* Mali
Upper Sind Frontier *see* Jaco-
babad District
Upper Tallassee Dam *see*
Yates Dam
Upper Volta *see* Burkina
(Faso)
Uralets. Urban settlement,
Sverdlovsk Oblast, Rus-
sia : Krasny Ural (–1933)
Uralmedstroy *see* Krasnou-
ralsk
Uralsk Oblast. Kazakhstan :
West Kazakhstan Oblast
(*1932–62)
Uramirt *see* Romit

Urbakh *see* Pushkino (2)

Ureña. Town, south-central
Costa Rica, Central
America : San Isidro
(–1931)

Urga *see* Ulan Bator

Urgench. Capital of
Khorezm Oblast, Uzbeki-
stan : Novourgench
(–1929)

Uriankhai *see* Tuva Autonomous Republic

Uritskoye (1). Village,
Gomel Oblast, Belorus-
sia : Volovitsky Krupets
(–1964)

Uritskoye (2). Village, Kustanay Oblast, Kazakhstan :
Vsekhsvyatskoye (–1923)

Urmia [Orūmīyeh]. City,
northwestern Iran :
Rezā'īyeh (1926–80)

Urozhaynaya (1). Village,
Minsk Oblast, Belorussia :
Bobovozovshchina
(–1964)

Urozhaynaya (2). Village,
Brest Oblast, Belorussia :
Voshkovtsy (–1971)

Urozhaynaya (3). Village,
Vitebsk Oblast, Belorus-
sia : Zashchesle (–1964)

Ursatyevskaya *see* Khavast

Uruaçu. City, central Brazil,
South America : Santana
(–1944)

Urundi *see* Burundi

Urupês *see* Mundo Novo

Urupskaya *see* Sovetskaya (4)

Urus-Martan. Village,
Chechen-Ingush Autono-
mous Republic, Russia :
Krasnoarmeyskoye
(1944–57)

Uryu *see* Kirillovo

Ushiro *see* Orlovo

Ushkovo. Village, Lenin-
grad Oblast, Russia :
Tyuriseva (–1948), Fin-
land (–1940)

Usküb *see* Skoplje

Usolye *see* Usolye-Sibirskoye

Usolye-Sibirskoye. Town,
Irkutsk Oblast, Russia :
Usolye (–1940)

Usolye-Solikamskoye *see*
Berezniki

Uspenka *see* Kirovsky (3)

USSR *see* Commonwealth of
Independent States

Ussuriysk. Town, Primorsky
Kray, Russia : Nikolsk
(–1926), Nikolsk-
Ussuriysky (1926–35),
Voroshilov (1935–57)

Ust-Abanskoye *see* Abakan

Ust-Bagaryak. Village,
Chelyabinsk Oblast, Rus-
sia : Nizhnyaya (–c. 1960)

Ust-Balyk *see* Nefteyugansk

Ust-Belokalitvenskaya *see* Belaya Kalitva

Ust-Borovaya *see* Borovsk

Ust-Dvinsk *see* Daugavgriva

Ust-Dzheguta. Town, Kara-
chayev-Cherkessk Auton-
omous Oblast, Stavropol
Kray, Russia : Ust-
Dzhegutinskaya (–1975)

Ust-Dzhegutinskaya *see* Ust-
Dzheguta

Ústí nad Labem. City,
northern Czech Lands :
Aussig (–1918, 1939–45),
Germany

Ústí nad Orlicí. Town,
northeastern Czech
Lands : Wildenschwert

(–1918, 1939–45), Germany

Ustinov *see* Izhevsk

Ustka. Town, northwestern Poland : Stolpmünde (–1945), Germany

Ust-Katav. Town, Chelyabinsk Oblast, Russia : Ust-Katavsky Zavod (–1943)

Ust-Katavsky Zavod *see* Ust-Katav

Ust-Labinsk. Town, Krasnodar Kray, Russia : Ust-Labinskaya (–1958)

Ust-Labinskaya *see* Ust-Labinsk

Ust-Medveditskaya *see* Serafimovich

Ust-Orda *see* Ust-Ordynsky

Ust-Ordynsky. Capital of Ust-Ordynsky Buryat Autonomous Okrug, Irkutsk Oblast, Russia : Ust-Orda (–1941)

Ustrzyki Dolne. City, southeastern Poland : Nizhniye Ustriki (1939–51), USSR

Ust-Sysolsk *see* Syktyvkar

Ust-Vorkuta. Settlement, Komi Autonomous Republic, Russia : Sangorodok (c. 1945–c. 1952)

Ust-Zhuya *see* Chara

Usumbura *see* Bujumbura

Utkinsky Zavod *see* Staroutkinsk

Uttar Pradesh. State, northern India : North-Western Provinces and Oudh (–1902), United Provinces (of Agra and Oudh) (1902–50)

Uuras *see* Vysotsk

Uzbekistan. Republic, west-central Asia : Uzbek SSR (*1924–91)

Uzbek SSR *see* Uzbekistan

Uzen *see* Tenge

Uzhgorod. Capital of Transcarpathian Oblast, Ukraine : Užhorod (1919–38), Czechoslovakia; Ungvár (1938–45), Hungary

Užhorod *see* Uzhgorod

Užice *see* Titovo Užice

Uzlovoye. Village, Kaliningrad Oblast, Russia : Rautenberg (–1945), Germany

Vaagni. Village, Armenia : Shagali (–c. 1960)

Vaasa. City, western Finland : Nikolainkaupunki [Nikolaistad] (c. 1860–1917)

Vabalninkas. Town, Lithuania : Vobolniki (–1917)

Vác. City, north-central Hungary : Waitzen (–?), Germany

Vaca Guzmán. Town, southeastern Bolivia, South America : Muyupampa (–c. 1945)

Vadinsk. Village, Penza Oblast, Russia : Kerensk (–c. 1940)

Vagarshapat *see* Echmiadzin

Vaila Voe Bay. Bay, Stewart Island, New Zealand : Avelavo Bay (–1965)

Vakhan. Village, Gorno-Badakhshan Autono-

mous Oblast, Tajikistan :
Zung (–c. 1935)

Vakhrushev. Urban settle-
ment, Sakhalin Oblast,
Russia : Tomarikishi
(1905–45), Japan

Vakhsh. Urban settlement,
Khatlon Oblast, Tajiki-
stan : Vakhstroy
(?–c. 1960)

Vakhstroy see Vakhsh

Valadim see Mavabo

Val-Brillant. Town, Quebec,
Canada : Cedar Hall
(–1913), Saint-Pierre-du-
Lac (1913–16)

Valdemārpils. Town, Latvia :
Sasmakken (–1917), Sas-
maka (1917–26)

Valdgeym see Dobropolye

Val d'Ifrane see Menzeh-
Ifrane

Val d'Or see Sehb Dheb

Valegotsulovo see Dolins-
koye

Valença see (1) Marquês de
Valença; (2) Valença do
Piauí

Valença do Piauí. City,
northeastern Brazil,
South America : Valença
(–1944), Berlengas
(1944–48)

Valencia. Municipality,
Negros Oriental, Philip-
pines : Nueva Valencia
(–1905), Luzurriaga
(1905–48)

Valera. Village, east-central
Spain : Valera de Arriba
(–c. 1960)

Valera de Arriba see Valera

Valgravé see Souk Eltnine

Valinhos see Guaraúna

Val-Jalbert. Community,
Quebec, Canada :
Ouiatchouan (–1909)

Valkatlen see Alkatvaam

Val-Laflamme see Barville

Valle di Pompei see Pompei

Valley Junction see West Des
Moines

Vallfogona see San Julián de
Vallfogona

Valmiera. Town, Latvia :
Wolmar (–1917), Ger-
many

Valparaíba see Cachoeira Paulista

Valverde see Mao

Valverde de la Virgen. Village, northeastern Spain :
Valverde del Camino
(–c. 1920)

Valverde del Camino see
Valverde de la Vir-
gen

Van Buren see Kettering

Vandenberg Air Force Base.
California, USA : Camp
Cooke (*1941–57)

Vandsburg see Więcbork

Vanier (1). City, Ontario,
Canada : Cummings' Is-
land (–1900), Eastview
(1909–69)

Vanier (2). Suburb of Quebec, Quebec, Canada :
Quebec West (–1966)

Vanilovo see Tsyurupy, imeni

Vannovsky see Khamza

Van Stadensrus. Town, Or-
ange Free State, South
Africa : Mook (–1925)

Vanuatu. Island republic,
southwestern Pacific :
New Hebrides (–1980),
Venarama (1980)

Varcar Vukuf *see* Mrkonić
Grad
Várdas. Village, southern
Greece : Vouprásion
(–1960s)
Vardenis. Urban settle-
ment, Armenia :
Basargechar (–1969)
Varena. Town, Lithuania :
Orany (–1917)
Varenne, La *see* El Meddah
Varna. City, eastern Bul-
garia : Stalin (1949–56)
Várnakas *see* Georgouláiika
Varttirayiruppu *see* Watrap
Várvaron *see* Myrtiá
Vasiliko *see* Michurin
Vasilkov pervy *see* Kalinovka
(2)
Vasilyevsko-Shaytansky *see*
Pervouralsk
Vasilyova Sloboda *see* Chka-
lovsk
Vasilyovo *see* Chkalovsk
Vaucluse *see* Fontaine-de-
Vaucluse
Vaudrevange. Town, eastern
France : Wallerfangen
(–1945)
Vayenga *see* Severomorsk
Vazovgrad *see* Sopot
Vedi. Urban settlement,
Armenia : Beyuk-Vedi
(–c. 1935)
Vegadea. Village, north-
western Spain : Vega de
Ribadeo (–c. 1920)
Vegas Verde *see* North Las
Vegas
Veglia *see* Krk
Veles *see* Titov Veles
Velika Kikinda *see* Kikinda
Velikaya Mikhaylovka. Ur-
ban settlement, Odessa

Oblast, Ukraine : Gro-
sulovo (–1945)
Velikaya Novosyolka. Ur-
ban settlement, Donetsk
Oblast, Ukraine : Bol-
shoy Yanisol (–1946),
Bolshaya Novosyolka
(1946–c. 1960)
Veliki Bečkerek *see* Zrenjanin
Velikiye Borki. Village, Ter-
nopol Oblast, Ukraine :
Borki Wielkie (–1944),
Poland
Velikiye Mosty. Town, Lvov
Oblast, Ukraine : Mosty
Wielkie (–1941), Poland
Velikoalekseyevsky *see* Bakht
Velikooktyabrsky. Urban
settlement, Tver Oblast,
Russia : Pokrovskoye
(–1941)
Veliko-Tŭrnovo. Town,
north-central Bulgaria :
Tŭrnovo (–1965)
Veliky Glubochok. Vil-
lage, Ternopol Oblast,
Ukraine : Hłuboczek
Wielki (–1944), Poland
Velilla de Guardo *see* Velilla
del Rio Carrión
Velilla del Rio Carrión. Vil-
lage, northern Spain :
Velilla de Guardo (–1960)
Velká Bíteš. Town, south-
ern Czech Lands : Gross-
Bitesch (–1918, 1939–45),
Germany
Velká Deštná. Mountain,
Czech Lands/Poland :
Deschnaer Kuppe
(–1918, 1939–45), Ger-
many
Velké Kapušány. Town,
eastern Slovakia :

Nagykapos (1938–45),
Hungary
Velké Karlovice. Village,
eastern Czech Lands :
Karlowitz (–1918, 1939–
45), Germany
Velké Meziříčí. Town, south-
central Czech Lands :
Gross-Meseritsch (–1918,
1939–45), Germany
Venarama see Vanuatu
Venet-Ville see Souk Tleta
Loulad
Venezia Tridentina see
Trentino-Alto Adige
Ventersburgsweg see Hennen-
man
Ventspils. City, Latvia :
Vindava (–1917)
Venustiano Carranza. City,
southern Mexico, North
America : San Bartolomé
(–1934)
Veranópolis. City, southern
Brazil, South America :
Alfredo Chaves (–1944)
Vérendrye see Union Jack
Vergel see Bom Jardim
Verin-Gusakyan see Gu-
sakyan
Verin-Talin see Talin
Veríssimo Sarmento see
Camissombo
Verkhne-Avzyano-Petrovsk
see Verkhny Avzyan
Verkhnedvinsk. Town,
Vitebsk Oblast, Belorus-
sia : Drissa (–1962)
Verkhne-Saldinsky Zavod see
Verkhnyaya Salda
Verkhnetoretskoye. Urban
settlement, Donetsk Ob-
last, Ukraine : Skotova-
taya (–1978)

Verkhneudinsk see Ulan-Ude
Verkhneufaleysky Zavod see
Verkhny Ufaley
Verkhneye Ablyazovo see Ra-
dishchevo (2)
Verkhny Avzyan. Urban set-
tlement, Bashkir Autono-
mous Republic, Russia :
Verkhne-Avzyano-
Petrovsk (–1942)
Verkhnyaya Khortitsa. Sub-
urb of Zaporozhye, Zapo-
rozhye Oblast, Ukraine :
Khortitsa (–1930s)
Verkhnyaya Pyshma. Town,
Sverdlovsk Oblast, Rus-
sia : Pyshma (–1946)
Verkhnyaya Salda. Town,
Sverdlovsk Oblast, Rus-
sia : Verkhne-Saldinsky
Zavod (–1938)
Verkhny Dashkesan see Dash-
kesan
Verkhny Ufaley. Town,
Chelyabinsk Oblast, Rus-
sia : Verkhneufaleysky
Zavod (*1933–40)
Verkhovina. Urban settle-
ment, Ivano-Frankovsk
Oblast, Ukraine : Zhabye
(–c. 1960)
Vermilion. Town, Alberta,
Canada : Breage (–1906)
Vermilion Valley see Holden
Verny see Alma-Ata
Vero see Vero Beach
Vero Beach. City, Florida,
USA : Vero (–1925)
Verőce. Town, northern
Hungary : Nógrádverőce
(–1965)
Verona see Cedar Grove
Verovka see Krasny Profin-
tern (3)

Verro *see* Võru

Vershino-Darasunsky. Urban settlement, Chita Oblast, Russia : Darasun (–c. 1960)

Vertyuzhany *see* Pridnestrovskoye

Verwoerdburg. Town, Transvaal, South Africa : Lyttelton (*1906–67)

Veselí nad Lužnicí. Town, west-central Czech Lands : Frohenbruck (–1918, 1939–45), Germany

Veselí nad Moravou. Town, southeastern Czech Lands : Wesseli (–1918, 1939–45), Germany

Vesit *see* Viesīte

Vesnovo. Village, Kaliningrad Oblast, Russia : Kussen (–1949), Germany (–1945)

Vest Agder. County, southern Norway : Lister og Mandals (–1918)

Vestfold. County, southeastern Norway : Jarlsberg og Larvik (–1918)

Vetluzhsky. Urban settlement, Kostroma Oblast, Russia : Golyshi (–c. 1960)

Veznikon *see* Hágion Pneúma

Vialar *see* Tissemsilt

Vibo Valentia. Town, southern Italy : Monteleone di Calabria (–1928)

Vicente Noble. Town, southwestern Dominican Republic, West Indies : Alpargatal (–1943)

Victor. Natural gasfield, North Sea, UK : Broken Bank (*c. 1975–83)

Victor Hugo *see* Hamadia

Victoria *see* Limbe

Victoria, Mount *see* Tomaniivi, Mount

Victoria Falls *see* Mosi-oa-Toenja (2)

Victoria West Road *see* Hutchinson

Victory *see* Doña Rosario

Videira. City, southern Brazil, South America : Perdizes (–1944)

Vidin. Mountain, northwestern Bulgaria : Acul (–1967)

Vidnoye. Town, Moscow Oblast, Russia : Rastorguyevo (–1965)

Viesīte. Town, Latvia : Vesit (–1917)

Vietz *see* Witnica

Vigia *see* Almenara

Viipuri *see* Vyborg

Vijayawada. Town, southeastern India : Bezwada (–1949)

Viktorovka *see* Taranovskoye

Vila Alferes Chamusca *see* (1) Chókué; (2) Guijá

Vila António Enes *see* Angoche

Vila Arriaga *see* Bibala

Vila Bugaco *see* Kemenongue

Vila Cabral *see* Lichinga

Vila Caldas Xavier *see* Muende

Vila Coutinho *see* Ulonguè

Vila da Maganja da Costa. Town, eastern Mozambique, southeastern Africa : Vila João Coutinho (–1969)

Vila Fontes *see* Caia
Vila Gouveia *see* Catandica
Vila João Coutinho *see* Vila da
   Maganja da Costa
Vila Junqueiro *see* Guruè
Vila Luísa *see* Marracuene
Vila Machado.   Village,
   south-central Mozam-
   bique, southeastern Af-
   rica : Nova Fontesvila
   (–1909)
Vila Marechal Carmona *see*
   Uige
Vila Norton de Matos *see* Ba-
   lombo
Vila Nova *see* Tchikala-
   Tcholohanga
Vila Nova de Gaza *see* Xai-
   Xai
Vila Nova do Seles *see*
   Uku
Vila Paiva de Andrada *see*
   Gorongosa
Vila Pery *see* Manica (1),
   (2)
Vila Salazar *see* (1) Dala-
   tando; (2) Sango
Vila Teixeira da Silva *see*
   Luau
Vila Trigo de Morais *see*
   Chókué
Vila Vasco da Gama.   Vil-
   lage, western Mozam-
   bique, southeastern
   Africa : Chiputo
   (–1924)
Vila-Vila *see* Villa Viscarra
Viljaka.   Town, Latvia :
   Marienhausen
   (–1917)
Viljandi.   Town, Estonia :
   Fellin (–1917)
Viljoensdorp *see* Newcastle
Vilkomir *see* Ukmerge

Villa Abecia.   Town, south-
   ern Bolivia, South Amer-
   ica : Camataquí
   (–c. 1945), Villa General
   Germán Busch (c. 1945–
   c. 1948)
Villa Americana *see* Ameri-
   cana
Villa Bella *see* Serra Talhada
Villa Bens *see* Tarfaya
Villa Canales.   Town, south-
   central Guatemala, South
   America : Pueblo Viejo
   (–1921)
Villa Cecilia *see* Ciudad Madero
Villa Cisneros *see* Dakhla
Villa de Don Fadrique.   Village, south-central Spain :
   Puebla de Don Fadrique
   (–c. 1920)
Villa del Nevoso *see* (Ilirska)
   Bistrica
Villa de María.   Town, cen-
   tral Argentina, South
   America : Río Seco
   (–c. 1945)
Villa di Briano.   Town,
   southern Italy : Frignano
   (–1950)
Villafranca de Ordizia.   Vil-
   lage, northern Spain : Vil-
   lafranca de Oria
   (–c. 1970)
Villafranca de Oria *see* Vil-
   lafranca de Ordizia
Villafranca Piemonte.   Vil-
   lage, northwestern Italy :
   Villafranca Sabauda
   (1934–50)
Villafranca Sabauda *see*
   Villafranca Piemonte
Villa General Germán Busch
   see Villa Abecia

Villa (General) Pérez.
Town, western Bolivia,
South America :
Charazani (–1930s)

Villa (General) Vicente Guerrero. Town, central
Mexico, North America :
San Pablo del Monte
(–1940)

Villaggio Mussolini see Arborea

Villahermosa. City, southeastern Mexico, North
America : San Juan Bautista [San Juan de Villa
Hermosa] (–1915)

Villa Isabel. Town, northwestern Dominican Republic, West Indies : Villa
Vásquez (–1938)

Villa la Trinidad. Town,
northwestern Argentina,
South America : La Trinidad (–c. 1945)

Villaluenga de la Vega. Village, northern Spain : Villanueva y Gaviños (–1920)

Villanueva de Alpicat see
Alpicat

Villanueva del Conde see Villanueva de Teba

Villanueva de los Infantes.
Village, south-central
Spain : Infantes
(–c. 1960)

Villanueva de Teba. Village, northern Spain :
Villanueva del Conde
(–c. 1920)

Villanueva y Gaviños see Villaluenga de la Vega

Villa Ramos. Barrio, Zamboanga del Norte, Philippines : Lipras (–1957)

Villar de Argañán. Village,
western Spain : Villar de
Puerco (–c. 1960)

Villar de Ciervos see Villar de
Samaniego

Villar de Puerco see Villar de
Argañán

Villar de Samaniego. Village, western Spain : Villar de Ciervos (–c. 1920)

Villa Rivero. Town, central
Bolivia, South America :
Muela (–1900s)

Villarreal de los Infantes.
Village, eastern Spain :
Villarreal (–c. 1960)

Villa Sanjurjo see Al-Hoceima

Villa Serrano. Town, southern Bolivia, South America : Pescado (–1940s)

Villa Vásquez see Villa Isabel

Villa Viscarra. Town, central Bolivia, South America : Vila-Vila (–c. 1940)

Vilnius. Capital of Lithuania : Wilno (1920–39),
Poland

Vindava see Ventspils

Vinodelnoye see Ipatovo

Vinogradnoye. Village,
North Ossetian Autonomous Republic, Russia :
Gnadenburg (–1944)

Vinogradov. Town, Transcarpathian Oblast,
Ukraine : Sevlyush
(–1946)

Vins see Vins-sur-Calamy

Vins-sur-Calamy. Village,
southeastern France :
Vins (–1937)

Vintar. Barrio, Bukidnon,
Philippines : Cawayanon
(–1968)

Vipacco *see* Vipava
Vipava. Village, western
Slovenia : Vipacco
(–1947), Italy
Virbalis. Town, Lithuania :
Veržbolovo (–1917)
Virgilio. Village, northern
Italy : Pietole (–?)
Virgin Islands (of the United
States). Island group,
West Indies : Danish
West Indies (–1917)
Virunga National Park.
Northeastern Zaïre, cen-
tral Africa : Albert Na-
tional Park (*1925–72)
Virungu. Town, southeast-
ern Zaïre, central Africa :
Baudouinville (–1966)
Visconde do Rio Branco.
City, southeastern Brazil,
South America : Rio
Branco (–1944)
Vishnevets (1). Village,
Grodno Oblast, Belorus-
sia : Gnoynitsa (–1964)
Vishnevets (2). Village,
Vitebsk Oblast, Belorus-
sia : Zherebtsy (–1964)
Vishnya (1). Village, Minsk
Oblast, Belorussia :
Malafeyevichi (–1964)
Vishnya (2). Village,
Vitebsk Oblast, Belorus-
sia : Podrassolay (–1964)
Vishnyovaya (1). Village,
Vitebsk Oblast, Belorus-
sia : Cherepni (–1964)
Vishnyovaya (2). Village,
Minsk Oblast, Belorussia :
Klyundevka (–1964)
Vishnyovoye (1). Urban set-
tlement, Dnepropetrovsk

Oblast, Ukraine : Eras-
tovka (–c. 1960)
Vishnyovoye (2). Suburb of
Pavlograd, Dnepropet-
rovsk Oblast, Ukraine :
Pavlogradskiye Khutora
pervyye (–c. 1960)
Visim. Urban settlement,
Sverdlovsk Oblast, Rus-
sia : Visimo-Shaytansky
Zavod (–1933)
Visimo-Shaytansky Zavod *see*
Visim
Visimo-Utkinsk. Urban set-
tlement, Sverdlovsk
Oblast, Russia : Visimo-
Utkinsky Zavod (–1946)
Visimo-Utkinsky Zavod *see*
Visimo-Utkinsk
Vislinsky Zaliv = Vistula La-
goon
Vista *see* Nsiom Fumu
Vistula Lagoon [Zalew Wi-
ślany, Vislinsky Zaliv].
Inlet, southwestern coast
of Baltic Sea, Poland/
Russia : Frisches Haff
(–1946), Germany (–
1945)
Vit. Village, Gomel Oblast,
Belorussia : Gnoyev
(–1964)
Vita. Village, Manitoba,
Canada : Szewczenko
[Shevchenko] (–1908)
Vitória *see* Vitória de Santo
Antão
Vitória da Conquista. City,
eastern Brazil, South
America : Conquista
(–1944)
Vitória de Santo An-
tão. City, northeastern

Brazil, South America :
Vitória (–1944)
Vitória do Alto Parnaíba *see*
Alto Parnaíba
Vitória do Baixo Mearim *see*
Vitória do Mearim
Vitória do Mearim.   City,
northeastern Brazil,
South America : Vitória
do Baixo Mearim
(–1944), Baixo Mearim
(1944–48)
Vittorio *see* Vittorio Veneto
Vittorio Veneto.   Town,
northeastern Italy : Vitto-
rio (–1923)
Vladikavkaz.   Capital, North
Ossetian Autonomous
Republic, Russia :
Ordzhonikidze (1931–44,
1954–90), Dzaudzhikau
(1944–54)
Vladimirovka *see* Yuzhno-
Sakhalinsk
Vladislavov *see* Kudirkos-
Naumiestis
Vlakháta *see* Karavómylos
Vlasova-Ayuta *see* Ayutinsky
Vlorë.   City, southwestern
Albania : Avlona (–1912)
Vobolniki *see* Vabalninkas
Vodopyanovo *see* Donskoye
(2)
Vogelkop *see* Doberai
Vohémar *see* Vohimarina
Vohibinany.   Town, eastern
Madagascar, southeast-
ern Africa : Brickaville
(–c. 1979)
Vohimarina.   Town, north-
eastern Madagascar,
southeastern Africa : Vo-
hémar (–c. 1979)

Volchyi Yamy *see* Krasnovichi
Volga-Baltic Water-
way.   Linking Volga
River and Baltic Sea,
Russia : Mariinsk Water
System (–1960)
Volgograd.   Capital of Vol-
gograd Oblast, Russia :
Tsaritsyn (–1925), Stalin-
grad (1925–61)
Volgograd Oblast.   West-
central Russia : Stalin-
grad Kray (*1934–36),
Stalingrad Oblast (1936–
61)
Volkhov.   Town, Leningrad
Oblast, Russia : Gostin-
opolye (–1923), Zvanka
(1927–36), Volkhovstroy
(1936–40)
Volkhovstroy *see* Volkhov
Volnyansk.   Town, Zapo-
rozhye Oblast, Ukraine :
Sofieyvka (–1935), Cher-
vonoarmeyskoye (1935–
66)
Volodarsk.   Town, Nizhe-
gorodskaya Oblast, Rus-
sia : Volodary (–1956)
Volodary *see* Volodarsk
Volovitsky Krupets *see*
Uritskoye (1)
Volta Blanche *see* Nakanbe
Volta Noire *see* Mouhoun
Volta Rouge *see* Nazinon
Volzhsk.   Town, Mari Au-
tonomous Republic, Rus-
sia : Lopatino (*c. 1935–
40)
Volzhsky.   Urban settle-
ment, Samara Oblast,
Russia : Bolshaya Tsar-
yovshchina (–c. 1960)

Vonki *see* Naberezhnaya

Voortrekkerhoogte. Military centre, Transvaal, South Africa : Roberts Heights (*1900–38)

Voortrekkerstrand. Town, Natal, South Africa : Munster (–1959)

Vorontsovka *see* Kalinino (2)

Vorontsovo-Aleksandrovskoye *see* Zelenokumsk

Voroshilov *see* Ussuriysk

Voroshilova, imeni *see* Voroshilovo

Voroshilovgrad *see* Lugansk

Voroshilovgrad Oblast *see* Lugansk Oblast

Voroshilovo. Village, Andizhan Oblast, Uzbekistan : Karasu (–1937), Voroshilova, imeni (1937–c. 1940)

Voroshilovsk *see* (1) Kommunarsk; (2) Stavropol

Voroshilovskoye. Village, Kirgizia : Lebedinovskoye (–1937)

Vorovskogo, imeni. Urban settlement, Moscow Oblast, Russia : Khrapunovo (–1941)

Võru. Town, Estonia : Verro (–1917)

Vose. Urban settlement, Khatlon Oblast, Tajikistan : Paituk (–c. 1935), Kolkhozabad (c. 1935–c. 1960)

Voshkovtsy *see* Urozhaynaya (2)

Voskresenovka *see* Oktyabrsky (9)

Voskresensk *see* Istra (1)

Voskresenskoye *see* Kirovo (2)

Vostochnaya (1). Village, Vitebsk Oblast, Belorussia : Tsutski (–1964)

Vostochnaya (2). Village, Mogilyov Oblast, Belorussia : Yazvy (–1964)

Vostochny. Urban settlement, Sakhalin Oblast, Russia : Motodomari (1905–45), Japan

Vostok *see* Neftegorsk

Votyak Autonomous Oblast *see* Udmurt Autonomous Republic

Vouga *see* Cunhinga

Vouprásion *see* Várdas

Voznesenskaya Manufaktura *see* Krasnoarmeysk (5)

Voznesensky *see* Krasny Oktyabr

Vrbno. Village, eastern Czech Lands : Würbenthal (–1918, 1939–45), Germany

Vrchlabí. Town, northern Czech Lands : Hohenelbe (–1918, 1939–45), Germany

Vrevsky *see* Almazar

Vrhnika. Village, western Slovenia : Oberlaibach (–1918), Germany

Vršac. City, northeastern Serbia : Werschetz (–1918), Germany

Vrysoúlai *see* Néai Vrysoúlai

Vsekhsvyatskoye *see* Uritskoye (2)

Vyatka. Capital of Kirov Oblast, Russia : Kirov (1934–91)

Vyborg. Town, Leningrad Oblast, Russia : Viipuri (1919–40), Finland

Vysochany (1). Village,
Vitebsk Oblast, Belorussia : Pentyukhi (–1964)

Vysochany (2). Village,
Minsk Oblast, Belorussia :
Shopa (–1964)

Vysoké Mýto. Town, east-central Czech Lands :
Hohenmauth (–1918,
1939–45), Germany

Vysoké nad Jizerou. Town,
northern Czech Lands :
Hochstadt (–1918, 1939–
45), Germany

Vysokogorny. Urban settlement, Khabarovsk Kray,
Russia : Muli (–c. 1960)

Vysoko-Litovsk see Vysokoye

Vysokoye. Town, Brest Oblast, Belorussia : Vysoko-Litovsk (–1939)

Vysotsk. Town, Vysotsky Island, Gulf of Finland,
Leningrad Oblast, Russia : Uuras (–1948),
Finland (–1940)

Vyšší Brod. Settlement,
southern Czech Lands :
Hohenfurth (–1918,
1939–45), Germany

Vyzna see Krasnaya Sloboda

Vzmorye (1). Village, Kaliningrad Oblast, Russia :
Grossheidekrug (–1946),
Germany (–1945)

Vzmorye (2). Urban settlement, Sakhalin Oblast,
Russia : Shiraura (1905–
45), Japan

Wąbrzeźno. Town, northern
Poland : Briesen (–1945),
Germany

Wadhwan see Surendranagar

Wadowice. Town, southern
Poland : Frauenstadt
(1939–45), Germany

Wafangtien see Fuhsien

Waghorn see Blackfalds

Wagstadt see Bílovec

Wainwright. Town, Alberta,
Canada : Denwood
(*c. 1905–09)

Waitzen see Vác

Wakeham Way see Maricourt

Waku Kungo. Town, west-central Angola, south-western Africa : Santa
Comba (–c. 1975), Uaco
Congo (c. 1975–c. 1979)

Wakura see Tazuruhama

Wałbrzych. City, southwestern Poland : Waldenburg
(–1945), Germany

Wałcz. Town, northwestern
Poland : Deutsch Krone
(–1945), Germany

Waldau see Nizovye

Waldenburg see Wałbrzych

Wallerfangen see Vaudrevange

Wanchow see Manning

Wan-ch'üan see Chang-chia-kou

Wanfow. Town, southeastern China : Tungon
(–1914)

Wangerin see Węgorzyno

Wangkü see Changan
[Ch'ang-an]

Wangshejenchwang see Lichen [Li-cheng]

Wangyehmiao see Ulan Hoto

Wankang. Town, southern
China : Pama (–1936)

Wankie see Hwange

Wanping [Wan-p'ing].
Town, northeastern

China : Lukowkiao
(–1928)
Wansen *see* Wiązów
Wanyüan. Town, central
China : Taiping (–1914)
Warmbad. Town, Transvaal,
South Africa : Hartings-
burg (–1903, 1905–20),
Warm Baths (1903–05)
Warm Baths *see* Warmbad
Warmbrunn *see* Cieplice
Ślaskie Zdrój
Warner Robins. City, Geor-
gia, USA : Wellston
(–c. 1940)
Wartenburg *see* Barczewo
Wartha *see* Bardo
Warthbrücken *see* Koło
Warthenau *see* Zawiercie
Washington Island *see* Teraina
Wasit. Province, eastern
Iraq : Kut (–1971)
Wąsosz. Town, western
Poland : Herrnstadt
(–1945), Germany
Watenstadt-Salzgitter *see*
Salzgitter
Water *see* Balindong
Waterhole *see* Fairview
Waterville *see* Cypress
Watkins *see* Watkins Glen
Watkins Glen. Village, New
York, USA : Watkins
(–1926)
Watrap. Town, southeast-
ern India : Vartti-
rayiruppu (–1920s)
Wawa. Village, Ontario,
Canada : Jamestown
(1948–60)
Wayaopu *see* Changtze
[Ch'ang-tzu]
Wayne. Village, Ohio,
USA : Freeport (–1931)

Webuye. Town, southern
Kenya, eastern Africa :
Broderick Falls (–1973)
Wedgeport. Town, Nova
Scotia, Canada : Tusket
Wedge (–1909)
Weedon Lake *see* Saint-Gérard
Węgliniec. Town, southwest-
ern Poland : Kohlfurt
(–1945), Germany
Węgorzewo. Town, north-
eastern Poland : Anger-
burg (–1945), Germany
Węgorzyno. Town, north-
western Poland : Wan-
gerin (–1945), Germany
Węgrów. Town, eastern Po-
land : Bingerau (–1945),
Germany
Wehlau *see* Znamensk
Weichang [Wei-chang].
Town, northeastern
China : Chutzeshan
(–1931)
Weifang. City, eastern
China : Weihsien (–1949)
Weihai. City, eastern China :
Weihaiwei (–1949)
Weihaiwei *see* Weihai
Weihsien *see* Weifang
Weisenstein *see* Paide
Weissenburg *see* Alba Iulia
Weiss-stein *see* Biały Kamień
Weisswasser *see* Bělá pod
Bezdězem
Weistritz *see* Bystrzyca
Weiyüan. Town, eastern
China : Pehtatung
(–1931)
Weiyüan *see* Kingku [Ching-
ku]
Wejherowo. Town, north-
ern Poland : Neustadt
(–1945), Germany

Wekelsdorf *see* Teplice nad Metují

Welfare Island *see* Franklin D. Roosevelt Island

Wellston *see* Warner Robins

Welungen *see* Wieluń

Welwitschia *see* Khorixas

Wenden *see* Cēsis

Wendisch Buchholz *see* Märkisch Buchholz

Wenling. Town, eastern China : Taiping (–1914)

Wenshan. Town, southwestern China : Kaihwa (–1914)

Werschetz *see* Vršac

Wesenberg *see* Rakvere

Weseritz *see* Bezdružice

Wesermünde *see* Bremerhaven

Wesseli *see* Veselí nad Moravou

West Allis. Suburb of Milwaukee, Wisconsin, USA : North Greenfield (–1902)

West Bengal *see* Bengal

West Columbia. Town, South Carolina, USA : (New) Brookland (–1938)

West Des Moines. Suburb of Des Moines, Iowa, USA : Valley Junction (–1938)

Western. Province, western Zambia, south-central Africa : Barotse (–1971)

Western *see* Copperbelt

Western Sahara. Territory, western Africa : Spanish Sahara (1958–75)

Western Samar *see* Samar

Western Test Range. Space research center, Point Mugu, north of Los Angeles, California, USA : Pacific Range (*1957–65)

West Hammond *see* Calumet City

West Irian *see* Irian Jaya West

Kazakhstan Oblast : Uralsk Oblast

Westlake. City, Ohio, USA : Dover (–1911)

West Lake *see* Kagera

Westlock. Town, Alberta, Canada : Edison (–1913)

West Lothian. Administrative district, southeastern Scotland, UK : Linlithgow (–1975)

West Malaysia *see* Peninsular Malaysia

West Memphis. City, Arkansas, USA : Bragg's Spur (*1910–29)

Westminster. City, Colorado, USA : Harris (–1911)

West Nimar *see* Khargone

West Shefford *see* Bromont

Westwold. Town, British Columbia, Canada : Grande Prairie (–1900), Adelphi (1900–26)

Whalers Bay. Stewart Island, New Zealand : Surveyors Bay (–1965)

Wharemoa. Town, South Island, New Zealand : Karoro (–1963)

Whatcom *see* Bellingham

Whyalla. City, South Australia, Australia : Hummock Hill (–1915)

Wiązów. Town, southwestern Poland : Wansen (–1945), Germany

Więcbork. Village, northern
Poland : Vandsburg
(–1945), Germany
Wielbark. Town, northeast-
ern Poland : Willenberg
(–1945), Germany
Wieleń. Town, northwest-
ern Poland : Filehne
(–1945), Germany
Wieluń. Town, south-
central Poland :
Welungen (1939–45),
Germany
Wiesengrund see Dobřany
Wildenschwert see Ústí nad
Orlicí
Wilhelmina Top see Trikora,
Puncak
Wilhelm-Pieck-Stadt Guben.
City, eastern Germany :
Guben (–1961)
Willemsdal see Greylingstad
Willenberg see Wielbark
Willingboro. Township,
New Jersey, USA :
Levittown (1959–63)
Williston. Town, Cape Prov-
ince, South Africa :
Amandelboom (–1919)
Willow Springs. Village, Illi-
nois, USA : Spring Forest
(–1937)
Willowvale see Gatyana
Wilmer. Settlement, British
Columbia, Canada :
Peterborough (–1902)
Wilno see Vilnius
Wilshamstead see Wilstead
Wilstead. Village, Bedford-
shire, England, UK :
Wilshamstead (–1978)
Winam. Town, southwest-
ern Kenya, eastern

Africa : Kavirondo Gulf
(–1975)
Windisch-Feistritz see (Slov-
enska) Bistrica
Windischgraz see Slovenj
Gradec
Wingon see Tzekam
Wińsko. Town, southwest-
ern Poland : Winzig
(–1945), Germany
Winterton. Village, Natal,
South Africa : Springfield
(–1910)
Winzig see Wińsko
Wirbeln see Zhavoronkovo
Wisconsin Dells. City, Wis-
consin, USA : Kilbourn
(–1931)
Wisconsin Rapids. City,
Wisconsin, USA : Grand
Rapids (–1920)
Wise. Town, Virginia, USA :
Gladeville (–1924)
Witnica. Town, western
Poland : Vietz (–1945),
Germany
Wittenberg see Nivenskoye
Wittenoom see Wittenoom
Gorge
Wittenoom Gorge. Town,
Western Australia, Aus-
tralia : Wittenoom
(–1951)
Wittingau see Třeboň
Wleń. Town, southwestern
Poland : Lähn (–1945),
Germany
Włocławek. City, central Po-
land : Leslau (1939–45),
Germany
Wodzisław Śląski. Town,
southern Poland : Loslau
(–1945), Germany

Wohlau *see* Wołow

Wołczyn. Town, southern
Poland : Konstadt
(–1945), Germany

Woldenberg *see* Dobiegniew

Wolframs-Eschenbach.
Town, southwestern
Germany : Eschenbach
(–1917)

Wolin. Town and island,
northwestern Poland :
Wollin (–1945), Germany

Wollin *see* Wolin

Wolmar *see* Valmiera

Wołow. Town, southwest-
ern Poland : Wohlau
(–1945), Germany

Woodburn (City). Town, Indiana, USA : Shirley City
(–1936)

Woodland Hills. Suburb of
Los Angeles, California,
USA : Girard (–1941)

Woodstock. Town, Cape
Province, South Africa :
Papendorp (–?)

Wrocław. City, southwest-
ern Poland : Breslau
(–1945), Germany

Wschowa. Town, western
Poland : Fraustadt
(–1945), Germany

Wuchan *see* Wusi [Wu-hsi]

Wucheng [Wu-ch'eng].
Town, eastern Tibet :
Sanyen (–1913)

Wu-ch'i = Wuki

Wuchow. City, southeastern
China : Ts'ang-wu (1913–
46)

Wuchuho *see* Shangchih

Wufeng. Town, east-central
China : Changlo (–1914)

Wufu *see* Nankiao [Nan-
chiao]

Wu-hsi = Wusi

Wuhsien *see* Soochow [Su-
chou]

Wu-hsing. City, eastern
China : Hu-chou (–1911)

Wuki [Wu-ch'i]. Town, central China : Taning
(–1914)

Wulung. Town, central
China : Siangkow (–1941)

Wuming. Town, southern
China : Wuyüan (–1913)

Wünschelburg *see* Radków

Würbenthal *see* Vrbno

Wushan. Town, north-cen-
tral China : Ningyüan
(–1914)

Wusheng. Town, central
China : Tingyüan
(–1914)

Wusi [Wu-hsi]. Town, northern China : Wuchan
(–1950)

Wutan. Town, northeastern
China : Wutancheng
(–1949)

Wutancheng *see* Wutan

Wuti. Town, eastern China :
Haifeng (–1914)

Wuting *see* Hweimin [Hui-
min]

Wutsin *see* Changchow
[Ch'ang-chou]

Wutu. Town, north-central
China : Kiechow (–1913)

Wutung. Town, northern
China : Kisiaying (–1949)

Wuwei. City, north-central
China : Liangchow
(–1913)

Wuyüan *see* Wuming

Xai-Xai. Town, southern
Mozambique, southeast-
ern Africa : Vila Nova de
Gaza (1922–28), João
Belo (1928–76)
Xangongo. Town, southern
Angola, southwestern Af-
rica : Roçadas (–c. 1979)
Xanthe. City, northeastern
Greece : Eskije (–1912),
Turkey
Xenía see Kalyvákia
Xerokhórion see Stauro-
drómion
Xhora. Town, southern
Transkei, southern Af-
rica : Elliotdale (–1976)
Xiririca see Eldorado
Xonrupt see Xonrupt-Longe-
mer
Xonrupt-Longemer. Village,
eastern France : Xonrupt
(–1938)

Ya-an. Town, southern China
: Ya-chou (–1913)
Yabalkovo. Village, south-
central Bulgaria : Almalii
(–c. 1945)
Yablochny. Urban settle-
ment, Sakhalin Oblast,
Russia : Rantomari
(1905–45), Japan
Yabu. Town, southern Hon-
shu, Japan : Yabuichiba
(–early 1940s)
Yabuichiba see Yabu
Ya-chiang = Yakiang
Ya-chou see Ya-an
Yaichow see Aihsien
Yakiang [Ya-chiang]. Town,
southern China : Hokow
(–1913)

Yakima. City, Washington,
USA : North Yakima
(–1918)
Yakkabag. Town, Kashka-
darya Oblast, Uzbeki-
stan : Stantsiya-
Yakkabag (–1978)
Yakovlevskoye see Privolzhsk
Yakunchikov see Krasny Ma-
yak
Yakut Autonomous Repub-
lic. Northeastern Rus-
sia : Yakut Autonomous
SSR (*1922–91)
Yakut Autonomous SSR see
Yakut Autonomous Re-
public
Yalu. Town, northeastern
China : Chalantun
(–1925, 1932–45)
Yama see Seversk
Yamankhalinka see Makham-
bet
Yamato. Town, west-central
Honshu, Japan : Takaki
(–1930s)
Yamburg see Kingisepp
Yamchow see Yamhsien
Yamhsien. Town, southeast-
ern China : Yamchow
(–1912)
Yamin, Puncak. Mountain,
Irian Jaya, Indonesia :
Prins Hendrik Top
(–1963)
Yaminskoye see Tselinnoye
(2)
Yang-chou. City, eastern
China : Kiangtu (1912–
49)
Yang-ch'u = Yangku
Yangchung. Town, eastern
China : Taiping (–1914)
Yanghopao see Yungning

Yang-hsin = Yangsin
Yangibazar *see* Ordzhoni-
kidzeabad
Yangi-Bazar *see* Soldatsky
Yangiyer. Town, Syrdarya
Oblast, Uzbekistan :
Chernyayevo (–c. 1917)
Yangiyul. Town, Tashkent
Oblast, Uzbekistan :
Kaunchi (–1934)
Yang-kü [Yang-ch'u] *see*
Taiyüan [Tai-yüan]
Yangon. Capital of Myan-
mar, southeastern Asia:
Rangoon (–1989)
Yangsin [Yang-hsin]. Town,
east-central China :
Hingkwo (–1912)
Yangyuan. Town, northeast-
ern China : Sining
(–1914)
Yanov *see* (1) Ivano-Frankovo;
(2) Ivanovo (2)
Yanovka *see* Ivanovka
Yantak *see* Buston
Yantarny. Urban settle-
ment, Kaliningrad Ob-
last, Russia : Palmnicken
(–1947), Germany
(–1945)
Yanushpol *see* Ivanopol
Yaoan. Town, southwestern
China : Yaochow (–1913)
Yaochow *see* (1) Yaoan; (2)
Yaohsien
Yaohsien. Town, central
China : Yaochow
(–1913)
Yaonan. Town, eastern
China : Changshan
(–1949)
Yarowie *see* Appila
Yaryksu-Aukh *see* Novola-
kskoye

Yasaka. Town, southern
Honshu, Japan : Minami-
oji (–early 1940s)
Yasen. Village, northern
Bulgaria : Plazigaz
(–c. 1945)
Yashalta. Village, Rostov
Oblast, Russia : Esto-
Khaginka (–1944),
Stepnoye (1944–58)
Yashkul. Urban settlement,
Kalmyk Autonomous Re-
public, Russia : Pescha-
noye (1944–c. 1960)
Yaski *see* Lesogorsky
Yasnogorsk. Town, Tula
Oblast, Russia : Laptevo
(–1965)
Yasnomorsky. Urban settle-
ment, Sakhalin Oblast,
Russia : Oko (1905–45),
Japan
Yasnoye. Village, Kalinin-
grad Oblast, Russia :
Kaukehmen (–1938),
Germany, Kuckerneese
(1938–45), Germany
Yass-Canberra *see* Australian
Capital Territory
Yates Dam. Dam, Ala-
bama, USA : Upper Tal-
lassee Dam (*1928–?)
Yavoshikha *see* Zalesovshch-
ina
Yaypan. Town, Fergana Ob-
last, Uzbekistan : Bazar-
Yaypan (c. 1940–75)
Yazvy *see* Vostochnaya (2)
Yegorshino *see* Artyomovsky
Yegri-Dere *see* Ardino
Yeh-hsien = Yehsien
Yehsien [Yeh-hsien]. Town,
eastern China : Laichow
(–1913)

Yekaterinburg. Capital of
Sverdlovsk Oblast, Rus-
sia : Sverdlovsk (1924–
91)
Yekaterinenshtadt see Marks
Yekaterinodar see Krasnodar
Yekaterinofeld see Bolnisi
Yekaterinoslav see
Dnepropetrovsk
Yekaterinovka see Ar-
tyomovsk (3)
Yekaterinovskaya see
Krylovskaya
Yekhegnadzor. Urban settle-
ment, Armenia : Kesh-
ishkend (–c. 1935),
Mikoyan (c. 1935–57)
Yelenendorf see Khanlar
Yelenovka see (1) Sevan; (2)
Zorinsk
Yelenovskiye Karyery see
Dokuchayevsk
Yelgava = Jelgava
Yelizavetgrad. Capital of
Kirovograd Oblast,
Ukraine : Zinovyevsk
(1924–36), Kirovo (1936–
39), Kirovograd (1939–
91)
Yelizavetpol see Gyandzha
Yelizavetpol Guberniya see
Gandzha Guberniya
Yelizovo. Town, Kamchatka
Oblast, Russia : Zavoyko
(–1924)
Yelkhovo. City, southeast-
ern Bulgaria : Kizil-agach
(–1925)
Yemen [South Yemen]
(1990†). Republic, Ara-
bian Peninsula : Southern
Yemen (*1967–70)
Yemva. Town, Komi Auton-
omous Republic, Russia :

Zheleznodorozhny
(–1985)
Yenakiyevo. Town, Don-
etsk Oblast, Ukraine :
Rykovo (c.1928–37),
Ordzhonikidze (1937–43)
Yenan. Town, central
China : Fushih (1913–48)
Yen-chiang = Yenkiang
Yen-ching = Yentsing
Yenchow see (1) Kienteh
[Chien-te]; (2) Tzeyang
[Tzu-yang]
Yenfeng. Town, southwest-
ern China : Paiyentsing
(–1913)
Yenije-i-Vardar see Yiannitsá
Yeni-Pazar see Novi Pazar
Yenkiang [Yen-chiang].
Town, northern China :
Taerhhu (–1942)
Yen-p'ing see Nanping [Nan-
p'ing]
Yenshan. Town, southwest-
ern China : Kiangna
(–1933)
Yenshan see Kingyüan
[Ching-yüan]
Yen-shou = Yenshow
Yenshow [Yen-shou]. Town,
northeastern China :
Changshow (–1914),
Tungpin (1914–29)
Yentsing [Yen-ching]. Town,
southwestern China :
Laoyatan (–1917)
Yenukidze see Ambrolauri
Yerevan. Capital of Arme-
nia : Erivan (–1936)
Yermolovsk see Leselidze
Yertarskoye see Yertarsky
Yertarsky. Urban settle-
ment, Sverdlovsk Oblast,
Russia : Yertarsky Zavod

(–c. 1928), Yertarskoye
(1928–40)
Yertarsky Zavod see Yertar-
sky
Yerzhar see Gagarin (2)
Yeski Dzhumaya see Tar-
govište
Yevdokimovskoye see Kras-
nogvardeyskoye (3)
Yezhovo-Cherkessk see Cher-
kessk
Yezupol see Zhovten (2)
Yiannitsá. City, northern
Greece : Yenije-i-Vardar
(–?), Turkey
Yichow see Yihsien [Ihsien]
Yihsien [Ihsien]. Town,
northeastern China :
Yichow (–1913)
Yin-chuan = Yinchwan
Yinchwan [Yin-ch'uan].
City, northwestern China :
Ningsia (–1945)
Ying-chiang = Yingkiang
Yingchow see (1) Fowyang
[Fou-yang]; (2) Yinghsien
Yinghsien. Town, northeast-
ern China : Yingchow
(–1912)
Yingkiang [Ying-chiang]. Vil-
lage, southwestern China :
Kanai (–1935)
Yingpankai see Pikiang
[Pi-chiang]
Yirga-Alam. Town, south-
ern Ethiopia, northeast-
ern Africa : Dalle (1936–
41)
Yitu [Itu]. Town, eastern
China : Tsingchow
(–1913)
Yiwu see Chenyüeh
Yochow see Yoyang
Yoshida see Shimo-yoshida

Yoshkar-Ola. Capital of
Mari Autonomous Re-
public, Russia : Tsar-
yovokokshaysk (–1919),
Krasnokokshaysk (1919–
27)
Youssoufia. Town, western
Morocco, northwestern
Africa : Louis-Gentil
(–c. 1959)
Yoyang. Town, south-cen-
tral China : Yochow
(–1913)
Yoyang see Antseh
Yüanchow see (1) Chihkiang
[Chih-chiang]; (2) Ichun
[I-chun]
Yüanling. Town, south-cen-
tral China : Shenchow
(–1913)
Yü-ch'i = Yüki
Yü-chiang = Yükiang
Yü-ch'ien = Yütsien
Yuchow see Fangcheng [Fang-
ch'eng]
Yüchow see Yütsien
Yüchung. Town, north-
central China : Kinhsien
(–1912), Kincheng (1912–
19)
Yudenichi see Sovetskaya (5)
Yudino see Petukhovo
Yüeh-chou see Yüeh-yang
Yüeh-yang. Town, south-
eastern China : Yüeh-
chou (–1911)
Yug. Urban settlement,
Perm Oblast, Russia :
Yugovskoy Zavod
(–1943)
Yugo-Kamsky. Urban settle-
ment, Perm Oblast, Rus-
sia : Yugokamsky Zavod
(–1929)

Yugokamsky Zavod *see* Yugo-
Kamsky
Yugovskoy Zavod *see* Yug
Yüki [Yü-ch'i]. Town, south-
western China : Sinsing
(–1913), Siuna (1913–
16)
Yükiang [Yü-chiang]. Town,
southeastern China :
Anjen (–1914)
Yuliya *see* Tsvetnogorsk
Yumrukchal *see* Botev
Yünchow *see* Yünhsien (1)
Yungan *see* Mengshan
Yunganpao *see* Langshan
Yungchang *see* Paoshan
Yüng-chi = Yüngtsi
Yungchow *see* Lingling
Yungkang *see* Tungcheng
[T'ung-cheng]
Yungki *see* Kirin
Yungnien. Town, northeast-
ern China : Kwangping
(–1913)
Yungning. Town, northwest-
ern China : Yanghopao
(–1942)
Yungning *see* (1) Lishih; (2)
Loning; (3) Nanning; (4)
Poshow; (5) Süyung
[Hsü-yung]
Yungpeh *see* Yungsheng
Yungping *see* Lulung
Yungsheng. Town, south-
western China : Yungpeh
(–1913)
Yung-shou = Yungshow
Yungshow [Yung-shou].
Town, central China :
Kienkünchen (–c. 1940)
Yungtai [Yung-tai]. Town,
southeastern China :
Inghok (–1941)

Yungteng. Town, north-
central China : Pingfan
(–1928)
Yungting *see* Tayung
Yüngtsi [Yüng-chi]. Town,
northeastern China :
Puchow (–1912)
Yungyün. Town, southeast-
ern China : Lungsinhü
(–1947)
Yünhsien (1). Town, south-
western China : Yünchow
(–1913)
Yünhsien (2). Town, east-
central China : Yünyang
(–1912)
Yunnan *see* (1) Kunming
[K'un-ming]; (2)
Siangyün [Hsiang-yün]
Yunokommunarovsk.
Town, Donetsk Oblast,
Ukraine : Bunge Rudnik
(*1908–?), Yunykh
Kommunarov, imeni
(?–1965)
Yünyang *see* Yünhsien (2)
Yunykh Kommunarov, imeni
see Yunokommunarsk
Yuryev *see* Tartu
Yuryuzan. Town, Chelyab-
insk Oblast, Russia :
Yuryuzansky Zavod
(–1943)
Yuryuzansky Zavod *see*
Yuryuzan
Yurzdyka *see* Zelenets
(2)
Yusta. Settlement, Kalmyk
Autonomous Republic,
Russia : Trudovoy
(–c. 1960)
Yutien *see* Changning
[Ch'ang-ning]

Yütsien [Yü-chien]. Town, eastern China : Yüchow (–1912)

Yuyü. Town, northeastern China : Shoping (–1911)

Yuzhno-Kurilsk. Urban settlement, Kuril Islands, Sakhalin Oblast, Russia : Furukamappu (1905–45), Japan

Yuzhno-Sakhalinsk. Capital of Sakhalin Oblast, Russia : Vladimirovka (–1905), Toyohara (1905–45), Japan

Yuzhny see (1) Adyk; (2) Dostluk; (3) Skuratovsky

Yuzovka see Donetsk (2)

Zabaykalsk. Urban settlement, Chita Oblast, Russia : Otpor (–c. 1960)

Ząbkowice Śląskie. Town, southwestern Poland : Frankenstein (–1945), Germany

Zablotye see Zabolotye

Zabolotye. Urban settlement, Volyn Oblast, Ukraine : Zablotye (–1944)

Zaborovtsy. Village, Vitebsk Oblast, Belorussia : Nevbily (–1964)

Zaboyshchik see Kurganovka

Zábřeh. Town, east-central Czech Lands : Hohenstadt (–1918, 1939–45), Germany

Zabrze. City, southern Poland : Hindenburg (1915–45), Germany

Zabuldychino see Olkhovskaya

Zachan see Suchan

Žacléř. Village, northern Czech Lands : Schatzlar (–1918, 1939–45), Germany

Zafarabad (1). Urban settlement, Leninabad Oblast, Tajikistan : Ayni (–c. 1960)

Zafarabad (2). Urban settlement, Bukhara Oblast, Uzbekistan : Kokcha (–1984)

Żagań. Town, western Poland : Sagan (–1945), Germany

Zagornaya. Village, Minsk Oblast, Belorussia : Bolvan (–1964)

Zagorodnaya. Village, Brest Oblast, Belorussia : Zlomyshle (–1964)

Zagorsk see Sergiyev Posad

Zagorsky see Krasnozavodsk

Zagreb. Capital of Croatia : Agram (1526–1918), Germany

Żagryazye see Bereznyanka

Zahana. Village, northwestern Algeria, northern Africa : Saint-Lucien (–c. 1962)

Zahirabad. Town, south-central India : Ekeli (–?)

Zainsk. Town, Tatar Autonomous Republic, Russia : Novy Zay (–1978)

Zaïre. Republic, central Africa : Congo Free State (–1908), Belgian Congo [Congo Belge] (1908–60), Congo (Léopoldville)

(1960–64), Congo (Kinshasa) (1965–71)

Zakamensk. Town, Buryat Autonomous Republic, Russia : Gorodok (–1959)

Zakarpatskaya Oblast = Transcarpathian Oblast

Zakaspiyskaya Oblast see Turkmenistan

Zakharovka see Frunzovka

Zakhedan. Town, eastern Iran : Dozdab (–?)

Zakhmatabad see Ayni

Zákupy. Town, northern Czech Lands : Reichstadt (–1918, 1939–45), Germany

Zaldíbar. Village, northern Spain : Zaldúa (–c. 1940)

Zaleshany. Village, Vitebsk Oblast, Belorussia : Bardily (–1964)

Zalesino. Village, Vitebsk Oblast, Belorussia : Glistenets (–1964)

Zalesnaya. Village, Vitebsk Oblast, Belorussia : Koleno (–1964)

Zalesovshchina. Village, Grodno Oblast, Belorussia : Yavoshikha (–1964)

Zalesovtsy. Village, Grodno Oblast, Belorussia : Plekhovo (–1964)

Zalesskaya. Village, Minsk Oblast, Belorussia : Pisyuta (–1964)

Zalesye. Village, Kaliningrad Oblast, Russia : Mehlauken (–1938), Germany, Liebenfelde (1938–45), Germany

Zalew Wiślany = Vistula Lagoon

Záloggon. Village, western Greece : Kamarína (–1960s)

Žamberk. Town, northeastern Czech Lands : Senftenberg (–1918, 1939–45), Germany

Zambia. Republic, southcentral Africa : Northern Rhodesia (*1911–64)

Zangelan. Town, Azerbaijan : Pirchevan (–1957)

Zangibasar see Razdan (2)

Zanow see Sianów

Zaouet el-Kahla see Bordj Omar Driss

Zapadno-Gruppsky see Shakhtyorsk (2)

Zapaluta see La Trinitaria

Zaporozhye. Capital of Zaporozhye Oblast, Ukraine : Aleksandrovsk (–1921)

Zaporozhye Guberniya (1922). Ukrainian SSR : Aleksandrovsk Guberniya (*1920–21)

Zapovednoye. Village, Kaliningrad Oblast, Russia : Seckenburg (–1945), Germany

Zara. Town, central Turkey : Kocgiri (–?)

Zarasai. Town, Lithuania : Novoaleksandrovsk (–1920), Ossersee (1941–44), Germany

Zárate. City, southeastern Argentina, South America : General Uriburu (1932–46)

Zarechnaya (1). Village, Minsk Oblast, Belorussia : Boldyuki (–1964)

Zarechnaya (2). Village,
Minsk Oblast, Belorussia :
Kulakovtsy (–1964)
Zarechnaya (3). Village,
Grodno Oblast, Belorus-
sia : Perkhayly (–1964)
Zarechnaya (4). Village,
Vitebsk Oblast, Belorus-
sia : Trukhanovichi
(–1964)
Zarechny. Urban settle-
ment, Ryazan Oblast,
Russia : Pobedinsky
(–c. 1960)
Zaritap. Village, Armenia :
Azizbekov (–c. 1960)
Zarkhanádes *see* Dasokhórion
Zarya *see* Leninsky (5)
Zashchesle *see* Urozhaynaya
(3)
Zaslav *see* Zaslavl
Zaslavl. Town, Minsk Ob-
last, Belorussia : Izyaslavl
(1920s), Zaslav (1920s–
c. 1935)
Zaslonovo. Village, Vitebsk
Oblast, Belorussia :
Kozodoi (–1945)
Žatec. Town, western Czech
Lands : Saaz (–1918,
1939–45), Germany
Zatishye *see* Elektrostal
Zatoka. Urban settlement,
Odessa Oblast, Ukraine :
Bugaz (–c. 1960)
Zatychino *see* Cheryomukha
Zave *see* Zawi
Zavitaya *see* Zavitinsk
Zavitinsk. Town, Amur Ob-
last, Russia : Zavitaya
(–1954)
Zavodoukovsk. Town,
Tyumen Oblast, Russia :
Zavodoukovsky (–1960)

Zavodoukovsky *see* Zavo-
doukovsk
Zavodskoy *see* Komsomolsky
(4)
Zavolzhsk. Town, Ivanovo
Oblast, Russia :
Zavolzhye (–1954)
Zavolzhye. Town, Nizhe-
gorodskaya Oblast, Rus-
sia : Pestovo (–1964)
Zavolzhye *see* Zavolzhsk
Zavoyko *see* Yelizovo
Zawi. Village, northeastern
Zimbabwe, southeastern
Africa : Zave (–1983)
Zawiercie. City, southern
Poland : Warthenau
(1939–45), Germany
Zbąszynek. Town, western
Poland : Neu-Bentschen
(–1945), Germany
Žd'ár. Town, central Czech
Lands : Saar (in Mähren)
(–1918, 1939–45), Ger-
many
Zehden *see* Cedynia
Zelaya. Department, east-
ern Nicaragua, Central
America : Bluefields
(–c. 1919)
Zelenets (1). Village, Brest
Oblast, Belorussia :
Terpilovichi (–1964)
Zelenets (2). Village,
Grodno Oblast, Belo-
russia : Yurzdyka
(–1964)
Zelenodolsk. Town, Tatar
Autonomous Republic,
Russia : Kabachishche
(–1932), Zelyony Dol
(1932–c. 1940)
Zelenogorsk. Town, Lenin-
grad Oblast, Russia :

Terijoki (–1948), Finland (–1940)

Zelenogradsk. Town, Kaliningrad Oblast, Russia : Kranz (–1946), Germany (–1945)

Zelenokumsk. Town, Stavropol Kray, Russia : Vorontsovo-Aleksandrovskoye (–1963), Sovetskoye (1963–65)

Zelensk see Leninsk (2)

Železná Ruda. Town, southwestern Czech Lands : Eisenstein (–1918, 1939–45), Germany

Železný Brod. Town, northern Czech Lands : Eisenbrod (–1918, 1939–45), Germany

Zelina. Village, northern Croatia : Sveti Ivan Zelina (–1948)

Zelman see Rovnoye

Zelyonaya (1). Village, Vitebsk Oblast, Belorussia : Pleshivtsy (–1964)

Zelyonaya (2). Village, Gomel Oblast, Belorussia : Zhezlenka (–1964)

Zelyony Bor. Village, Minsk Oblast, Belorussia : Gaden (–1964)

Zelyony Dol see Zelenodolsk

Zelyony Log. Village, Vitebsk Oblast, Belorussia : Khokhulki (–1964)

Zemen. Village, western Bulgaria : Belovo (–c. 1945)

Zemgale see Jelgava

Zemlya Imperatora Nikolaya II see Severnaya Zemlya

Zempelburg see Sepolno (Kraińskie)

Zenkovka see Chkalovskoye (2)

Zernograd. Town, Rostov Oblast, Russia : Zernovoy (–1960)

Zernovoy see Zernograd

Zestafoni. Town, Georgia : Dzhugeli [Kvirily] (–1921)

Zhabovka see Partizanka

Zhabye see Verkhovina

Zhavoronkovo. Village, Kaliningrad Oblast, Russia : Wirbeln (–1945), Germany

Zhdanov see Mariupol

Zhdanovsk see Beylagan

Zhelaniya, Cape. Northern Severnaya Zemlya, Arctic Ocean, Nenets Autonomous Okrug, Arkhangelsk Oblast, Russia : Mauritius, Cape (–c. 1918)

Zheleznodorozhny (1). Urban settlement, Kaliningrad Oblast, Russia : Gerdauen (–1946), Germany (–1945)

Zheleznodorozhny (2). Town, Moscow Oblast, Russia : Obiralovka (–1939)

Zheleznodorozhny see (1) Kungrad; (2) Yemva

Zheleznogorsk see Zheleznogorsk-Ilimsky

Zheleznogorsk-Ilimsky. Town, Irkutsk Oblast, Russia : Zheleznogorsk (–1965)

Zherdevka. Town, Tambov
Oblast, Russia : Chi-
bizovka (–1954)
Zherebilovichi *see* Sosnovaya
(3)
Zherebtsy *see* Vishnevets (2)
Zhezlenka *see* Zelyonaya (2)
Zhigulyovsk. Town, Samara
Oblast, Russia :
Otvazhnoye (1946–49),
Otvazhny (1949–52)
Zhilyanka *see* Kargalinskoye
Zhirnovsk. Town, Vol-
gograd Oblast, Russia :
Zhirnoye (–1954),
Zhirnovsky (1954–58)
Zhirnovsky *see* Zhirnovsk
Zhirnoye *see* Zhirnovsk
Zhirospyory *see* Partizanskaya
(4)
Zhivkovo. Village, west-
central Bulgaria : Avli-
koi (–c. 1945)
Zhivoglodovichi *see* Per-
vomaysk (5)
Zhob. Town, northeastern
Pakistan : Fort Sandeman
(–c. 1948)
Zholkev *see* Nesterov (2)
Zholkva *see* Nesterov (2)
Zhovten (1). Village,
Odessa Oblast, Ukraine :
Petroverovka (–c. 1928)
Zhovten (2). Urban settle-
ment, Ivano-Frankovsk
Oblast, Ukraine : Ye-
zupol (–1940), Stakha-
novo (1938–47)
Zhovtnevoye (1). Town,
Nikolayev Oblast,
Ukraine : Bogoyavlensk
(–1938), Oktyabrskoye
(1938–61)

Zhovtnevoye (2). Village,
Dnepropetrovsk Oblast,
Ukraine : Izluchistaya
(–c. 1928), Stalindorf
(c. 1928–44), Stalinskoye
(1944–61)
Zhukovo. Village, Kaluga
Oblast, Russia : Ugodsky
Zavod (–1974)
Zhukovsky. Town, Moscow
Oblast, Russia : Otdykh
(–1938), Stakhanovo
(1938–47)
Zhyoltaya Reka *see* Zhyoltyye
Vody
Zhyoltyye Vody. Town,
Dnepropetrovsk Oblast,
Ukraine : Rudnik imeni
Shvartsa (–1939), Zhy-
oltaya Reka (1939–57)
Zhyoltyye Vody *see* Mirnoye
(2)
Židlochovice. Town, south-
ern Czech Lands : See-
lowitz (–1918, 1939–45),
Germany
Ziębice. Town, southwest-
ern Poland : Münsterberg
(–1945), Germany
Ziebingen *see* Cybinka
Ziegenhals *see* Głuchołazy
Zielenzig *see* Sulęcin
Zielona Góra. Town, west-
central Poland : Grünberg
(in Schlesien) (–1945),
Germany
Zighout Youcef. Village,
northeastern Algeria,
northern Africa : Condé-
Smendou (–c. 1962)
Žilina. Town, northern Slovakia : Sillein (–1918,
1939–45), Germany

Zimbabwe. Republic, south-eastern Africa : Southern Rhodesia (*1900–64, 1979–80), Rhodesia (1964–79), Zimbabwe Rhodesia (1979)

Zimbabwe Rhodesia *see* Zimbabwe

Zimigui-Ziwanan *see* Masi

Zimnitsa. Village, eastern Bulgaria : Kashla-koi (–1906)

Zimogorye. Town, Lugansk Oblast, Ukraine : Cherkasskoye (–1961)

Zinder *see* Niger (1)

Zinovyevsk *see* Yelizavetgrad

Zinten *see* Kornevo

Zirke *see* Sieraków

Zirknitz *see* Cerknica

Ziwa Magharibi *see* Kagera

Ziyautdin *see* Pakhtakor

Zlaté Hory. Village, north-eastern Czech Lands : Zuckmantel (–1919, 1939–45), Germany

Zlaté Moravce. Town, western Slovakia : Aranyosmarót (–1918), Hungary

Zlatna. Village, central Romania : Klein-Schlatten (–1920), Germany

Zlatograd. City, southern Bulgaria : Dara Dere (–1934)

Zlín. Town, southeastern Czech Lands : Gottwaldov (1948–90)

Zlodin *see* Krasnoberezhye

Zlokuchen *see* Ivanski

Zlomyshle *see* Zagorodnaya

Złotoryja. Town, southwestern Poland : Goldberg (–1945), Germany

Złotów. Town, northwestern Poland : Flatow (–1945), Germany

Złoty Stok. Town, southwestern Poland : Reichenstein (–1945), Germany

Žlutice. Town, western Czech Lands : Luditz (–1918, 1939–45), Germany

Zmajevo. Village, northern Serbia : Pašićevo (–1947)

Żmigród. Town, southwestern Poland : Trachenberg (–1945), Germany

Zmiyov. Town, Kharkov Oblast, Ukraine : Gotvald (1976–91)

Znamenka (1). Village, Brest Oblast, Belorussia : Durichi (–1964)

Znamenka (2). Village, Mogilyov Oblast, Belorussia : Kobylyanka (–1964)

Znamenka (3). Village, Minsk Oblast, Belorussia : Podonki (–1969)

Znamenka (4). Village, Gomel Oblast, Belorussia : Sleptsy (–1958)

Znamensk. Urban settlement, Kaliningrad Oblast, Russia : Wehlau (–1946), Germany (–1945)

Znamensky *see* Pamyati 13 Bortsov

Znamya. Village, Minsk Oblast, Belorussia : Startsevichi (–1964)

Znauri. Village, South Ossetian Autonomous Oblast, Georgia : Znaur-Kau (–c. 1945)

Znaur-Kau *see* Znauri

Zobten *see* Sobótka
Zolotushino *see* Gornyak (2)
Zomba. Town, southwestern Hungary : Döryzomba (*1940–41)
Zongo Rapids. River, northwestern Zaïre, central Africa : Grenfell Rapids (–?)
Zorinsk. Town, Lugansk Oblast, Ukraine : Yelenovka (–1963)
Zorndorf *see* Sarbinowo
Zory. Village, southern Poland : Sohrau (–1945), Germany
Zrenjanin. City, northeastern Serbia : Veliki Bečkerek (–1930s), Petrovgrad (1930s–c. 1947)
Zschornegosda *see* Schwarzheide
Zuckmantel *see* Zlaté Hory
Zudañez. Town, south-central Bolivia, South America : Tacopaya (–1900s)
Züllichau *see* Sulechów
Zülz *see* Biała
Zung *see* Vakhan
Zvanka *see* Volkhov
Zvenigovo. Town, Mari Autonomous Republic, Russia : Zvenigovsky Zaton (–c. 1940)
Zvenigovsky Zaton *see* Zvenigovo
Zvishavani. Town, south-central Zimbabwe, southeastern Africa : Shabani (–1982)
Zvolen. Town, central Slovakia : Altsohl (–1918, 1939–45), Germany
Zvyagi *see* Roshchino (3)
Zwischenwässern *see* Medvode
Zwittau *see* Svitavy
Żywiec. Town, southwestern Poland : Saybusch (–1945), Germany

APPENDIX : OFFICIAL NAMES OF COUNTRIES

(as of January 1, 1993)

The names below are given in the official language or languages of the country concerned. Most countries have a single official language, but some have two, a few three, and one, Singapore, no less than four, respectively Mandarin Chinese, Malay, Tamil, and English.

Afghanistan	Da Afghānestān Jamhawrīyat/Jomhūrī-ye Afghānestān
Albania	Republika e Shqipërisë
Algeria	al-Jumhūrīyah al-Jazā'irīya ad-Dīmuq-rātīyah ash-Sha'bīyah
Andorra	Principat d'Andorra
Angola	República de Angola
Antigua and Barbuda	Antigua and Barbuda
Argentina	República Argentina
Armenia	Hayastani Hanrapetut'yun
Australia	Commonwealth of Australia
Austria	Republik Österreich
Azerbaijan	Azärbayjan Respublikasi
Bahamas	The Commonwealth of the Bahamas

Bahrain
Dawlat al-Baḥrayn

Bangladesh   Gana Prajātantrī Bangladesh

Barbados   Barbados

Belarus
  (Belorussia)   Respublika Belarus

Belgium   Koninkrijk België/Royaume de Belgique

Belize   Belize

Benin   République du Bénin

Bhutan   Druk-Yul

Bolivia   República de Bolivia

Bosnia and
  Herzegovina   Republika Bosna : Hercegovina

Botswana   Republic of Botswana

Brazil   República Federativa do Brasil

Brunei   Negara Brunei Darussalam

Bulgaria   Republika Bŭlgaria

Burkina Faso   Burkina Faso

Burundi   Republika y'u Burundi/République du Burundi

Cambodia   Roat Kampuchea

Cameroon   République du Cameroun/Republic of Cameroon

Canada   Canada

Cape Verde   República de Cabo Verde

Central African Republic	République Centrafricaine
Chad	Jumhūrīyah Tshad/République du Tchad
Chile	República de Chile
China	Chung-hua Jen-min Kung-ho-kuo
Colombia	República de Colombia
Comoros	Jumhurīyat al-Qumur al-Ittihādīyah al-Islāmīyah/République Fédérale Islamique des Comores
Congo	République du Congo
Costa Rica	República de Costa Rica
Côte d'Ivoire	République de Côte d'Ivoire
Croatia	Republika Hrvatska
Cuba	República de Cuba
Cyprus	Kypriakí Dimokratía/Kıbris Cumhuriyeti
Czechoslovakia	Čescá a Slovenská Federativní Republika/Česká a Slovenská Federatívna Republika
Denmark	Kongeriget Danmark
Djibouti	Jumhūrīyah Jībūtī/République de Djibouti
Dominica	Commonwealth of Dominica
Dominican Republic	República Dominicana
Ecuador	República del Ecuador
Egypt	Jumhūrīyah Miṣr al-'Arabīyah

El Salvador	República de El Salvador
Equatorial Guinea	República de Guinea Ecuatorial
Estonia	Eesti Vabariik
Ethiopia	YeĒtiyop'iya
Fiji	Sovereign Democratic Republic of Fiji
Finland	Suomen Tasavalta/Republiken Finland
France	République Française
Gabon	République Gabonaise
Gambia	Republic of the Gambia
Georgia	Sakartvelos Respublikis
Germany	Bundesrepublik Deutschland
Ghana	Republic of Ghana
Greece	Ellinikí Dimokratía
Grenada	Grenada
Guadeloupe	Département de la Guadeloupe
Guatemala	República de Guatemala
Guinea	République de Guinée
Guinea-Bissau	República da Guiné-Bissau
Guyana	Co-operative Republic of Guyana
Haiti	Repiblik Dayti/République d'Haïti
Honduras	República de Honduras
Hungary	Magyar Köztársaság

Iceland	Lýdhveldidh Ísland
India	Bhārat/Republic of India
Indonesia	Republik Indonesia
Iran	Jomhūrī-ye Eslamī-ye Irān
Iraq	Al-Jumhūrīyah al- 'Irāqīyah
Ireland	Republic of Ireland/Poblacht na hEireann
Israel	Medinat Yisra'el
Italy	Repubblica Italiana
Jamaica	Jamaica
Japan	Nihon
Jordan	Al-Mamlakah al-Urdunnīyah al-Hāshimīyah
Kazakhstan	Qazaqstan Respublikasï
Kenya	Jamhuri ya Kenya/Republic of Kenya
Kiribati	Republic of Kiribati
Korea, North	Chosŏn Minjujuŭi In'min Konghwaguk
Korea, South	Taehan Min'guk
Kuwait	Dowlat al-Kuwayt
Kyrgyzstan (Kirgizia)	Kyrgyzstan Respublikasy
Laos	Sathalanalat Paxathipatai Paxaxôn Lao
Latvia	Latvijas Republika
Lebanon	Al-Jumhūrīyah al-Lubnānīyah
Lesotho	Lesotho/Kingdom of Lesotho

Liberia	Republic of Liberia
Libya	Al-Jamāhīrīyah al-'Arabīyah al-Lībīyah ash- Shabī'yah al-Ishtirākīyah
Liechtenstein	Fürstentum Liechtenstein
Lithuania	Lietuvos Respublika
Luxembourg	Groussherzogtum Lëtzebuerg/Grand-Duché de Luxembourg/Grossherzogtum Luxemburg
Macau	Ao-men/Macau
Macedonia	Republika Makedonija
Madagascar	Repoblika Demokratika Malagasy/République Démocratique de Madagascar
Malawi	Republic of Malawi
Malaysia	Malaysia
Maldives	Divehi Jumhuriyya
Mali	République du Mali
Malta	Repubblika ta' Malta
Marshall Islands	Majōl/Republic of the Marshall Islands
Martinique	Département de la Martinique
Mauritania	Al-Jumhūrīyah al-Islāmīyah al-Mūrītanīyah
Mauritius	Republic of Mauritius
Mexico	Estados Unidos Mexicanos
Moldova (Moldavia)	Republica Moldova
Monaco	Principauté de Monaco

Mongolia	Mongol Uls
Morocco	Al-Mamlakah al-Maghribīyah
Mozambique	República de Moçambique
Myanmar	Pyidaungzu Myanma Naingngandaw
Namibia	Republic of Namibia
Nauru	Republic of Nauru
Nepal	Nepāl Adhirājya
Netherlands	Koninkrijk der Nederlanden
New Zealand	New Zealand/Aotearoa
Nicaragua	República de Nicaragua
Niger	République du Niger
Nigeria	Federal Republic of Nigeria
Norway	Kongeriket Norge
Oman	Salṭanat 'Umān
Pakistan	Islām-ī Jamhūrīya-e Pākistān
Panama	República de Panamá
Papua New Guinea	Independent State of Papua New Guinea
Paraguay	República del Paraguay
Peru	República del Perú
Philippines	Republika ng Pilipinas
Poland	Rzeczpospolita Polska
Portugal	República Portuguesa

Puerto Rico	Estado Libre Asociado de Puerto Rico
Qatar	Dawlat Qaṭar
Réunion	Département de la Réunion
Romania	România
Russia	Rossiyskaya Federatsiya
Rwanda	Repubulika y'u Rwanda/République Rwandaise
Saint Kitts and Nevis	Federation of Saint Kitts and Nevis
Saint Lucia	Saint Lucia
Saint Vincent and the Grenadines	Saint Vincent and the Grenadines
San Marino	Serenissima Repubblica di San Marino
São Tomé and Príncipe	República Democrática de São Tomé e Príncipe
Saudi Arabia	Al-Mamlakah al-'Arabīyah as-Sa'ūdīyah
Senegal	République du Sénégal
Seychelles	Repiblik Sesel/Republic of Seychelles/ République des Seychelles
Sierra Leone	Republic of Sierra Leone
Singapore	Hsin-chia-p'o Kung-ho-kuo/Republik Singapura/Singapore Kudiyarasu/Republic of Singapore
Slovenia	Republika Slovenija
Solomon Islands	Solomon Islands

Somalia	Jamhuuriyadda Dimuqraadiga Soomaaliya/ Jumhūrīyah aṣ-Ṣūmāl ad-Dīmuqrā- ṭīyah
South Africa	Republiek van Suid-Afrika/Republic of South Africa
Spain	Reino de España
Sri Lanka	Sri Lankā Prajathanthrika Samajavadi Jana- rajaya/Ilangai Jananayaka Socialisa Kudiarasu
Sudan	Jumhūrīyat as-Sūdān
Suriname	Republiek Suriname
Swaziland	Umbuso weSwatini/Kingdom of Swaziland
Sweden	Konungariket Sverige
Switzerland	Confédération Suisse/Schweizerische Eidgen- ossenschaft/Confederazione Svizzera
Syria	Al-Jumhūrīyah al-'Arabīyah as-Sūrīyah
Taiwan	Chung-hua Min-kuo
Tajikistan	Jumhurii Tojikistan
Tanzania	Jamhuri ya Muungano wa Tanzania/United Republic of Tanzania
Thailand	Prathet Thai
Togo	République Togolaise
Tonga	Pule'anga Fakatu'i 'o Tonga/Kingdom of Tonga
Trinidad and Tobago	Republic of Trinidad and Tobago
Tunisia	Al-Jumhūrīyah at-Tūnisīyah

Turkey	Türkiye Cumhuriyeti
Turkmenistan	Türkmenistan Jumhuriyäti
Tuvalu	Tuvalu
Uganda	Republic of Uganda
Ukraine	Ukrayina
United Arab Emirates	al-Imārāt al- 'Arabīyah al-Muttaḥida
United Kingdom	United Kingdom of Great Britain and Northern Ireland
United States of America	United States of America
Uruguay	República Oriental del Uruguay
Uzbekistan	Ozbekistan Jumhuriyäti
Vanuatu	Ripablik blong Vanuatu/République de Vanuatu/Republic of Vanuatu
Vatican City	Stato della Città del Vaticano
Venezuela	República de Venezuela
Vietnam	Công Hòa Xã Hôi Chu Nghĩa Viêt Nam
Western Samoa	Malo Sa'oloto Tuto'atasi o Samoa i Sisifo/ Independent State of Western Samoa
Yemen	al-Jumhūrīyah al-Yamanīyah
Yugoslavia	Federativna Republika Jugoslavija
Zaïre	République du Zaïre
Zambia	Republic of Zambia
Zimbabwe	Republic of Zimbabwe

BIBLIOGRAPHY

There are hundreds of books on place-names, ranging from general gazetteers and atlases to specialized etymological dictionaries. Those listed below, together with more general reference works and articles, were found to be the most useful in compiling and checking material for the present book. Readers interested in the place-names of a specific region, such as an individual country, state, or administrative district, are recommended to consult the titles listed in the work by Emil Meynen below, as one of the most comprehensive geographical bibliographies of its type.

Addleton, Jonathan. "The Fate of British Place Names in Pakistan," *Asian Affairs,* XVIII, Pt. 1 (February 1987).

Allen, Jenny *et al.* (comps). *Geographical Digest 1990–91.* Oxford, UK: Heinemann Educational, 1990.

Armstrong, G.H. *The Origin and Meaning of Place Names in Canada.* Toronto: Macmillan, 1930.

Atlas mira (Atlas of the world). Moscow: Glavnoye upravleniye geodezii i kartografii pri Sovete Ministrov SSSR, 1984.

Atlas SSSR (Atlas of the USSR), 3d ed. Moscow: Glavnoye upravleniye geodezii i kartografii pri Sovete Ministrov SSSR, 1983.

Barraclough, Geoffrey (ed.) *The Times Atlas of World History,* rev. ed. London: Times Books, 1984.

Bartholomew, John C., *et al.* (eds). *The Times Atlas of the World,* 8th ed. London: Times Books, 1990.

Bohannon, John. "What's in a name?" *Saturday Evening Post* 260, no. 5 (July–August 1988).

Bol'shaya Sovetskaya Entsiklopediya (Great Soviet Encyclopedia), 3d ed. Moscow: Sovetskaya Entsiklopediya, 1970–78. 30 vols.

Bushmakin, S.K. (ed.) *Slovar' geograficheskikh nazvaniy SSSR* (Dictionary of geographical names of the USSR), 2d rev. & enld. ed. Moscow: Nedra, 1983.

Cabral, Antonio. *Dicionário de nomes geográficos de Moçambique: sua origem* (Dictionary of geographical names of Mozambique: their origin). Lourenço Marques: Empresa Moderna, 1975.

Chazov, Ye. I. (chief ed.) *Kurorty: Entsiklopedicheskiy slovar'* (Health resorts: an encyclopedic dictionary). Moscow: Sovetskaya Entsiklopediya, 1983.

Cherpillod, A. *Dictionnaire étymologique des noms géographiques* (Etymological dictionary of geographical names). Paris: Masson, 1986.

Clark, Bruce. "Lenin's city of revolution chooses return to its imperial identity," *The Times*(London), June 14, 1991.

Collins Road Atlas Europe, rev. ed. Edinburgh, UK: Bartholomew, 1992.

Columbia-Lippincott Gazetteer of the World. New York: Columbia University Press, 1952; with 1961 supplement.

Dauzat, A., and Ch. Rostaing. *Dictionnaire étymologique des noms de lieux en France* (Etymological dictionary of place-names in France), 2d. ed. Paris: Librairie Guénégaud, 1978.

Encyclopaedia Britannica, 15th ed. Chicago: Encyclopaedia Britannica, 1974; with revisions, 1984.

Florinsky, Michael T. (ed.) *McGraw-Hill Encyclopedia of Russia and the Soviet Union,* New York: McGraw-Hill, 1962.

Fullard, Harold (ed.) *Geographical Digest.* London: George Philip, 1971–79.

Gazetteer of Official Standard Names approved by the United States Board on Geographical Names, Washington, DC, 2d ed. 1970. (No. 42: USSR)

"Guide to USAF bases at home and abroad," *Air Force Magazine* (Washington, DC), vol. 60. no. 5 (May 1977).

Hamilton, William B. *The Macmillan Book of Canadian Place Names.* Toronto: Macmillan, 1978.

Harder, Kelsie B. (ed.) *Illustrated Dictionary of Place Names: United States and Canada.* New York: Van Rostrand Reinhold, 1976.

Hunter, Brian (ed.) *The Statesman's Year-Book 1991–1992.* London: Macmillan, 1991

Johnson, S. *Where Is It? A Geographical Reference Book for Young and Old.* Exeter, UK: A. Wheaton & Co., 1948.

Kalesnik, S.V. (chief ed.) *Entsiklopedicheskiy slovar' geograficheskikh nazvaniy* (Encyclopedic dictionary of geographical names). Moscow: Sovetskaya Entsiklopediya, 1973.

Keesing's Contemporary Archives. Vols. 1–32. Harlow, UK: 1931–86.

Keesing's Record of World Events. Vols. 33–38. Harlow, UK: 1987–92.

Kidron, Michael, and Ronald Segal. *The New State of the World Atlas,* 4th ed. London: Simon & Schuster, 1991.

King, Jan. "Name That Hill—But First..." *New York Times,* August 14, 1983

Kirchherr, Eugene C. *Place Names of Africa, 1935–1986: A Political Gazetteer.* Metuchen, NJ: Scarecrow Press, 1987.

Komkov, A.M. (ed.) *Slovar' geograficheskikh nazvaniy zarubezhnykh stran* (Dictionary of geographical names of foreign countries), 3d ed. Moscow: Nedra, 1986.

Lexikon tōn Dēmōn, Koinotētōn kai oikismōn tēs Hellados (Register of the boroughs, communities and settlements of Greece). Athens: Ethnikē Statistikē Hypēresia tēs Hellados, 1974.

Losique, Serge. *Dictionnaire étymologique des noms de pays et de peuples* (Etymological dictionary of names of countries and peoples). Paris: Éditions Klincksieck, 1971.

A Magyar Nepköztársaság Helységnévtáta (The place-names register of the Hungarian People's Republic). Budapest, 1973.

Mason, Oliver (comp.) *Bartholomew Gazetteer of Britain.* Edinburgh, UK: John Bartholomew & Son, 1986.

Meynen, Emil. *Gazetteers and Glossaries of Geographical Names of the Member Countries of the United Nations and the Agencies in Relationship with the United Nations: Bibliography 1946–1976.* Wiesbaden, Germany: Franz Steiner Verlag, 1984.

Nienaber, P.J. *Suid-Afrikaanse Pleknaamwoordeboek* (Dictionary of South African place-names), 2d rev. ed. Cape Town: Tafelberg, 1972.

Nikonov, V.A. *Kratkiy toponimicheskiy slovar'* (Concise toponymical dictionary). Moscow: Mysl, 1966.

Orth, Donald J. "The Mountain Was Wronged: The Story of the Naming of Mt. Rainier and Other Domestic Names Activities of the US Board on Geographic Names," *Names,* vol. 32, no. 4 (December 1984).

Paxton, John (ed.). *The Statesman's Year-Book,* London: Macmillan, 1969–90.

Paxton, John (ed.). *The Statesman's Year-Book Historical Companion.* London: Macmillan, 1988.

Paxton, John (ed.) *The Statesman's Year-Book World Gazetteer.* 4th rev. ed. London: Macmillan, 1991.

Peterson, Charles B. "The Nature of Soviet Place-Names," *Names,* vol. 25, no. 1 (March 1977).

Petrunko, Oksana. "What's in a name?," *Soviet Weekly,* August 30, 1990.

Pospelov, Ye.M. *Shkolnyy toponimicheskiy slovar'* (School toponymical dictionary). Moscow: Prosveshcheniye, 1986.

Quindlen, Anna. "A Day for Renaming Places," *New York Times,* April 23, 1983

Raper, P.E. *Dictionary of Southern African Place Names.* 2d ed. Johannesburg: Jonathan Ball, 1989.

Rayner, Caroline, *et al.* (comp.). *Philip's Geographical Digest 1992–93.* Oxford, UK: Heinemann Educational, 1992.

Reed, A.W. *Place Names of Australia.* Frenchs Forest, New South Wales, Australia: Reed Books, 1988.

"Remember Christmas Island? It's Now Kiritimati," *New York Times,* December 31, 1990.

Rennick, Robert M. "On the Success of Efforts to Retain the Names of Several American Communities in the Two World Wars," *Names,* vol. 32, no. 1 (March 1984).

Room, Adrian. *Dictionary of Irish Place-Names.* Belfast: Appletree Press, 1986.

Room, Adrian. *Dictionary of World Place Names Derived from British Names.* London: Routledge, 1989.

Room, Adrian. *Place-Names of the World.* North Ryde, New South Wales, Australia: Angus & Robertson, 1987.

Rosenthal, Eric (comp.) *Encyclopaedia of Southern Africa,* 7th rev. ed. Cape Town: Juta, 1978.

Schofield, Clive. Borderline cases, *Geographical* (London), vol. LXIV, no. 6 (June 1992).

Shadbolt, Maurice (ed.). *The Shell Guide to New Zealand.* London: Michael Joseph, 1969.

Sivin, Nathan *et al.* (eds). *The Contemporary Atlas of China.* London: Weidenfeld and Nicolson, 1988.

Spaull, Hebe. *New Place Names of the World.* London: Ward Lock, 1970.

Stewart, George R. *American Place-Names.* New York: Oxford University Press, 1970.

Stewart, John. *African States and Rulers.* Jefferson, NC: McFarland, 1989.

Sturmfels, Wilhelm, and Heinz Bischof. *Unsere Ortsnamen* (Our place-names). Bonn: Dümmlers, 1961.

Thakore, M.P. "Changes in Place-Names in India," *The Indian Geographer,* vol. 1, no. 1 (August 1956).

"The Names They Are A-Changin'," *Time,* January 27, 1992.

The New World Map, presented with *Geographical Magazine* (London), vol. LXIV, no. 6 (June 1992).

Treharne, R.F., and Harold Fullard (eds). *Muir's Historical Atlas, Medieval and Modern,* 11th ed. London: George Philip & Son, 1969.

Trëshnikov, A.F. (chief ed.) *Geograficheskiy entsiklopedicheskiy slovar'* (Geographical encyclopedic dictionary), 2d rev. & enld. ed. Moscow: Sovetskaya Entsiklopediya, 1989.

Trillin, Calvin. "Map maker, map maker, I'm not a sap," *Star Ledger* (Newark, NJ), March 25, 1991.

"U.S. Board Changes Names of One Hundred Twenty-One Places," *Washington Post,* January 18, 1982.

Webster's New Geographical Dictionary. Springfield, MA: Merriam-Webster, 1988.

What's in a change? *The Guardian* (London), June 17, 1991.

Where's Where: A Descriptive Gazetteer. London: Eyre Methuen, 1974.

Whitaker's Almanack. London: J. Whitaker & Sons, 1970–93.

Wilcocks, Julie. *Countries and Islands of the World: A Guide to Nomenclature,* 2d ed. London: Clive Bingley, 1985.

Wilford, John Noble. "Map Makers Get Lost as the World Turns on Them," *New York Times,* June 21, 1992.

Willett, B.M. (ed.) *Geographical Digest.* London: George Philip, 1980–84.

Willett, B.M. (ed.) *The New Geographical Digest.* London: George Philip, 1986.

Wolk, Allan. *The Naming of America.* Nashville, TN: Thomas Nelson, 1977.

The World Almanac and Book of Facts. New York: World Almanac, 1970–93.

Yerofeyev, I.A. *Imya Lenina na karte rodiny* (The name of Lenin on the map of the motherland), 2d rev. ed. Moscow: Prosveshcheniye, 1985.

Yusupov, E. Yu. (ed.) *Imeni Lenina* (Named for Lenin). Tashkent, Uzbek SSR: Uzbekistan, 1980.

Zhuchkevich, V.A. *Kratkiy toponimicheskiy slovar' Belorussii* (Concise toponymical dictionary of Belorussia). Minsk, Belorussian SSR: Izdatelstvo Belorusskogo gosudarstvennogo universiteta imeni V.I. Lenina, 1974.

ABOUT THE AUTHOR

ADRIAN ROOM (M.A., Oxford University, England) is the author of around 40 popular reference books, mainly on the origins of words and names. He has taught English and modern foreign languages at a number of schools and colleges, and in 1984 left his post as Senior Lecturer in Russian with the Ministry of Defence to pursue writing fulltime. He has long specialized in the field of place-names, and his first book on the subject, which was his first book overall, was *Place Names of the World* (David & Charles, 1974). His third book, *Place-Name Changes Since 1900,* was published by Scarecrow Press in 1979, and the present book is an updating and expansion of that work. His recent publications include *Dictionary of Place-Names in the British Isles* (Blooms-bury, 1989) and *Street Names of England* (Paul Watkins, 1992). His largest work ever on the subject of names was published as *Brewer's Dictionary of Names* (Cassell, 1992). He is currently working on a dictionary of African place-names, to be published by McFarland, NC. Adrian Room is a Fellow of the Royal Geographical Society, a member of the English Place-Name Society, and a member of the American Name Society.